Singing Early Music

MUSIC: SCHOLARSHIP AND PERFORMANCE
Thomas Binkley, general editor

Willi Apel. *Italian Violin Music of the Seventeenth Century.*
A. Peter Brown. *Performing Haydn's* The Creation.
David Ledbetter. *Harpsichord and Lute Music in 17th-Century France.*
George Houle. *Meter in Music, 1600–1800.*
Meredith Little and Natalie Jenne. *Dance and the Music of J.S. Bach.*
Timothy J. McGee. *Medieval Instrumental Dances.*
Betty Bang Mather. *Dance Rhythms of the French Baroque.*
Nigel North. *Continuo Playing on the Lute, Archlute and Theorbo.*
Jason Paras. *The Music for Viola Bastarda.*
Dolores Pesce. *The Affinities and Medieval Transposition.*
Sandra Rosenblum. *Performance Practices in Classical Piano Music.*
Beverly Scheibert. *Jean-Henry D'Anglebert and the Seventeenth-Century Clavecin School.*
Jeremy Yudkin. *De musica mensurata.*

Singing Early Music

THE PRONUNCIATION OF EUROPEAN LANGUAGES IN THE LATE MIDDLE AGES AND RENAISSANCE

edited by Timothy J. McGee
with A. G. Rigg and David N. Klausner

INDIANA UNIVERSITY PRESS
Bloomington and Indianapolis

The paper used in this publication meets the
minimum requirements of American National Standard
for Information Sciences—Permanence of Paper for
Printed Library Materials, ANSI Z39.48-1984.

Manufactured in the United States of America

Library of Congress Cataloging-in-Publication Data

Singing early music : the pronunciation of European languages in the Late Middle Ages and Renaissance / edited by
Timothy J. McGee with A. G. Rigg and David N. Klausner.
p. cm. +1 sound disc (digital ; 4 3/4 in.) — (Music—
scholarship and performance)
Includes bibliographical references and index.
ISBN 0-253-32961-2 (cl : alk. paper).
1. Singing—Diction. 2. Romance languages—Pronunciation.
3. Germanic languages—Pronunciation. I. McGee, Timothy J.
(Timothy James), date . II. Rigg, A. G. III. Klausner, David
N. IV. Series.
MT883.S56 1996
783'.043—dc20 95-22575
3 4 5 01 00 99 MN

To Thomas Binkley

whose insight and leadership in the field of early music have been a constant inspiration.

CONTENTS

Iberian Peninsula

Italy

Germany and the Low Countries

PREFACE

The original desire to undertake this book grew from my interest in the performance of medieval and Renaissance music. It seemed to me that if we are to recreate the music of those early centuries as faithfully as possible to the intentions of the composers, our first concern should be to perform it with the sounds the composers expected to hear. And whereas a number of scholars and instrument makers have been involved in the reproduction of authentic musical instruments over the past century, far less attention has been given to singing the texts with the correct pronunciation. It was this thought that prompted me to propose this book to the language specialists who have written the individual chapters.

Correct pronunciation will not by itself guarantee a historically correct vocal performance any more than will the use of the correct instrument; numerous other matters must also be taken into account: tone color, musical style, appropriate techniques, ornamentations, etc. But pronouncing the words correctly is definitely a step in the right direction, and the correct pronunciation will also influence some of the other vocal elements, especially tone color.

As can be seen in the following pages, when period pronunciations are substituted for modern pronunciations, poetic lines will often have both a different metric flow and a different set of rhymes, aspects that greatly change the sound properties of the musical line. Poetry was written to be heard, and poets had specific sound as well as meaning in mind when they wrote. In that light, although directed mainly at singers of early music, this guide should also be of major assistance to those interested in early drama, poetry, and literature.

A guide to pronunciation must have two dimensions: geography and chronology. All languages differed according to locale and evolved through the centuries. The pronunciation of French, for example, would have been different in the north and the south, and even within those areas there would have been local differences; southern French (Occitan) would have been influenced differently according to the proximity of Spain, Italy, or Germany. An example of the chronological dimension would be the influence of French and Latin on English leading over the centuries from the highly accented Anglo-Saxon to the smoother sounds of Early Modern English. Some of the changes and variations in pronunciation are reflected in the spellings of words that were altered according to area and century, but after the invention of the printing press the standardization that gradually appeared no longer reflected even the massive changes.

The end date for this guide is somewhat different for each language, depending upon when the pronunciation had finally evolved to the point where it is close to modern use. That is not to say that nothing has happened to languages in the past three hundred years, but the most significant changes were all in place by the middle to end of the seventeenth century. Thus this introductory guide deals with the pronunciation of the principal languages of Europe between the twelfth and the seventeenth century. The selection of dialects to include was determined by whether there is an adequate amount of extant musical repertory and whether we could locate a qualified scholar.

The pronunciation of languages from hundreds of years ago poses many unanswered (and sometimes unanswerable) questions. Our authors have consulted many sources in order to ferret out pronunciation rules, to take note of exceptions, and to chart the gradual changes as the languages evolved over the centuries of the Late Middle Ages and Renaissance. The amount of information they were able to find is extremely uneven, both from one language to another and for certain kinds of details within a single language. In some cases they have been able to make quite sophisticated distinctions with great confidence, while on other occasions the choice of one sound over another may be no more than an informed guess. To avoid burdening the reader with authors' frequent claims of uncertainty, they have been edited down to a minimum. We ask you to believe that in mixing together secure fact and unclear guesses we have not intended to mislead but to give assistance. When an unambiguous answer was not available we instructed our authors to give the best available advice, believing that our principal audience—singers—would prefer the opinion of an authority to no clear answer at all. In most cases it is ascertainable when the evidence is incomplete; the sources of information and the degree of detail that can be derived from them are described briefly by each author.

One extremely important area not covered here is that of changes in pronunciation caused by sentence structure—the concept that pronunciation of certain words changes with context. For example, just as the pronunciation in modern English is different for *day* and Mon*day, found* and New*found*land, *have* and *have* to, in some areas the pronunciation of *saint* changes in the following contexts:

Saint Michael and All Angels
The saint was a holy man
Saint Michael will fight against Antichrist

After considering how to approach this area and whether it would be appropriate to attempt it, since for many of the languages there is not enough information to begin, we reluctantly decided that the dynamics of sentence structure is beyond the scope of this book.

The issue of spelling found in the sources has been addressed by all of the authors, since the instructions given relate to how one pronounces what is written. If the reader is working from the original, there will be no problem in applying the instructions given here. If, however, an edition is used, the reader may be faced with an "adjusted" spelling. In many of the most available secondary sources an editor has silently adjusted the text for a modern reader, adding accent marks in French, for example, or using High German as standard spellings for Low German originals. An ideal performance should start with the original sources, but when that is not practical the reader is advised to be wary of possible editorial changes and to attempt to return the texts to their original spellings before settling on pronunciation. When possible, instructions for doing that have been included in the chapters.

The task confronting our authors has not been easy; in most cases it has involved a great deal of original work. It is my pleasure to thank them publicly at this time. In order to standardize the format for the sake of the readers everyone was asked to adopt a uniform approach and a standard set of pronunciation markings. That task alone required several revisions on the part of each author before we arrived at the format you see here. I am grateful for their patience and for the cooperation and suggestions I have received from each of the contributors over the years it has taken to bring this book to publication.

The editorial work has been shared by my two collaborators: A. G. Rigg created the initial design and format of the chapters and produced a preliminary draft of his Anglo-Latin chapter as a starting model. David N. Klausner provided the phonetic alphabet and the model for the diachronic sound charts, helped refine the chapter format, and, with George Rigg, checked all chapters for technical consistency. Without these two linguistic specialists, their expertise, and their unfailing enthusiasm, it is doubtful that there would ever have been a book. Responsibility for all final choices and the accuracy of details is mine.

TJM
Toronto
April 1993

ACKNOWLEDGMENTS

The editors and authors are grateful for the assistance of numerous people over the years of preparation. In particular, we thank Thomas Binkley for his encouragement and advice through every stage of the preparation, and Alice Colby-Hall for her meticulous reading of the entire manuscript.

We are grateful to Massimo Ossi for assistance with the selection of Italian texts and dialects; Elizabeth Aubrey for assistance with Provençal and Occitan; Steven Dworkin for assistance with Galician-Portuguese; Joseph Gulsoy for assistance with Catalan; Acting Dean Robert Falck, in the Faculty of Music, University of Toronto, for financial assistance; Josiah Blackmore for assistance with the recording; Bryden Baird, who did the recording and editing; and the Electroacoustic Music Studio at the Faculty of Music, University of Toronto. Thanks are also due to the many students in the Historical Performance Ensembles of the University of Toronto over the past eight years who have consulted various chapters while preparing their performances and offered useful suggestions.

HOW TO USE THIS GUIDE

A *chart of the International Phonetic Alphabet* (IPA) is printed on the final pages of this book so you can locate it easily as you read the text. Please read the opening section of Chapter 1, "Phonetics," first, for assistance in understanding the symbols and terminology, and listen to the CD recording in the back pocket, index numbers 1–66.

At the end of each chapter you will find sample texts for each of the major languages, followed by transcriptions in IPA, as indicated on the phonetic chart. Most of these texts are read on the CD to help you interpret the phonetic symbols.

All the authors have used a common outline, expanding or omitting sections to fit the demands of their particular languages. In addition to the detailed discussion of each consonant and vowel, which is the basis of each chapter, some languages permitted the creation of a diachronic sound chart, which provides a compact view of pronunciation changes. These charts can be used for further refining the pronunciation of a text for which the approximate date is known. In English, for example, the closer the date of the text is to 1500, the closer the pronunciation of *a* will be to [æ], as compared to the [a] in earlier texts.

COMMON ABBREVIATIONS

L = Latin
Eng = Modern English
OE = Old English
AE = American English
BE = British English
ME = Middle English
E Mod Eng = Early Modern English
Fr = Modern French
OFr = Old French
Fr.L = French Latin
M. Pic = Middle Picard
Sp = Modern Spanish
Pr = Modern Portuguese
It = Modern Italian
FIt = Florentine Italian
NIt = Northern Italian
Ger = Modern German
MHG = Middle High German
OHG = Old High German
NHG = New High German
ENHG = Early New High German
Dut = Modern Dutch

Singing Early Music

1—

Introduction

PHONETICS

David N. Klausner

The simplest and most obvious way to describe a phonetic sound would be to give a clear example of it in Modern English. Unfortunately, pronunciation of Modern English varies so widely between speakers that in many cases a clear example can only be given with an elaborate explanation of the intended dialect or speech group. For example, it would be very useful to be able to define the vowel [ɔ] as the sound of *a* as in *all,* but that would indicate entirely different sounds to a reader in Birmingham, England, and to one in Birmingham, Alabama. Thus it is necessary to define sounds by the precise position of the organs of speech (principally the mouth and tongue) needed to produce the sound. This introduction provides a brief explanation of the standardized descriptions of sounds phoneticians use. Contributors have used Modern English examples when they are relatively unambiguous, but in each chapter there are some sounds that can only be made clear by a phonetic description.

Consonants

Consonants are defined as the full or partial closure of the passage of air that flows from the lungs through the larynx (voice-box) and the mouth. Three elements go into the description of a consonant: the extent of the closure, the parts of the mouth which cause the closure, and whether the larynx is activated or not. Let us look at these elements in reverse order. If you place your fingers on your larynx (the Adam's apple) and say the word *thin* and then the word *then,* you will feel that the larynx vibrates for the *th* in the second word but not in the first. This "activation" of the larynx is called "voicing," and a consonant in which the activation occurs is said to be "voiced." Conversely, a consonant that does not activate the larynx is said to be "unvoiced." This simple distinction defines the difference between such pairs as *b/p, v/f, g/k,* and *d/t.*

The parts of the mouth that cause closure of the air channel are identified by adjectives derived from their Latinate anatomical names: the lips *(labial),* the teeth (*dental,* usually referring in fact to a position just behind the teeth), the alveolar ridge about a half-inch behind the teeth *(alveolar),* the hard bony roof (palate) of the mouth *(palatal),* the soft tissue (velum) farther back on the roof of the mouth *(velar),* the soft flap (uvula) hanging down at the back of the mouth *(uvular).* Closure is produced in two ways: By bringing two of these parts of the mouth together—the lips, producing a *bilabial* sound *(p, b),* or the lips and the teeth, producing a *labiodental* sound *(v, f);* or by bringing part of the tongue in contact with one of the other points. The tongue is often not included in the phonetic description; if a sound is said to be *alveolar (t, d), palatal (ch, j), velar (k, g),* or *uvular* (*r* in some dialects of French), it is assumed that it is the tongue that is making contact with the specified point in the mouth. The prefix *apico-* is sometimes added to indicate that it is the tip of the tongue rather than its flat upper surface that makes contact with the stationary part of the mouth, as in *apico-dental.* A consonant may also be said to be *palatalized* if the tongue moves toward the hard palate (the roof of the mouth) during its production (as in the sound of *-ll-* in *colliery* or of *-tch-* in *kitchen*).

A consonant may also be produced by fully closing the air passage, in which case it is said to be a *stop* or an *occlusive,* or by partially closing the passage and forcing air through it, in which case the consonant is a *fricative.* Thus *t* is a stop, while *th* is a fricative. Fricatives like *s* or *z,* which have a high proportion of upper harmonics, are sometimes called *spirants;* the strength of their articulation can be indicated by the terms *fortis* (strong) and *lenis* (weak).

This mode of description does not quite cover all the possibilities. Consonants produced by partially closing the passage in order to redirect the air stream may be called *approximants* or *continuants,* depending on the nature of the closure. Consonants produced by redirecting the air stream through the nose are defined as *nasal* (most languages have a bilabial form *m* and a dental form *n*), while those in which the air stream is redirected sideways within the mouth are called *laterals* (*l* is the most common).

Many of the other terms used in defining consonants are self-explanatory; thus an *r* in which the tongue makes a single brief contact with the alveolar ridge is called a *flap,* but if the contact is repeated (as in a Scottish or Italian *r*) it is a *trill* or *roll.* In some languages the difference may be important, as in Spanish *perro* (dog), where the double consonant indicates a roll, and *pero* (but), where the single consonant indicates a flap. One sound *(h)* is produced with the breath alone, by suddenly increasing the rate of exhalation, and is therefore called an *aspirate.* In some languages a stop may also be accompanied by aspiration; frequently the aspirate form of a consonant (*bh* with strong aspiration as in *bam!* for example) is quite distinct from the unaspirated form *(b* as in *but).* The strength of the aspiration is sometimes indicated by the terms *fortis* (for a strong aspiration) and *lenis* (for a weak aspiration).

Compound consonants are also frequent, consisting most commonly of a stop and a spirant. When the stop is the first element, these sounds are called *affricates.* Since the spelling of affricates is often not immediately obvious, they are included in the chart of phonetic symbols ([dʒ] as in *edge,* or [tʃ] as in *itch*—notice that the difference lies in the voicing). The reverse, a spirant followed by a stop, can almost always be indicated by a simple pair of consonants and is therefore unambiguous ([st] as in *lost,* or [ft] as in *laughed*). These are not included in the phonetic chart.

These relatively simple rules will allow the accurate definition of consonants where necessary. Thus for a non–German speaker, it is much better to describe the phonetic symbol [x] as an unvoiced velar fricative than to say it is the sound *ch* in *noch,* when there may be no one around to ask what the word really sounds like. Though the terminology may be a bit daunting at first, it does allow for much more precision.

Vowels

Since vowels do not involve a closure of the air passage, they are best defined by the shape of the mouth cavity required to produce them. Since the tongue is the principal moveable organ inside the mouth, most vowels can be defined by its position. The mouth can produce an infinite number of vowel sounds. Start with your tongue as far forward in your mouth as it will go, producing the sound *ee,* then move the tongue backwards through the sequence *ee, eh, ah, oh, oo.* The tongue begins relatively high in the mouth, then moves lower, with *ah* at the bottom (this is why the doctor asks you to say "Ah" to get your tongue out of the way and provide a good view of the nether regions of your throat). Then, since it is becoming bunched up at the back, your tongue is forced to move up again toward *oo.* This vowel sequence is a continuum, and each language utilizes a limited number of specific places along it. Vowel positions are generally defined by two axes in the mouth: *front* and *back,* and *high* and *low.* Thus the sound *ee* is a high front vowel, while *ah* is a mid-low vowel. The front-back distinction is particularly important, since in many languages it governs the quality of adjacent consonants (compare the syllables *-ci-* and *-co-* in Italian, with front and back vowels respectively). Front and back vowels are occasionally called *anterior* and *posterior.*

As you move in the vowel sequence from *ah* through *oh* to *oo,* your lips become progressively more rounded. Many languages make a distinction between *rounded* and *unrounded* vowels. English for the most part limits this distinction to the back vowels, but it is very important there, distinguishing between the sound of *but* (unrounded) and *put* (rounded). Other languages use rounding in different ways; the French vowel of *tu* is a rounded high front vowel.

Some languages, French and Portuguese especially, also have *nasalized* vowels in which a following nasal sound (usually *n*) forces the production of the vowel into the nose without the consonant actually being pronounced (Fr. *un, en*). These are indicated symbolically by placing a tilde (~) over the vowel. This is quite different from the use of the tilde in Spanish, where it indicates a palatalization of the consonant over which it is placed (as in *niño,* pronounced like the first *n* in English *onion*).

Compound vowels are called *diphthongs* when two vowel sounds are present, or *triphthongs* with three vowel sounds. Note that both diphthongs and triphthongs operate phonetically as if they were single vowels and are not split by syllable breaks. Diphthongs can be confusing, since in most languages they have little to do with spelling. English is particularly egregious in this respect: the vowel in *lead* is not a diphthong in either of the word's possible pronunciations even though it is spelled with two vowels, whereas the vowel of *ride* is a diphthong, even though it is spelled with a single vowel. Say the word *ride* slowly, and notice that the vowel immediately following the *r* (an "ah" sound) is not the same as the vowel immediately preceding the *d* (an "ee" sound). There is a smooth glide from the first to the second vowel without a break. Two adjacent vowels that do not form a diphthong are separated by a slight break, called a *hiatus;* compare the difference between the diphthong [ai] of *ride* and the two distinct vowels of *Aida.* When the first vowel element in a diphthong is the more important one, some contributors call it a "falling" diphthong. The reverse, in which the second element is the more important, usually begins with a semivowel *(y* or *w).* Phoneticians differ in whether it should be called a "rising" diphthong or a semivowel followed by a vowel.

The description of both vowels and consonants may be further amplified by indicating their relative position in a word, which may in some cases have an important bearing on their pronunciation. They may be defined by the position of the syllable in which they occur: the first syllable—*initial;* the last syllable—*final;* an intervening syllable—*medial.* Conversely, vowels especially may be defined by their relationship to the accent: in an accented syllable—*tonic;* in an unaccented syllable—*atonic;* preceding an accented syllable—*pretonic;* following an accented syllable—*posttonic.*

The purpose of phonetic descriptions is not to confuse the reader but to provide a degree of precision in an area in which present-day speech allows an extremely wide range of usage. Our hope is that a reader in Glasgow will be able to come to the same conclusions in the pronunciation of a particular text as a reader in Chicago.

Bibliography

Peter Ladefoged. *A Course in Phonetics.* 3rd ed. Fort Worth, TX, 1993.
Henry Rogers. *Theoretical and Practical Phonetics.* Toronto, 1991.

OVERVIEW OF EUROPEAN LANGUAGES
A.G. Rigg

Common linguistic features (most noticeable in the numerals and names for familial relationships, but also evident in grammatical and structural elements) have led scholars to posit a hypothetical original language known as Indo-European, which includes not only Western languages but also Sanskrit. From this hypothetical origin are descended all Western European languages except Basque and Finno-Ugric. Indo-European thus embraces Germanic (e.g., German, Dutch, Icelandic, Norwegian, other Scandinavian languages, and English), Italic (including Latin), Celtic (e.g., Irish, Welsh, Cornish), and Greek. For the purposes of the present book, the most important branches are Italic and Germanic. Diagrammatically, they appear thus:

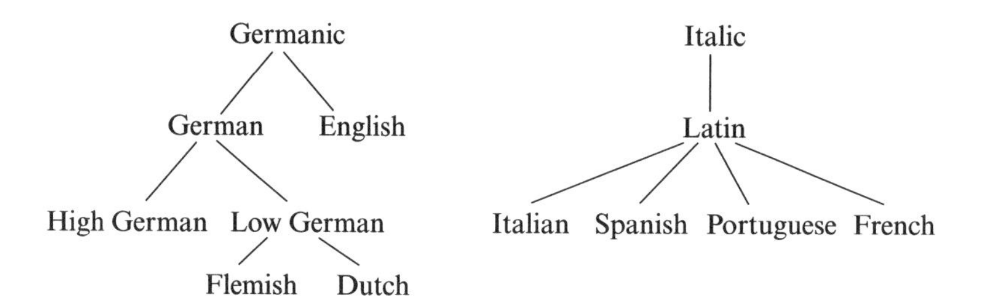

The spread of these two linguistic families arose from immigration and invasion. The Latin-speaking Romans conquered first Italy, then the Iberian peninsula (present-day Spain and Portugal), then Gaul (present-day France) and finally large parts of what is now Britain. The tongues spoken in these countries, with the exception of Britain, are what are now known as the Romance languages. Germanic-speaking people moved west and north across Europe, occupying Germany, Scandinavia, the Netherlands, and most of what is now Belgium; during the fourth and fifth centuries A.D. they also began to settle in what is now England, displacing the Celtic-speaking population (some of whom may have spoken a descendant of Latin); these Celts moved westward and were confined to Wales, Brittany, and Cornwall (Ireland and northern Scotland had remained Celtic). German-speaking races (specifically, the Franks) also penetrated northern Gaul, giving the whole country the name France and influencing, though not replacing, the Latin-derived tongue that was to develop into French. Another influential movement of Germanic people was that generally known as the Viking invasions: Danes settled in northern and eastern England, and Norsemen settled Normandy, in both cases adopting the native languages but considerably influencing pronunciation in both regions.

This neat picture—of Europe divided between Germanic and Romance languages—must, however, be modified further. Languages do not remain static, but continually evolve and change. No doubt for many generations the Latin speakers who settled Italy, Spain, and Gaul were mutually intelligible, perhaps differing only in accent (much like the present-day speakers of English in England, Scotland, the U.S.A., Canada, and Australia), but in time these "dialects" diverged sufficiently to be regarded as distinct languages. There are many reasons for linguistic change and for the varying pronunciations that make a book such as this necessary. The first is inherent to any language: a strong stress on one syllable causes other syllables to become unstressed or even to disappear entirely (compare the spellings and pronunciations of words like *Wednesday, laboratory, February);* anticipation by the mouth of a sound about to be formed causes the sound before it to be modified (compare the glide formed, in British and some Canadian English, between *t* and *u* in *tune*). Second, and this is important for the development of distinct languages across Europe, there is the phenomenon of substrates; for example, if Latin is learned by speakers of different native languages, their pronunciation of Latin (and perhaps also their syntactic structures) will differ from each other. Third, there is the constant influence of neighboring languages and dialects, through invasion or trade. For England, the most important influence was the Norman Conquest of 1066, which introduced French as the language of government and administration for the next two centuries: the French would speak English like Frenchmen, and the English would speak French like Englishmen, and both languages were influenced by the other. A similarly dramatic juxtaposition of linguistic groups was seen in Spain during the Moorish (Muslim) occupation. Less dramatic but equally important is the intermingling of people in commerce and trade (as in the pidgins or Creoles that developed in West Africa) or in employment: for example, London in the Middle Ages attracted tradesmen from many parts of Europe (especially French and Dutch speakers) and also migrants from all parts of England seeking work. If, as is often the case, the large city is also an administrative and cultural center, this rapidly developing dialect becomes the "standard" for the rest of the country.

The reconstruction of the pronunciation of early forms of languages is a hazardous and uncertain business. Sometimes we can make inferences from the study of related languages; from English *stone, father, set,* Old English *stān, fæder, settan,* German *Stein, Vater, setzen,* we can build up a picture of sound changes that shows them all deriving from the same original Germanic words. Sometimes modern spellings give a clue to a pronunciation that has now been lost: *night* once had a palatal spirant before the *t.* (This must be used with caution: English never had a *b* in *debt* or an *s* in *island*). Sometimes we can use puns, word play, alliteration, rhymes, and similar literary devices to infer pronunciations. Our best evidence is contemporary comment, but this is rare until the sixteenth and seventeenth centuries, when philological studies began properly; even here there can be problems, as the early philologists tended to use vague words, like "soft," or give as examples other words whose exact pronunciations we do not know. The whole business is full of uncertainties and guesses, but some guesses are more informed than others: these informed guesses, we hope, are what you will find in this book.

LATIN
A.G. Rigg

Latin held a unique position in Western civilization in the Middle Ages and Renaissance, perhaps similar to that of English nowadays in Africa and India. Although it was the principal official and literary language in Western Europe, it was no one's first tongue: people did not learn Latin at their mother's or nurse's knee; no one spoke Latin at home. It was taught in school to a very small class of society; theoretically it was spoken at school and in the universities, but it did not come naturally to anyone.

Medieval Latin must be distinguished from "Vulgar Latin," the ancestor of the Romance languages—Italian, Spanish, French, and so on. Vulgar Latin developed and changed in grammar, syntax, pronunciation, and spelling, so that in the end it became scarcely recognizable as Latin at all. Medieval Latin, however, is simply Classical Latin, the language of Roman civilization 100 B.C. TO A.D. 100, as learned and practiced in the Middle Ages, though somewhat modified. The basic texts on which instruction in Latin depended were the grammars of Priscian and Donatus, both compiled in late Antiquity on Classical models; the texts studied in schools were usually Classical (Cicero, Terence, Ovid, Virgil), patristic (Augustine and the church fathers, early Christian poets), and the Bible itself and the liturgy, both known through Latin translations made in late Antiquity. Thus, there was a constant check on changes in the Latin language.

Nevertheless, changes in society—in political, social, judicial, and ecclesiastical organization, and in science and technology—forced Latin to develop new vocabulary. Also, the constant use of Latin by speakers of vernacular languages caused it to adapt its syntax to vernacular patterns. There were very minor modifications to the spelling system (most noticeably, *e* for *ae* and *oe,* and *-ci-* for *-ti-*).

The least restraint was on pronunciation: although information on the pronunciation of Classical Latin was available (e.g., in the widely used *Etymologiae* of Isidore), it seems to have been largely ignored. Thus, it was in pronunciation, which developed along lines parallel to the speaker's own vernacular, that Medieval Latin differed most from Classical Latin. In his *De recta latini graecique sermonis pronuntiatione dialogus,* published in 1528, Erasmus protested against the great diversity of Latin pronunciations across Europe (thus incidentally providing us with some of the best evidence for contemporary practice). He tried to reestablish Classical pronunciation as the norm and was eventually successful, though in England, France, and Germany the reform was not completed until the early twentieth century. In James Hilton's novel *Goodbye Mr. Chips,* the headmaster tries to persuade the Latin master, Mr. Chips, to "move with the times" and give Cicero the correct Classical pronunciation ['kɪkɛro:] rather than the traditional ['sɪsɛro:]. Elsewhere things were moving in a different direction: in 1903 Pope Pius X issued a decree *motu proprio* (on his own initiative) on the performance of sacred music. The *Liber usualis* of 1896 was eventually expanded to include pronunciation, and it resulted in the uniform adoption of an Italianate pronunciation of Latin throughout the Roman Catholic church.

Neither reformed Classical pronunciation nor the pronunciation of the twentieth-century *Liber usualis* has any validity for the Latin of the Middle Ages or Renaissance. As vernacular speakers spoke Latin according to their own idiom, the pronunciation of Latin divided according to national and regional languages and dialects. Indeed, there were as many pronunciations of Latin across Europe as there were languages—let alone dialects—thus leading to Erasmus' complaints. The principal division is between those countries whose vernacular language was ultimately derived from Vulgar Latin (the Romance tongues of Italy, Spain, France, and the Picard/Walloon area of the Netherlands), and those whose native language was Germanic (Germany, England, and the Flemish area of the Netherlands).

In Romance countries there was a tendency to assimilate the pronunciation of Latin to that of its contemporary derivation, e.g., for the French to perceive *dicere, contra,* as *dire, contre,* and to pronounce them accordingly. Roger Wright has argued convincingly that in pre-Carolingian Spain, the Latin spelling system was simply a formal way of writing Spanish (just as in English we use the ancient spelling *night* for the sound [nait] and the single spelling *tune* for the various pronunciations [tu:n] [tju:n] and [tʃu:n]). Sixteenth-century puns in French Latin show that at many times it was pronounced just like French. Awareness remained, however, that Classical Latin had originally been different—that grammatical relationships depended on a clear articulation of endings, and that the scansion of quantitative verse required a distinction between long and short vowels—and so there were periodic attempts at reform, most notably during the Carolingian "renaissance" of the eighth and ninth centuries but also at other times. This meant that some Latin words, as in Spanish, were treated differently according to their status in the vernacular: recently adopted Latin words might no longer be perceived as the roots of contemporary words, and so be pronounced in a more "Latinate" manner, whereas older words would participate in the vernacular pronunciation (comparable examples in English are the three words *leal, loyal,* and *legal,* of which only the last shows its evident origin in Latin *legalis*).

In the Germanic-speaking regions, however, there was no possibility of assimilating Latin to the native language. Here Latin was learned as a foreign language and pronounced—and learned in school—as it was spelled. Thus, in England, Germany, and the Flemish Netherlands, the inflexional endings of Latin were given full expression. The primary divergences from the pronunciation of Classical Latin in these areas, therefore, arose when the *letters* of Latin corresponded to those in the native language and were pronounced accordingly; thus, a German would perceive *ge-* as [gɛ] or as some kind of fricative, and an Englishman as [dʒɛ], the way *ge-* was pronounced in their respective tongues.

The exact reproduction of the sounds of Medieval and Renaissance Latin is bedeviled by the constant possibility of reform according to the principles of Classical Latin, of spelling, or of some other system. This topic is mentioned in all the sections on Latin in this book. It is particularly important after the Reformation, when exiled Catholics and Protestants adopted the pronunciations of their new homes and then brought them back to their native countries.

The spelling of Latin through the Middle Ages and Renaissance was, on the whole, remarkably consistent, though it differed in several respects from the spelling of Classical Latin. In a few cases spellings reflect national and regional pronunciations, and where this is the case such spellings are discussed in the appropriate chapter.

The principal differences between Medieval and Classical spelling are: Classical *ae* and *oe* are regularly spelled *e (hec* instead of *haec),* and Classical *-ti-* is commonly spelled *-ci- (eciam* instead of *etiam).*

Two further common spelling variants reflect neither Medieval nor Classical Latin, but the traditional spelling of modern "Schoolbook" Latin: Both Medieval and Classical Latin tend to use *u* and *v* interchangeably. Until the late fourteenth century, Medieval manuscripts make no distinction between consonantal [v] and vocalic [u], writing both as *u* (e.g., *iuuenis, uiuere*). From about 1400 to the middle of the seventeenth century, *v* and *u* are positional variants, with *v* used initially and *u* medially, without reference to their phonetic value. Medieval and Renaissance manuscripts consistently use *i* for both vocalic [i] and consonantal *j* ([dʒ] or [j]), giving common spellings like *Iesum, iusticia, cuius.* Modern editors frequently distinguish between the two, using *i* and *j.*

For the performer, the chief difficulty is not the spelling of Medieval Latin but the varied practices of modern editors. It has become common practice for editors to "classicize" the texts; that is, to adjust the manuscript spellings to conform more or less to Classical (or more often Schoolbook) Latin. This practice is seen in series such as *Analecta Hymnica:* for the medieval spellings *racio, equs, mechus, celum,* editors often substitute the Classical forms *ratio, aequus, moechus, caelum.* This forces Medieval Latin into an alien mold and separates the spelling from its phonetic base. The modern reader will be alerted to "classicization" by the presence of *ae* and *oe* spellings, and should be prepared (mentally at least) to make substitutions of the following type: for *prae-, caedo, haec, quae, caelum, oboedire, ratio, retia,* read *pre-, cedo, hec, que, celum, obedire, racio, recia.*

Nineteenth-century editors often write *eius, cuius,* etc., as *ejus, cujus;* the value of this intervocalic *i/j* depends on the linguistic area. In England it is [dʒ].

The text examples at the end of each Latin chapter have been given in the form in which the performer will most likely encounter them, that is, in modern edited form.

Bibliography

Harold Copeman. *Singing in Latin.* Oxford, 1990.
Roger Wright. *Late Latin and Early Romance.* Liverpool, 1982.
W. S. Allen. *Vox Latina,* 2nd ed. Cambridge, 1978. On Classical Latin.
A. G. Rigg. "Latin Language," in *Dictionary of the Middle Ages,* Vol. 7 (1986), 350–59. The remarks on pronunciation are very general, but the article is useful on the general development of the language.

Britain

2

English

DAVID N. KLAUSNER

Between the tenth and the eighteenth century, English underwent significantly more changes than any other European language. These changes were both internally and externally motivated; among the most important were an almost complete loss of inflectional endings at the beginning of the period, a considerable input of foreign loan-words, especially from French, and, during the fifteenth century, a complete shift in the pronunciation of the long vowels.

Before the sixteenth century, written English was for the most part phonetic; that is, the spelling of a word was a more or less accurate reflection of the way it was pronounced. In the best of all possible worlds this might be seen as a considerable advantage, with the pronunciation of a word immediately visible in its spelling and vice versa, but in practice phonetic spelling creates as many problems as it solves. Modern English spelling is certainly illogical, but it has a certain consistency; that is, a word will be spelled the same way (ignoring a few differences of national practice) throughout the English-speaking world. Imagine the differences in the phonetic spelling of the word *well* as pronounced by a BBC announcer and by a resident of the American South! The spelling of early English is, however, logical in a way that the spelling of Modern English is not, since it can reflect the writer's pronunciation, dialect features and all. During the sixteenth century a degree of standardization entered the written language, and a literate writer (or printer) was more likely to spell according to this standard than according to his spoken dialect.

Bear in mind that for earlier periods, certainly up to the mid-eighteenth century, and perhaps later, pronunciation was far more flexible than it is today. Although we now are accustomed to variant pronunciations between dialects of English, the speaker of a particular dialect is usually relatively strict in the pronunciation of any word. For earlier periods there were many words for which there were several possible pronunciations within the same speech group; we can only distinguish between them when they are indicated in the spelling or metrics, but their existence means that we must take early spelling seriously and not as a debased form of modern "systematized" spelling.

The Great Vowel Shift

Documenting the pronunciation of early English is complicated by a major sound-change, known as the Great Vowel Shift. Even during a period in which spelling is largely phonetic, writers tend to be very conservative and continue to spell words the same way throughout their lives, even though the pronunciation changes. For this reason, the vowel shift is very difficult to date accurately. It certainly took place primarily during the fifteenth century, but there is considerable debate over whether it occurred early or late in the century, as well as over how long it took. It is, of course, highly likely that the timing and duration of the vowel shift were different in different parts of the country. Proximity to a major urban center like London could have been a contributing factor. But because pronunciation before and after the vowel shift can be reconstructed with some accuracy, by extrapolation it is possible to say, in a general way, what the language of the fifteenth century must have sounded like. For performers dealing with the English repertoire of the fifteenth century (including most of the carols), it is probably more sensible to postulate a performance either before the vowel shift (for works from early in the century) or after it, rather than to attempt the reconstruction of a transitional pronunciation.

In essence, the Great Vowel Shift affected long vowels only, shifting the pronunciation of both back and front vowels higher in the mouth so that, for example, the sound of long *a* as in *name* moved upwards from [ɑ:] in the late fourteenth century to [ɛ:] by about 1500. As the other vowels moved higher, those which had been in the highest position, *i* at the front and *u* at the back, became diphthongs, accounting for the Modern English pronunciation of words like *rise* and *house* (in which the Middle English pure vowels [i:] and [u:] became diphthongs [ai] and [au]).

Evidence

The evidence for the pronunciation of early English consists primarily in rhyme and meter, spellings, and Renaissance authorities.

Rhyme and Meter

Especially in the earlier part of the period, before the advent of printing, the principal relationship between a poem and its audience was aural, not visual, and thus eye-rhymes *(dead/mead)* were generally not a part of the poet's repertoire. Even after the sixteenth century, rhymes are often a good indication of pronunciation, as in the well-known example of Alexander Pope's rhyming of *tea* with both *away* and *obey* (indicating a pronunciation *tay*). Similarly his rhyme *venture/enter* gives us a strong clue to the lateness of the development of palatalization in the unaccented *-ture* syllable (Modern English [-tju:r] or [-tʃu:r]) since the rhyme would be impossible with this pronunciation.

Rhyme evidence is even more important for earlier periods. It shows us, for example, that the diphthong *-oi-* (largely found in French loan-words) had by the sixteenth century become unrounded to [ʌi] (and later to [ai]), so that *boil* could rhyme with *mile,* and *join* with *line,* as they still do in modern dialects like Cockney, Australian, and Newfoundland English.

In using the evidence of rhymes to establish pronunciation we must be aware that some rhyme pairs become traditional, and persisted as acceptable rhymes long after their pronunciations had separated. The common late sixteenth century rhyme of *wind/kind* is such a traditional rhyme, and Shakespeare's *food/good* may well be another.

Meter provides vitally important information, especially after the late fifteenth century, when the gap between spelling and pronunciation began to widen. Before the middle of the eighteenth century, poets tended to write in relatively strict meters, and what appear at first glance to be metrical anomalies often signal a pronunciation that is not reflected in the spelling. There are, for example, many words that are regularly contracted in sixteenth- and seventeenth-century pronunciation, though this contraction may not be indicated in the spelling, such as one-syllable pronunciations of *spirit* [sprʌit] (sometimes spelled *sprite*) or *evil* [i:ɪl] or [i:l]. The meter of a poem is often the only indication that such an alternate pronunciation is intended.

Spellings

The evidence of spelling is particularly important, though it must be used with some care. During the Middle Ages, phonetic spellings often point to differences of pronunciation between dialects, but we must be careful to distinguish between substantive differences in spelling and those that merely indicate a lack of standardization. A word spelled several ways by the same writer will often indicate nothing more than a lack of standardization, though in some cases it may be useful. Take, for example, the common alternations *and/ond* and *land/lond* in early Middle English. Both forms frequently occur in the work of a single writer, indicating that the actual vowel lay on the boundary between the writer's expectations of the two sounds.

Throughout the period, the spellings of foreigners and semiliterate persons are especially useful, since such writers are consciously attempting to reproduce what they hear.

Renaissance Authorities

Among other aspects of language that caught the attention of scholars of the sixteenth and seventeenth centuries was pronunciation, and these two centuries saw the publication of numerous tracts by so-called orthoepists (scholars of pronunciation). These tracts tend to be reformist in tone and rarely give a thorough description of the pronunciation of their day, concentrating on what the authors consider to be abuses of "correct" pronunciation. They are, nonetheless, extremely useful in providing evidence of what pronunciations existed (the catalogued "abuses") as well as of what a scholarly mind, in most cases educated and conservative, thought the pronunciation ought to be. A full list of Renaissance writings on the English language, including the works of the orthoepists, is given in E. J. Dobson, *English Pronunciation, 1500–1700,* pp. 1011–22, esp. 1020–22, and in A. J. Ellis, *Early English Pronunciation,* vol. 1, pp. 31–48.

Stress and Scansion

The accentuation of English words has been relatively stable; thus in many cases we can assume that the accentuation of an early word is the same as that of its modern cognate. There are some exceptions: compound adverbs and conjunctions could be accented on either syllable *(therefore, wherefore);* variable stress is occasionally found in compounds made up of two nouns (especially monosyllables), such as *mankind.* In such cases it may be assumed that the accentuation when sung followed the stress of the musical phrase. The textual underlay of English songs seems to indicate that composers were well aware of the accentuation of the texts they were setting, and serious disagreements between music and text are relatively rare. Note that this is not necessarily the case in other languages.

The situation with loan-words, especially those from French, is less clear. In Old French the accent generally fell on the final syllable, though many words ending in an *e* had a penultimate accent. A final accent would have sounded strange to English speakers, and quite soon after the adoption of a word into English its stress was likely to shift to reflect English norms. Poets were not slow to take advantage of this period of shifting stress and used loan-words with variable stress as it suited them.

For the Middle English period, the scansion of poetry is also affected by the pronunciation of unstressed *-e* [ɛ], or in some cases [ə]. For the most part, unstressed *-e* (especially final *-e*) represented the remnants of the lost inflectional system of Old English and therefore appeared generally in grammatical situations where an Old English ending would previously have been used. During the fourteenth and fifteenth centuries, even this last remnant of the inflections was disappearing. At the beginning of the fourteenth century final *-e* seems to have been generally pronounced, while by the fifteenth century it had become an archaism. Through much of the fourteenth century, then, it was in the process of being lost, and poets frequently took advantage of this variability. The scansion of a line of fourteenth-century verse often requires a decision concerning which final *-e*'s are silent and which are to be pronounced. Though final *-e* was lost in speech by the fifteenth century, it remained a common element of verse scansion for some time. This subject is discussed in more detail below under "Other Considerations."

Bibliography

Charles Barber. *Early Modern English.* London, 1976. Esp. pp. 288–338.
E. J. Dobson. *English Pronunciation, 1500–1700,* 2d ed. Oxford, 1968.
E. Ekwall. *A History of Modern English Sounds and Morphology,* trans. A. Ward. Oxford, 1980.
A. J. Ellis. *On Early English Pronunciation,* 5 vols. London, 1869–89; repr. New York, 1969.
Manfred Görlach. *Introduction to Early Modern English.* Cambridge, 1991. Esp. pp. 61–78.
C. Jones. *A History of English Phonology.* London, 1989.
H. Kökeritz. *A Guide to Chaucer's Pronunciation.* New York, 1962.
S. Moore. *Historical Outlines of English Sounds and Inflexions,* rev. A. Marckwardt. Ann Arbor, 1957.
T. Pyles. *The Origins and Development of the English Language.* 4th ed. San Diego, 1993.
B. Strang. *A History of English.* London, 1970.
H. Sweet. *A History of English Sounds.* Oxford, 1888.

Sounds

Some phonetic terminology will be necessary in order to describe the sounds of early English, and thus it would be a good idea to review "Phonetics" (pp. 1–4, above), although some of the more important points are repeated here. The position of a sound in a word is said to be initial, medial, or final, depending on whether the sound comes at the beginning, in the middle, or at the end of the word (such as, respectively, the *t* in *term, water,* and *wait*). Vowels are described according to the relative position of the tongue in the mouth needed to produce them; thus if one starts with the tongue toward the front of the mouth (as in the sound *ee*) and moves it back, a sequence of vowels is produced moving from *ee* (really a long *i* as in *machine*) through *e, a, o,* and finally to *u.* Within this sequence *i* and *e* are normally described as "front vowels" and *a, o,* and *u* as "back vowels"; as will be seen shortly, the difference is important, since front and back vowels often have different effects on neighboring consonants. As the tongue moves back to produce the long *u* (as in *boot*), the lips become rounded. This further distinction is also important, that is, between vowels that are rounded (*u* as in *put* [ʊ]; *o* as in *go* [o:]) and unrounded (*u* as in *but* [ʌ]; *o* as in *broad* [ɔ:]). Finally, tongue position also dictates whether a vowel is high or low, and changes along this axis are called "raising" or "lowering." The highest vowels are the farthest to the front and back, *i* and *u* respectively; *e* and *o* are mid-vowels, and *a* is the lowest. In the following list, sounds are traced from early Middle English up to the early eighteenth century. Phonetic equivalents are indicated by square brackets ([ ]).

Consonants

English consonants remain relatively stable throughout the period, with a few exceptions in which the significance of a compound consonant changes. No description is given if the pronunciation of the consonant is identical to Modern English usage.

b [b] as in Modern English.

c The hard consonant [k] was used before back vowels *a, o,* and *u (can, come),* and before the consonants *l, r,* and *n.*

The soft consonant [s] was used before front vowels *e* and *i (city, certain).* To indicate the sound [k] before a front vowel, the letter-form *k* would normally be used *(kin).*

ch As with *c,* the quality of the sound is sometimes determined by the following vowel; hard [k] before a back vowel *(character),* and soft [tʃ] before a front vowel *(chin).* This is not a reliable criterion, however, since a large number of loan-words, especially from French, have a soft *ch* [tʃ] followed by a back vowel *(charm, chain, change).* Conversely, a few words borrowed from Greek and Italian have a hard *ch* [k] followed by a front vowel *(chimera).* Modern English usage is usually a reliable guide to the quality of *ch; -ch-* was also sometimes used in Middle English as an alternate spelling for *-gh-;* see below.

d [d], as in Modern English.

f [f] or [v], as in Modern English. The consonant is usually pronounced [v] when it occurs medially between voiced sounds (that is, all vowels plus some consonants like *l* and *r*), thus *wolf/wolves.* The difference may or may not be indicated in the spelling.

g In general, the hard consonant [g] was used before back vowels *a, o,* and *u (goes, goose),* and before the consonants *l, r,* and *n.* The soft consonant [dʒ] was used before front vowels *e* and *i (gentil).* The sound is also spelled with *j* or *i;* see below under *j.* Modern English usage is a good guide to the quality of early English *g.*

gh In Middle English, the combination *gh* was pronounced [x] after a back vowel (as in Scottish *loch*), [ç] after a front vowel (as in German *nicht*). The sound generally disappeared (in the case of [ç]) or became [f] (in the case of [x]) during the fifteenth century; and Modern English usage is usually a reliable guide to the pronunciation of individual words (compare *laughter* and *daughter*). It is clear from the works of the orthoepists that the older pronunciation [x] was retained late into the sixteenth century by some conservative speakers *(enough).* Note that the sounds [ç] and [x] were often spelled *-h-, -ch-, -z-,* and sometimes *-y-* in Middle English.

gn Both elements were pronounced in initial position until late in the sixteenth century *(gnawen, gnaw).* At least until the end of the fourteenth century the French pronunciation [ɲ] may have remained with some frequency in French loan-words like *signe, digne.*

h Weakly aspirated in native words, generally silent in loan-words *(honor).* In early Middle English texts sometimes used interchangeably with *-gh-* to indicate the sounds [ç] or [x]; see *gh* above.

j [dʒ] Throughout the Middle Ages and Renaissance, the letter-form *j* was simply a variant of the letter *i,* and the two were used interchangeably to indicate this sound. Thus the spellings *ioly* and *Iesus* indicate pronunciations with [dʒ], not with [j] as in *yet.*

k [k]. See above under *c.*

kn As with *gn,* both elements were pronounced until late in the sixteenth century *(knowen, know)* but were lost by the beginning of the seventeenth century, allowing Shakespeare to pun on *knight/night.*

l At the end of the fourteenth century *l* was probably still pronounced before *f, k,* and *m (half, folk, palmer).* By the early sixteenth century *l* had generally been lost in the combinations *-al* and *-ol* + *f, k, m,* or *t (half, walk, calm, fault).* The *l* was restored in some words like *fault* and *vault* in the nineteenth century (compare Swift's eighteenth-century rhyme *thoughts/faults*).

m [m], as in Modern English.

n [n], as in Modern English.

ng At the beginning of the Middle English period the *g* was still pronounced in this consonant pair (that is, as in *finger* rather than *singer*), a pronunciation which still survives in some British dialects, such as Lancashire. By the end of the fourteenth century the *g* had been lost in final position (especially in the common *-ing* verbal ending), though it may well have remained in medial positions. By the sixteenth century final *-g* was no longer pronounced in almost all cases and *-ing* was pronounced [in]. The orthoepist Christopher Cooper, writing in 1685, tells us that *jerkin* and *jerking* are pronounced alike. Compare, for example, modern English colloquial *singin';* the pronunciation [ŋ] was restored in "polite" speech in the nineteenth century.

p [p], as in Modern English.

ph [f], as in Modern English.

r [r̥] or [rr]. The flat palatal *r* common today through most of North America was unknown in the Middle Ages and Renaissance, at which time the *r* was pronounced at the front of the mouth using the tip of the tongue either to trill or flick the consonant, as in modern Scots. The sound was weaker (less strongly trilled) before consonants and in final position. From the sixteenth century on it was often lost before *-s (horse, purse, verse).* This characteristic can still be heard in upper-class British and in some North American dialects *(horse/hoss; arse/ass).*

s [s] or [z], following for the most part the practice of Modern English. Pronounced [s] in weakly stressed words like *is* and *was* at least into the seventeenth century, as can be seen in frequent rhymes like *is/kiss/bliss/his/miss* or *was/grass.* On the quality of the *a*'s in this last rhyme see below under short *a.*

sh [ʃ], as in Modern English; also spelled *sch.*

t [t], as in Modern English.

th By the fourteenth century the differentiation between the voiced form [ð] *(then)* and the unvoiced form [θ] *(thin)* already corresponded to the practice of Modern English. Earlier than the fourteenth century it would not have been uncommon (following the practice of Old English) for *th-* in initial position to have been unvoiced. Editions of musical works from the fourteenth century or earlier sometimes follow the manuscripts in using the graphemes þ and ð instead of *th;* these letter-forms were used interchangeably by medieval scribes and in most cases do not indicate a difference between voiced and unvoiced pronunciation.

v [v]; throughout the Middle Ages and Renaissance, little distinction was made between the letter-forms *v* and *u,* especially in medial positions. Thus spellings like *loue* or *vnder* do not indicate a difference in pronunciation.

w Until around the end of the fourteenth century, *w* was still pronounced in initial position before a consonant *(writen).* Initial *w* continued to be pronounced by some conservative speakers until the end of the sixteenth century.

wh Although the spelling of this consonant group changed from the Old English *hw,* in some regions its pronunciation has remained the same (as in Modern English *whether*).

y This letter-form was variously used in early Middle English as an alternative form of *i* and, sometimes, *gh,* as well as having its modern use as [j]. The obsolete letter-form *ʒ* is occasionally found for it as well.

Vowels

Modern English is sometimes, though not always, a good guide to the length of vowels at earlier periods. Especially during the early Middle English period, there was a considerable amount of instability in some vowels in certain positions. For example, short vowels followed by *l, m, n,* or *r* and a second consonant were particularly unstable and tended during the late Old English period to become long. In many cases this lengthening did not last, and the vowel again became short. These variations account for the apparent inconsistency of pronunciations like *wind* (verb) and *wind* (noun), and *yield* and *friend.* In both cases the first word has preserved the lengthened form, while the second has been shortened again. The lengthening did not occur when the consonant pair was followed by a third consonant, thus *child/children.*

Conversely, in the Middle English period there was a strong tendency to lengthen vowels occurring in open syllables (that is, syllables that end in a vowel rather than a consonant). In many cases this happened before the loss of final inflections and final unstressed *-e,* changes that turned many two-syllable words into monosyllables. When the final *-e* was lost in pronunciation, it often came to be used to indicate a long vowel. Compare the difference between the long vowel of *wine* (from wi-ne, in which the first syllable is open), and *win* (a single closed syllable). The opposite tendency existed as well, that is, to shorten vowels in closed syllables (ending with a consonant rather than a vowel).

Toward the end of this period, in the early fifteenth century, vowels before palatal sounds like [ç] and [x] (usually spelled *-h-, -ch-,* or *-gh-*) also tended to become long, and were therefore affected by the Vowel Shift. Shortly afterward many of these palatal sounds disappeared in pronunciation, though they were often retained in spelling. Compare Middle English *briht* [bṛɪçt] with a short *i,* with Early Modern English *bright* [bṛʌit], in which the vowel has become a diphthong and the palatal consonant has disappeared in pronunciation. Since the Vowel Shift only affected long vowels, this change must indicate that the short *i* in this phonetic situation had become lengthened before the Vowel Shift occurred.

During the Middle English period it became common to write double vowels to indicate long vowels (in particular, *ee* and *oo*). Unfortunately, both of these spellings are ambiguous and can indicate a variety of sounds (see below, under long *e* and long *o*).

Short Vowels

On the whole, short vowels in English have changed relatively little over the last thousand years, and their pronunciation in Modern English is in many cases a reliable guide to their pronunciation at earlier stages of the language. The common tendency in Modern English to reduce most unstressed vowels to a neutral sound [ə] (the sound of the unstressed vowels in *ba'nana*) had probably begun by the middle of the fourteenth century.

By the early sixteenth century, short vowels other than *a* were often reduced to a neutral vowel [ə] before *r,* thus obscuring the differences in the vowels of *mirth, heard,* and *word* which in earlier pronunciation would have been quite distinct.

a Short *a* had none of the wide variation it has in Modern English *(fat, all, want).* In most positions the Old English short *a* [ɑ] moved slightly to the front in the period immediately following the Norman Conquest, to [a] (the short *a* of German *Mann*), and moved farther to the front by 1500 to become our normal short *a* [æ] as in *at, cat,* or *pat.* Conservative speakers, however, kept the pronunciation [a] until well into the seventeenth century. The [a] pronunciation was generally retained before *-r,* so *are, far,* and *war* would have had the same vowel.

The situation was rather different when the vowel was followed by *-l;* there the Middle English vowel was a full back vowel [ɑ], as in American English *got* (thus *all, call, fall* would have been pronounced [ɑl], [kɑl] and [fɑl]). By about 1500 this had become [ɔ] as in Modern English *coffee* or *all.* From about 1500 on, short *a* after *w-* was rounded to [a], giving a pronunciation of [want] for *want,* and [was] for *was.* This is especially noticeable in seventeenth-century rhymes like *guarded/rewarded, regard/ward.*

e In stressed syllables, pronounced [ɛ] with little of the variation found in Modern English (compare *bed* and *serve*). Short *e* was commonly raised to *i* before *-ng (England);* modern usage is generally a good guide to this. From the fifteenth century on, it was very common to lower short *e* to short *a* [a] when followed by *-r.* This change is sometimes, though not always, indicated in the spelling, thus *sarve* for *serve, sarjent* for *sergeant.* Shakespeare's rhyme *deserts/parts* is a good example; both words would have had [a].

In unstressed syllables, short *e* presents some specific problems, which are discussed below under "Other Considerations," pp. 25–27.

i [ɪ]; spelling commonly alternated with *y,* especially in Middle English. This is merely a spelling variant and does not indicate a difference in pronunciation. Both *i* and its long form *j* were used to indicate the consonant [dʒ], and spellings like *Iesus* do not necessarily indicate a pronunciation with [j] as in *yet,* though in very early texts they may do so.

o Until the late sixteenth century pronounced [ɔ]. Before *-gh* it was pronounced [ɔu] and was often written *-ough* (as in *broghte/broughte*). In the late sixteenth century this vowel was often unrounded to [a], giving spelling variants like *stop/stap.*

A major exception to the pronunciation of *o* as [ɔ] occurs in words which in Modern English have *o* pronounced [ʌ] *(love, yong).* In these cases the vowel would have been pronounced [ʊ] without the unrounding of Modern English. On the evidence of the orthoepists, this unrounding began around the 1640s, so until about that time words that now contain the unrounded vowel [ʌ] would have been pronounced with [ʊ], whether spelled with *o* or *u.* Thus *love* would be [lʊv] rather than [lʌv]. The same vowel was also found in words spelled with *-or-,* such as *world* and *worth,* for which the pronunciation would in later Middle English have been [wʊr̩ld] and [wʊr̩θ]. This change is difficult to date; before about 1500 the pronunciation may still have been [ɔ], thus [wɔr̩ld] and [wɔr̩θ]. Note that this pronunciation survives in the Lancashire dialect of British English.

u Until the seventeenth century this was the rounded vowel of *put* [ʊ], rather than the unrounded vowel of *but* [ʌ]. The Modern English unrounded sound may have begun to appear in speech soon after 1600, but the older rounded vowel remained, especially in conservative speech, until the 1640s. Note that this is the same vowel that is spelled *o* in words like *love.*

Long Vowels

Most difficulties with the pronunciation of earlier English occur in the sounds of long vowels, for they were changed markedly by the Great Vowel Shift during the fifteenth century. The situation is complicated by the fact that the conservatism in spelling brought in, at least in part, by the introduction of printing, preserved many spellings that reflect pronunciations in use before the Vowel Shift. As we will see, the Modern English pronunciation of a word is frequently a useful guide to the path it has taken in earlier centuries.

a The history of the pronunciation of long *a* is probably the most complex of any sound in English, and accuracy in its various sounds is the most critical single factor in a convincing recreation of early pronunciation. The principal thing to remember is that the long *a* of Modern English (as in *name*) did not exist until the nineteenth century.

In a great many words pronounced with long *a* in Old English, the vowel moved quite far back in the mouth to become a sound closer to *o* [ɔ:]; this change had already begun in the later Old English period and was common except in the north of England and Scotland by the twelfth century *(stan/stone),* although with some words, like *and/ond,* the *o* spelling did not become standard. The spelling is sometimes a guide to just how far back in the mouth the writer considered this vowel to lie.

In words retaining long *a* in Modern English, the Old English sound had by the later fourteenth century become [ɑ:], the sound of Modern English *father.* The two sounds are not easily distinguished, especially in singing, and the [ɑ:] vowel may be considered the norm for texts before the middle of the fifteenth century. Words that retained long *a* are pronounced [e:i] in Modern English *(name, take).*

By the middle of the fifteenth century the pronunciation of long *a* was beginning to move toward [æ:]. This shift was complete by about 1500, though the pronunciation [ɑ:] was retained in conservative speech. The [æ:] pronunciation was short-lived, and by the middle of the century had moved farther up in the mouth to [ɛ:]. This sound became the norm for the rest of the sixteenth and seventeenth centuries. It is easy enough to reproduce this vowel by sounding the Modern English vowel (as in *name*) and moving the tongue down slightly. Early in the eighteenth century the vowel moved up to its modern position as [e:], but without the slight diphthongization [e:i], which most modern speakers introduce into words like *name* and *take.* This vowel would have also served for words in which long *a* has become [æ:] as in Modern English *(have),* so that *have* could rhyme with *save,* pronounced [hɛ:v] and [sɛ:v].

e In the Middle English period there were two forms of long *e,* generally called "open" and "close." The two are not usually difficult to distinguish if a Modern English cognate is available, since words with Middle English open *e* (*speke, dreme, pece;* pronounced [ɛ:]) generally came to be spelled with *ea* during the sixteenth century *(speak, dream, peace),* while words with Middle English close *e* (pronounced [e:]) came to be spelled with *e, ee,* or sometimes *ie (he, see, grief).* Unfortunately this was not unambiguous, for the *ea* combination was already in common use for two other sounds: [ɛ:] as in *yea, break, great,* and the short *e* [ɛ], which had appeared in closed syllables in early Middle English in words like *death* and *head.*

The history of the open *e* is more complex, for it took several routes. In most words with open *e,* the [ɛ:] pronunciation was retained well into the seventeenth century by most speakers (allowing Falstaff's pun on *reason/raisin*). The upward shift to [e:], which became the norm later in the seventeenth century, may have begun in the pronunciation of some speakers as early as the 1570s. In words that have the vowel [i:], as in Modern English *(teach, dream),* the [ɛ:] pronunciation may have been retained at least into the eighteenth century (for example, in Swift's rhyme of *creature* and *nature,* and Pope's rhyme of *pleased* and *raised*). There is, however, considerable argument about this, and some scholars date the upward shift from [ɛ:] to [e:] to the fifteenth century.

Close *e,* which was pronounced [e:] through the Middle English period, moved up by the early sixteenth century to its present sound [i:]. In final position (usually spelled *-y* or *-ie*) and in unaccented positions, this sound was probably shortened slightly to [i], as in *every* [ɛvri] or *methinks* [miθɪnks].

i Long *i,* also frequently spelled *y* as in *hide/hyde,* was pronounced [i:] through most of the Middle English period. From the early fifteenth century it underwent a series of small changes, eventually resulting in the diphthong of Modern English, [ai] as in *rise.* Early in the fifteenth century a slight diphthongization developed to [ii:], which by the middle of the century became [ʌi]. Both of these diphthongs were pronounced without a stress on the initial element of the diphthong; that is, the two elements were of approximately equal weight. Early in the sixteenth century, the sound moved to [ʌi] with initial stress, that is, the first element of the diphthong became the more important. This sound remained until the late eighteenth century, at which time it moved to its present sound, [ai].

Final long *i* is a problem. Rhymes from the late sixteenth and early seventeenth centuries would suggest that both [i:] and [ai] were possible *(he/harmony* as well as *eye/victory).* The problem arises when two words with ambiguous final *-y* (or *-ie*) rhyme. It is likely that in a rhyme like *beautifies/harmonies* both words would be pronounced with [ai], but since both pronunciations existed we cannot be certain. These variations probably indicate flexibility in pronunciation of final *-y/-ie;* they are unlikely to indicate that [i:] was accepted as a rhyme for [ai].

o As with long *e,* we must distinguish between open and close forms of long *o.* The open form, which became Modern English long *o* as in *most, stone,* or *roast,* was pronounced [ɔ:] until the fifteenth century. The close form gave Modern English words spelled with *oo* as in *food, good, blood* (note the wide variation of Modern English pronunciation) and a few words pronounced with [u:] though spelled with a single *o (do).* Until the fifteenth century this vowel was pronounced [o:].

By the end of the fifteenth century, the open *o* had moved from [ɔ:] to [o:], with the exception of a very few words like *hot,* in which the vowel became short. Words with closed syllables in which the *o* had been shortened early in the Middle English period retained that quality *(soft).*

The situation with the close *o* is more complex. By the end of the fifteenth century the Middle English vowel [o:] had moved up to [u:] as in *food,* though this was sometimes shortened to [ʊ] as in *foot.* There seems to have been a good deal of inconsistency in the pronunciation of this sound during the sixteenth and seventeenth centuries (as with the Modern English pronunciation of *roof*), and it is not clear whether Shakespeare's rhymes of *reprove/love, mood/blood,* and *food/good* represent real or traditional rhymes.

At least until the eighteenth century the word *one* was pronounced with a long *o* [o:n], rather than [wʌn] as in Modern English, giving rhymes like *one/own/grown.*

u The Old English long *u* [u:] remained through the Middle English period in native words like *hus* (house). In French loan-words *u* was probably pronounced with the French vowel [y:] by upper-class speakers (especially those who knew some French) perhaps until as late as the end of the fourteenth century *(vertu).*

From the beginning of the fifteenth century, long *u* underwent a series of changes toward a diphthong, similar to the changes seen in long *i.* By the end of the century the sound had become [əu:]. As with long *i,* this diphthong did not have an initial stress and both its elements were weighted about equally. Early in the sixteenth century the pronunciation shifted to [ʌu] with initial stress, a pronunciation now heard in some forms of Canadian English (as in *house, about*). This sound remained the norm until the end of the eighteenth century, when it shifted in British (and American) speech to its present position [au].

Diphthongs

A diphthong consists of two vowel sounds with a glide between that act like a single sound. The first vowel sound is the principal element of the diphthong, taking about two-thirds of the length of time it takes to pronounce the whole diphthong. Diphthongs are never broken by syllable divisions. Generally, the second element of a diphthong is rarely fully long, thus Modern English *ride* is [raid] rather than [rai:d]. Before the Great Vowel Shift, diphthongs were indicated by the spelling with fair consistency. That was no longer true after the Vowel Shift, as can be seen by the treatment of the diphthongs created from the Middle English high long vowels *i* and *u.* Long *u,* which in Modern English became [au], is consistently spelled *ou* (as in *house*), while Middle English long *i,* which became Modern English [ai] as in *ride,* is spelled as a single vowel.

Diphthongs can occasionally be difficult to recognize in some positions. In a word like *eye,* the *y* is in effect a consonant, so the combination *ey* is not a diphthong. The syllable break is *e·ye,* so the Middle English pronunciation would have generally been [i:e]. It is quite likely, however, that the same apparent ambiguity we see in the word existed for speakers in the fourteenth century as well, and the pronunciation [ʌi:e] (where the word has been read as diphthong *ey* + *e*) may have existed alongside the more usual [i:e].

ai/ay/ei/ey These four spellings all represented the same sound, which until the early fifteenth century was pronounced [æi] as in *maiden, sayde, fair.* At some point, most likely during the fifteenth century, the diphthong [æi] became a single sound [ɑ:], falling in with the long *a* of *name.* From then on its history follows the same course as long *a,* becoming successively [æ:] by about 1500 and moving to [ɛ:] shortly after, retaining that sound until it became [e:] in the early eighteenth century.

au/aw This diphthong was pronounced [au] until the late sixteenth century, though before *n, m,* and *gh (=f)* it may well have been pronounced [ɑ:] as in *daunce, chaumbre, straunge, laughter.* By the early seventeenth century it had become [ɔ:].

eu/ew Until the seventeenth century this diphthong was pronounced in two ways: [iu] in words like *newe, knew,* or *trewe;* [ɛu] in words like *fewe, lewed, bewte.* Spellings like *true* would suggest that after *r* the diphthong could often become a single vowel [u:]. In the seventeenth century these two sounds fell together as [iu], the [ɛu] pronunciation disappearing entirely. In colloquial speech, at least from the late sixteenth century on, the diphthong [iu] was probably often sounded as [ju] as in Modern English *(beauty).*

oi/oy This diphthong fell into two groups in Middle English: words like *choise, joy,* or *cloister,* in which it was consistently pronounced [oi], and words like *anoint, boil, join* (many of them derived from Anglo-Norman), in which it could be pronounced either as [oi] or [ui]. The [oi] pronunciation remained unchanged, but during the sixteenth century the pronunciation [ui] was unrounded to [ʌi], just as happened with [ʊ]. The result was that it became identical with the pronunciation of long *i,* giving rhymes like *boil/bile, join/line.* Note that the pronunciation with the diphthong [oi] existed side by side with [ai]; a poet's rhymes can be a good guide to the pronunciation of these words.

ou/ow/ough For the Middle English period, these forms could indicate both a diphthong and a single sound. The diphthong occurred in words in which the vowel is now pronounced [o:] as in *know,* [oʌ] as in *soul,* and [ɔ:] before *-ght* as in *thought.* In these words, the sound was [ɔʊ] in Middle English and became [oʊ] by early in the fifteenth century. This diphthong tended by the early sixteenth century to become the single sound [o:], or [ɔ:] before *-ght.*

The single sound [u:] occurred in words that today have the sounds [au] as in *house,* [ɔ:] as in *course,* or [u:] as in *through.* The spelling of this sound could vary considerably, but the Modern English pronunciation is a reliable guide. This pronunciation [u:] fell together with that of long *u* in some cases (giving [ʌu] not only in words like *proud,* but also in *wound,* which could thus rhyme with *sound*). In other cases it remained [u:], especially before *-gh (through).*

Other Considerations

Unstressed short *e:* In Middle English, short *e* was frequently unpronounced in unstressed syllables; the situation was somewhat different depending on whether the *e* occurred in a medial or a final position. In medial positions, short *-e-* was the weakest vowel in the language, with the result that it was very easily lost. In a great many cases, the loss of unstressed *-e-* was a characteristic both of the individual speaker and of the formality of speech (compare the differences between *every* and *ev'ry, lovèd* and *lov'd*). Thus pronunciations with and without the unstressed *-e-* frequently existed simultaneously. Poets often took advantage of this situation, anticipating a pronunciation with or without the *-e-* (which normally created an extra syllable) as metrically appropriate. The dropping of an unstressed *-e-* was sometimes indicated in the spelling, but not with any consistency. For such contraction the metrics usually provide a better guide than the spelling. It is not certain whether an unstressed *e* always retained the pronunciation [ɛ] or was frequently reduced to neutral vowel [ə]; though this reduction is likely, it could not have been indicated in spelling.

For unstressed *-e* in final position the situation is slightly different. One of the major changes in the English language during the Middle Ages was the widespread loss of inflections (or "endings," as they are most commonly known), which in Old English had distinguished the different functional cases of nouns, pronouns, and adjectives as well as the different forms of verbs. The loss of many of these inflections began in the late Old English period and continued into the thirteenth century, by the end of which most of the grammatical functions previously indicated by an ending were now shown by the order of the words in the sentence. Some inflections remained, of course, and have done so into Modern English (such as *'s* to indicate possession and *-ed* to indicate the past tense of a weak verb). Through much of the fifteenth century the inflections that did remain, such as *-es* as a plural ending and *-ed* for the past tense of a verb, were still pronounced.

Those inflections whose grammatical purpose was lost did not, however, immediately disappear, but remained in a great many cases as a final unstressed *-e*. The pronunciation of this final *-e* disappeared slowly through the fourteenth century (and perhaps the early fifteenth), though it is clear that even when it was no longer sounded in speech it was used by poets for metrical purposes, though it generally seems to have been dropped before a word beginning with a vowel or *h-*. Thus the metrics (and in some cases the music) is usually the best guide to whether or not to pronounce a final *-e*. By 1500 or shortly thereafter, the metrical use of final *-e* had ceased.

-ure: The combination *-ure* occurs most frequently in French loan-words, and until well into the fourteenth century was probably pronounced as in French [-yr̩]. In later periods the pronunciation of this group depended on whether the syllable in which it occurred was stressed (as in *sure*) or not (as in *nature*).

In stressed syllables, the vowel *u* became palatalized (that is, preceded by a "y" sound [j]), but the consonant before it did not. Since the effect of palatalization on consonants varies from consonant to consonant, some examples will make this clearer. Note the difference in the American and British pronunciations of a word like *tune:* [tu:n] in American English, with no palatalization, and [tju:n] or [tʃu:n] in British English, with, in the first case, a palatalization of the vowel, and in the second, a palatalization of the initial consonant. Thus in a word like *sure,* the *s* remained [s] rather than being palatalized to [ʃ] and the pronunciation would have been [sju:r̩] rather than Modern English [ʃu:r]; similarly the *d* in *endure* would not have been palatalized to [dʒ], giving [ɛndju:r̩] rather than [ɛndʒu:r] as in some dialects of Modern English.

In unstressed syllables no palatalization at all took place, so that well into the seventeenth century and probably later the normal pronunciation was [ər], allowing Swift to rhyme *venture* and *centre.* The Modern English pronunciation of both stressed and unstressed *-ure* with palatalization of a preceding consonant certainly existed by the late seventeenth century but, as the orthoepist Christopher Cooper remarked in 1685, it was considered a barbarism.

Other combinations of long *u* + consonant (in which the length of the vowel is indicated by a final silent *e*) were pronounced the same in both stressed syllables *(tune, tube, dupe)* and unstressed *(fortune)*.

-ion, -ioun: Consonants followed by the group *-ion* or *-ioun* are not palatalized and retain their full syllabic value. Thus *habitacioun* would contain five syllables, [habıtası·u:n] rather than [hæbıta:ʃʌn].

DIACHRONIC SOUND CHART FOR ENGLISH

An asterisk (*) indicates that the change is not universal; the appropriate section of the text should be read for clarification.

1100 1200 1300 1400 1500 1600 1700

VOWELS

SHORT VOWELS

Spelling	Development
a	[a] --- [æ]* ---→
(before *l*)	--- [o] --- [ɑ]* ---→
e	[ɛ] ---→
(before *r*)	--- [a] (often) ---→
(in unstressed syllables, see pp. 25–26)	
i	[ɪ] ---→
(can also represent *j*)	
o	[ɔ] --- [a] (often) ---→
	[ʊ]* --- [ʌ] ---→
u	[ʊ] --- [ʌ] ---→

LONG VOWELS (Great Vowel Shift)

Spelling	Development
a	[ɔ:] --- [o:] --- [æ:] --- [ɛ:] --- [e:]→
e (open*)	[ɛ:] --- [e:]* ---→
e (close*)	[e:] --- [i:] ---→
i	[i:] --- [ii:] - [ʌi:] - [ʌi] ---→
(for final *i*, see p. 23)	
o (open*)	[ɔ:] --- [o:]* ---→
o (close*)	[o:] --- [u:]* ---→
u	[u:] --- [ʌu:] - [ʌu] ---→
	[y:] in Fr loan-words --- [u:] ---→

DIPHTHONGS

Spelling	Development
ai, ay, ei, ey	[æi] --- [o:] - [æ:] --- [ɛ:] --- [e:]→
au, aw	[au] --- [ɔ:] ---→
eu, ew	[iu] or [ɛu]* --- [iu] ---→
oi, oy	[oi] or [ui]* --- [oi] or [ʌi]* ---→
ou, ow, ough	[ɔʊ] --- [oʊ] --- [o:] or [ɔ:]*- →
	or*
	[u:]* ---→

CONSONANTS

Spelling	Development
b	[b] ---→
c	[k] before *a, o, u;* [s] before *e, i* ---→
ch	[tʃ] or [k] ---→
d	[d] ---→
f	[f] or [v] ---→
g	[g] before *a, o, u;* [dʒ] before *e, i* ---→

	1100 1200 1300 1400 1500 1600 1700
gh	[x] ------ | (disappears or becomes [f])
h	weak [h] ------→ (can also indicate [ç] or [x] to about 1300)
j	[dʒ], but often interchangeable with *i* ------→
k	[k] ------→
l	[l] ------→
m	[m] ------→
n	[n] ------→
ng	[ŋg] ------ [ŋ] (final) ------ [ŋ] (all positions) - →
p	[p] ------→
ph	[f] ------→
q	[k] ------→
r	[r̥] ------→
s	[s] or [z] ------ →
sh	[ʃ] ------→
t	[t] ------→
th	[θ] or [ð] ------ →
þ	
ð	
v	[v] ------→ (can also represent *u*)
w	[w] ------→
y	[j] ------→ (can also represent *i*)

SAMPLE TEXTS

A St. Godric hymn

The three short hymns of St. Godric, dating from about the third quarter of the twelfth century, are the earliest texts in English with musical setting. They survive in several manuscripts; this transcription is based on British Library, Royal MS. 5 f vii, f. 85. CD #2.

Sainte marie uirgine
moder ihesu cristes nazarene,
onfo, scild, help þin Godric;
onfang, bring heȝelic wið þe in Godes riche.

5 Sainte marie, christes bur,
maidenes clenhad, moderes flur,
dilie min sinne, rix in min mod,
bring me to winne wiþ þe selfe God.

sɑintɛ mɑṛi:·ɛ vi:ṛgi:nɛ
mo:dɛṛ dʒe:zu: kṛi:stɛz nɑzɑṛɛnɛ
ɔnfo ʃɪld hɛlp ði:n go:dṛɪtʃ
ɔnfɔŋg bṛɪŋg he:jɪlɪtʃ wɪð ðe: ɪn gɔdɛz ṛi:tʃɛ

5 sɑintɛ mɑṛi:·ɛ kṛi:stɛz bu:ṛ
mɑidɛnɛz kle:nhɑd mo:dɛṛɛz flu:ṛ
dɪli:·ɛ mi:n sɪnnɛ ṛɪks ɪn mi:n mo:d
bṛɪŋg me: tɔ wɪnnɛ wɪð ðɛ sɛlvɛ gɔd

NOTES

1 *uirgine: u* is merely a spelling variant for *v.*
2 *ihesu:* the *h* derives from a common misinterpretation of the Greek letter eta (η) and is of no significance.
5 *christes:* the manuscript uses the Greek letters χρ for *chr.*
7–8 *sinne, winne:* double consonants seem to have indicated a doubled sound (as in *pen-knife*).
8 *selfe:* the manuscript reads *selfd,* an obvious error.

Mirie it is

This secular lyric of about 1225 is found in MS. Rawlinson G 22, f. 1v. The lower part of the page is missing, so it is not clear if there were further verses. CD #3.

Mirie it is while sumer ilast
wið fugheles song!
oc nu necheþ windes blast
and weder strong.
5 Ej! ej! what þis nicht is long,

and ich wiþ wel michel wrong
soregh and murne and fast.

mıṛi: ıt ıs hwi:lɛ sʊmɛṛ ılast
wıð fu:xɛlɛs sɔŋg
ɔk nu: nɛtʃɛθ wındɛs blast
and wɛdɛṛ stṛɔŋg
5 ai ai hwat ðıs nıçt ıs lɔŋg
and ıtʃ wıð wɛl mıtʃɛl wṛɔŋg
sɔṛɛx and mu:ṛn and fast

NOTES

6 *wiþ*: the manuscript reads *wid,* but see l. 2, which gives the normal form.
7 *soregh:* the final consonant may be silent.

Edi beo thu

This devotional song from the second half of the thirteenth century is found in Oxford, Corpus Christi College, MS 59, f. 113v. It was probably composed at Llanthony Priory, Gloucestershire. The first two of its eight stanzas are given here; the manuscript's ʒ has been replaced with *y* where it indicates the sound [j]. CD #4.

Edi beo þu, heuene quene,
folkes froure and engles blis,
moder unwemmed and maiden clene,
swich in world non oþer nis.
5 On þe hit is wel eþ-sene
of alle wimmen þu hauest þet pris.
Mi swete leuedi, her mi bene
and reu of me yif þi wille is.

Þu asteye so þe daiy-rewe
10 þe deleð from þe deorke nicht.
Of þe sprong a leome newe
þat al þis world haueð ilizt.
Nis non maide of þine heowe,
swo fair, so sschene, so rudi, swo bricht.
15 <Mi> swete leuedi of me þu reowe
and haue merci of þin knicht.

e:dı be: ðu: hɛvɛnɛ kwe:nɛ
fɔlkɛs fṛu:ṛ(ɛ) and ɛŋglɛs blıs
mo:dɛṛ ʊnwɛmɛd and mæidɛn cle:nɛ
swıtʃ ın wɔṛld no:n o:ðɛṛ nıs

5 ɔn ðe: hɪt ɪs wɛl ɛθse:nɛ
ɔv alɛ wɪmɛn ðu: hɑ:vɛst ðɛt pṛi:s
mi: swe:tɛ le:vɛdi hɛ:ṛ mi: be:nɛ
and ṛɛu ɔv me: jif ði: wɪlɛ ɪs

ðu: aste:jɛ sɔ: ðɛ dæi ṛiu·ɛ
10 ðe: de:lɛθ fṛɔm ðɛ dɛṛkɛ nɪçt
ɔv ðe: spṛɔŋg a le:mɛ niu·ɛ
ðat al ðɪs wɔṛld havɛθ ɪlɪçt
nɪs no:n mæid ɔv ði:nɛ hiu·ɛ
sɔ: fæiṛ sɔ: ʃe:nɛ sɔ: ṛʊdi: sɔ: bṛɪçt
15 mi: swe:tɛ le:vdi ɔv me: ðu: ṛiu·(ɛ)
and havɛ mɛṛsi: ɔv ði:n knɪçt

NOTES

1 *beo:* the *o* is an archaism that was probably not pronounced.
1, 6, 7, etc. *heuene, hauest, leuedi,* etc.: the *u* here is a common spelling variant for *v.*
4 or possibly [wɔṛuld].
9 *daiy-rewe:* the *y* is redundant and may be ignored; the word would normally be spelled either *dai* or *day.*
10 þe: it is, or course, vital to distinguish here between the definite article [ðɛ] and the second person pronoun [ðe:]. Their spelling was not clearly differentiated until well into the sixteenth century.
11 *leome:* see note to l. 1.
13 *maide:* the music would suggest the elision of the final *-e* before a following vowel.
14 *swolso:* the *w* is an archaism preserved from Old English; the occurrence of the normal spelling in the same line would imply that it is not to be pronounced.
15 *levedi:* medial vowels in weak positions (especially short *-e-*) were frequently dropped; the music would suggest here that the word has only two syllables.
15 *reowe:* see note to l. 1, as well as the spelling of l. 8.

I haue set my hert so hye

This song from Bodleian MS. Douce 381, f. 20 is from about 1400, before the Great Vowel Shift. It shows some northern dialectal forms *(hert* for *hart,* þenk for *think)* that would not necessarily be found in texts written farther south. E. J. Dobson is surely right (given the music) that the last line of the poem is intended as a refrain to be sung at the end of each stanza; I have also accepted his adjustment of the verb of this refrain for the second stanza.

I haue set my hert so hye,
me likyt no love þat lower ys;
and all þe paynes þat y may dry,
me þenk hyt do me good, ywys,
5 me þenk yt do, ywis.

For on that lord þat loved us all
so hertely have I set my þowʒt,

yt ys my joie on hym to call,
for love me haþ in balus browȝt,
10 me þenk yt haþ, ywis.

i: hav sɛt mi: hɛ:ṛt sɔ: hi:
me: li:kɪt nɔ: lʊv ðat lɔ:wɛṛ ɪs
and al ðɛ pæinz ðat i: mai dṛi:
me: θɛnk (h)ɪt do: me: go:d ɪwɪs
5 me: θɛnk (h)ɪt do: ɪwɪs

fɔṛ ɔn ðat lɔṛd ðat lʊvɪd ʊs al
sɔ: hɛ:ṛtɛli hav i: sɛt mi: θɔʊxt
ɪt ɪs mi: dʒoi ɔn hɪm tɔ: kal
fɔṛ lʊv me: haθ ɪn balʊs bṛɔʊxt
10 me: θɛnk (h)ɪt haθ ɪwɪs

NOTES

4–5, 10 *hyt, yt:* the variation in the spelling here would suggest a very weakly aspirated *h.*
6–8 *loved, hertely, joie:* these are all representative cases in which decisions about the pronunciation of an unstressed short *e* must be made on metrical grounds.
9 *balus:* or [baləs]; the plural ending would more often be spelled *-es.*

Owt of your slepe

Two phonetic transcriptions follow for this fifteenth-century carol (Oxford, Bodleian Library, MS. Arch. Selden B 26, f. 14v). The first represents a pronunciation from early in the century, before the Great Vowel Shift; the second a pronunciation from the end of the fifteenth century or early in the sixteenth, after the Vowel Shift. CD #5 and #6.

Owt of your slepe aryse and wake,
For God mankynd nowe hath ytake
Al of a maide without eny make;
Of al women she bereth the belle.
5 Nowel!

And thorwe a maide faire and wys
Now man is made of ful grete pris;
Now angelys knelen to mannys seruys,
And at this tyme al this byfel.
10 Nowel!

Now man is brighter than the sonne;
Now man in heuen an hye shal wone;
Blessyd be God this game is begonne;
And his moder emperesse of helle.
15 Nowel!

That euer was thrall, now ys he fre;
That euer was small, now grete is she;
Now shal God deme bothe the and me
   Vnto his blysse yf we do wel.
20   Nowel!

Now man may to heuen wende;
Now heuen and erthe to hym they bende;
He that was foo now is oure frende;
   This is no nay that Y yowe telle.
25   Nowel!

Now, blessyd brother, graunte vs grace
A domesday to se thy face
And in thy courte to haue a place,
   That we mow there synge nowel.
30   Nowel!

Pre-Vowel Shift

u:t ɔv yuṛ sle:p aṛi:z and wɑ:k
fɔr gɔd manki:nd nu: haθ ɪtɑ:k
al ɔv a mæid wɪðu:t ɛni mɑ:k
   ɔv al wɪmɛn ʃe: bɛ:ṛɛθ ðɛ bɛl
5   nɔ:wɛl

and θɔṛu a mæidɛ fæiṛ and wi:s
nu: man ɪs mɑ:d ɔv fʊl gṛɛ:t pṛi:s
nu: andʒɛlɪs kne:lɛn to: manɪs sɛṛvi:s
   and at ðɪs ti:m al ðɪs bifɛl
10   nɔ:wɛl

nu: man ɪs bṛiçtɛṛ ðan ðɛ sʊn
nu: man ɪn hɛvɛn an hi: ʃal wɔ:n
blɛsɪd be: gɔd ðɪs gɑm ɪs bigʊn
   and hɪs mo:dɛṛ ɛmpṛɛs ɔv hɛl
15   nɔ:wɛl

ðat ɛvɛṛ was θṛal nu: ɪs he: fṛe:
ðat ɛvɛṛ was smal nu: gṛɛ:t ɪs ʃe:
nu: ʃɑl gɔd de:m bɔ:θ ðe: and me:
   ʊnto: hɪs blɪs ɪf we: do: wɛl
20   nɔ:wɛl

nu: man mæi to: hɛvɛn wɛnd
nu: hɛvɛn and ɛ:ṛθ to: hɪm ðæi bɛnd
he: ðat was fɔ: nu: ɪs u:ṛ fṛɛnd

ðɪs ɪs nɔ: næi ðat i: ju: tɛl
25 nɔ:wɛl

nu: blɛsɪd bṛo:ðɛṛ gṛant ʊs gṛɑ:s
a do:mɛzdæi to: se: ði: fɑ:s
and ɪn ði: ku:ṛt to: hav a plɑ:s
ðat we: mɔʊ ðɛṛ(ɛ) sɪŋ no:wɛl
30 nɔ:wɛl

Post-Vowel Shift

ʌut ɔv yuṛ sli:p aṛʌiz ænd wæ:k
fɔṛ gɔd mænkʌind nʌu hæθ ɪtæ:k
ɔl ɔv a mæ:d wɪðut ɛni mæ:k
ɔv ɔl wɪmɛn ʃi: bɛṛɛθ ðɛ bɛl
5 no:wɛl

ænd θṛu: a mæ:dɛ fæ:ṛ ænd wʌiz
nʌu mæn ɪs mæ:d ɔv fʊl gṛe:t pṛʌis
nʌu æ:ndʒɛls kni:lɛn tu: mænz sɛṛvʌis
ænd æt ðɪs tʌim ɔl ðɪs bifɛl
10 no:wɛl

nʌu mæn ɪs bṛʌitəṛ ðæn ðɛ sʊn
nʌu mæn ɪn hɛvən an hʌi ʃæl wo:n
blɛsɪd be: gɔd ðɪs gæ:m ɪs bɛgʊn
ænd hɪs mʊdəṛ ɛmpṛɛs ɔv hɛl
15 no:wɛl

ðæt ɛvəṛ was θṛal nʌu ɪs hi: fṛi:
ðæt ɛvəṛ was smal nʌu gṛe:t ɪs ʃi:
nʌu ʃæl gɔd dɛ:m bo:θ ði: ænd mi:
ʊntu: hɪs blɪs ɪf we: du: wɛl
20 no:wɛl

nʌu mæn mæ: tu: hɛvən wɛnd
nʌu hɛvən ænd ɛṛθ tu: hɪm ðæ: bɛnd
hi: ðæt was fo: nʌu ɪs ʌuṛ fṛɛnd
ðɪs ɪs no: næ: ðæt ʌi juu: tɛl
25 no:wɛl

nʌu blɛsɪd bṛʊðəṛ gṛaunt ʊs gṛæ:s
a du:mzdæ: tu: si: ðʌi fæ:s
ænd ɪn ðʌi ku:ṛt tu: hæv a plæ:s
ðæt wi: mo: ðɛṛ sɪŋ no:wɛl
30 no:wɛl

NOTES

14 *moder:* this vowel must have been shortened before the Vowel Shift; the *-d-* may indicate [ð] as in the common spelling variants *murder/murther.*

26 *brother:* see note to l. 14.

Pastime with good company

One of the best-known pieces in Henry VIII's manuscript (British Library, MS. Add. 31922, ff. 14v–15), this song is also found in two versions in Ritson's manuscript (British Library, MS. Add. 5665, ff. 136v-137 and 141v–142). CD#7.

Pastime with good company
I love and shall until I die.
Gruch so will, but none deny;
So God be pleas'd, so live will I;
5 For my pastance,
Hunt, sing and dance;
My heart is set
All goodly sport
For my comfort:
10 Who shall me let?

Youth must have some dalliance,
Of good or ill some pastance;
Company methinks then best
All thoughts and fancies to digest,
15 For idleness
Is chief mistress
Of vices all:
Then who can say
But mirth and play
20 Is best of all?

Company with honesty
Is virtue, vices to flee;
Company is good and ill,
But every man hath his free will.
25 The best ensue,
The worst eschew,
My mind shall be;
Virtue to use,
Vice to refuse,
30 Thus shall I use me.

pæstʌim wɪð gud kumpæni
ʌi luv ænd ʃæl untɪl ʌi dʌi

gṛutʃ so: wɪl bʊt nʊn di:nʌi
so: gɔd bi: pli:zd so: lɪv wɪl ʌi
5 fɔṛ mʌi pæstɑ:ns
hʊnt sɪŋ ænd dɑ:ns
mʌi hɛ:ṛt ɪs sɛt
ɔl gʊdli spɔṛt
fɔṛ mʌi kʊmfɔṛt
10 hu: ʃæl mi: lɛt

ju:θ mʊst hæv sʊm dæli·ɑ:ns
ɔv gʊd ɔṛ ɪl sʊm pæstɑ:ns
kʊmpæni miθɪnks ðɛn bɛst
ɔl θɔts ænd fænsiz tu: dɪdʒɛst
15 fɔṛ ʌidlnɛs
ɪs tʃi:f mɪstṛɛs
ɔv vʌisɛz ɔl
ðɛn hu: kæn sæ:
bʊt mɪṛθ ænd plæ:
20 ɪs bɛst ɔv ɔl

kʊmpæni wɪð ɔnɛsti
ɪs vɛṛtu: vʌisɛz tu: fli:
kʊmpæni ɪs gʊd ænd ɪl
bʊt ɛvṛi mæn hæθ hɪs fṛi: wɪl
25 ðɛ bɛst ɛnsu:
ðɛ wʊṛst ɛstʃu:
mʌi mʌind ʃæl bi:
vɛṛtu: tu: ju:z
vʌis tu: ṛɛfju:z
30 ðʊs ʃæl ʌi ju:z mi:

NOTES

21 *company, honesty:* I have slightly shortened these final long *i*'s, but given the rhyme with *flee* (which cannot be shortened), it may be preferable to keep them long.

All creatures now are merry-minded

This well-known madrigal was John Bennet's contribution to the *Triumphs of Oriana* of 1601. CD #8.

All creatures now are merry, merry-minded.
The shepherds' daughters playing,
The nymphs are fa-la-la-ing,
Yond bugle was well winded.
5 At Oriana's presence each thing smileth.

The flowers themselves discover,
Birds over her do hover;
Music the time beguileth.
See where she comes, with flowery garlands crowned
10 Queen of all queens renowned.
  Then sang the shepherds and nymphs of Diana:
  Long live fair Oriana!

ɔl kṛɛ:təṛz nʌu aṛ mɛṛi mɛṛi mʌindɛd
ðə ʃɛpəṛdz dɔ:təṛz plɛ:·ɪŋ
ðə nɪmfs aṛ falalaɪŋ
jɔnd bju:gl wɔs wɛl wʌindɛd
5 æt ɔṛi:ænaz pṛɛzɛns i:tʃ θɪŋ smʌi:lɛθ
ðə flʌuṛz ðɛmsɛlvz dɪskᴜvɛṛ
bəṛdz o:vəṛ həṛ du: hᴜvəṛ
mju:zɪk ðə tʌim bɪgʌilɛθ
si: hwɛ:ṛ ʃi: kᴜmz wɪð flʌuṛi gaṛlənds kṛʌunɛd
10 kwi:n ɔv ɔl kwi:nz ṛinʌunɛd
  ðɛn sæŋ ðə ʃɛpəṛdz ænd nɪmfs ɔv di:·æna
  lɔŋ lɪv fɛ:ṛ ɔṛi:·æna

NOTES

2, etc. *the, shepherds,* etc.: By this time, the short vowels were definitely pronounced as [ə], but it is not certain whether they were sung that way. They may have retained their short vowel sound in singing, [ðɛ] and [ʃɛpɛṛdz]; in l. 7 [bɪṛdz].

3

Sixteenth-Century Scots

DAVID N. KLAUSNER

Sixteenth-century Scots was a dialect of Early Modern English. Most of its consonants and some of its vowels follow closely the history of English sounds. The following outline discusses only the sounds that differ from those of English.

The spelling of Middle Scots is often a good indication of the places in which it differs from English in pronunciation. Since none of the Scottish music of the sixteenth century was ever printed, and survives only in manuscript copies, the spelling of its texts is more strongly phonetic than that of English of the same period. For the same reason, Scots spelling also exhibits individual vagaries that are less likely to occur in printed sources. The following characteristics of the language are usually reflected in the spelling:

1. *i* following *e, o, u,* and often *a* indicates a long vowel. Thus we commonly find spellings like *feir, befoir, puir,* and *mair.* This usage also indicates the pronunciation of words like *devoir* [dεvo:r̩] and *rejois* [r̩εdʒo:s], though the latter also appears as *rejoyce* or *rejoyis,* which would be pronounced [r̩εdʒois]. These spellings are discussed below under the individual long vowels.

2. There are few or no silent consonants or consonant clusters. Thus groups like *-ch, -gh,* and *-cht* continued to be pronounced after their disappearance in some English words (such as *through* or *knight/knicht*). The common ending *-is* (or *-ys*) is syllabic.

3. Some final consonants (especially [i:]) are frequently omitted in Middle Scots, so spellings like *gloir* for *glory* indicate a monosyllabic pronunciation [glo:r̩]. This tendency can also reduce a final diphthong to a single vowel, as in *jo* for *joy* (pronounced [dʒo:]). Medial vowels are occasionally omitted as well, *sprit* or *spreit* (pronounced [spr̩i:t]) for *spirit.*

4. Metathesis (the transposition of adjacent sounds) is common in Middle Scots. In most cases it probably indicates a difference in pronunciation, as in *birst/brist,* or *-gn,*

which is sometimes spelled *-ng,* as in *ring* for *reign.* Here the pronunciation [r̩iŋ] is indicated, since the word rhymes with *king.*

5. The common spelling *ane* for the indefinite article does not indicate its pronunciation, which would have been [ə] or [ʌ].

Bibliography

A. J. Aitken. "How to Pronounce Older Scots," in A. J. Aitken, M. P. McDiarmid, and D. S. Thomson, eds., *Bards and Makars.* Glasgow, 1977, pp. 1–21.

K. Elliott and H. M. Shire, eds. *Music of Scotland, 1500–1700, Musica Britannica,* vol. xv. London, 1957.

H. M. Shire. *Song, Dance and Poetry of the Court of Scotland under James VI.* Cambridge, 1969.

G. Gregory Smith. *Specimens of Middle Scots.* Edinburgh and London, 1908.

Consonants and Consonant Groups

The tendency for all consonants to be sounded lasted considerably longer in Scots than in English, so groups like *kn-* and *gn-* were probably pronounced through most of the sixteenth century.

ch, gh Following the front vowels *i* and *e,* pronounced [ç] *(bricht);* following the back vowels *a, o,* and *u,* pronounced [x] *(eneugh, pleuch).*

quh- Appears occasionally as a variant for *wh-*. Strongly aspirated, closer to [xw] than to [hw].

r Always either trilled [rr] or flicked [r̩] with the tip of the tongue.

s, sh Note that words which have *sh-* in Modern English occasionally have *s-* [s] in Middle Scots *(shall/sall).*

wh- More strongly aspirated than in English, approaching [xw] rather than [hw].

Vowels

Short Vowels

The system of short vowels was identical to the short vowels of Middle and Early Modern English with the following exceptions: short *a* remained [a] through the period, rather than moving up to [æ]. During the sixteenth century short *u* [ʊ] tended to become fronted to [œ]; a similar fronting occurred with long *u.*

Long Vowels

Because of the vagaries of Middle Scots spelling, it is often difficult to know at a glance precisely what sound is intended, and whether an individual vowel is long or short. In many cases, vowels which are long in English are also long in Scots. The exceptions are governed by a change which occurred during the latter part of the sixteenth century, when the length of vowels became more a function of the surrounding sounds, their "phonetic environment," than of the history of the individual word. According to this "Scottish Vowel-length Rule," the earlier Scots long vowels remained long in accented positions when they were followed by voiced sounds other than stops *(p, t, k, b, d, g).*

A following *l* also inhibited this change. Vowels remained long in final accented positions (as in *die* [di:]), and in medial positions they remained long when they fell immediately before syllabic and morphemic boundaries (that is, before inflectional endings), as well as before [r̥d] and [dʒ]. Thus the verb *defe* ("to deafen") retained the long vowel [di:v], since the final consonant is voiced and is not a stop; but the adjective *deif* ("deaf") was shortened to [dif] because the final consonant is unvoiced. Notice that [i] is not the short vowel of *sit,* but the high front vowel of French *si,* shorter in duration than the full long vowel of *meet.* Similarly, the verb-form *deid* ("died") was pronounced [di:d] because the vowel precedes an inflectional ending, but the adjective *deid* ("dead") became [did].

a As in English, by the end of the fifteenth century the Middle English long *a* [ɑ:] had shifted upward to become [ɛ:], where it remained through the sixteenth century. At some point in the later seventeenth or early eighteenth century it moved farther up to its present position, [e:]. Long *a* is indicated in a variety of ways in the manuscripts, by the common form *a* + consonant + *e* (the usual modern indication, as in *made*) and by *ai, ay,* and sometimes *e.* That the spelling *hart* occurs, as well as *hert* and *hairt,* suggests that sometimes it can appear simply as *a.* In final position it regularly appears as *-a* *(sa/sae,* pronounced [sɛ:], for Modern English *so).*

e By the beginning of the sixteenth century, close *e* had moved up from [e:] to [i:]. Open *e* by the late fifteenth century had moved up from [ɛ:] to [e:], and during the sixteenth century it continued to rise to join the close *e* as [i:]. Both open and close long *e* are variously spelled *ei, ey,* and *e* + consonant + *e*. Close *e* in final position is spelled either *-e* or *-ee.*

i As in English, the Great Vowel Shift forced long *i* to become a diphthong. By the late fifteenth century, long *i* had become [ei], moving to [æi] by the end of the sixteenth century. It was spelled *i, y, yi, i,* or *y* + consonant + *e.* In final position it normally appears as *-y.*

o Middle English open *o* [ɔ:] had become [o:] by the beginning of the fifteenth century in Scots, as in English. The spelling was *oi, oy, o* + consonant + *e,* or, in final position, *-o.* Thus the vowels of *moste* and *lorde* would be the same. Close *o* provides one of the most characteristic sounds of early Scots. This sound, which became *-oo-* (usually [u:], [ʊ], or [ʌ] in Modern English as in *food, good,* or *blood*), became [ø] in Scots and was generally spelled with *-u-.* See below under *u.*

Note that many words in which long *a* had moved up to long *o* during the Middle English period sometimes preserve the *a* form in Scots (*sa* [sɛ:]/*so* [so:]). There seems to have been considerable freedom with these forms, and both *a* and *o* forms can be found in the same piece *(mair/moir).*

u Unlike the situation in English, long *u* in Scots was not affected by the Great Vowel Shift and remained [u:], usually spelled *ou* or *ow.* Long *u* followed by *l* + consonant tended during the sixteenth century to move forward in the mouth to become [œ], affecting words like *shulter* (shoulder) and *full.*

Words with [u:], [ju:], [ʌ], and [ʊ] in Modern English, principally deriving from the Middle English close *o* [o:], such as *fool, move, do; sure, creature; blood;* or *good* had [ø:] in Middle Scots. The first of these groups was most commonly spelled *o* + consonant + *e (fole)* or, in final position, *-o (do);* the second and third groups *u* + consonant + *e, w* + consonant + *e, ui, uy, wi,* and *wy (gude, guid).*

Note that, as in English, a consonant before *-ure* did not become palatalized until considerably later. Thus Modern English *sure* [ʃu:r] would have been pronounced [sør], or possibly with the vowel (not the consonant) slightly palatalized, [sjøɽ].

Diphthongs

ai, ay By the late fifteenth century, the first element of this diphthong had shifted up to [æi:], becoming a single vowel, [ɛ:], during the course of the sixteenth century.

au, aw By the late fifteenth century this had in most cases become a single vowel, [ɔ:].

eu, iu These two diphthongs, separate in earlier forms of Scots, had coalesced early in the fifteenth century to [iu:]. By the end of the sixteenth century, the pronunciation could be either [iu:] or [ju:].

ou Although normally pronounced [ɔ:] or [u:], as in Early Modern English, when it indicates Modern English *-ow (bow, grow), four,* and *over* (variously spelled *our, owr, ouir, owir*) it was pronounced as a diphthong as in Modern English *our,* [ouɽ] or more probably [ʌuɽ].

SAMPLE TEXTS

Woe worth the tyme

This consort song in four parts is found in several sources, the earliest being Thomas Wode's partbooks, copied between 1562 and 1590. A later source adds a fifth part (National Library of Scotland, MS Panmure 11).

Woe worth the tyme and eik the place
That shee wes to me knowne,
For sine I did behold her face,
My hart was never my owne,
5 My owne, jo, my owne,
My hart wes never my owne.

Sumtyme I livd at libertie
Bot now I doe not soe.
Sche hes my hart so faithfullie
10 That I cane loue no moe,
No moe, jo, no moe,
That I cane loue no moe.

To be refuist of loue, allace,
All earthlie joyes, adewe.
15 My mistris sho is merciles
And will not on me rew,
  Me rew, jo, me rewe,
And will not on me rewe.

Now am I left all comfortles
20 And no remeid cane crave.
My paines they are remediles
And all the wyte yowe have,
  You have, jo, you have,
And all the wyte you have.

wo: wurrθ ðɛ tæim and e:k ðɛ plɛ:s
ðat ʃe: wɛz tø mi: kno:n
fɔrr sɪn æi dɪd bɛhɔld hɛṛ fɛ:s
mæi hɛ:rrt wɛz nɛvɛrr mæi o:n
5   mæi o:n dʒo: mæi o:n
mæi hɛ:rrt wɛz nɛvɛrr mæi o:n

sʊmtæim æi lɪvd at lɪbɛṛti:
bʊt nʌu æi dø nɔt so:
ʃe: hɛz mæi hɛ:ṛt so: fɛ:θfʊli:
10 ðat æi kɛ:n lʊv no: mo:
  no: mo: dʒo: no: mo:
ðat æi kɛ:n lʊv no: mo:

tø bi: ṛɛføzt ɔv lʊv alæs
al ɛ:rrθli: dʒoiz adiu:
15 mæi mɪstṛɪs ʃe: ɪz mɛ:rrsɪlɛs
and wɪl nɔt ɔn mi: rriu:
  mi: rriu: dʒo: mi: rriu:
and wɪl nɔt ɔn mi: rriu:

nʌu am æi lɛft al kʊmfɔṛtlɛs
20 and no: ṛɛme:d kɛ:n kṛɛ:v
mæi pɛ:nz ðɛ: ɛ:ṛ ṛɛmɛdɪlɛs
and al ðɛ wæit ju: hɛ:v
  ju: hɛ:v dʒo: ju: hɛ:v
and al ðɛ wæit ju: hɛ:v

NOTES

1 *worth,* etc.: [ṛ] or [rr] should be used as the performer feels appropriate in this and the following example.

15 *sho:* The vowel no longer indicates the pronunciation; see 1. 2 for the normal form.

Balulalow (Ane Sang of the Birth of Christ)

The earliest source for the music of this lovely lullaby is John Gamble's commonplace book from about 1660. The text had appeared in George Bannatyne's collection of 1578, *Ane Compendious booke of godly and spirituall songs,* also known as "The Gude and Godlie Ballatis." CD #9.

I come from hevin heich to tell
The best nowells that e'er befell.
To you thir tythings trew I bring
And I will of them say and sing.
5 This day to you is born ane child
Of Marie meik and Virgin mild
That blissit bairn bening and kind
Sall you rejoyce baith hart and mind.

Lat us rejoyis and be blyth
10 And with the Hyrdis go full swyth
And see what God of his grace hes done
Throu Christ to bring us to his throne.
My saull and life stand up and see
What lyis in ane cribbe of tree.
15 What Babe is that, sa gude and fair?
It is Christ, God's Son and Air.

The silk and sandell thee to eis
Ar hay and sempill sweilling clais
Wharin thou gloris greitest King
20 As thou in hev'n war in thy ring.
And war the warld ten times sa wide
Cled ouer with gold and stanes of pride,
Unworthie yit it were to thee
Under thy feet ane stule to be.

25 O my deir hart, yung Jesus sweit,
Prepair thy creddill in my spreit!
And I sall rock thee in my hart
And never mair fra thee depart.
Bot I sall praise thee evermoir
30 With sangis sweit unto thy gloir.
The Kneis of my hart sall I bow,
And sing that rycht Balulalow.

æi kʊm fṛɔm hɛvın hi:ç tø tɛl
ðɛ bɛst no:wɛlz ðat ɛ:ṛ bɛfɛl

tø ju: ðɪrr tøðɪŋz tṛiu: æi bṛɪŋ
and æi wɪl ɔv ðɛm sɛ: and sɪŋ
5 ðɪs dɛ: tø ju: ɪz bɔṛn ə tʃæild
ɔv maṛi mi:k and vɪṛdʒɪn mæild
ðat blɪsɪt bɛ:ṛn bɛnɪŋ and kæind
sæl ju: ṛɛdʒois bɛ:θ hɛ:rrt and mæind

læt ʊs ṛɛdʒois and bi: blæið
10 and wɪð ðɛ hɪṛdɪz go: fœl swæið
and si: hwat gɔd ɔv hɪz gṛɛ:s hɛz do:n
θṛu: kṛæist tø bṛɪŋ ʊs tø hɪz θṛo:n
mæi sɔl and læif stand ʊp and si:
hwa læi·ɪz ɪn ə kṛɪb ɔv tṛi:
15 hwat bɛ:b ɪz ðat sɛ: gø:d and fɛ:rr
ɪt ɪz kṛæist gɔdz sʊn and ɛ:rr

ðɛ sɪlk and sandɛl ðe: tø i:z
aṛ hɛ: and sɛmpɪl swi:lɪŋ klɛ:z
hwaṛ ɪn ðu: glo:ṛi:z grrɛ:tɛst kɪŋ
20 az ðu: ɪn hɛvn waṛ ɪn ðæi rrɪŋ
and waṛ ðɛ waṛld tɛn tæimz sɛ: wæid
klɛd ɔurr wɪð gɔld and stɛ:nz ɔv pṛæid
ʊnwʊrrði jɪt ɪt wɛṛ tø ði:
ʊndɛṛ ðæi fi:t ə støl tø bi:

25 o: mæi dʒi:ṛ hɛ:rrt jʊŋ dʒi:zʊs swi:t
pṛɛpɛ:ṛ ðæi kṛɛdɪl ɪn mæi spṛi:t
and æi sæl ṛɔk ði: ɪn mæi hɛ:rrt
and nɛvɛṛ mɛ:rr fṛɔm ði: dɛpɛ:rrt
bʊt æi sæl pṛɛ:z ði: ɛvɛṛmo:ṛ
30 wɪð saŋɪz swi:t ʊntø ðæi glo:ṛ
ðɛ kni:z ɔv mæi hɛ:rrt sæl æi bʌu
and sɪŋ ðat ṛɪçt baløIalʌu

NOTES

5 *ane:* despite the spelling, the indefinite article is pronounced [ə] or [ʌ].

4

Anglo-Latin

A. G. RIGG

The portion of Britain now known as England was originally Celtic-speaking, but in the fourth and fifth centuries the Celtic population (the present Welsh) was driven out by the invasions of the Angles (hence, *Engla-land,* the land of the Angles), Saxons, Jutes, and Frisians. From then on the population was Germanic-speaking. A knowledge of Latin was reintroduced primarily by the Christianizing mission of St. Augustine of Canterbury in 597, although it had also been widely used by Irish missionaries. The pronunciation of Latin by the Angles and Saxons is not the topic of this chapter, as it was displaced at the time of the Norman Conquest of 1066.

In abbeys and cathedrals William the Conqueror replaced the monks and clergy, at least at the higher administrative levels, by Normans. For example, by the end of his reign in 1100, of thirty-five abbeys only three still had English abbots. The Norman abbots and bishops in turn brought over their followers. The effect, at the educated level in society, was the Normanization of England. These foreigners spoke French (though it was Norman French, not that of Paris), and presumably their teaching of Latin reflected their origin. In 1205, however, King John lost Normandy, and thereafter the French nature of the upper classes gradually diminished, especially during the fourteenth century; between about 1250 and 1400 we see the reemergence of the class that spoke English as its mother tongue, though even in the twelfth century native Englishmen rose to high rank. Until the middle of the fourteenth century the teaching of Latin in school was done in French, but we have no way of knowing the quality of the French accent and pronunciation employed. It is thus very debatable whether one should pronounce twelfth- and thirteenth-century Anglo-Latin in a French or an English manner: for example, is *qui* [ki:] as in French, or [kwi:] as in English? I have opted to give a modified French pronunciation for the twelfth century (but preserving the inflected endings), but

English thereafter. By the fourteenth and fifteenth centuries we can be fairly sure of an English pronunciation.

After the beginnings of humanism and the Reformation of the sixteenth century, the picture becomes clouded again. The violence of the Reformation and the Counter-Reformation resulted in the exile of religious adherents of both persuasions, Catholic and Protestant. They received their educations in Italy, Holland, Switzerland, and all over Europe, and they brought back to England a variety of Latin pronunciations, including the Classically based reformed pronunciations recommended by Erasmus. In the examples below I have chosen to present the traditional "Old Latin" style, which is reflected in present-day legal Latin. From pronunciations such as [ˈnaisai], [ˈsaini dai·i:], and [ˈsɛrsiɔrˈɑrai] for *nisi, sine die,* and *certiorari* we can (with caution) infer the Renaissance and Medieval sounds that preceded them.

Evidence

The evidence for the pronunciation of Medieval and Renaissance Latin in England consists in rhymes and alliteration, spellings, loan-words, comparative philological developments, and Renaissance authorities.

Rhymes and Alliteration

The general prevalence of disyllabic rhyme after about 1150, in both rhythmic and rhymed quantitative verse (such as the Leonine hexameter), helps to confirm the pronunciation of both vowels and consonants (though poets did not hesitate to rhyme short with long vowels). The medieval rhymes *sancte : ante, decus : moechus, decus : aequus,* and *caelum : telum* show the following changes from Classical Latin:

nct	has changed to [nt] or [ŋt]
oe	has changed to [e:]
ch	has changed to [k]
qu	before *u* has changed to [k]
ae	has changed to [e:]

The heavily alliterated *Melos Amoris* of the fourteenth-century mystic Richard Rolle shows that the initial consonants of *iudicium* and *gero* are the same, [dʒ], not Classical [j] and [g] respectively, and that initial *c* before a front vowel is [s]. For example,

sanctus secernitur a seculi singultu et singulare solacium
scilicet celeste sumit incessanter
iuvenis iusticiam iuravi gestare genusque iudicii
per omne habere

ˈsaŋtʊs seˈsɛṛnɪtʊṛ ɑ: ˈsɛkʏli: sɪŋgˈʊltʏ ɛt sɪŋgʏˈlɑ:ṛe sɔˈlɑ:sɪʊm
ˈsi:li:sɛt seˈlɛste ˈsʏmɪt ɪnsɛsˈsantɛṛ
ˈdʒʏvenɪs dʒʊsˈtɪsɪam dʒʏˈṛɑ:vi: dʒɛˈstɑ:ṛe ˈdʒɛ:nʊskwe dʒʏˈdɪsi·i:
pɛṛ ɔmne aˈbɛ:ṛe

Spellings

The spelling of Medieval Latin, compared to that of medieval vernacular languages, is relatively stable. It diverges from Classical Latin in regularly having *e* for *oe* and *ae*, and *-ci-* for *-ti-*, and in a few other minor matters, but it tends to be fairly uniform across Europe. Thus, divergences from this "standard," if supported by other evidence, can often indicate pronunciation. A good idea of common Anglo-Latin spellings can be gathered by glancing through the pages of Latham's *Revised Medieval Latin Word-list.* Thus, *abet* (for *habet*) and, conversely, *honus* (for *onus*) demonstrate the common loss of initial *h-*, as in words that have initial *h-* in French. The use of *ngn* for *gn* (in *angnus, dingnus,* for *agnus, dignus*) shows the development of [ŋ] before [gn]; that is, not [agnʊs], [dɪgnʊs] but [aŋgnʊs], [dɪŋgnʊs].

Loan-words

The present pronunciation of a vernacular word borrowed directly from Latin probably indicates the pronunciation of the Latin word at the time of the borrowing. Thus, English *verbal, judicial, germinate,* and *quality* show that *verbum* had initial [v] not Classical [w], that *iudicium* and *germen* had initial [dʒ], not Classical [j] and [g], and that *qualitas* had [kw] not French [k].

Comparative Philological Developments

In the absence of any restraint against change, Latin was subject to the same sound changes that affected the vernacular languages, except that, as a learned language, Latin was probably pronounced somewhat more carefully than the mother tongue. For example, when all the Middle English long vowels changed position in the fifteenth century in the Great Vowel Shift (see above, p. 14), there is every reason to believe that their Latin equivalents did the same. Thus, Modern English has a diphthong [ei] in *labor,* and the early phonetician Robert Robinson (1617) shows a long vowel in *calor,* where both have short *a* in Classical Latin. The sequence of development would be: [ɑ] up to about 1200, then [ɑ:] by Middle English lengthening in open syllables, then early Modern English [æ:] (which is probably what Robinson intended), and finally [ei] in present English. Similarly, we can infer from present legal Latin [naisai] for Classical *nisi* that the sixteenth- and seventeenth-century pronunciation was [ɔi] or [ʌi], and the pronunciation before the Vowel Shift was [i:], which probably goes back to an earlier [i].

Renaissance Authorities

The few direct comments on pronunciation by medieval writers usually go back to Classical sources (e.g., Isidore of Seville) or comment on specific points of vowel length. "Differential verses" (like those by Serlo of Wilton) help to distinguish short and long vowels, but they are intended for the scansion of quantitative verse and have little relevance to ordinary pronunciation. In the Renaissance, however, there was a renewed interest in the subject. Erasmus' *De recta latini graecique sermonis pronuntiatione* (1528) tried to restore Classical sounds, and in so doing gave an entertaining but unsystematic survey of "vices" in pronunciation in all European countries, which gives us many clues to contemporary pronunciation. Many writers in the next two centuries, both English and Continental, entered the debate; the evidence they provide is collected in Copeman, *Singing in Latin,* Chapters 6–8. Sometimes their evidence is hard to interpret, especially on the vowels, as it is not clear what some of their terms mean, and their analogies (in vernacular languages) are equally problematic. Their statements about consonants, however, are much more useful. Robert Robinson's *The Art of Pronuntiation* (1617) has an invaluable phonetic transcription of a Latin poem, given in an "old" style pronunciation, which is especially informative. (Dobson's interpretations of Robinson's phonetic symbols are given in a form of the International Phonetic Alphabet that does not match the one used in this book. Consequently, where there is a risk of confusion, I have placed Dobson's phonetic transcriptions in double square brackets [[. . .]]).

No one sort of evidence is sufficient to establish pronunciation: we have to allow for inexact rhymes, for simple incompetence in spellings, for the possibility that vernacular languages and Latin did not necessarily behave in the same way, and for the difficulty in interpreting statements about language by unscientific observers. When they support each other, however—as in the case of [s] for *c* before *e* and *i*—we can obtain, within broad phonemic bands, a fairly probable picture.

Bibliography

F. Brittain. *Latin in Church: The History of Its Pronunciation,* rev. ed. Alcuin Club Tracts. London, 1955.

H. Copeman. *Singing in Latin.* Oxford, 1990. The evidence for English Latin is in Chapter 9, pp. 111–34. Although I do not follow Copeman in every detail, I have modified many of my earlier interpretations (as in the *Dictionary of the Middle Ages)* in several ways in light of his evidence and discussions.

E. J. Dobson. *Phonetic Writings of Robert Robinson,* Early English Text Society 238 (1957), pp. xviii-xxi, 27–28.

Ross W. Duffin. "National pronunciations of Latin ca. 1490–1600." *Journal of Musicology* 4 (1985–86):217–26.

G. Herbert Fowler. "Notes on the Pronunciation of Medieval Latin in England." *History* n.s. 22 (1937):97–109.

R. E. Latham. *Revised Medieval Latin Word-list from British and Irish sources.* London, 1965.

Sounds and Spellings

Between about 1100 and the early fifteenth century England had no fixed spelling system, and changes in sound often resulted in changes in spelling. (The "diversity" in spelling, often of the same word by the same writer, was not fully reduced to uniformity until the emergence of the first great dictionaries in the eighteenth century.) Latin, however, had a spelling system essentially derived from that of ancient Rome. One might expect, therefore, that there would be a great gap between spelling and pronunciation when sounds changed but spellings remained the same (as is the case in English, whose spelling system reflects pronunciations current about 1400). This is not, in fact, so. Latin was learned from books and in school, and England did not have a vernacular language clearly derived from Latin, as did France and Italy. Consequently, the spelling system exercised a strong conservative effect, restraining the speaker from departing too far from the written form. In addition, teachers tried to ensure that inflexional endings were clearly enunciated, so that the grammatical structure of a sentence would be preserved.

Stress and Accent

The rules for quantitative (metrical) verse, that is, verse that depends on syllable length, are irrelevant to performers of music.

A few words on stress, however, may be useful in order to show how rhythmical verse was composed. If the penultimate syllable of a word is long, the stress falls on it (e.g., amā́bat); if the penultimate is short, the stress falls on the antepenultimate (amábĭtur).

Consonants

Until the loss of final *-e* in English (in the late fourteenth century), double consonants in Anglo-Latin, as in English, were pronounced double (e.g., *ad-do*); the effect was to shorten the preceding vowel, and this happened also before any consonant "cluster" except those in which the second element was a liquid or labial (*r* and *l*). The combination *st-*, however, could begin a syllable and did not cause shortening. Sometimes a double consonant is written in order to indicate a preceding short vowel. By Robinson's time, double consonants were single.

b [b]

c [k] before back vowels *a, o, u,* and before *r* and *l,* e.g., *carus* [ˈkɑ:ṛʊs], *contra* [kɔntṛɑ], *cum* [kʊm], *cresco* [kṛɛsko:], *clarus* [ˈklɑ:ṛʊs].

[ts] to about 1200, and thereafter [s], before the front vowels *e* (including Classical Latin *ae* and *oe*) and *i,* both long and short. Thus, *cedo, sedo,* and *caedo* are homophones [ˈsɛ:do:], *cibus* is [si:bʊs], and *cignum* and *signum* are also homophones [sɪŋgnʊm]. There is no direct evidence for the early pronunciation [ts]; it is inferred from contemporary French. There is no justification for the pronunciation [tʃ].

ci Before a vowel, [sɪ] until about 1500; thereafter [sj]; by the early seventeenth century this had developed to [ʃj], as recorded by Robinson for *Graecia* and *liceat.* See also *-ti-* below.

cc [ks] after a back vowel and before a front vowel (as can be seen in the loan-words *accede, accident, occident*). Copeman (p. 51) also argues for [ks] between front vowels, including *ecce* (*behold*); this is probably correct, but it should be noted that his evidence is entirely from spellings of words compounded from *ex-* + *c-*.

ch Normally [k] when it is in a learned spelling in a word derived from Greek or falsely connected with Greek (as in *charus* for *carus,* as though it were connected with Greek χαρις; there may also be influence from French *charite.* The word is also sometimes spelled *karus*).

In *michi, nichil* (the normal Medieval spellings for Classical *mihi, nihil*), it is probably the palatal spirant [ç]: [mi:çɪ], [ni:çɪl].

-c Final *c* is always [k] in *ac, hec,* etc.

d Normally [d]. In final position it was unvoiced to [t], as is shown by frequent rhymes such as *Dauid: lauit* and by the common spellings *quicquit* (= *quicquid*), *nequit* (= *nequid,* and conversely *nequid* for *nequit*), *haut* or *aut* (for *haud*); *sed* is normally spelled *set.*

di- In certain words this had the value [dʒ], e.g., *diabolus,* often spelled *zabulus,* and derivatives of *dies* such as *diurnalis,* spelled *jornalis,* and *dieta* (*room*), spelled *zeta.* It is unlikely, however, that the pronunciation should be extended to other *di-* words.

f [f]. On *ph,* see below.

g [g] before back vowels *a, o, u,* and consonants *r* and *l,* e.g., gubernator [gʊbɛr̩ˈnɑ:tɔr], *gloria* [ˈglɔr̩iɑ], *grauis* [ˈgr̩ɑ:vɪs].

[dʒ] before front vowels *e* (including Classical Latin *ae* and *oe*) and *i.* Thus, *gener* [ˈdʒɛnɛr̩], *gero* [dʒɛr̩o:], *agit* [ˈɑ:dʒɪt]. Note that this never advanced to [ʒ], as it did in French Latin.

Note: the variation in pronunciation of *c* and *g* according to the nature of the following vowel must have meant variation in the conjugation of verbs. Thus, [ɑ:go:], but [ˈɑ:dʒɪt]; [ˈdi:ko:], but [ˈdi:sɪt].

gn [ŋgn] after both front and back vowels; for *dignus* and *agnus* we often find the spellings *dingnus* and *angnus,* i.e., [ˈdɪŋgnʊs], [ˈaŋgnʊs]. The pronunciation is commented on by Renaissance writers, but Robinson actually records [gn].

h This is not a consonant in Medieval or Renaissance Latin, and there is strong evidence that it was not pronounced at all: Erasmus complains about its omission in pronunciation. It is often omitted in spelling (e.g., *ac, abet,* for *hac, habet*) or added (e.g., *honus* for *onus*). It is often used to indicate diaeresis, that is, the separate pronunciation of two adjacent vowels, e.g., *trahicit* [tr̩ɑ:ˈi:sɪt].

hi- [dʒ] in personal and place names in *hiero-;* the spelling is simply to indicate the prefix "holy," e.g., *Hierusalem, Hiericho, Hieronimus* [dʒɛr̩ˈʏsalɛm], [ˈdʒɛr̩ɪko:], [dʒɛˈr̩ɔ:nɪmʊs].

On *mihi, nihil,* see under *ch.*

i/j Initial *i* before a vowel, sometimes spelled *j,* is a consonant [dʒ]. Thus *iudex* = [dʒʏdɛks], *ianua* = [dʒɑ:nwɑ]. This is shown by loan-words into English (e.g., *judicial*), by Richard Rolle's alliteration (above, p. 47), and by Robert Robinson. Similarly, intervocalic *i* is [dʒ] in *cuius* [kʏdʒʊs], *eius* [ɛdʒʊs]. The exclamation *eia,* however, is probably [j], as it is sometimes spelled *eya.* On post-consonantal *i,* see below (p. 55) on semivowels.

Note that *ij* is simply a spelling or orthographic variant for *ii.*

Ih/Jh [dʒ] in names like *Ihesus* (*Jesus*) [ˈdʒɛ:sʊs]. The *h* has no phonetic significance;

it is a misunderstanding of the Greek letter H (*eta*) when the name *Jesus* is spelled in Greek capitals IHCOC.

k [k] when it occurs, which is rarely.

l [l]

m [m]. In Anglo-Latin (in contrast with the Romance languages) it was a bilabial plosive, as is shown by the spellings *tempto, ympnus* (= *hymnus*). In classical Latin quantitative verse (mainly hexameters and elegiac couplets), final post-vocalic *m* was elided before a following vowel in the next word; this practice was followed by careful (i.e., not all) English writers of quantitative verse, but it was clearly not a natural pronunciation, as it was never followed in rhythmical verse.

n [n]. On *gn,* see above.

nct [ŋt], at least according to Robinson (who distinguishes it from the sound in English *into*), but rhymes like *ante: sancte* show that it must have been close to [nt].

p [p]. See also above on *m.*

ph [f] except in the word *sphera* (Classical *sphaera*), whose common spelling *spera* indicates [p].

ps [s] as in *psalmus* [salmʊs], as shown by many *s-* spellings.

qu [kw] before *a, e,* and *i,* but [k] before *o* and *u.* Before 1200, under French influence, it may have been [k] in all positions. Evidence that English Latin retained [kw] (where French had [k]) is provided by the early Middle English spellings *quene* and *quik* for Old English *cwen* and *cwic,* and by Bullokar (1580). On the other hand, Bullokar (cited by Copeman, pp. 95–96) seems to make an exception for *quu* and *quo,* and we have the common spelling *equs* for *equus,* and frequent rhymes in *decor: aequor, decus: aequus,* and (from Michael of Cornwall) *tenebrasco: cras quo.* Loan-words from Latin seem to have retained [kw], e.g., *quality* (where the [w] has caused rounding of [a] to [ɔ]), *quintessence.*

r [r̩]. There is no evidence for the loss of post-vocalic *r.*

s [s]. Medially between vowels, *s* was voiced to [z], as shown by Robinson [[ekspózitríks]] (= *expositrix*). In final position, after an unstressed vowel, the evidence is ambiguous; by the sixteenth century English had [z] in *is, was,* etc., but Robinson shows both [z] in [[fasìlēzkwì]] (= *facilesque*), [[dēkùz]] (= *decus*), and [s] in [[sēlȍs]] (= *caelos*).

sc [sk] before back vowels *a, o, u,* and consonants *r* and *l,* e.g., *scando* [skando:], *scribo* [skri:bo:].

[s] before front vowels *e* (including Classical Latin *ae* and *oe*) and *i.* Evidence includes rhymes, loan-words such as *science, disciple,* and Robinson. Medially, *sc* [s] may have been doubled, but *discit* and *dicit* are near-homophones, [ˈdi:sɪt], as are *esce* and *esse* [ɛse].

t [t]. In final position after a vowel, this had become [θ] by the sixteenth century; [θ] is mentioned by some sixteenth-century writers and it is shown in Skelton's rhymes (Copeman, p. 35, who also gives an example from Chaucer). The change is similar to that of final *d.*

-ti- [si], later [sj], except after *s* and *x* (where it is still [ti] as in *ustio* [ˈʊsti·o:] and *mixtio* [ˈmɪksti·o:]). The usual [si] is shown by the normal spellings *racio, sencio,* etc. By the seventeenth century this had developed to [ʃj], as Robinson has *inscitiam* as [ɪnsˈɪʃjam] and has even absorbed the [j], as he also has *ratione* as [ṛaʃo:ni].

th [t]. This is shown in common spellings *tronus, teatrum,* etc. (for Classical Latin *thronus, theatrum*).

v (u) [v] in prevocalic and intervocalic position, never [w]. This is shown by loan-words (e.g., *verbal*), by Robinson, and by spelling confusion between *u* and *b.* As noted above, the normal spelling is *u,* but *v* is sometimes found initially.

x [ks]. The group *exst-, ext-,* is sometimes simplified to [ɛst].

z [z]. This occurs only in words of Hebrew or Greek origin, e.g., *azyma.*

Vowels

Stressed Vowels

For the composition of quantitative verse, Medieval Latin retained—with a few minor divergences—the Classical distinction between short and long vowels. It also kept the rule of lengthening "by position," i.e., a syllable is treated as long, whatever the length of the vowel, if the vowel is followed by two or more consonants (except before a consonant followed by *l* or *r* in the same syllable). These rules do not concern performers.

In spoken and sung Latin, however, there is strong evidence that vowels behaved much like their English equivalents. Stressed vowels followed by two or more syllables were treated as short, e.g., [paˈsɪfɪko:] (Classical Latin *pācifico*). Similarly, vowels before double consonants and clusters of consonants were short: Robinson gives [mɪsɪs] for *missis.* Conversely, after about 1200, vowels in open syllables in penultimate position were lengthened, even if they were short in Classical Latin: Robinson gives [[seīmùl]] for *sĭmul,* [[bōneì]] for *bŏni,* etc. This lengthening is confirmed by loan-words such as *labor,* which had a short *ă* in Classical Latin. This lengthening must have obscured important lexical and grammatical distinctions, for example, between *vĭdeo/vīdi, vĕnio/vēni, mălus/mālus.*

The exact quality (as opposed to the length) of the vowels is irrecoverable; the best we can do is to posit a series of contrastive phonemes that correspond (in a fairly conservative way, seeing that Latin was still a learned language) to those of the contemporary English vernacular pronunciation. The following chart gives stressed vowels, first potentially long (in open syllables and not followed by more than one syllable), then short (in closed syllables or followed by more than one consonant). The dates are of course approximate.

		before 1200	13th–14th centuries	15th–16th centuries	17th century
a	*cado*	kɑdɔ:	kɑ:dɔ:	kæ:do:	ke:do:
	castrum	kastṛʊm	kastṛʊm	kastṛʊm	kæstṛʊm
e	*sedet*	sɛdɛt	sɛ:dɛt	se:dɛt	si:dɛt
	pectus	pɛktʊs	pɛktʊs	pɛktʊs	pɛktʊs
i	*videt*	vɪdɛt	vi:dɛt	vəidɜt	vʌidɛt
	victus	vɪktʊs	vɪktʊs	vɪktʊs	vɪktʊs
o	*solus*	sɔlʊs	sɔ:lʊs	so:lʊs	so:lʊs
	coctus	kɔktʊs	kɔktʊs	kɔktʊs	kɔktʊs
u	*fugit*	fʏdʒɪt	fʏdʒɪt	fʏdʒɪt	fjʏdʒɪt
	fulsit	fʊlsɪt	fʊlsɪt	fʊlsɪt	fʊlsɪt

Note that [ʊ] was not lengthened to [u:], since this would have gone to [au] in the Modern period. Robinson shows a front vowel for *Judea* [[dž iwdḗa]]. Robinson also provides the evidence for a glide vowel before [ʏ] in *tenuisque* [[tenyìwiskwi]].

au	*gaudet*	gaudɛt	gaudɛt	gɔudɛt	gɔ:dɛt

eu *deus* is normally two syllables, with *e* as in open *e* above; if monosyllabic,

		dɛws	dɛws	dy:s	dʒy:s

ae/oe see above, p. 47

Unstressed Vowels

There is a tendency in English pronunciation for unstressed vowels to be reduced to indistinctness; the back vowels *a, o, u,* to [ə]; and front *e* to [ɪ]; cf. the *a* in *above,* the *u* in *subordinate,* the *e* in *cricket.* Something similar may have happened in Latin: cf. spellings such as *discendo* (for *descendo*) and *sepero* (for *separo*). On the other hand, as Latin was a learned language and there was always a need to preserve distinct inflexional endings, I suspect that full values were usually maintained. Robinson's evidence is ambiguous: it shows *i* (probably [ɪ]) for *e* in words like [[disìri]] (for *dicere*), but at other times preserves distinct sounds in [[lēisèt]] *(licet),* [[terìbilḗz]] *(terribiles),* [[sēlȍs]] *(caelos),* etc. In some cases, Robinson may represent a "reformed" sound. My suggestions are tentative.

NON-FINAL POSITION

a [a] at all periods; perhaps [æ] by the seventeenth century.

e [ɛ]; probably [e] in open syllables, as this would be the sound most likely to raise to [ɪ] in the seventeenth century (cf. Robinson [[rimíseī]] for *remissi*).

Final *-es* is long in Robinson [[terȉbilḗz]], perhaps representing [i:], earlier [e] or [e:].

er: Robinson gives [[ur]] in tonic position in [[katùrva]] *(caterva);* cf. the present pronunciation of *refer,* etc.

i [ɪ] at all periods, thus failing to make a distinction between the dative/ablative plural *-īs* and the genitive singular *-is.* Despite his apparent reformed pronunciation in some respects, Robinson shows misis [[misìs]] for *missīs*, etc.

o [ɔ] at all periods, but Robinson shows a long [o:] in [[sēlȍs]] (for *caelos*), perhaps suggesting an earlier [ɔ:].

u [ʊ] at all periods. Perhaps [ʏ] in open syllables.

FINAL POSITION, OPEN

a [a] at all periods.

e [e], by the seventeenth century raised to [ɪ]: Robinson has [[disìri]], i.e. [dɪsɪṛɪ] for *dicere.*

i Perhaps [i:]. Robinson distinguishes Classical [ɪ] and [i:] in [[meīhì]] *(mihi)* and [[boneī̀]] *(boni),* but he may reflect a reformed pronunciation.

o [ɔ:] until about 1400, [o:] thereafter. Robinson gives [o:] in *recto* but [[u]] (? [ʊ]) in [[mōdù]] for *modo.*

u Perhaps [y], e.g. [mɑ:ny] for *manu,* but this is a guess.

Note: *cui* (dative singular) was [kʌi], later [kai].

GLIDE VOWELS

Between a consonant and [ʏ] a glide vowel [j] developed, probably by the late sixteenth century. Robinson writes [[tenyìwiskwi]], [[instítyiwít]] for *tenuisque, instituit.* I have given [fjʏdʒɪt] for *fugit.* This glide also developed between a consonant and [i] or [ɪ]; Robinson has [[sapyìens]] for *sapiens* and [[vāryieī]] for *varii.*

Unstressed *i* or *e* after a consonant and before a vowel developed into a semivowel [j], causing the preceding consonant to palatalize (Robinson's [[lišìat]], [[prōpíšiṍ]], for *liceat, propitio*); sometimes the semivowel was itself absorbed (Robinson's [[rāšȍni]] for *ratione*).

DIACHRONIC SOUND CHART FOR ANGLO-LATIN CONSONANTS

	1100	1200	1300	1400	1500	1600	1700
b	[b]		→				
c + a, o, u, l, r	[k]		→				
c + e, i	[ts]	→[s]	→				
ci + vowel	[si]				→ [ʃj]		→
ch	[k]		→				
-c final	[k]		→				
d	[d]		→				
-d final after vowel	[t]		→				
f	[f]		→				
g + a, o, u, l, r	[g]		→				
g + e, i	[dʒ]		→				
gn	[ŋgn]		→				
h	[-]		→				
hi- + vowel	[dʒ]		→				
i- + vowel	[dʒ]		→				
-i- between vowels	[dʒ]		→				
Ih-, Jh-	[dʒ]		→				
k	[k]		→				
l	[l]		→				
m	[m]		→				
n	[n]		→				
nct	[ŋt]		→				
p	[p]		→				
ph	[f]		→				
ps	[s]		→				
qu + a, e, i	[kw]		→				
qu + o, u	[k]		→				
r	[r]		→				
s	[s]		→				
-s- between vowels	[z]		→				
-s final after vowel	[s]				→ ? [z]		→
sc + a, o, u, l, r	[sk]		→				
sc + e, i	[s]		→				
t	[t]		→				
-t final after vowel	[t]				→ [θ]		→
-ti-	[si]					[ʃj]	→[ʃ]
th	[t]		→				
v, u	[v]		→				
x	[ks]		→				
z	[z]		→				

SAMPLE TEXTS

Hymn to St. Oswald

Before 1173. London, British Library, MS Trinity O. 3. 55, fol. 68v. (Photo facsimile in Iain Fenlon, ed., *Cambridge Music Manuscripts 900–1700* [Cambridge, 1982].) CD #10.

Sceptriger Oswalde celo terraque sacrate
trans mare Germanis Gallis
Fulgescis ab angelis
et quecumque tuam gens poscit opem subit amplam
rex bone propicium nobis regem pete regum

A few French values (e.g., for *qu*) have been given in order to indicate the probable French influence on teaching in the twelfth century:

ˈsɛptṛɪdʒɛṛ ɔsˈwalde ˈtsɛlɔ: tɛṛˈṛɑ:ke saˈkṛɑ:te
tṛans ˈmɑṛe dʒɛṛˈmɑ:ni:s ˈgalli:s
fʊlˈdʒɛssɪs ab ˈãndʒɛli:s
ɛt kɛˈkʊŋke tʏãm dʒɛ̃ns ˈpɔssɪt ˈɔpɛ̃m ˈsʏbɪt ˈãmplam
ṛɛks ˈbɔne pṛɔˈpɪtsɪʊm ˈnɔbi:s ˈṛɛdʒɛ̃m ˈpɛte ˈṛɛgʊm

O potores exquisiti

Fourteenth century. London, British Library, MS Egerton 3309, fol. 72, 75. CD #11.

O potores exquisiti,
Licet sitis sine siti
En bibatis expediti
Et ciphorum inobliti;
Ciphi crebro repetiti
  Non dormiant
Et sermones inauditi
  Prosiliant

Qui potare non potestis
Ite procul ab his festis,
Procul ite ! Quid hic estis ?
Non est locus hic modestis:
Inter letos mos agrestis
  Modestie
Judex est et certus testis
  Ignavie

Si quis latitat hic forte
Qui recusat vinum forte

Ostendantur ei porte,
Exeat hac de cohorte;
Plus est nobis gravis morte
   Si maneat.
Ergo sic a nobis eat
   Ne redeat

ɔ: pɔˈtɔ:ṛɛs ˈɛkskwɪˈzi:ti:
ˈli:sɛt ˈsi:tɪs ˈsi:ne ˈsi:ti:
ɛn bi:ˈbɑ:tɪs ɛkspeˈdi:ti:
ɛt sɪˈfɔ:ṛʊm ɪnɔˈbli:ti:
ˈsi:fi: ˈkṛɛbṛɔ: ṛepeˈti:ti:
   nɔn ˈdɔṛmɪant
ɛt sɛṛˈmɔ:nɛs ɪnauˈdi:ti:
   pṛɔˈsi:lɪant

kwi: pɔtɑ:ṛe nɔn pɔˈtɛstɪs
ˈi:te ˈpṛɔ:kʊl ab i:s ˈfɛstɪs
ˈpṛɔkʊl ˈi:te kwɪt i:k ˈɛstɪs
nɔn ɛst ˈlɔ:kʊs i:k mɔˈdɛstɪs
ˈɪntɛṛ ˈlɛ:tɔ:s mɔ:s aˈgṛɛstɪs
   mɔˈdɛstɪe
ˈdʒʏdɛks ɛst ɛt ˈsɛṛtʊs ˈtɛstɪs
   ɪŋˈgnɑ:vɪe

si: kwɪs ˈlɑ:tɪtat i:k ˈfɔṛte
kwi: ṛeˈkʏzat ˈvi:nʊm ˈfɔṛte
ɔstɛnˈdantʊṛ ˈɛ:·i: ˈpɔṛte
ˈɛkse·at ɑ:k dɛ: kɔ·ˈɔṛte
plʊs ɛst ˈnɔ:bɪs ˈgṛɑ:vɪs ˈmɔṛte
   si: ˈmɑ:ne·at
ˈɛṛgɔ: si:k ɑ: ˈnɔ:bɪs ˈɛ:·at
   nɛ: ˈṛɛ:de·at

Risum fecit Sare

Fourteenth century, London, British Library MS Arundel 248, fol. 201v. CD #12.

Risum fecit Sare
sue Deus care
   quo conrident omnia.
Novum fecit mirum:
plenum alvo virum
   circumdedit femina

femina non quevis
non fallax aut levis,
   imo plena gracia,
cuius distillatur
nobis quicquid datur
   ex gracie copia

ˈṛi:zʊm ˈfɛ:sɪt ˈsɑ:ṛe
ˈsʏ·e ˈdɛ:ʊs ˈkɑ:ṛe
   kɔ: kɔnˈṛi:dɛnt ˈɔmni·ɑ
ˈnɔ:vʊm ˈfɛ:sɪt ˈmi:ṛʊm
ˈplɛ:nʊm ˈalvɔ: ˈvi:ṛ:ʊm
   sɪṛkʊmˈdɛ:dɪt ˈfɛ:mɪnɑ

ˈfɛ:mɪnɑ nɔn ˈkwɛ:vɪs
nɔn ˈfallaks aut ˈlɛ:vɪs
   ˈɪmmɔ: ˈplɛ:nɑ ˈgṛɑ:sɪɑ
ˈkʏdʒʊs dɪstɪlˈlɑ:tʊṛ
ˈnɔ:bɪs ˈkwɪkwɪt ˈdɑ:tʊṛ
   ɛks ˈgṛɑ:sɪ·e ˈkɔ:pɪɑ

O Maria Deo grata

Robert Fayrfax (ca. 1464–1521). CD #13.

O Maria Deo grata
Mater Christi praesignata,
   mihi tuo famulo
Clemens esto supplicanti
et succurre deprecanti,
   ut sic in hoc seculo

Christo possim militare,
ne a cultu deviare
   videar justitiae;
Isto mundo consummato
et antiquo debellato
   principe malitiae,

Te Maria mihi duce,
regnum Dei plenum luce
   introire valeam,
ubi sanctam trinitatem
ejusdemque majestatem
   sine fine videam.

O Maria, mater bona,
virgo vera et sincera,
me juvare propera,
ut adversa non me laedant,
sed ut prosperis succedant
mihi semper prospera.

o: maˈrəi·ɑ ˈde·o ˈgræ:tɑ
ˈmæ:tɛr ˈkrəisti: presiŋˈgnæ:tɑ
ˈməiçi: ˈtʏo: ˈfæ:mʏlo:
ˈkle:mɛns ˈe:sto: ˈsʏpliˈkanti:
ɛθ sʊˈkʊre ˈde:preˈkanti:
ˈʊθ sɪk ɪn o:k ˈse:kʏlo:

ˈkrəisto: ˈpɔsɪm ˈmi:li:ˈtæ:re
ne: ɑ: ˈkʊlty ˈde:vɪˈæ:re
ˈvəidɪ·ar dʒʏˈstɪsɪ·e
ˈɪsto: ˈmʊndo: ˈkɔnsuˈmæ:to:
ɛθ anˈtəiko: ˈde:bɛˈlæ:to:
ˈprɪnsɪpe mɑˈli:sɪ·e

te: maˈrəi·ɑ ˈməiçi: ˈdʏse
ˈrɛŋgnʊm ˈde:i: ˈple:nʊm ˈlʏse
ɪntro:ˈəire ˈvæ:lɪ·am
ˈʏbi: ˈsaŋtam ˈtrɪnɪˈtæ:tɛm
ˈe:dʒʊsdɛmkwe ˈmadʒɛˈstæ:tɛm
ˈsəine ˈfəine ˈvəidɪ·am

o:maˈrəi·ɑ ˈmæ:tɛr bo:nɑ
ˈvɪrgo: ˈve:rɑ ɛθ sɪnˈse:rɑ
me: dʒʏˈvæ:re ˈprɔperɑ
ʊθ adˈvɛrsɑ nɔn me: le:dant
sɛt ʊθ ˈprɔsperɪs sʊkˈse:dant
məiçi: sɛmpɛr ˈprɔsperɑ

Suscepimus

From William Byrd, *Gradualia ac Cantiones Sacrae* (London, 1605). CD #14.

Suscepimus, Deus, misericordiam tuam
in medio templi tui secundum nomen tuum
Ita et laus tua in fines terrae, justitia, justitia,
plena est dextera tua
Magnus Dominus et laudabilis nimis in civitate Dei nostri
In monte sancto ejus, ejus,

Gloria patri et filio et spiritui sancto
sicut erat in principio, et nunc et semper
et in saecula saeculorum. Amen

sʏˈsi:pɪmʊs ˈdi:ʊs mɪzɛṛˈkɔṛdjam ˈtjy·am
ɪn ˈmi:djo: ˈtɛmplʌi ˈtjy·ʌi se:kʊndʊm ˈno:mɛn ˈtjy·ʊm
ˈʌitɑ ɛθ lɔ:z ˈtjy·ɑ ɪn ˈfʌini:z ˈtɛṛe dʒʏˈsti:sjɑ dʒʏˈsti:sjɑ
ˈpli:nɑ ɛst ˈdɛksteṛɑ ˈtjy·ɑ
ˈmaŋgnʊs ˈdɔmɪnʊz ɛθ lɔ:de:bɪlɪs ˈnʌimɪz ɪn si:vɪˈte:te
　ˈdi:·ʌi ˈnɔstṛʌi
ɪn ˈmɔnte ˈsaŋto: ˈi:dʒʊs ˈi:dʒʊs
ˈglo:ṛjɑ ˈpe:tṛʌi ɛθ ˈfʌiljo: ɛθ ˈspʌiṛɪtjy·ʌi ˈsaŋto:
ˈsʌikʊθ ˈe:ṛaθ ɪn pṛɪnˈsi:pjo: ɛθ nʊŋk ɛθ ˈsɛmpɛṛ
ɛθ ɪn ˈsi:kʏlɑ si:kʏˈlo:ṛʊm ˈe:mɛn

France

5—

Old French

ROBERT TAYLOR

French is one of the Romance languages, all of which evolved from the familiar variety of spoken Latin called Vulgar Latin. The common source of the nine languages was more or less homogeneous in nature during the middle period of the Roman Empire, although some regional variations of vocabulary and pronunciation undoubtedly developed over time because of differences in social and commercial activity. Variations were also caused by varying structures of the native languages that underlay the common use of Latin; their speech patterns influenced its natural and continuous evolution, even after they had been completely replaced by official Latin usage.

As long as the Empire lasted, this spontaneous evolution of the living Latin language was held in check by centralized social structures, not only administrative ones, but also the schools and the Church. With the fall of the Empire came the loss of centralized stability and social order; the various parts of the Empire were isolated from one another and were subject to varying sorts of political and linguistic influence from the outside. Among its neighboring Romance languages, French evolved more rapidly and more radically than the others, for reasons that are not entirely known. The geographical openness of northern Gaul made it prone to invasion by various ethnic groups, resulting in an ethnic and linguistic mix that tended to be less stable than those of other areas. In fairly recent times, the Celtic tribes moved into western Europe and settled more densely in the northern part of Gaul than in the south. In any case, their language seems to have exerted a greater influence on the development of Vulgar Latin in the North than it did in the South. On the other hand, the Latin presence was more solidly established in the South, where Roman colonization had been accomplished almost a century before the conquest of northern Gaul in 52 B.C. To these factors must be added the powerful influence of the Germanic language of the Franks, which was imposed solidly on the

North by extensive settlement and intermarriage, in contrast to the more limited administrative presence of the Frankish control over the South. In the North there seems to have been several centuries of bilingualism in the mixed population of Gallo-Romans and Franks. Ultimately the conquerors abandoned their language in favor of Gallo-Roman, but the sounds, the vocabulary, and the structures of the vernacular language had been profoundly destabilized, leading to rapid and radical evolution, particularly in the area of pronunciation. Many phonetic changes found in all Romance languages are found in a more extreme form in French. Unaccented vowels were weakened everywhere, but in French they often disappeared completely. Similarly, consonants in weak position, which evolved to some extent in all Romance languages, frequently disappeared or became vocalized in French. The diphthongization of certain accented vowels and the palatalization of some consonants moved through several stages in French, with radical effect on the phonological system.

Regional Varieties

There were about eleven dialects in Old French, but not all were of literary importance, and all were increasingly dominated from the end of the twelfth century by Francien, the language used by the royal court and the centralized administration in and around Paris. The eastern dialects, from Wallonia (Belgium) down through Lorraine to Burgundy, had many common features that distinguished them from Francien. The northern group, from Wallonia westward through Picardy to Normandy, was even more characteristic and exerted considerable influence on the development of the literary language.

Aside from Picard, the various regional varieties of Old French are not of great practical importance for performers of medieval music, for a number of reasons. First, strong dialectal features are commonly found only in the twelfth and early thirteenth centuries, and were avoided more and more after the thirteenth in favor of standardized Francien. Second, other regions, except for Picardy, did not have strong lyric traditions. While literature in other genres, and particularly prose works, may show a variety of strongly marked dialectal variants even into the fifteenth century, lyric poetry was normally written in Francien or Picard. Features from other dialectal regions are more likely to be due to scribal variation than to poetic intent. Finally, even in the case of "Picardized" texts, the regional features may have been largely artificial, used to impart a characteristic sound for artistic reasons during performance, rather than represent the poet's spontaneous usage or artistic intent. It was commonly held in the early Medieval period that certain languages were better suited for certain literary genres than others, and both Picard and Francien seem to have been considered as worthy vehicles for lyric poetry. Later, this prestige was to pass exclusively to Francien, while Picard was to retain a position of strength only in the domain of dramatic literature.

For performance purposes, artistic freedom of interpretation may be assumed to include that of regularizing regional characteristics or of coloring a text with regional pronunciations in response to an artistic preference for characteristic sounds, or in the interests of responding to a local preference for adaptation to the audience's habitual speech patterns.

Following the overall presentation of vowels and consonants, a list of the most characteristic Picard features has been added to aid in the recognition of the typical Picard flavor. Regionally flavored poems are never consistent in all aspects of their pronunciation. Performers will have to decide whether to pronounce the forms as they are written, or to regularize them by consistently using Francien or Picard sounds.

Evidence

There is no standard phonology of Medieval French, and there were only the beginnings of scientific accuracy of phonetic description by the sixteenth century. There seems to have been a good deal of regional and social flexibility of usage, and one of the Medieval poets goes so far as to recommend tolerance in matters of pronunciation; Conon de Béthune was embarrassed by the mockery by court people (even by the queen) of his regionalized Artois or Picard speech, and he claims in a poem that it is uncourtly to make fun of someone else's pronunciation.

The written text itself is of course the most reliable guide to pronunciation. Early texts in Old French are reasonably phonetic; that is, we may pronounce what we see—all letters that are written are meant to be pronounced, "silent" letters are simply omitted, and for a certain time, changes in pronunciation were reflected faithfully in the spelling. However, spelling soon became traditional, and from the thirteenth century onward, only texts written or copied by uneducated people continued to reflect new sounds with any accuracy. Thus we may find indications of evolved pronunciations in the "incorrect" spellings of some of the mystery plays of the fifteenth century and in diaries and personal correspondence of the sixteenth century. Occasionally words are transcribed in a non-Roman alphabet, such as in a number of Hebrew glosses of the thirteenth century; they may furnish clues to actual pronunciation because of the distinctions made between sounds in these different languages. In later periods, similar clues to exact pronunciation may be gleaned from the way in which Middle English or Middle High German writers spell words borrowed from Middle French, or from the letters used to transcribe into French words borrowed from other languages; *artichault* from Italian *articiocco* in the sixteenth century indicates that the spelling *au* in French no longer indicates the diphthong [au], but has simplified to [o].

Much precision can be established through a careful analysis of poetic language. From a study of assonances we may find clear evidence of the nasalization of vowels, the differentiation of *e* sounds, and the simplifying of diphthongs to monophthongs. From the analysis of rhymes, which began to be used in French poetry in the early twelfth century, we may examine the status of consonants after the tonic vowel, to establish the period of their disappearance. Nothing may be proved about the exact sound of pretonic vowels or consonants, however, except in the rare cases where poets have used leonine rhymes consistently. Since the poets usually showed scrupulous care in the regularity of syllable count in versification, we may establish the period in which the neutral *e* in hiatus disappeared from pronunciation, or in which the closed vowels [i, u, y] became semi-vowels and ceased to form a separate syllable.

The rest of our knowledge has come of necessity from the painstaking philological and comparative study of language evolution over the past two centuries. The body of knowledge built up in this way is extremely detailed and precise, filling many volumes of basic reference manuals, grammars, and dictionaries, but it has to do with transformational information for the most part, that is, the ways in which languages have evolved step by step from their origins to the present day, and the processes that govern the evolution.

Bibliography

Jeannine Alton and Brian Jeffery. *Bele Buche e Bele Parleure. A Guide to the Pronunciation of Medieval and Renaissance French for Singers and Others.* London: Tecla Editions, 1976. 79 pp.
Joseph Anglade. *Grammaire élémentaire de l'ancien français.* Paris: A. Colin, 1917; 12th ed. 1965. 248 pp. See pp. 67–71.
Henri Bonnard. *Synopsis de phonétique historique.* 3d ed., rev., with the addition of exercises. Paris: SEDES, 1985. 64 pp.
Edouard Bourciez. *Précis historique de phonétique française.* 8th ed., rev. and corr. Paris: Klincksieck, 1955. xlvii, 333 pp.
Charles Bruneau. *Petite histoire de la langue française.* 2 vols. Paris: E. Colin, 1955. xi, 284 pp.
Ferdinand Brunot. *Histoire de la langue française des origines à nos jours.* New ed. Paris: A. Colin, 1966–. See tomes I, II, and III. 548, 510, 456, and 320 pp.
Jacques Chaurand. *Histoire de la langue française.* Que Sais-Je? 167. Paris: PUF, 1969. 128 pp. 2d ed., 1972.
François de la Chaussée. *Initiation à la phonétique historique de l'ancien français.* Paris: Klincksieck, 1974.
Fletcher Collins. *A Medieval Songbook: Troubadour and Trouvère.* Charlottesville: University Press of Virginia, 1982. See pp. 159–61.
Pierre Fouché. *Phonétique historique du français.* 3 vols. Paris: Klincksieck, 1952, 1958, 1961.
Charles T. Gossen. *Grammaire de l'ancien picard.* Reprint with minor corrections and additions. Paris: Klincksieck, 1976. 226 pp.
A. J. Greimas. *Dictionnaire de l'ancien français.* Paris: Larousse, 1968 (with frequent revisions since that date).
Rebecca Harris-Warrick. "A Guide to the Pronunciation of Old French for Singers." A term project for the D.M.A., Stanford University, 1977. vii, 53 pp.
Mireille Huchon. *Le Français de la Renaissance.* Que Sais-Je? 2389. Paris: PUF, 1988. 128 pp. See pp. 83–95.
Christiane Marchello-Nizia. *Histoire de la langue française aux XIVe et XVe siècles.* Paris: Bordas, 1979. 378 pp.
Kristoffer Nyrop. *Grammaire historique de la langue française.* Vol. I: *Histoire de la langue; phonétique historique.* Paris: Picard, 1914. 594 pp.
Mildred K. Pope. *From Latin to Modern French with Especial Consideration of Anglo-Norman.* Manchester: Manchester University Press, 1934. Rev. ed. 1952. xxxii, 571 pp.
Georges Straka. "Les rimes classiques et la prononciation française de l'époque." *Travaux de linguistique et de littérature* 23/1 (1985):61–138.
———. "Remarques sur les voyelles nasales, leur origine et leur évolution en français." *Revue de linguistique romane* 19 (1956):245–74.
Charles Thurot. *De la Prononciation française depuis le commencement du XVIe siècle d'après les témoignages des grammairiens.* Paris: Imprimerie royale, 1881. Reprint, Slatkine, 1966.

Chronological Divisions

Within the period covered (1100–1650), the vowels and consonants of French seem to be in continuous motion; the language of 1100 bears little resemblance to that of 1650. For the practical purposes of this book, this span is divided into three periods: Period One, 1100 to 1250, Old French proper; Period Two, 1250 to 1450, which may be called loosely Middle French; and Period Three, 1450 to 1650, Renaissance French. Within each of these periods, the language may be envisaged as a relatively cohesive unit. It is generally easy to place a poem within one of the three periods, even if the precise date of composition is not known, and the relevant information will then be more easily identified in the following presentation of sounds. The diachronic chart below will assist the reader in further refining pronunciation.

The three periods are not entirely arbitrary designations. Each one contains a number of clearly characteristic sound features: the first has affricated consonants [ts], [tʃ], [dʒ]; typical diphthongs [ɔj], [aw], [ɛw], [wɛ]; neutral [ə] pronounced in all positions; final *s* and preconsonantal *s* always pronounced; Germanic *h* strongly aspirated; and in general a direct correlation between spelling and pronunciation. The second has a disconcerting number of spellings that do not reflect pronunciation; simplified affricates [s], [ʃ], [ʒ] from the older [ts], [tʃ], [dʒ]; simplified diphthongs; effacement of [ə] in hiatus; silent *s* before consonants and in some final positions; and loss of many final consonants. The third has silent final *s* in all categories; a shift in the pronunciation of [ə] by labialization (rounding of the lips); a restructuring of nasalization patterns and effects; the appearance of posterior [ɑ] (see below, "Vowels"); and a generally new tendency to "rationalize" pronunciation and spelling by reference to analogy with general patterns within French and to Latin etymology.

Aside from phonetic reasons, the three periods may each be thought of as centered on a significant musical repertory: the first includes songs by Gace Brulé, Chastelain de Coucy, Blondel de Nesle, Richart de Fournival, Thibaut de Champagne, Colin Muset, and others, mostly monophonic works; the second has both monophonic and polyphonic works by such poets as Adam de la Halle, the *Fauvel* group, Guillaume de Machaut, Gilles Binchois, Baude Cordier, and Guillaume Dufay (unfortunately, for the important poets Eustache Deschamps and Charles d'Orléans, no melodies are extant); the third includes Josquin des Prés, Nicolas Gombert, Claude Lejeune, Pierre de la Rue, Johannes Ockeghem, Orlando di Lasso, and others, in a period of international musical style.

Sounds vs. Spellings

As a general rule, the spellings of Old French tend to reflect the actual pronunciation; until the thirteenth century, shifts in pronunciation were reflected dependably in the spelling. However, even in the earliest period, notational patterns soon became traditional and rigid; after the mid-thirteenth century, spelling lagged further and further behind phonetic changes and ceased to give a predictable indication of the sounds. This trend has continued into modern French in spite of periodic attempts to rationalize and simplify spellings, especially during the Renaissance period; modern French spellings are in many cases a poor guide to pronunciation. For example, the Latin *rege (king)* had evolved to the sound [rej] in early Old French and is noted *rei* according to its pronunciation; we may observe its subsequent shift to the sound [rɔj] during the early twelfth century because the spelling *roi* changes to reflect the new sound. But from then on, no further change was made to the spelling, even though the actual pronunciation shifted to [rwɛ] in the late twelfth century and to its modern sound [rwa] in the eighteenth century.

Even in Old French, there were hesitations in the notation of new sounds that had no close equivalent in Latin tradition, such as the diphthongized vowels and the palatalized consonants. Sometimes there were quite different solutions to the problems in different areas, or simply from one scribe to another, and these sometimes became typical of a region or of a *scripta,* even if they did not reflect any difference in the actual pronunciation. The palatalized *n* [ɲ], for example, was written frequently as *gn* or *ng,* but sometimes as simple *n,* or *ni, in, ign;* or in the Walloon area as *nh.*

In the Middle French period, many artificial learned spellings were introduced through the wider judicial and administrative uses of French to replace Latin. Often these are an attempt to restore the Latin appearance of the words by the use of etymological forms, as in the spelling *temps (<tempus)* for Old French *tens,* but often the attempt was approximate or faulty or merely for decorative effect, as in *faulx* for *faus (<fals), subject* for *sujet* or *avecques* for *avec.*

Stress and Accent

As early as the first Old French poetic texts, the stress patterns typical of modern French are to be used. That is, instead of an accented syllable that belongs to each word and helps to identify it, Old French automatically puts the stress on the final syllable of a word or of a linked group of words (ignoring, of course, the unstressed final *e,* which is not counted as a syllable), so that the accent ceases to have any function in determining meaning.

Even more important for singers is the fact that the traditional Latin verse meters (iambic, dactylic, etc.), which depend on successions of accented and unaccented syllables, or long and short syllables, cannot function effectively in French; at least they cannot function in a spontaneous fashion, since they do not reflect the actual spoken pronunciation patterns. This is not to say that the traditional metrical verse forms cannot be imposed artificially, as they were indeed at various periods; but in general, French versification depends, from the earliest poems, on syllabic count for its basic rhythmic form.

There is no reason to assume, however, that this basic normal pattern was not sometimes ignored or modified in response to the stronger demands of musical form. An unusual stress pattern may in fact be intended in some cases to draw particular attention to that part of the text or, conversely, to draw a particular effect from the musical passage itself.

Consonants

Many consonants in Medieval French pose no problems of pronunciation, being spoken approximately as in modern French and English; only those that are difficult by reason of their articulation or because of a shift in sound during the period of coverage have been presented below.

In general, Period One is characterized by phonetic spellings; that is, all consonants that are written are to be pronounced as they stand. But during the thirteenth century, spelling traditions tended to become fixed and did not necessarily change to reflect subsequent shifts in pronunciation. In addition, as time passed, more and more learned spellings from Latin were admitted, especially in the fourteenth and fifteenth centuries, causing further difficulties in the interpretation of pronunciation from the written forms.

Double consonants were simplified to single sounds before 1100, except for *rr* (see below). Therefore, with this exception, no doubles are to be pronounced, no matter what the spelling. Note that double *ss* is often used in spelling to denote simple [s], as opposed to the spelling with single *s* denoting [z] (see below).

Final consonants were progressively weakened throughout the centuries that interest us. In Period One, all written final consonants are to be pronounced, with the proviso that any voiced consonants for which there are voiceless equivalents *(d, g, v)* are to be pronounced as voiceless [t], [k], [f]. For example, *grant* and *grand* are pronounced [grãnt], *sanc* and *sang* [sãnk], *lief* and *liev* [ljɛf]. In popular usage, all final consonants had fallen by the mid-thirteenth century, but in literary usage they were pronounced at the end of a line of verse, at a distinct pause, and before a word beginning with a vowel, right up to the sixteenth century. During Period Three (and into the Classical period), the general rule is that *all* final consonants are silent, except for rare cases when they were restored consciously for the sake of clarity or as a result of spelling. For details concerning final *s* and *r,* see below.

Implosive consonants, that is, those that closed a syllable and were followed by another consonant that opened the next syllable, were pronounced at the beginning of the Old French period, but they gradually weakened and fell, at least in popular speech, by the end of the twelfth century (e.g., Cha*r*les, chambe*r*lan, i*s*le, bla*s*me, la*r*ge, fo*r*ce). For detailed remarks on implosive *s* and *l,* see below.

From the fourteenth century onward, many etymological consonants were restored to spelling, but only a few were subsequently pronounced (e.g., modern French a*b*sorber, su*b*til, pronounced [apsɔrbe, syptil] with a sound assimilated to that of the following consonant); most, however, were purely orthographic (e.g., modern doi*g*t, earlier frui*c*t, su*b*je*c*t).

Assimilation of implosive consonants to the sound of the following consonant (voicing or unvoicing) was undoubtedly common practice from the earliest period on, and should be practiced in performance (e.g., *absolu* [apsɔly].

c Before *a, o,* or *u,* the letter *c* was pronounced [k]; before *e* or *i* it was pronounced [ts] during the Old French period, and [s] thereafter. E.g., *citét* [tsitɛθ] > [site], *ciel* [tsjɛl] > [sjɛl], *place* [platsə] > [plasə].

ch The notation *ch* was invariably pronounced [tʃ] during the Old French period, and [ʃ] thereafter. E.g., *riche* [ritʃə] > [riʃə], *chief* [tʃjɛf] > [ʃjɛf], *sache* [satʃə] > [saʃə].

g Before *a, o,* and *u, g* was pronounced [g]; before *e* and *i,* it was pronounced [dʒ] during the Old French period, and [ʒ] thereafter. E.g., *gesir* [dʒezir] > [ʒezir], *jugier* [dʒydʒjɛr] > [ʒyʒjɛr].

gu The pronunciation is a simple [g], the letter *u* merely indicating the unpalatalized [g] as opposed to the palatalized [dʒ]. E.g., gant/guant, guide, guise, garder/guarder.

h Latin *h* disappeared from the language as early as the first century B.C., and thus it has never been pronounced in French at any period. Traditional spellings have maintained it very frequently in the written language, and even restored it in many instances where it had disappeared from Old French notation, especially in the fourteenth and fifteenth centuries. (E.g., Latin *habile* and *homine,* noted and pronounced *able* and *ome* in Old French, restored to *habile* and *homme* in Middle French.

Germanic *h* has quite a different history. It is to be found in French in numerous words of Germanic or exotic origin, such as *honte, hibou, hasard.* In Old French it was strongly pronounced, probably more harshly than in modern German or English, but gradually it weakened in force, from the thirteenth century on, until it disappeared entirely at the end of the eighteenth century. In Renaissance French it still has a strong enough articulation to be compared to English *h.* (In Modern French, although it is never pronounced, the "Germanic," or aspirate, *h,* noted with an asterisk in most dictionaries, still has a disjunctive effect, preventing liaison and elision [*les hiboux, la honte*], as opposed to the Latin *h,* which has no effect whatever on pronunciation.)

j The letter *j* was invariably pronounced [dʒ] during the Old French period, and [ʒ] thereafter. E.g., *jardin* [dʒardin] > [ʒardĩn], *joie* [dʒoiə] > [ʒweə], *jorn* [dʒɔrn] > [ʒɔrn].

l At the beginning of a word or syllable, the normal *l* was pronounced as in modern French with a light, clear, front sound.

When followed by another consonant, or at the end of an atonic form such as *al* or *del* linked phonetically to a following word with an initial consonant, *l* vocalized early to the semi-vowel sound [w], which then combined with the preceding vowel in various ways. The letter *l* was frequently maintained in spelling, especially in Periods One and Two, but its pronunciation was invariably [w]. For example, *altre/autre* were pronounced [awtrə] before simplifying to [otrə]; *colp/coup* [kɔwp], then [kup], then [ku]; *del/deu* [dɛw] > [dy]; *vielz/vieuz* [vjɛwts] > [vjɛws] > [vjø]; *fils/fius* [fiws] > [fis].

Palatalized *l* [ʎ], similar in pronunciation to the English sound in mi*lli*on, the Spanish *ll,* and the Italian *gl,* was pronounced thus in literary usage right up to the end of the eighteenth century, after the French Revolution, even though it had been reduced to [j] in popular speech as early as the fourteenth century. Normally it is signaled in medieval texts by the spellings *il* or *ill,* but other spellings are sometimes found, such as *li, lli, l, ll, lh,* etc.

n, m The nasal consonants *n* and *m* were pronounced even after a nasalized vowel, in contrast to modern French, where they are silent after a nasalized vowel, pronounced only after an oral vowel or at the beginning of the word. The modern practice was not accepted into literary usage until some time during the sixteenth century, and thus applies only to our Period Three.

ɲ Palatalized *n* [ɲ], similar in pronunciation to the English sound in mi*ni*on, Spanish *ñ,* and Italian *gn,* was spelled normally *-gn-* or *-ign-* in early French, although other spellings are found, such as *-ng-, -in-, -ni-, -n-, -nh-,* etc. The sound itself has been constant from Old French through to Modern French.

q/qu Whether written with a *u* or not, the pronunciation is a simple [k]. E.g., *quatre, qui, quant, qatre, qi, qant, katre, ki, kant, cant.*

r Throughout the period of coverage, *r* was the traditional rolled apical consonant [r̥], similar to that of present-day Spanish and Italian, and to that which is still in common usage in southern France. The velar or uvular *r* [R], typical of modern French, did not make its appearance until the mid-sixteenth century and was not accepted into cultivated speech (i.e., poetry and song) until the end of the seventeenth century.

In final position *r* became silent, like all other consonants, as early as the thirteenth century in popular speech and regularly in literary usage from the sixteenth century. In our Period Three (Renaissance), *r* was silent in infinitives of the first conjugation *(chanter, parler),* as well as in nouns and adjectives ending in *-er* and *-ier;* the disappearance was extended gradually to include infinitives ending in *-ir,* nouns in *-oir* and *-eur (finir, comptoir, menteur).* Only later, in the mid-eighteenth century, were some of these restored for purposes of clarity or identification of function.

rr Double *rr* was pronounced strongly throughout our reference period as [rr], with two or three flips of the tongue instead of one. Even though this double sound was simplified to a single one [r̥] in popular usage as early as the end of the twelfth century, it was not accepted in the cultivated language of song until the mid-seventeenth century.

s In final position in the word, *s* is to be pronounced [s] in texts from Period One. During Period Two, all final consonants, including *s,* disappeared from the popular language, but in literary usage, the situation was more complex. Inside a line of verse where there was no grammatical pause, *s* was only pronounced if the following word began with a vowel, and it was voiced to [z] (e.g., *plus agreable* [plyzagre·ablə] as in modern French). At a pause or at the end of a line, final *s* was fully pronounced [s]. In Period Three, final *s* at a pause or at the end of a line was silent along with all other final consonants; but when final *s* disappeared, the preceding vowel (except for unstressed *e*) was lengthened as a sort of syllabic compensation, and this lengthened vowel was perceptible until the end of the eighteenth century. In the case of *a,* pure rhymes were impossible between singulars and plurals such as *soldat* [sɔlda] and *soldats* [sɔldɑ:], in part because of the difference in vowel length, in part because this difference was accompanied by a shift in articulation from [a] to [ɑ].

Inside a word followed by *t, p,* or *k,* the consonant *s* maintained its pronunciation in Period One (*teste* [tɛstə]). When it was followed by any other consonant, *s* was silent even in the oldest of poetic texts of Period One (e.g., bla*s*me, i*s*le, a*s*ne, hi*s*dous, ma*s*le). By Period Two, *s* was silent in all these cases, even though it generally remained in spelling until the eighteenth century. Before its complete disappearance, *s* was pronounced in an aspirated form similar to an *h* or a German [x], and even after it had disappeared completely, it caused a lengthening of the preceding vowel which was still pronounced in Period Three. For example, the verb form *est,* pronounced [ɛst] in Period One, was transcribed in Period Two as *eght* in the treatise *Orthographia Gallica,* and in Period Three as *eee* by the Renaissance scholar Erasmus.

x This is a common spelling equivalent for *-us.* E.g., *miex* [mjews], *Dex* [dews].

z The letter *z* at the end of a word was pronounced as an affricate [ts] during Period One, simplifying thereafter to [s] in Period Two, becoming silent in Period Three. For example, *chantez* was pronounced [tʃãntɛts] > [ʃãntɛs] > [ʃãte]; *dolz* was pronounced [dowts] > [dus] > [du].

Vowels

a A short open vowel [a] pronounced toward the front of the mouth. In Period Three the posterior long [ɑ:] was formed as a consequence of the disappearance of a following implosive *s,* which lengthened the vowel by compensation and drew the articulation toward the back of the mouth by assimilation to the guttural [x] sound of the weakened *s.*

e The letter *e* was never silent, as it may sometimes be in modern French. However, it did stand for a variety of actual sounds that tended to evolve and fluctuate in usage, making the precise sounds at times difficult to identify. Note that modern editors of medieval French texts use an acute accent to distinguish a tonic *e* in the final syllable from a post-tonic vowel [ə]. This does not imply a closed [e] as distinct from an open [ɛ], as it does in modern French usage. For example, *celé, celés (hidden)* were pronounced [səle], [səlɛs] as opposed to *cele, celes (this, these),* pronounced [sɛlə], [sɛləs].

Early in Period One, three pronunciations were possible in tonic syllables:

[e] the closed vowel was found originally in words like *dete, vert,* coming from Latin long *e* or short *i* in a closed syllable

[ɛ] the open vowel was found in words like *perte, bele, teste,* coming from Latin short *e* in a closed syllable

[ɛ:] a third sound was found in words like *mer, tel, pere, chanter,* coming from Latin *a* in a free syllable; it was unstable, evolving from a very open to a very closed sound, and more importantly, it was a long vowel and did not assonate in early texts with the other two varieties of *e.*

In a complex evolution lasting until late in the sixteenth century, all three varieties of *e* were redistributed into two sounds according to position, [e] being used in a free syllable, [ɛ] in a checked syllable, that is, when a consonant was pronounced after the vowel. As final consonants gradually disappeared during Periods One and Two (see above), many [ɛ] sounds evolved to [e]. For example *bontét* [bontɛθ] became *bonté* [bonte], *chanter* [tʃãntɛr] became [ʃãnte]. In the case of nouns like *essai* the original diphthong [aj] simplified to [ɛ] early in Period One, then closed to [e] by the end of the period, whenever it was in final position; however, the plural form *essais* kept its [ɛ] as long as the final *s* was pronounced, and in traditional literary usage for some time afterward; thus in Periods Two and Three and right into the seventeenth-century Classical period, the singular *essai* [ɛse] could not rhyme with the plural *essais* [ɛsɛ].

In initial position, *e* maintained a full vocalic sound, but it is impossible to say whether it was open or closed. Most linguists agree that a "central" *e,* neither very open nor very closed, was probably the norm, but with a good deal of fluctuation depending on neighboring sounds and local traditions.

In all other unaccented syllables, *e* very early took on a short and indistinct pronunciation, probably like a very abbreviated "central" *e*. Since it is not discussed in early grammatical treatises, no one can be entirely sure of the particular sound that this vowel had in Periods One and Two, but it does not seem to have been labialized like the modern French sound, a sort of abbreviated [ø], until Period Three. In this presentation, the symbol [ə] has been used to represent both sounds, that is, the short, neutral, front vowel with no rounding of the lips, typical of Periods One and Two, and the slightly labialized sound typical of Period Three and of modern French.

Disappearance of [ə]: In Period One, all vowels that appear in the texts are to be pronounced, including final [ə] *porte* [pɔrtə], [ə] in hiatus *vëu* [vəy], and even in final position after another vowel *vëue* [vəyə], *portee* [purteə]. In Period Two, [ə] disappeared in non-final hiatus, although it was frequently maintained in spelling: *eu* [y], *receu* [rəsy]. In Period Three there were no further disappearances, but the pronunciation of [ə] in final position after a consonant or another vowel became very weak. In poetry the traditional "feminine" rhymes, consisting of a tonic syllable plus an atonic [ə], ensured the preservation of final [ə] until the twentieth century. In a few cases, by analogy with the reformed pronunciation of Latin instituted by Erasmus, many [ə] vowels became [e] in Period Three, as in *ferir, perir, gesir.* And despite the normal rules, there seems to have been a good deal of poetic freedom to pronounce or elide [ə] as required by the tyrannical French syllabic versification.

i A very closed vowel, [i], as in modern French. As part of a diphthong or triphthong it corresponds to the semi-vowel [j].

o Latin accented ŏ in a closed syllable continues as the open sound [ɔ], e.g., *mort* [mɔrt]. Latin accented ō and ŭ merged into the closed sound [o], but in Period One, the sound was more closed than the *o* of modern French, approaching the sound of [u]. In initial position, *o* did in fact close to [u] during Period One; the new sound was sometimes signaled by the spelling *ou,* but often the traditional spelling was retained: *soleil/souleil, cort/court, voloir/vouloir, boche/bouche.* In Period Three the reforms made to Latin pronunciation by Erasmus caused a corresponding shift in French from [u] back to [o], as in *couloque* > *colloque, coupie* > *copie, chouse* > *chose,* with some confusions, such as *fornir/fournir, formi/fourmi.*

u The very closed, front, rounded vowel [y] as in modern French.

Diphthongs

Diphthongs are typical of Period One; in Period Two, most were simplified to a single vowel. Spellings are not a reliable guide to pronunciation, since they become relatively fixed after about 1200 and do not change to reflect shifts in pronunciation.

ai Simplified to [ɛ] by the start of Period One: *fait* [fɛt].

au A diphthong [aw] in Period One, thereafter simplified to [o]: *autre/altre* [awtrə] > [otrə].

eau The triphthong [ɛaw] in Period One, thereafter [əo]: *beau* [bɛaw] > [bəo] (not simplified to [bo] until the end of the sixteenth century). Note the typical Picard variation *iau,* pronounced [jaw] in Period One, thereafter [jo].

eu The diphthong [øw] during Period One, thereafter [ø]: *fleur* [fløwr̥] > [flør].

ie The diphthong [jɛ] from Period One on: *ciel* [tsjɛl] > [sjɛl].

ieu The triphthong [jøw] during Period One, thereafter [jø]: *dieu* [djøw] > [djø].

oi The diphthong [ɔj] during most of Period One, thereafter [wɛ]: *roi* [rɔj] > [rwɛ], *chantoit* [tʃãntɔjt] > [ʃãntwɛ].

ou Simplified to [u] by the start of Period One: *coup* [kup] > [ku].

ue Probably the diphthong [wø], simplified during the course of Period One to [ø]: *nuef* [nwøf] > [nøf].

ui The diphthong [ɥi] from Period One on: uit/huit [ɥit].

Vowels in Hiatus

Two vowels in contact were pronounced separately in Period One, that is, they were counted as separate syllables in versification. From Period Two on, they were reduced to a single vowel, though the spellings often remained unchanged. Some poetic license prevailed, allowing such vowels to be counted as syllables if required in versification; e.g., *aïde* [a·idə] > [ɛdə], *haïne* [ha·inə] > [ɛnə], *paour* [pa·ur] > [pør], *recëu* [rəsə·y] > [rəsy].

This series of reductions includes that of ə before a vowel (see above). As with other reductions, the remaining vowel was lengthened by compensation, and this typical long vowel often remained for some time after the shift (Period Two), preventing rhyme with the corresponding short vowel and imparting a musically important characteristic to the rhythm.

Nasalization

Nasalization of vowels by a following [m], [n], or [ɲ] took place progressively over several centuries, affecting all vowels except [u] and [ə]. (The vowel [u] did not occur before the thirteenth century, and the shift from [o] in a closed syllable, which created it, was impeded by a following nasal. The vowel [ə] was not susceptible to phonemic nasalization because it was by nature unaccented, short and indistinct.)

In Period One the open vowels and diphthongs were already nasalized before *n* or *m* in all positions. Note that the nasal consonant continued to be pronounced: *an/am* [ãn/ãm]; *en/em* [ãn/ãm], originally [ɛ̃n/ɛ̃m] but opened to [ãn/ãm] by the time of the earliest lyric poems; *ain/aim* [ɛĩn/ɛĩm], originally [aĩn/aĩm] but closed to [ɛĩn/ɛĩm] by the time of the earliest lyric poems; *ein/eim* [ɛĩn/ɛĩm]; *ien/iem* [jɛ̃n/jɛ̃m].

Early in Period One (by 1150) two further nasalizations took place: *on/om* nasalized to [õn/õm]; *oin/oim* [wɛ̃n/wɛ̃m]. In Period Two, the closed vowels were progressively nasalized (*i* by the mid-thirteenth century, and *u* [y] during the fourteenth century): *in/im* [ĩŋ/ĩm], *un/um* [ỹn/ỹm].

During Period Three, nasalized vowels followed by *n* or *m* plus vowel were progressively denasalized, starting with the closed sounds. At the same time, the nasal consonant in implosive position (i.e., at the end of a word, or followed by another consonant) ceased to be pronounced, and in disappearing caused a lengthening of the nasalized vowel. In addition to this structural shift, a number of nasalized vowels were opened or simplified in articulation, giving essentially the modern pattern of French nasalization: *an/am* [ã:], *ain/aim* [ɛ̃:], *ein/eim* [ɛ̃:], *in/im* [ɛ̃:], *ien/iem* [jɛ̃:], *un/um* [ø̃:], *on/om* [õ:], *oin* [wɛ̃:].

DIACHRONIC SOUND CHART FOR FRENCH

An asterisk (*) indicates that the change is not universal; the appropriate section of the text should be consulted for clarification.

	1100		1250	1450	1650
VOWELS					
a	[a]				→
(before *s*)	[a]			[ɑ]	→
e accented	[e]	[e] (open syllable)			→
	[ɛ]	[ɛ] (closed syllable)			→
	[ɛ:]				
unaccented	[ə] (indistinct)			[ə] (rounded)	→
i	[i]	→			
o*					
u	[y]	→			
DIPHTHONGS					
ai	[ɛ]				→
au	[aw]		[o]		→
eau	[ɛaw]		[o]		→
eu	[ɛw]		[ø]		→
ie	[jɛ]				→
ieu	[jɛw]		[jø]		→
oi	[ɔj]		[wɛ]		→
ou	[u]*				→
ue	[wɛ]		[ø]		→
ui	[ɥi]				→
NASALS					
an, am, en, em	[ãn], [ãm]			[ɑ̃:]	→
ein, eim	[ẽn], [ẽm]			[ɛ̃:]	→
on, om		[õn], [õm]		[õ:]	→
oin		[wẽn]		[wɛ̃:]	→
in, im			[ĩn], [ĩm]	[ɛ̃:]	→
un			[ỹn]	[œ̃:]	→
CONSONANTS					
c before *i, e*	[ts]		[s]		→
before *a, o, u*	[k]				→
ch	[tʃ]		[ʃ]		→
g before *i, e*	[dʒ]		[ʒ]		→
before *a, o, u*	[g]				→
h Latin	silent		→		
Germanic	[x]			[h]	→
j	[dʒ]		[ʒ]		→
l implosive	[w]* (combines with preceding vowel)			→	
palatalized	[ʎ]		→		
r final	[ṛ]			often silent*	→
s final	[s]		silent except at pause, end of line*	silent	→
	[s]		[z] (liaison)		→
implosive	[s]*		silent		→
Final consonants	pronounced		pronounced only at pause*	silent	→
Implosive consonants	pronounced		silent		→

TYPICAL PICARD SOUNDS

(For Picard Latin, see Chapter 19, “Netherlands Latin.”)

Retention of *k* and *g* instead of Francien [tʃ] and [dʒ] (simplified to [ʃ] and [ʒ] in Periods Two and Three). E.g.: *canter* (for *chanter*), [kãntɛṛ] for [ʃãntɛṛ]; *gardin* (for *jardin*), [gaṛdĩn] for [ʒaṛdĩn]; *vaque* (for *vache*), [vakə] for [vaʃə]. Similarly [tʃ > ʃ] instead of Francien [ts > s]: *pieche* (for *piece*), [pjɛʃə] for [pjɛsə]; *cacher* (for *chacier*), [kaʃɛṛ] for [ʃasjɛṛ].

Retention of Germanic *w* instead of Francien *g*: *warder* (for *garder*), [waṛdɛṛ] for [gaṛdɛṛ]; *were* (for *guerre*), [wɛṛə] for [gɛṛə].

Reduced forms *iu* and *u* instead of the Francien triphthongs *ieu* and *ueu*: *liu* (for *lieu*), [lju] for [ljø]; *fu* (for *feu*), [fu] for [fø].

Triphthong *iau* instead of *eau*: *biau* (for *beau*), [bjo] for [bəo].

Unstressed feminines identical with masculines: *le, me, te* (for *la, ma, ta*), [lə, mə, tə] for [la, ma, ta].

Groups *ml, nr, lr* without the Francien glide: *asamlent* > *asanlent* (for *asamblent*), [asãmlə] > [asãnlə] for [asãmblə]; *tenront* (for *tendront*), [tãnṛõn] for [tãndṛõn]; *sorrai* (for *soldrai*), [sɔṛṛe] for [sɔwdṛe].

Metathesis of *r*: *aprechoive* (for *aperçoive*), [apṛɛʃwɛvə] for [apɛṛswɛvə]; *govrener* (for *governer*), [gɔvṛənɛṛ] for [gɔvɛṛnɛṛ]; *kerstienté* (for *chrestienté*), [kɛṛtjɛ̃nte] for [kṛetjɛ̃nte]; *pernons* (for *prenons*), [pɛṛnõn] for [pṛənõn].

Key “signal” forms (used frequently by poets to stress, or to add Picard “flavor”): *jou* (for *je*), [ʒu] for [ʒə]; *no, vo* (for *nostre, vostre*), [no], [vo] for [nɔtṛə], [vɔtṛə]; first plural verb ending, *-iemes* (imperfect), [-jɛmə].

SAMPLE TEXTS

Period One

Gace Brulé, “De bone amour”

Twelfth-century chanson. Paris, Bibl. Nat. Ms Fr. 846. fol. 41v. CD #15.

De bone amour et de lëaul amie
Me vient sovant pitiez et remembrance,
Si que jamais a nul jor de ma vie
N'oblïerai son vis ne sa semblance;
Por ce, s'Amors ne se vuet plus sosfrir
Qu'ele de touz ne face son plaisir
Et de toutes, mais ne puet avenir
Que de la moie aie bone esperance.

Coment porroie avoir bone esperance
A bone amor et a lëal amie,
Ne a biaus yeuz n'a la douce semblance
Que ne verrai jamés jor de ma vie?

Amer m'estuet, ne m'en puis plus sosfrir
Celi cui ja ne vanra a plaisir;
Siens sui, coment qu'il m'en doie avenir,
Et si n'i voi ne confort ne ahie.

də bõn ãmuṛ e də le·au ãmiə
mə vjɛ̃nt suvãn pitjɛts e ṛəmãmbṛãnsə
si kə dʒa mɛs a nyl dʒuṛ də ma viə
nubliəṛe sõn vis nə sa sãmblãnsə
puṛ sə sãmuṛs nə sə vuɛt plys susfṛiṛ
kɛlə də tuts nə fasə sõn plɛziṛ
e də tutəs mɛs nə puɛt avəniṛ
kə də la mɔj ɛ·ə bõn ɛspɛṛãnsə

kõmãnt purrɔj avɔjr bõn ɛspɛṛãnsə
a bõn ãmuṛ e a le·au ãmiə
nə a bjaus jœts na la dusə sãmblãnsə
kə nə vɛrrɛ dʒamɛs dʒuṛ də ma viə
ãmɛṛ mɛstuɛt nə mãn pɥis plys susfṛiṛ
səli kɥi dʒa nə vãnṛa a plɛziṛ
sjɛ̃ns sɥi kõmãnt kil mãn dɔj avəniṛ
e si ni vɔj nə kõnfɔṛt nə a·i·ə

Period Two

From *Roman de Fauvel*

Early fourteenth century, Paris, Bibl. Nat. fonds Fr. 146, fol. 29v. CD #16.

Se mes desirs fust a souhais,
mener devroie grant joie;
mais nenil, ainçois m'est a fais
quer je sai que ne pourroie
venir a mon desir jamais
s'amours ne me donnoit voie
et grace de venir a pais
a celi qui me guerroie
cruelment en dis et en faiz;
si qu'amours un seul don proie:
que se je sui de riens meffaiz
envers lui, corrigiez soie
a son plaisir de touz meffaiz.

Bonne est amours ou dangier ne maint mie
ne mautalens qui n'i font fors grever
les vrais amanz pleins de grant courtoisie

qui nuit et jour servent sanz nul fausser.
Dangier ne met nul service en prisie
quer vilains est, ne sait guerredonner.
Quant voit l'amant qu'a li tout s'umilie,
adont orgueil se paine de moustrer
et mautalens d'autre part pleins d'envie
envers l'amant pité ne lait ouvrer.
Se tel vilain ne se feïssent partie
encontr' amanz, trop bon feïst amer
et de legier on recouvrast amie.

sə me dəziṛ fyta su·ɛs
mənɛrdəvṛwɛ·ə gṛãn ʒwɛ·ə
mɛ nənil ɛ̃nswɛ mɛt a fɛs
kɛṛ ʒə sɛ kə nə purrwɛ·ə
vəniṛ a mõn dəziṛ ʒãmɛs
sãmuṛ nə mə dõnwɛ vwɛ·ə
e gṛasə də vəniṛ a pɛs
a səli ki mə gɛrrwɛ·ə
kṛy·ɛlmãnt ãn dize ãn fɛs
si kãmuṛz ỹn søl dõn pṛwɛ·ə
kə sə ʒə sɥi də ṛjɛ̃n mefɛs
ãnvɛṛ lɥi kɔṛiʒje swɛ·ə
a sõn plɛziṛ də tu mefɛs

bõn ɛt ãmuṛz u dãnʒjɛṛ nə mɛ̃n mi·ə
nə motalãn ki ni fõn fɔṛ gṛəvɛṛ
le vṛɛz ãmãn plɛ̃n də gṛãn kuṛtwɛzi·ə
ki nɥit e ʒuṛ sɛṛvə sãn nyl fosɛṛ
dãnʒjɛṛ nə mɛ nyl sɛṛvis ãn pṛizi·ə
kɛṛ vilɛ̃nz ɛt nə sɛ gɛṛədõnɛṛ
kãn vwɛ lãmãn ka li tu symili·ə
adõnt ɔṛgøλ sə pɛ̃nə də mutṛɛṛ
e motalãn dotṛə paṛ plɛ̃n dãnvi·ə
ãnvɛṛ lãmãn pite nə lɛt uvṛɛṛ
sə tɛl vilɛ̃n nə sə fə·isə paṛti·ə
ãnkõntṛ ãmãns tṛo bõn fə·it ãmɛṛ
e də ləʒjɛṛ õn ṛəkuvṛat ãmi·ə

Guillaume de Machaut, "Phyton, le mervilleus serpent"

Ballade from second half of the fourteenth century. (Source: Machaut manuscripts.) CD #17.

Phyton, le mervilleus serpent
Que Phebus de sa flesche occit,

Avoit la longueur d'un erpent,
Si com Ovides le descrit.
Mais onques homs serpent ne vit
Si fel, si crueus ne si fier
Com le serpent qui m'escondit,
Quant a ma dame merci quier.

Il ha sept chiés, et vraiement,
Chascuns a son tour contredit
La grace, ou mon vray desir tent,
Dont mes cuers an doleur languit:
Ce sont Refus, Desdaing, Despit,
Honte, Paour, Durté, Dangier,
Qui me blessent en l'esperit,
Quant a ma dame merci quier.

Si ne puis durer longuement,
Car ma tres douce dame rit
Et prent deduit en mon tourment
Et es meschiés, ou mes cuers vit.
Ce me destruit, ce me murdrit,
Ce me fait plaindre et larmoier,
Ce me partue et desconfit,
Quant a ma dame merci quier.

fitõn lə mɛṛviλø sɛṛpãnt
kə feby də sa flɛʃ ɔkit
avwɛ la lõngøṛ dỹn ɛṛpãnt
si cõm ovidə lə dekṛit
mɛzõnkəz õm sɛṛpãnnə vit
si fɛl si kṛy·ø nə si fjɛṛ
kõm lə sɛṛpãn ki mɛskõndit
kãnt a ma dãmə mɛṛsi kjɛṛ

il a sɛ ʃjɛs e vṛeəmãnt
ʃakỹnza sõn tuṛ kõntṛədit
la gṛas u mõn vṛe deziṛ tãnt
dõn me køṛzãn duløṛ lãngit
sə sõn ṛəfy dedɛ̃n depit
õntə pa·uṛ dyṛte dãnʒjɛṛ
ki mə blɛsətãn lɛspəṛit
kãnt a ma dãmə mɛṛsi kjɛṛ

si nə pɥi dyṛɛṛ lõngəmãnt
kaṛ ma tṛɛ dusə dãmə ṛit

e pṛãn dedɥit ãn mõn tuṛmãnt
e ɛs mɛʃjɛs u me køṛ vit
sə mə detṛɥit sə mə myṛdṛit
sə mə fɛ plɛ̃ndṛ e laṛmwɛjɛṛ
sə mə paṛty e dekõnfit
kãnt a ma dãmə mɛṛsi kjɛṛ

Baude Cordier

Early fifteenth century. Chantilly, Musée Condé 1047, fol. 11v. CD #18.

Belle, bonne, sage, plaisant et gente,
a ce jour cy que l'an se renouvelle
vous fais le don d'une chanson nouvelle
dedans mon cuer qui a vous se presente.
De recepvoir ce don ne soyés lente,
je vous suppli, ma doulce damoyselle,
belle, bonne, sage, plaisant et gente,
a ce jour cy que l'an se renouvelle,
car tant vous aim qu'aillours n'ay mon entente,
et si scay que vous estes seule celle
qui fame avés que chascun vous appelle:
flour de beauté sur toutes excellente.
Belle, bonne, sage, plaisant et gente,
a ce jour cy que l'an se renouvelle
vous fais le don d'une chanson nouvelle
dedans mon cuer qui a vous se presente.

bɛlə bõnə saʒə plɛzãnt͜e ʒãntə
a sə ʒuṛ si kə lãn sə ṛənuvɛlə
vu fɛ lə dõn dỹnə ʃãnsõn nuvɛlə
dədãn mõn køṛ ki a vu sə pṛezãntə
də ṛəsəvwɛṛ sə dõn nə swɛje lãntə
ʒə vu sypli ma dusə dãmwɛzɛlə
bɛlə bõnə saʒə plɛzãnt͜e ʒãntə
a səʒuṛ si kə lãn sə ṛənuvɛlə
kaṛ tãn vuz ɛ̃m kaʎuṛ ne mõn ãntãntə
e si se kə vuz ɛtə sølə sɛlə
ki fãm ave kə ʃakỹn vuzapɛlə
fluṛ də bote syṛ tutəz ɛksɛlãntə
bɛlə bõnə saʒə plɛzãnt͜e ʒãntə
a sə ʒuṛ si kə lãn sə ṛənuvɛlə
vu fɛ lə dõn dỹnə ʃãnsõn nuvɛlə
dədãn mõn køṛ ki a vu sə pṛezãntə

Period Three

Josquin des Prés

Ca. 1500. Florence, Bibl. Nat. Ms. XIX 164–67. CD #19.

Entré je suis en grant pensée
Pour faire ung nouvel amy
Dont je seray courrouchée
Et auray le cueur marry
Je crois que n'est point par luy
Pour faire ma destinée
J'assairay aultre que luy
Je le mettray en oubly

ã:tre ʒə sɥi ã gr̥ã: pã:seə
pur̥ fɛr̥ ø̃: nuvɛl ami
dõ ʒə sər̥e kur̥uʃeə
e ɔr̥e lə kør̥ mar̥i
ʒə crwe kə nɛ pwɛ̃: par lɥi
pur̥ fɛr̥ə ma dɛstineə
ʒasɛr̥e otr̥ə kə lɥi
ʒə lə mɛtr̥e ãn ubli

Pierre de la Rue, "Ce n'est pas jeu"

Late fifteenth–early sixteenth century. Brussels, Royal Library, Ms 228, fol. 5v–6.

Ce n'est pas jeu d'estre sy fortunée,
Qu'eslonger fault ce que l'on aime bien;
Et sy suis sceure que pas de luy ne vient
Mais me procede de ma grant destinée.

Dictes vous donc que je suis esgarée
Quant je me voy separée de mon bien:
Ce n'est pas jeu...

J'ay le rebours de toute ma pensée,
Et sy n'ay nul qui me conforte en rien;
De tout cecy je le porteray bien,
Mais que de luy je ne soye oublyée:
Ce n'est pas jeu...

sə nɛ pɑ ʒø dɛtrə si fɔrtyneə
kelɔɲe fo sə kə lõnɛmə bjɛ̃:
e si sɥi syr(ə) kə pɑ də lɥi nə vjɛ̃:

mɛ mə prosɛdə də ma grã: dɛstine·ə

ditə vu dõ kə ʒə sɥi zegareə
kã: ʒə mə vwɛ səpareə də mõ: bjɛ̃:

ʒe lə rəbur də tutə ma pã:seə
e si ne nyl ki mə kõ:fɔrt ã: rjɛ̃:
də tu səsi ʒə lə pɔrtəre bjɛ̃
mɛ kə də lɥi ʒə nə swɛ ubli·e·ə

Johannes Ockeghem, "J'en ay dueil"

Late fifteenth-century rondeau. Brussels, Royal Library, Ms 228, fol. 15v–16. CD #20.

J'en ay dueil que je ne suis morte;
Ne doy-je pas vouloir morir?
Dueil a mon cueur voulu saisir
Qui de tous biens me desconforte.

Ma douleur est plus que trop forte
Car sans avoir aucun plaisir
J'en ay dueil...

Je n'ay rien qui plus me conforte.
D'oeil ne voy plus que desplaisir.
Mort est le plus que mon desir,
Car quelque chouse qu'on m'aporte,
J'en ay dueil...

ʒãn e døʎ kə ʒə nə sɥi mɔṛtə
rnə dwɛ ʒə pɑ vulwɛr muṛiṛ
døʎ a mõ: køṛ vuly sɛziṛ
ki də tu bjɛ̃: mə dekõ:fɔrtə

ma dulør ɛ ply kə tro fɔrtə
kar sã:z avwɛr okø̃: plɛzir

ʒə ne rjɛ̃: ki ply mə kø̃:fɔrtə
døʎ nə vwɛ ply kə deplɛzir
mɔr ɛ lə ply kə mõ: dɛzir
kar kɛlkə ʃuzə kõ: mapɔrtə
ʒãne døʎ

Orlando di Lasso, "Que dis-tu"

Late sixteenth-century dialogue, text by Ronsard. CD #21.

Que dis-tu, que fais-tu, pensive Tourterelle,
dessus cest arbre sec? —Las! passant je lamente.

He pourquoi dy le moy? —De ma compagne absente
plus chere que ma vie. —En quelle part est elle?

Un cruel oyseleur par glueuse cautelle
l'a prinse et l'a tuee, et nuict et jour je chante
son trespas dans ces bois, nommant la mort meschante
qu'elle ne m'a tuee avecques ma fidelle.

Voudroys tu bien mourir avecques ta compagne?
Ouy, car aussi bien je languis en douleur,
et toujours le regret de sa mort m'accompagne.

O gentilz oyseletz que vous estes heureux
d'aymer si constamment, qu'heureux est vostre coeur
qui sans point varier est toujours amoureux.

kə di ty kə fɛ ty pãsivə tuṛtəṛɛlə
dəsy sɛt aṛbṛə sɛk la pasã ʒə lamãtə
e puṛkwɛ di lə mwɛ də ma kõpaɲ apsãtə
ply ʃɛṛə kə ma viə ã kɛlə paṛ ɛtɛlə

ø̃ kry·ɛl wɛzələøṛ paṛ gly·øzə kotɛlə
la pṛɛ̃z e la ty·e·ə e nɥit e ʒuṛ ʒə ʃãtə
sõ tṛepa dã se bwɛ nɔmã la mɔṛ meʃãtə
kɛlə nə ma ty·e·ə avɛkə ma fidɛlə

vudṛwɛ ty bjɛ̃ muṛiṛ avɛkə ta kõpaɲə
wi kaṛ osi bjɛ̃ ʒə lãgi ã duløṛ
e tuʒuṛ lə ṛəgṛɛ də sa mɔṛ ma kõpaɲə

o ʒãtiz wɛzəlɛ kə vuz ɛtəz øṛø
dɛme si kõstamã kørøz ɛ vɔtṛə køṛ
ki sã pwɛ̃ vaṛi·e·ɛ tuʒuṛz amuṛø

Orlando di Lasso, "Une puce"

Late sixteenth-century villanelle, text by De Baïf.

Une puce j'ay dedans l'oreill' helas!
Qui de nuit et de jour me fretill' et me mord
Et me faict devenir fou.

Nul remede n'i puis donner.
Je cours deça, je cours dela.
Ote la moy, retire la moy, je t'en pri!
O toute belle, secour moy!

Quand mes yeux je pence livrer au someil,
Elle vient me piquer, me demange, me poingt
Et me garde de dormir.

Nul remede...

D'une vielle charmeresse aidé me suis,
Qui guerit tout le monde et de tout guerissant,
Ne m'a sçeu me guerir moy:

Nul remede...

Bien je sçay que seule peux guerir ce mal,
Je te pri de me voir de bon oeil, et vouloir
Amolir ta cruauté:

Nul remede...

ynə pysə ʒɛ dədã:lɔṛɛʎ elɑ
ki də nɥit e də ʒuṛ məfṛətiʎ e mə mɔṛ
e mə fɛ dəvəniṛ fu

nyl ṛəmɛdə ni pɥi dɔne
ʒə kuṛ dəsa ʒə kuṛ dəla
otə la mwɛ ṛətiṛə la mwɛ ʒə tã:pṛi
o tutə bɛlə səkuṛ mwɛ

kã: mez jø ʒə pã:sə livṛe o sɔmɛʎ
ɛlə vjɛ̃: mə pike mə dəmã:ʒə mə pwɛ̃:
e mə gaṛdə də dɔṛmiṛ

dynə vjɛʎə ʃaṛmərɛs ɛde mə sɥi
ki gɛṛi tu lə mõ:d e də tu gɛṛisã:
nə ma sy mə gɛṛiṛ mwɛ

bjɛ̃: ʒə sɛ kə sølə pø gɛṛiṛ sə mal
ʒə tə pṛi də mə vwɛṛ dəbõ:n øʎ e vulwɛṛ
amɔliṛ ta kṛy·ote

Picard, Period Two

Perrin d'Angicourt, "Il couvient k'en la candeille"

Rome, Vatican Reg. 1490, fol. 97r–98r. CD #22.

Il couvient k'en la candeille
  Ait treble sustance,
Ains k'ele soit en vaillance
  Ne k'ele ait pooir

K'ele fache son devoir;
Car il i doit par raison
Avoir cire et lumignon,
Et el cief met on le fu;
  Et dont a vertu
De faire l'autrui service
Tant qu'ele est arse et remise.

Et je sui tout en tel guise
  Et en tel samblanche:
Espris d'un fu k'Amours lanche,
  Ke me fait ardoir
Le cuers et le cors doloir
Et fondre sans garison.
Cis fus me vint par enson,
Car jou m'en senti feru
  Loés que j'euc veü
Çou dont li mons s'esmerveille,
Dont j'art et souspir et veille.

il kuvjɛ̃n kãn la kãndɛʎə
ɛ trɛblə systãnsə
ɛ̃n kɛlə swɛt ãn vaʎãnsə
nə kɛl ɛ puwɛr
kɛlə faʃə sõn dəvwɛr
kar il i dwɛ par rɛzõn
avwɛr sir e lymiɲõn
e ɛl kjɛf mɛt õn lə fy
e dõnt a vɛrty
də fɛrə lotrɥi sɛrvisə
tãn kɛl ɛt ars e rəmizə

e ʒə sɥi tut ãn tɛl gizə
e ãn tɛl sãmblãnʃə
epri dỹn fy kãmur lãnʃə
kə mə fɛt ardwɛr
lə cørs e lə kɔr dulwɛr
e fõndrə sãn garizõn
si fy mə vĩn par ãnsõn
kar ʒu mãn sãnti fɛry
lwɛs kə ʒyk və·y
su dõn li mõn semɛrvɛʎə
dõn ʒart e supir e vɛʎə

Magister Antonius Zachara de Teramo, "Je suy navrés"

Early fifteenth-century macaronic verse in French and Italian. Lucca Codex, fol. 9–10.

Je suy navrés tan fort o dous amy.
—De quoy? —de Aitnerolf et de les dames.
—Hay las, chantés, or non crier, ciantés!
—Vraiemant mourray per celles, moy amy.

La nobiltà con tutte le scientie
et l'art liberal con le richezze,
la libertà, vertù con le prudentie,
Chaliopè poeta e le forteç
çe,

tout l'estourmant du mondo et gionesse,
biau sir, or que vous plet, et tout le nimphes,
oy vraiement, or sus chantés appres
grant parlament de sens, o vray ami.

Je suy navrés tan fort, o dous amy.
—De quoy? —De Aitnerolf et de les dames.
—Hay las, chantés, or non crier, ciantés!
—Vraiement mourray per celles, moy amy.

ʒə sɥi navṛe tãn fɔr o duz ãmi
də kwɛ də ɛtnərɔlf e də le dãmə
e las ʃãnte ɔṛ nõn kṛie ʃãnte
vṛɛmãn murrɛ pɛr sɛlə mwɛ ãmi

la nɔbilte (a?) kõn tutə le sijãnsə
e laṛ libeṛal kõn le ṛiʃɛsə
la libɛṛte (a?) vɛrty kõn la prydãnsə
kaljope pɔɛt e la fɔrtɛsə

tu le tuṛmãn dy mõnd e ʒø̃nɛsə
bjo siṛ ɔṛ kə vu plɛ e tu le nĩmfə
ɔi vrɛəmãn ɔṛ sys ʃãntez apṛɛ
gran parləmãn də sãn o vṛɛ ãmi

ʒə sɥi navṛe tãn fɔṛ o duz ãmi
də kwɛ də ɛtnɛrɔlf e də le dãmə
e las ʃãnte ɔṛ nõn kṛie ʃãnte
vrɛmãn murrɛ pɛr sɛlə mwɛ ãmi

This text willfully mixes French and Italian spellings. It is often hard to determine what pronunciation was intended; in fact, it is likely that performers would have the liberty to play with such a poem, to "ham it up" for humorous or other purposes.

6

French Latin

HAROLD COPEMAN

The Gallic pronunciation of Latin was notorious from early times, when the Celtic Gauls came to speak the language of their Roman conquerors, and it was later affected by the waves of Germanic settlers and invaders from the fifth to the tenth centuries.

By the twelfth century, as in Norman England, *c* had already been palatalized and sibilized from [k] to [ts] when followed by a front vowel *(e, i),* as in *celum.* (I exclude the Picard speech of northern France, which is covered in Chapter 19, "Netherlands Latin.") In the thirteenth century this sound moved farther forward in the mouth, again as in England, to [s].

The consonant *g* before *e* and sometimes *i* had changed from [g] to [dʒ]; in the thirteenth century it moved to simple [ʒ].

Vowels in French and French Latin then developed differently from those in English, particularly in the nasalization of vowels before *n* and *m.* The nasalization began gradually and affected *a* and *e* before *o, i,* and *u* (in that order; see Alton and Jeffery, *Bele buche,* 35–37).

Particularly in the ninth and sixteenth centuries the efforts of Classical reformers complicated the story. Around a.d. 800, when spoken Latin was developing toward French and the other Romance tongues, Emperor Charlemagne (a Frankish German) enlisted scholars from Britain and Ireland to restore the Latin language proper for use in Church and State. They started the great medieval "schools" to educate the clergy (who were also the natural administrators of his Christian Empire). The linguistic reform concentrated on getting all the letters of the Latin word pronounced; the effect seems to have differed from Classical Latin, giving a French flavor to vowels and to *c* and *g.*

In the political chaos of the centuries after Charlemagne's death, a few of the schools sought to preserve this strict pronunciation, but the natural tendency was to pronounce

Latin words as French itself was spoken, including the dropping of many consonants and the further development of vowels. As some of the letters in French had become silent, the Latin, with its need for inflected word-endings, became difficult to understand, especially for foreigners. For this reason and in order to foster the learning and enjoyment of Classical verse, the reformers of the mid-sixteenth century tried to introduce a Classical, or sometimes an Italian, Latin pronunciation. This had some effect in schools and universities, though it was probably not until the seventeenth century that the Church, with its Latin singing, changed from the old French-style Latin. The mongrel pronunciation that grew up after the partial reform was defended until modern times as part of the French cultural heritage.

French Latin had a distinctive treatment of stress. Instead of stressing a syllable in the way familiar in Italian, German, and English Latin, the French tended (unless the final vowel was nasal) to emphasize the last syllable in a word, especially at the end of a phrase. This is not so much a stress as a substantial lengthening of the vowel. In measured music, this may appear in the note values; in chant, the same habit needs to be borne in mind. The origin of this pattern in the early centuries was the dropping of weak syllables toward the end of a Latin word, which left the accented syllable at the end; a similar accentuation at or near the end of a word was applied to the new French language, and then to unabbreviated Latin itself. The Latin word *dominicus* and the later *demenium* lost their last two syllables and became the (Anglo-French) *demesne;* so through this linguistic habit we have, for instance, a long ending, [y:z], in the Latin *Dominus* or *Sanctus.*

Regional Varieties

Both before and after the collapse of the Roman Empire northern Gaul was occupied by Germanic settlers from the east and later from the north. Starting in the fifth century, this involved long-continued violence and oppression, but those invaders who stayed absorbed the Latin tongue from the governing Romans and, as they became Christianized, from the Church. They dropped their own Germanic dialects in favor of versions of the emerging French vernacular, notably Walloon/Picard. A later wave, the Normans, settled farther west before conquering England in 1066.

Various degrees of Germanic speech remained in the regional dialects, of which Picard is important to singers because it was the tongue of many of the great Franco-Flemish composers, including Josquin des Prés and Lassus.

The Francien tongue of central France came to be accepted as standard French, and the suggested pronunciation below is based on it. For Norman and Provençal Latin one can follow the data on the vernacular in Alton and Jeffery, *Bele buche e bele parleur.*

Evidence

There are two types of evidence not included in Chapter 4, "Anglo-Latin." First, there is a report by John Hart (dated 1569, but probably compiled some years earlier) of "how the French do pronounce their Latin." He gives, in an early (and of course crude) attempt at phonetic transcription, the Lord's Prayer in French and in (French) Latin. In the text below, the first line is the Latin text, the second is Hart's French Latin, and the third is a modern phonetic transcription of the second line.

Hart's version does not always agree with the recommendations on pronunciation later in the present chapter because of regional and individual variety at the time, as well as the disagreement between reforming grammarians and the traditionalists (in the Church and outside).

In the following text, vowels are lengthened as indicated by Hart. Lengthening occurs at or near the end of some words; some consonants are dropped, but perhaps a degree of reform had set in. For example, Hart gives *et* as [ɛt] before *nos, ne,* though it has no [t] before *in terra.* The final *s* appears phonetically as *z.* He gives *iu* for *u* in both open and closed syllables. But he does not indicate the qualities of all vowels; his *iu* has been entered as [y], though he may have intended a diphthong, [iu].

Pater noster qui es in celis, sanctificetur nomen tuum
pạter noster kiez in seḷiz santifisetiur nomen tiuium
pa:tɛṛ nɔstɛṛ ki·ɛz ɪn seli:z santifisetyṛ nomɛn ty·ym

adveniat regnum tuum, fiat voluntas tua sicut in celo et in terra
atveniat reínium tiuium fiat voluntạz tiuạ sikiut in selo e in tára
atveniat ṛeinym ty·ym fi·at volʊnta:z ty·a: sikyt ɪn selo e ɪn taṛa

panem nostrum quotidianum da nobis hodie
panem nostrium kotidianium da nobịz odịe
panɛm nɔstṛym kɔtɪdi·anym da nobi:z ɔdi:·e

et dimite nobis debita nostra
& dimịte nobị debịta nostra
e dimi:te nobi: debi:ta nɔstṛa

sicut et nos dimitimus debitoribus nostris
sikiut et noz dimịtimiuz debitoribiuz nostrịz
sikyt ɛt nɔz dimi:timyz debɪtɔrɪbyz nɔstri:z

et ne nos inducas in temptationem: sed libera nos a malo.
et ne noz indiukạz in tentasionem: set libera noz a malo
ɛt ne nɔz ɪndyka:z ɪn tɛntasi·onɛm sɛt lɪbeṛa nɔz a malo

The second source of evidence is Latin-French puns, which became fashionable in the late sixteenth century. The efforts of reformers had focused attention on the old French-Latin pronunciation, which became a matter for amusement. It was exploited by Etienne Tabourot in *Les Bigarrures* (The mix-ups), a collection of puns first published in 1583, with reprints up to 1628. A simple example is *laboravi/laboure envy,* which shows the Latin *o* spoken as French *ou,* and French *en* as Latin *a.* Similarly *habitaculum/habit à cul long,* and *omnia tentate/on y a tant tasté* tell us about *-um, mn, en, -e,* and the elision of consonants such as the *s* in *tasté.* These puns confirm that Latin (when unreformed) was spoken as if it were French. Etienne's uncle Jehan Tabourot (by anagram Thoinot Arbeau) was Canon of Langres in eastern France (and author of *Orchésographie,* on dancing and its tunes). One may assume that the nephew was familiar with the way Latin was spoken and sung in church at that time.

However, regional variations and speech habits were changing (particularly for *-um*), and we cannot take Tabourot, a late sixteenth-century source, as representative of pronunciation in, say, northern France around 1500. The nasalization of vowels is a particular complication; it started at different times and varied regionally; some denasalization started in the sixteenth century. To reach detailed conclusions we have to apply the results of detailed linguistic studies. Synoptic keys are given in Alton and Jeffery, *Bele buche.*

Bibliography

(See also the works listed in Chapter 4, "Anglo-Latin.")

J. Alton and B. Jeffery. *Bele buche e bele parleure.* London, 1976. Text and tape.
Ch. Beaulieux. "Essai sur l'histoire de la prononciation française du latin." *Revue des études latines* 5 (Paris, 1927).
H. Copeman. *Singing in Latin.* Oxford, 1990; rev. ed., 1992. Especially chaps. 2 and 10b, and Appendixes 2 and 3.
P. Damas. "La prononciation du latin avant la réforme du XVIe siècle." *Revue du chant grégorien,* May–June 1933, pp. 71–82.
———. *La prononciation française du latin depuis le XVIe siècle.* Paris, 1934.
G. du Guez (du Gues, de Vadis, de Wes, du Wés, Dewes). *An Introductorie for to lerne, to rede, to pronounce and to speake frenche.* Ca. 1530; reprinted in the 1852 ed. of Palsgrave, pp. 891–1079. Also see Copeman, pp. 257–60.
J. Fox and R. Wood. *A Concise History of the French Language.* Oxford, 1968.
J. Marouzeau. *La prononciation du latin,* 3d ed. Paris, 1943.
J. Palsgrave. *Lesclarcissement de la langue Francoyse.* 1530 (facs. ed., London, Scolar Press, 1969), ed. F. Génin and P. Lorain, Paris, 1852. See Copeman, pp. 247–56.
M. K. Pope. *From Latin to Modern French.* Manchester, 1952.
P. Rickard. *A History of the French Language.* London, 1974.
R. Wright. *Late Latin and Early Romance.* Liverpool, 1982.

Sounds and Spellings

As Gallo-Roman Latin developed gradually into French, some consonants and even syllables became silent; Latin *Deus* became French *Dieu, gloria* became *gloire, homo, filius, pater* became *homme, fils, père,* and so on. Apart from the effect on accentuation noted above, this affected groups of consonants, which might survive in vernacular writing (once that had started) but be simplified in speech. The Latin *temptatio* (where *p* was already silent) gave the French word *temptation,* whose pronunciation was carried back into the Latin word. John Hart in the mid-sixteenth century heard *temptationem* as *tentasionem.*

Generally the French have been reluctant to allow consonants to cut into the smooth flow of speech, and so into the line of chant or other song. B. Lamy, writing as Messieurs du Port Royal in *The Art of Speaking* (Eng. tr. 1676, Third Part, 108) explained their approach in the seventeenth century:

> Among the letters, some are pronounced with ease, others with pain: Those whose pronunciation is easy, have an agreeable sound; those which are pronounced with difficulty, do grate upon the ear. Consonants are pronounc'd with more difficulty than Vowels, and therefore their sound is less soft and fluent. It is convenient to temper the harshness of the one by the sweetness of the other, and that is to be done by placing the Vowels betwixt the Consonants,

> that there may not be too many of them together. This harshness arising from the concourse of consonants is obvious in the Northern Languages. Dutch and English are very unpleasant to them whose ears have not been accustomed to those Languages. . . . according to the different degrees of the peoples inclination to delicacy, their words are compos'd of Letters more or less soft; they having had less regard to follow reason, than to tickle their ears. In respect of this softness of pronunciation the Romans used *aufero* for *abfero, colloco* for *cumloco,* as analogy oblig'd them to speak [i.e., as the components of the words suggest]. Analogy has remitted of its rights in favour to the softness of pronunciation. . . .

Sometimes the simplification of pronunciation turns what had been a closed syllable into an open one, so that the quality of the vowel is affected (see "Word Division," below). In *expecto* the *c* has become silent, so the second syllable is *-pe-*; *-xp-* is sounded [sp] not [ksp]. The pronunciation of the word (in terms of modern French) becomes *espéto.* In the next word in the Creed, *resurrectionem/resurrexionem, ct* or *x* is pronounced [z], and (as for *expecto*) the preceding syllable, *-re,* becomes open: so the *e* is the closed vowel [e] as in *é.* (If the *c* and *t* had been separately pronounced, the syllabification would have been *re·sur·rec·ti·o·nem,* and the vowel in *-rec* would have been pronounced *è* [ɛ].)

After about 1200, non-nasal consonants at the ends of words were only sounded before an initial vowel in a following word, or at the end of a phrase. For nasal consonants before other consonants at various times, see below on *an,* etc.

In consonantal groups one or more consonants may drop. The details depended on the period and the social context; the singer should bear in mind the analogy with French pronunciation and particularly the remarks by Lamy (above) on "softness of pronunciation" and avoidance of "harshness arising from the concourse of consonants." Some detailed rules were given about 1530 by Palsgrave and by du Guez, who did not entirely agree (see Copeman, pp. 252–53 and 258–60); we suggest the following practice:

1. When, within a word or phrase, *s* is followed by *t* (or *p, c/k*), the *s* is silent *(e(s)t, o(s)tende, no(s)tram, Chri(s)te,* and probably *po(s)t).* (Picard Latin in northern France differs; see Chapter 19, "Netherlands Latin.") After about 1550 the *s* might be restored for a time in places influenced by the reformers, but these may have been exceptional.

2. Both consonants are sounded when a stop and a liquid consonant initiate the syllable: *gl*adius, pa·*tr*em (see "Word Division"), *pr*o(p)ter, *cl*amavit. They are also sounded if a liquid closes the syllable, followed by another consonant: mo*rs,* mo*r*·*t*em, inca*r*·*n*atus, pa*r*·*t*em, pa*r*·*c*e, te*r*·*t*ia ([tɛrsia]), a*l*·*t*issimus, sepu*l*·*t*us.

3. In many other groups the first consonant in a pair became silent (is elided) where the two sounds together would have sounded harsh or have been difficult to articulate: *fa(c)tus, san(c)tus, a(d)vocata, re(g)ni, o(m)nes, pro(p)ter, redem(p)tor.* This is even more common when a word ending with a consonant is followed by an initial consonant: *ex Patre* might become *e Patre.* In *Et in unu(m) Dominu(m) Jesu(m) Christum, Filiu(m) Dei unigenite* (see below) there is elision within the two phrases but not between them *(Christum, Filium).* If the music suggested a break after *Dominum* the final *m* would of course be sounded. In the sample text *Credo in unu(m) Deum, Pater omnipotentem,* below, there would be elision at *Deu(m), Pater* if the sentence is set in one single musical phrase. Similarly in *a(d) te suspiramu(s) gementes et flentes.* (Note that *et* seems to have had a silent *t* in all positions, at least before sixteenth-century reforms.)

4. In a group of three consonants one will usually be dropped: *redem(p)tor, co(n)glorificatur* ([kɔ̃gl-], *san(c)tam, benedictu(m) fructum.* Similarly, with a compound consonant: de*x*teram will reduce, probably to [-t-]. But some initial groups will survive: in *str*icte, *scr*iptum, *spl*endidus the French might be tempted to introduce an initial [e] and drop the [s], but this would add a syllable and might not fit the music.

5. When a final *m* or *n* is followed by an initial consonant, the consonants will govern the quality of the preceding vowel. So, in *et unam sanctam catholicam,* the ending of *unam* is nasal but that of *sanctam* is non-nasal because the second consonantal sound is [k]. So is *-em* in *remissionem peccatorum,* because [p] follows. See *am* below.

6. When an initial consonant follows *-um, -us,* we have generally elided the *-m, -s.*

The modern singer must make decisions on matters like elision and liaison despite the sometimes conflicting or incomplete character of the historical indications. Comfort may be drawn from the realization that some points remained contemporaneously in doubt or in dispute in France itself. The phonetic transcriptions below aim at a coherent linguistic style for each period. The singer should note the sharp contrast with German Latin, where a glottal stop before an initial vowel takes the place of the liaison practiced in French Latin. The need for international intelligibility was one of the humanist arguments in the sixteenth century in favor of reform (which by the end of our period seems unlikely to have affected much of the Latin used in church).

The nasalization of vowels when the syllable is closed by *m* or *n* is discussed under each vowel. (Nasalization may be deferred until near the end of the vowel, merging with the nasal consonant.) There are four nasal vowels that are not known in modern French: [ã] (as distinct from nasal back *a,* [ɑ̃]), [ĩ], [ũ], and [ỹ]. They are produced from the oral vowels by opening the nasal passages.

Word Division

The French practice was to end a syllable on a vowel wherever possible. Erasmus (1528) contrasted this with the Dutch system, which would give *Chris·te;* whereas the French would say *Chri·ste.* This division may affect the quality of the preceding vowel: for instance, *ve·stra* would give [vetra] whereas *ves·tra* would give [vɛztra], and the French system implies the former.

Consonants (when not dropped, see above)

b [b]

c [k] if before *a, o, u,* or *r, l.* [ts] if before *e, i* or *ae/æ, oe/œ* to about 1250, thereafter [s].

cc [ks] or [ts] in *ecce, accipit,* etc., to 1250, thereafter [s].

ch [k] before *a, o* or a consonant *(chorus, Christe).* [tʃ] before *e, i (cherubim, michi, nichil)* to about 1250, then [ʃ].

d A forward sound compared with the English [d]; sometimes unvoiced to [t]. (Hart gives *adveniat* as *atveniat.*)

f [f]

g [g] if before *a, o, u.* [dʒ] before *e* and *i,* to about 1250; [ʒ] thereafter.

gn [n] in this period rather than [ɲ] or the reformed [gn]. During the period of sixteenth-century reform, the practice became confused.

h Silent, but in *mihi, nihil* as if with *ch* (above).

i as consonant *j* [dʒ] to 1250, then [ʒ], including *cujus, ejus, eia,* etc.

k [k], if used.

l [l], on the teeth, not a backward sound as in southern English *mill.*

m, n [m], [n] except after a vowel in the same syllable; see relevant vowel below and "Word Division," above. *n* before [k], [g] becomes [ŋ] (but *-nct-* simplifies to [nt]).

nc, nq, ng Probably [ŋ] before these velar stops, thus [ŋk], [ŋk], [ŋg].

p [p], not too explosive.

qu [k], not [kɥ] at this time.

r [r̩], trilled, not the uvular sound of modern French speech. Final *r* weakened from 1300 except before an initial vowel.

s [s] at the start of words, and in careful circles also in compounds like *re·surrectio.* [z] between vowels and at the ends of words when *s* is sounded.

t, th [t], but final *t* is often silent (including *et;* but sounded in endings *-at, -et* unless elided before a following consonant). In *-tia, -tio t* is pronounced [s].

u as consonant *v* [v]. The difference is orthographic only.

x [z]; compounds with *ex* were pronounced with the French vowel of *yeux,* according to Tory, 1529.

z [z]

Liaison: When a final consonant is pronounced and the next word in the phrase starts with a vowel, the consonantal sound is joined to the new word. Thus, in the text "Credo in unum Deum," below, the first two words in line 12, "Crucifixus etiam," are joined; but the opening word in line 14, "Et," and the "et" in the middle of line 15 each start a new phrase, so there would be no liaisons (unless the musical phrase is continuous). (Note that this is quite different from German Latin, see p. 263.)

Consonantal groups: see guidance on elision, p. 95.

Double consonants: pronounced single; e.g., *terrae* as [tɛr̩e].

Vowels

General note on nasal vowels: The singer should sing most of the note on the relevant oral vowel ([a], [e], [i], [o], [ɔ], [oe], [u], [y]) and move to the nasal vowel just before the consonant is sounded.

a A fairly forward vowel, [a].

ae, oe As for *e.*

am, an [ãm], [ãn]: a forward sound, not the modern back nasal vowel [ɑ̃]. Nasalization was strongest in a closed syllable, but was also present in open syllables, in contrast to modern French, e.g., *A*men, cl*e*mens, though probably not g*e*mentes. The nasal consonant itself was also sounded until the early sixteenth century. (From the mid-sixteenth century the sound of *am, an* became merely [ã], and [m], [n] were omitted before most following consonants: thus *ante* moved from [ãnte] to [ãte].) But before [k], [g], and [p], [a] was denasalized, and *m, n* were sounded, so *tanquam, amplius* became [taŋkã, ampli·yz]; similarly in dexter*am P*atris.

au [au] to about 1300, [ao] from 1300 to 1500, then [o] as in modern French.

e The quality seems to have varied over time, but for an open syllable a rather open *é*/[e] can be used (rather than *è*/[ɛ]): thus the vowel in *celi* would be pronounced as in *été.* For a syllable closed by a non-nasal consonant *(pater, es), e* is [ɛ]; and *er* indeed was indicated by Hart (1569) as opening further, to [ar]; *terra* was *tara.* See also "Unstressed Vowels," below.

em, en As for *am, an* above; but the endings *ens, ent* should probably be [ɛnz], [ɛt]. Thus *cle·mens* might be [klãmɛnz], but *fle·ntes* would be [flãntɛz] until the early sixteenth century, then [flãtɛz]. The rule about a following [k], [g], or [p] meant that *tem·pus,* for example, remained [tɛmpyz]; also *consubstantialem·Patri.*

est, et [ɛt] and [e] respectively. Before a consonant in the next word *est* may become [ɛ]. On the other hand Damas gives *et* as *é* even before a vowel.

i [i], whether short or long.

in [in] to about 1250, then [ĩn]; from 1500 *in* could be sounded [i] or [ĩ], or as the modern [ɛ̃].

o [o] in an open syllable, closing toward [u] from 1200 to the sixteenth century. [o] or [u] in a syllable closed by a non-nasal consonant *(prop·ter, Crea·tor;* see next entry*).*

om, on The complete nasalization of *o* took some centuries from 1200, and the consonant continued to be sounded until around 1500. The vowel then developed in Paris from [õ] to [ɔ̃]. In the provinces it generally remained [ũ]. So in Paris *con·verte* may be sung [kõnvɛrte], then [kɔ̃vɛrte]; in the provinces [kũnvɛrte], then [kũvɛrte]; similarly, though less strongly nasalized, *do·minus.* Before two nasal consonants *(omnia),* these nasal vowels were used c.1300–1450; they then denasalized over centuries. Singers may use, for Paris, [õnia], then from 1500 [ɔ̃nia]; for the provinces from 1200 to 1650, [ũnia].

u as vowel [y] in an open syllable. But *-us* could be sounded as in French *-euse,* [øz]. See also *qu.*

um, un [ym], [yn] to 1400; [ỹm], [ỹn] from 1400 to at least 1550. From 1550 to 1650, the modern [œ̃], as in the French *un,* was known (though Hart, writing in 1569, still gives *tuum* as *tiuium*).

y [i] rather than the Greek [y].

Unstressed Vowels

Beaulieux says that the final Latin *-e* was the close *e (é),* [e], not [ə] (one of very few differences from the French of the time). One may suspect that this pronunciation was what the schools taught, but that it was not always observed in everyday Latin. In the prefix *ex,* at least, a weak vowel ([œ] or [ə]) is recorded (see *x* above), and [ə] can be used with discretion, e.g., in *ante,* the second *e* in *benedictus,* and the second in *terre.*

DIACHRONIC SOUND CHART FOR FRENCH LATIN

An asterisk(*) indicates that reference to the text is particularly desirable.

	1200	1300	1400	1500	1600	1700
VOWELS						
a	[a] - - - - - -					→
am, an	[ãm, ãn][ffi]				[ã]*	[ɑ̃]
au	[au]	[ao]			[o] - - - - - -	→
e, ae, oe	[e], rather open* - - - - - -					→
em, en	[ãm, ãn]†				[ã]	[ɑ̃]
i, y	[i] - - - - - -					→
im, in	[im, in] [ĩm, ĩn]			[i],[ĩ],[ɛ̃] - - - - - -		→
o, open syllable	[o] closing to - - - - - -			[u] - - - - - -		→
o before non-nasal consonant	[ɔ]			[ɔ], [u] - - - - - -		→
om, on (Paris)	[ɔ̃m, ɔ̃n]*†				[ɔ̃]*† - - - - - -	→
(provinces)	[ũm, ũn]*†				[ũ]*† - - - - - -	→
u	[y]* - - - - - -					→
um, un	[ym, yn]		[ỹm, ỹn]		[ỹm, ỹn], [œ̃] -	→
CONSONANTS (see text for consonantal group)						
b	[b] - - - - - -					→
c before *e, i*	[ts]	[s] - - - - - -				→
cc before *e, i*	[ks], [ts] - -	[s] - - - - - -				→
ch before *e, i*	[tʃ]	[ʃ] - - - - - -				→
c, cc, ch, other	[k] - - - - - -					→
d	[d] - - - - - -					→
f, ph	[f] - - - - - -					→
g before *e, i*	[dʒ] - - - - - -	[ʒ] - - - - - -				→
other	[g] - - - - - -					→
gn	[n]				[n],[ɲ],[gn] -	→
h	silent* - - - - - -					→
i, j	[dʒ] - - - - - -	[ʒ] - - - - - -				→
l	[l] - - - - - -					→
m	[m]* - - - - - -					→
n	[n]* - - - - - -					→
p	[p] - - - - - -					→
qu	[k] - - - - - -					→
r	[r]* - - - - - -					→
s	[s],[z]* - - - - - -					→
t, th	[t] - - - - - -					→
v	[v] - - - - - -					→
x, z	[z] - - - - - -					→

† Nasalization may be deferred, in the interests of singing tone, until near the end of the vowel, merging with the nasal consonant.

SAMPLE TEXTS

In the phonetic transcriptions, nasal vowels are indicated by a tilde (~) and elision by the symbol ‿ . See the above text on vowels (some of which are not found in modern French), on elision, and on liaison.

Salve Regina

Francien Latin. Text by a French writer of the late eleventh century. This medieval pronunciation is suitable until 1300. CD #23.

Salve, regina misericordie
vita, dulcedo et spes nostra, salve!
ad te clamamus exsules filii Eve
ad te suspiramus gementes et flentes
in hac lacrimarum valle.
Eia ergo, advocata nostra,
illos tuos misericordes oculos ad nos converte
et Iesum, benedictum fructum ventris tui,
nobis post hoc exsilium ostende,
o clemens, o pia,
o dulcis Maria.

salve ṛɛdʒinã mizəṛikɔṛdi·e
vita dyltsedo e spɛ̃‿nɔtṛa salve
a‿te klãmãmyz ezylɛz fili·i eve
a‿te sypiṛãmy‿dʒemãntɛz e flãntɛz
in ak lakṛimary‿vale
ɛdʒa ɛṛgo avokatã nɔtṛa
ilɔ‿ty·ɔ‿mizɛṛikɔṛdez okylɔz ã‿nɔ‿kɔnvɛṛte
e dʒezy‿benedity‿fṛyty‿vɛ̃ntṛi‿ty·i
nobi‿pɔt ɔk ezili·ym otɛ̃nde
o klãmɛnz o pi·a
o dytsi‿maṛi·a

Credo in unum Deum

Francien Latin, suitable for central French music of late medieval times, before the reforms of the mid-sixteenth century. This version differs somewhat from that for 1500 notated in imitative modern French by Damas in 1933; in particular, during the sixteenth century Latin *-um* turned into [õ] (modern French *on,* used by Damas) or into other sounds, including French *un* [œ̃]. There is some argument on the timing of these changes; see Copeman, *Singing in Latin,* pp. 288–89, 286–87 (Picard text); and the note on Franco-Flemish composers, below, in Chapter 19, "Netherlands Latin." See also p. 92, above, for a sixteenth-century pronunciation of the *Pater Noster.* The text below uses a reformed orthography; in manuscript sources *æ, œ* appear as *e.* CD #24.

Credo in unum Deum, Patrem omnipotentem,
Factorem cæli et terræ,
Visibilium omnium et invisibilium.
Et in unum Dominum Jesum Christum, Filium Dei unigenitum.
Et ex Patre natum ante omnia saecula.
Deum de Deo, Lumen de lumine, Deum verum de Deo vero.
Genitum, non factum, Consubstantialem Patri:
Per quem omnia facta sunt.
Qui propter nos homines et propter nostram salutem
descendit de cælis; et incarnatus est de Spiritu Sancto
ex Maria Virgine, et Homo factus est.
Crucifixus etiam pro nobis sub Pontio Pilato
passus et sepultus est.
Et resurrexit tertia die secundum Scripturas et ascendit in caelum.
Sedet ad dexteram Patris, et iterum venturus est
cum gloria judicare vivos et mortuos
cujus regni non erit finis.
Et in spiritum sanctum Dominum et vivificantem,
qui ex Patre Filioque procedit.
Qui cum Patre et Filio simul adoratur, et conglorificatur,
qui locutus est per prophetas.
Et unam sanctam catholicam et apostolicam ecclesiam.
Confiteor unum baptisma in remissionem peccatorum.
Et exspecto resurrectionem mortuorum.
Et vitam venturi saeculi. Amen.

kṛedu ĩn‿ỹnỹ‿de·ỹm patṛãm ũniputãntãm
faturãm‿seli e‿tɛṛe
vizibili·ỹm ũni·ỹm e ĩvizibili·ỹm
e ĩn ỹnỹ‿dũminỹ‿ʒezỹ‿kṛitỹm fili·ỹ‿de·i yniʒãnitỹm
e ɛs patṛe natỹm ãnte ũni·a sekyla
de·ỹ‿de de·u lymã‿de lỹmĩne de·ỹ‿vɛṛỹ‿de de·u vɛṛu
ʒãnitỹ‿nɔ̃‿fatỹm kɔ̃nsystãnsi·alɛm patṛi
pɛ‿kɛm ũni·a fata sỹnt
ki pṛutɛ‿nuz ũminɛz e pṛutɛ‿nɔtṛãm salytãm
desãndi‿de seliz e ĩŋkaṛnatyz ɛ‿de spiṛity sãntu
ɛz maṛi·a viṛʒĩne e ũmu fatyz ɛt
kṛysifizyz esi·am pṛũ nubi‿sy‿pɔ̃nsi·u pilatu
pasyz e sepyltyz ɛt
e ṛezyṛezi‿tɛṛsi·a di·e sekỹndỹ‿skṛityṛaz e asãndit ĩn selỹm

sedet a‿deteṛam‿patṛiz e iteṛỹ‿vãntyṛyz‿ɛt
kỹm gloṛi·a ʒydikaṛe vivuz e mɔṛtyɔz
kyʒy‿ṛɛ̃ni nũn eṛi fĩniz
e ĩn spiṛitỹ‿sãntỹ‿dũmĩnỹm e vivifikãntãm
ki ɛs patre fili·uke pṛusedit
ki kỹ‿patṛe e fili·u simyl aduṛatyr e kɔ̃gloṛifikatyṛ
ki lukytyz ɛ‿pɛ‿pṛufetaz
e ynãm sãntam katulikãm e aputulikãm ɛklezi·ãm
kɔ̃nfite·uṛ ỹnỹ‿batĩma ĩn ṛɛ̃misi·ũnɛm pekatuṛỹm
e ɛspetu ṛezyṛezi·ũnã‿mɔṛtyuṛỹm
e vitãm vãntyṛi sekyli ãmãn

7 Occitan

ROBERT TAYLOR

The Occitan language evolved by a natural and continuous process from Latin, as did the other Romance languages. Its linguistic base was not the polished literary language that we know as Classical Latin, but the familiar spoken variety that coexisted with it on a lower social level of usage.

In Roman Gaul, Latin language and culture had taken firmer root in the South than in the North, because the areas of modern-day Provence and Languedoc had been Romanized almost a century before the northern parts. Provincia was established between 154 and 125 B.C., whereas northern Gaul was not conquered until the campaign of Julius Caesar in 52 B.C. This early split between North and South was one of several factors causing the linguistic differentiation of France into two distinct languages. According to Pierre Bec, the geographical openness of the North, in contrast to the more inaccessible, mountainous terrain of the South, led over time to a different ethnic mix, characterized by stability and conservatism in the South, as opposed to a more restless, innovative character in the North. The Celtic substratum may have had a stronger influence on the evolution of Latin in the North, and the later Germanic superstratum of the Franks penetrated much more profoundly into the lives and language of the northern Gallo-Romans than did that of the Burgunds and Visigoths into the language of the South. Whatever the underlying reasons, the result was a radical split between an ultraconservative Occitan language in southern France and a highly innovative French language in the North, which moved further away from its Latin origins.

Occitan has closer linguistic ties with the other Mediterranean Romance languages than with French. In particular, it is closely related to Catalan, since the Catalan-Occitan area developed almost as an ethnic unit until the eleventh century and did not differentiate seriously into two linguistic entities until the political realignments of the thirteenth century. During the Medieval period, in fact, Gascon, theoretically one of the dialects of Occitan, was considered a foreign language by the troubadours and was more likely to be incomprehensible to Occitan speakers than Catalan.

At present, the Occitan region covers about one-third of France, along with Monaco and small border areas of Italy and Spain. It includes between ten and fourteen million French citizens who speak or understand Occitan, more than one-quarter of the population of France. Although its official functions have become severely limited, there is a strengthening movement to preserve and restore the Occitan language as the instrument and expression of an enduring ethnic culture.

Regional Varieties

Although the Occitan region may be divided into at least five dialectal regions in the Middle Ages (six, if Gascon is included as a dialect, or seven, if medieval Catalan is considered part of an Occitano-Catalan linguistic unit), there is little necessity for taking this into consideration for the practical purposes of performing troubadour songs. From the earliest extant works, the troubadours used a unified poetic language, which came to be regarded in Europe as the natural language of lyric poetry, just as other languages were felt to be uniquely suited for the expression of other literary genres. The few dialectal differences recorded in the poems do not seem to be related to the poets' geographic origins. Regional variants even occur within the same poem, and some poets seem to have used them at will as a means of enriching their fund of expressive words and sounds.

There has been some controversy concerning the linguistic base of the troubadour language, but no region has been shown to be more influential than another. Additionally, some scholars have tried to discover Poitevin forms in the poems of the earliest troubadour, Guilhem de Peitieus, but no proof has yet been offered to indicate that Guilhem used anything but the standardized literary *koiné.*

Likewise, the poet Marcabrun was of Gascon origin, but his poetry does not contain the regional forms most characteristic of this area. Some of the Catalan troubadours (e.g., Cerveri de Girona) show traces of Catalanized spellings in their works, just as the Italian poets who composed in Occitan (e.g., Sordello) may have admitted a few Italianisms into their poems, but these are infrequent, and they rarely influence the actual pronunciation.

Evidence

We have been able to ascertain the approximate pronunciation of troubadour poetry from variant spellings; rhymes, assonances, and alliterations; metrics; non-Occitan scripta conventions; medieval authorities; and comparative philology.

Variant Spellings

The confusion of spellings, such as *se* for *ce, voluntat* for *volontat,* indicate the accomplishment of a phonetic evolution (here: [ts] > [s] and atonic [o] > [u].

Rhymes, Assonances, and Alliterations

When we note that tonic *-a* followed by unstable *n* does not rhyme with regular tonic *-a,* we have confirmation of two *a*-phonemes, the normal [a] (anterior *a*) and the posterior [ɑ], as well as confirmation that Old Occitan does not nasalize vowels followed by nasal consonants, as Old French does.

Metrics

The care with which the troubadours counted syllables in each line of the verse forms may be utilized to determine loss of vowels, elision, or shift from disyllabic pronunciation of contiguous vowels to a monosyllabic pronunciation (diphthong or monophthong).

Non-Occitan Scripta Conventions

The Italianized notation *gl* and the Catalanized *ll,* both indicating [λ], give evidence of the palatalized sound of Occitan *lh.* Likewise, the transcription of Occitan words in non-Latin alphabets such as Hebrew or Greek may confirm their pronunciation with more precision.

Medieval Authorities

Old Occitan grammatical treatises, such as *Leys d'Amors,* sometimes contain detailed comments on the nature of certain vowels and consonants.

Comparative Philology

The nature of many phonetic evolutions may be determined by hypothesis through the comparative study of Latin and modern Occitan, the points of departure and arrival, both known in precise detail, and by comparison with similar evolutions in the other Romance languages.

Bibliography

Jeanine Alton and Brian Jeffery. *Bele buche e bele parleure. A Guide to the Pronunciation of Medieval and Renaissance French for Singers and Others.* London, 1976. See pp. 24–26.
Pierre Bec. *La Langue occitane.* Que Sais-Je?, 1059. Paris, 1963.
———. *Anthologie des troubadours.* Paris, 1979. See pp. 9–12.
Edouard Bourciez. *Eléments de linguistique romane.* 4th ed. Paris, 1956. See pp. 141–80, 285–313.
Ake Grafström. *Etude sur la graphie des plus anciennes chartes languedociennes avec un essai d'interprétation phonétique.* Uppsala, 1958.
R. T. Hill and T. G. Bergin. *Anthology of the Provençal Troubadours.* 2d rev. and enl. ed. New Haven and London, 1973. See pp. xix–xxiv.
Max Pfister. "Beiträge zur altprovenzalischen Grammatik." *Vox romanica* 17 (1958):281–362.
Nathaniel B. Smith and Thomas G. Bergin. *An Old Provençal Primer.* New York and London, 1984. See pp. 1–61.
Walther von Wartburg. *Evolution et structure de la langue française.* Berne, 1946. See pp. 60–65.

Pronunciation and Spelling

Old Occitan notation is largely phonetic; that is, in most cases the spelling reflects the actual pronunciation. Diphthongs and triphthongs are noted as such and are to be pronounced as written. Evolved forms of consonants, such as voiced, opened, or palatalized states, are generally identified by the medieval scribes, and are to be pronounced as written. As in all medieval vernaculars, however, variant spellings are found for many words, sometimes in disconcerting numbers. In Old Occitan, most of them represent actual differences in pronunciation, but a few do not:

The letter *h* is never pronounced, and there is no distinction between the usage of Germanic and Latin *h,* as there is in French. Most often, it represents simply a graphical tradition from Latin *(onor/honor; om/hom);* sometimes it serves to indicate hiatus when placed between two vowels *(traïr/trahir),* or to prevent the misreading of a word beginning with a semi-vowel *u* or *i (uelh/huelh; ieu/hieu);* it is also utilized in some of the digraphs that identify palatalized consonants such as *ch, lh,* and *nh* (see below).

The letter *u* after *q* is traditional but generally unpronounced *(qui, que,* also written *qi, qe, ki, ke),* except for the form *qui,* or more usually *cui,* representing the indirect object pronoun "to whom," pronounced [kuj].

The letter *u* after *g* serves only to indicate the pronunciation [g] before the vowels *e* and *i;* before the vowel *a* it is superfluous but is often found *(aguessen, venguen, guidar, gardar/guardar).*

A small number of learned forms, chiefly in later texts, reinstate superfluous etymological letters, probably unpronounced *(autor/auctor, semana/setmana/septmana).*

Some sounds were not consistently represented, and interpreting their various notations may be confusing. Palatalized *n* may be spelled *nh, inh, ign, ingn;* thus *senhor, seinhor, seignor, seingnor* are all pronounced [seɲor]. Similarly, palatalized *l* may be spelled *l, lh, il, ill;* the forms *vol, volh, voil, voill* may all be pronounced [vɔʎ]. The palatal affricate [tʃ] is most often spelled *ch,* but in final position it may be found as *ch, ich, g, ig,* etc. (*fach, faich, fag, faig* all pronounced [fatʃ]). The sound [dʒ] is normally *g* (before *e, i*) or *j* (before *a, o, u*), but may be spelled *tg (messatge).*

In other cases, variant spellings represent regional or chronological evolutions that *do* represent different sounds. Although we would expect a poet to use only one spelling at a given time or in a given place, the troubadours utilized many of the available forms interchangeably, even within a single poem, as a means of enriching the poetic language. Thus forms with [k] and [g], such as *canso, cantar, gauzir, gauch,* are typical of the southern Occitan regions (Languedoc, Provence), while those with [tʃ] and [dʒ], such as *chanso, chantar, jauzir,* and *jau,*, are more typical of the northern dialects (Auvergne, Limousin). However, all are part of the standardized literary language and are used at will by poets from any area. Similarly, intervocalic *d* was opened to *z* or even disappeared entirely during the time of the troubadours, but older forms such as *espada, guidar, vida* are found alongside the more recent *espaza, guizar/guiar, via.* All of them should be pronounced as written.

Stress and Accent

The stressed syllable in an Occitan word is almost always the same as in the Latin and therefore the same as in the other Romance languages. As a rule of thumb, words ending in a vowel are stressed on the second-last syllable, except for certain verb forms and adverbs stressed on a final vowel *(lau'séta, en'veja; au'rai, a'gui; ai'ssi, de'sse).* Words ending in a consonant are stressed on the last syllable *(mo'ver, ai'las, mi'ralh);* this includes words ending in "unstable *n*" even though it may not be noted in the spelling *(Limo'zi, Limo'zin),* but it does not include words ending in flexional *s ('alas, mera'vilhas)* or the third-person plural verb forms ending in flexional *n ('cantan, 'vendon, can'tavan).* A few learned words are stressed on the third-last syllable *('lagrema, 'monegue, 'glezia).* A few common exceptions are the subjective cases *'molher, 'senher,* as opposed to the accusative *mol'her, sen'hor;* the infinitives *'planher, 'volver;* the adjectives *'frevol, 'avol, 'joven* (the noun is *jo'ven*); the religious words *a'postol, ca'tolic.*

A secondary stress falls on the initial syllable, on the original tonic syllable of any recognizable element in a compound word, and on a prefix. All other syllables are atonic; that is, those in intertonic position between the initial and stressed syllables, in post-tonic position after the accent, and in final position.

It is important to note that stress can be phonemic in Occitan, unlike the case in French, where the accent has ceased to be distinctive. For example, the difference in stress can distinguish *ˈcantan (they sing)* from *canˈtan (singing), partiˈra* (future) from *parˈtira* (conditional), *ˈvias (ways)* from *viˈas* or *viˈatz (quickly), ˈqueri (I seek)* from *queˈri (I sought).*

Metrics

The basic form of the troubadours' poems depended on a recurring line of identical syllabic length from stanza to stanza. Syllables were therefore counted with great care. Feminine endings, that is, final unaccented *-a* or *-e,* did not count in the measuring of the line, although they were in fact pronounced distinctly.

Except at a pause or at the end of a line, final unaccented *-a* and *-e* were elided before a word beginning with a vowel. Such elided vowels were normally omitted by the poet and are indicated in modern editions by an apostrophe. Even if they are written, such vowels are regularly elided and have no phonetic value. However, there was some flexibility available to the poet; if such a vowel was needed for the sake of metrics, it could be pronounced, in which case it counted as a syllable, forming a hiatus with the following vowel.

Text Editions

The following comments concerning pronunciation of medieval Occitan are based on spellings as they are commonly found in good critical editions. However, the principles of textual editing are not rigidly fixed. Some editors regularize spellings to avoid ambiguous forms or to give greater unity to the presentation, but most try to remain close to the manuscript practices. All are obliged to add punctuation, which is almost totally lacking in the chansonniers. The letter *i* was used by medieval scribes to note the vowel [i], the semi-vowel [j], and the consonant [dʒ]; the letter *j* was used occasionally for the same sounds, and *y* more rarely for the first two. Similarly, the letter *u* was used for [u], which later evolved to [y]; for the semi-vowel [w], which evolved to [ɥ]; and for the consonant [v]. The letter *v* could be used for the same sounds. Many modern editors regularize the presentation by using *i* for the vowel and semi-vowel, reserving *j* for the consonant; in the second case they use *u* for the vowel and semi-vowel, *v* for the consonant. But others choose to maintain the spellings as they are found in the manuscripts, leaving it to the reader to decide on the pronunciation. Usually the transposition is easy to make; at least the vowels *i* and *u* are immediately recognizable, but sometimes it is very difficult to tell whether a consonant or a semi-vowel was intended by the scribe.

These editorial problems will be discussed further (see, in particular, under *j* and *v* below). In any case the reader should be aware of the decisions affecting the preparation of the printed text being used and should realize that some aspects of the textual reading are still open to interpretation.

Consonants

Most consonants in Occitan pose no problems in pronunciation, being articulated approximately as in English; only those that are difficult are noted below. All final consonants are pronounced, but the voiced ones that have an equivalent unvoiced partner are pronounced as unvoiced in final position, whether they are written as such or not. For unstable *n* and unstable *t,* see below.

c Before *e* or *i, c* was pronounced [ts] from a very early period, simplifying to [s] during the time of the troubadours. The alternating spellings *ce/se, ci/si, aiço/aisso* indicate the transitional state of the evolution. In view of the difficulty of dating the shift precisely, it is preferable to pronounce [s] in all cases.

Before *a, o* or *u,* before a consonant, or in final position, *c* was pronounced [k].

ch Before *a,* the digraph *ch* indicates the pronunciation [tʃ], which alternates with *c* [k] in some very common words: *chanso/canso, chastel/castel, chara/cara, charn/carn.* The palatalized [tʃ] is typical of northern Occitan, while [k] is normal in the southern area, but both forms are used interchangeably in the poetry and should be pronounced as written. In final position, *-ch* likewise indicates the pronunciation [tʃ], but in this case there are numerous other spellings of the same sound (see above).

d Intervocalic *-d-* weakens to [z] (or falls completely) in some words during the period of the troubadours. It was probably affected in some regions more than in others, but both spellings are found in the poetry. It may be preferable to pronounce [z] for both spellings, but no consonant should be reinstated if it has fallen in the spellings; e.g., *espada/espaza (sword), adorar/azorar/aorar (to worship).*

In a somewhat analogous situation, the letters *d* and *z* (and occasionally *t*) are used to avoid hiatus between vowels when a short word ending in a vowel or consisting of a vowel, comes into contact with a word beginning with a vowel; the word *e (and)* becomes *et, ed, ez; a (to)* becomes *ad, az; o (or)* becomes *od, oz; que (that)* becomes *qued, quez.* All of these liaison sounds should be pronounced lightly as [z].

g Before *e* or *i, g* was pronounced [dʒ]: *gent, getar, Lemoges, gingibre, ginhos;* before *a, o,* and *u* and before a consonant, *g* was pronounced [g]. In final position *g* was sometimes used to note the sound [tʃ] (see above).

i, j In the manuscripts, *i* and *j* were used interchangeably for the vowel [i], the semi-vowel [j], and the consonant [dʒ]. In initial position before a vowel, the consonant [dʒ] was intended: *joc, jazer, jurar.* In final position, they denote the semi-vowel [j] in a diphthong: *rei, joi* [rɛj, dʒɔj].

In intervocalic position, it is sometimes very difficult to decide whether the semi-vowel or the consonant was intended. In fact, the two pronunciations may have alternated in some words, e.g., *maior/major* (both written with either *i* or *j* in the manuscripts!), the first being northern, the second southern. In most cases, the consonant [dʒ] is preferred: *sojorn, ploja, domnejar, cujar, vejaire, autrejar;* but the semi-vowel [j] is preferable in derivatives whose root word has [j]: *joios* [dʒɔjos] from *joi* [dʒɔj], *reial* [rɛjal] from *rei* [rɛj], *veraia* [veraja] from *verai* [veraj], and in certain suffixes (see Smith, p. 34).

Before *a,* the letter *i/j* alternates with *g* in a number of common words: *jardin/gardin, jau/gaug, jal/gal, jauzir/gauzir.* The palatal affricate [dʒ] is typical of northern Occitan, while [g] is typical of the South. As with the alternating [tʃ] and [k], both forms are used interchangeably in the poetry, perhaps for aesthetic reasons, and should be pronounced as written.

l Two types of *l* were distinguished: the regular Latin [l] and a palatalized variety [λ]; the first is written simply as *l* or occasionally *ll,* while the second has a large variety of spellings, including *lh, ll, il, ill, illi, gl, igl,* and *l.* In these spellings, the *i* and *g* are part of the notation of [λ] and are not pronounced. Since *ll* and occasionally *l* itself can denote either [l] or [λ], it is sometimes difficult to distinguish the two. In a few cases, there seem to have been alternating regional forms: *caval/cavalh, il/ilh, melor/melhor, fil/filh,* which should be pronounced as written, but normally the two sounds were carefully separated. Before another consonant, *l* may have had a velar pronunciation, similar to the English sound; in any case, it vocalized during the twelfth century to the semi-vowel [w], forming a diphthong with the preceding vowel. The older and newer forms alternate in the poetry, perhaps by aesthetic choice, and should be pronounced as they are written: *beltat/beutat, molt/mout, dols/dous.*

n One of the most characteristic traits of Old Occitan phonology is the unpredictable disappearance of the so-called unstable *n,* in words such as *pa/pan, bo/bon, bos/bons, Ventador/Ventadorn, Limozi/Limozin, us/uns.* It normally occurs in final position after a vowel, as above, but is sometimes found in interior position before a consonant: *cofortz/confortz, efan/enfan,* and may even affect unrelated words by hypercorrection: *fo/fon* from Latin *fuit, pro/pron* from *prode.* For reasons not entirely clear, final *n* is stable in many words, especially when followed by unstable final *t* (written or not): *quan/quant, aman/amant* and adverbs ending in *-men/-ment.* The phenomenon must have had some effect on the preceding vowel, since words with stable and unstable *n* do not normally rhyme. It seems to have been responsible for the creation of a new phoneme, the posterior [ɑ] (see below).

nh Alongside the regular Latin [n] was the palatalized variety [ɲ], identified by a disconcerting number of spellings, including *nh, gn, ign, ingn, ing, ng, in, nn,* and *n;* as with [λ], the *i* and *g* in these notations are part of the graph and are not to be pronounced. Also as with [λ], there is some evidence of regional unpalatalized forms alongside the palatalized ones: *gen/genh (skill), fen/fenh (he pretends), plans/planhs (lament).*

qu The *u* is a purely traditional part of the spelling and is not pronounced, except in the form *qui* (more frequently *cui*), the indirect object pronoun corresponding to the Latin dative case meaning *to whom,* pronounced [kuj].

r Occitan uses the traditional Indo-European apical *r,* as in modern Italian and Spanish. It is pronounced with a single vibration or flap of the tip of the tongue against the alveolar ridge [ɾ], except when it is actually doubled, as in certain future tenses, or at the beginning of the word, when it should be produced forcefully, with several vibrations [rr].

s Initial and final *s* are pronounced [s]; before a consonant, *s* is fully pronounced, but it is influenced by the following sound, being pronounced [s] before a voiceless consonant, [z] before a voiced: *estela, esperanza* with [s]; *almosna, isla, blasmar* with [z].

In intervocalic position, it is pronounced [s] or [z] according to Latin etymology. Scribal spellings are not a sure guide, since both *s* and *z* may be used for the sound [z]. In theory, [s] should be identified by the spelling *ss,* but in fact the double *ss* is very frequently reduced in spelling to *s* by the scribes, as with most other double consonants. Thus *doussa* often appears as *dousa;* and *baizar (to kiss)* and *baissar (to lower)* may both be spelled *baisar.*

After a prefix, a root beginning with *s* is still pronounced [s] even if it has become intervocalic.

Note the scribal use of *ç* interchangeably with *s.*

t In final position, *t* is unstable after *n: quan/quant, manh/maint,* at the end of adverbs ending in *-men/-ment,* and occasionally in other words, such as *for/fort, cru/crut, drei/dreit, esgar/esgart.* These should be pronounced as written.

z Although *z* originally denoted the voiced affricate [dʒ], it simplified to [z], as [ts] simplified to [s], but at an earlier date. The spellings *s* and *z* alternate even in the earlier troubadours, indicating the pronunciation [z] in such words as *cortesia/cortezia, rosa/roza, gilosa/giloza.*

In final position *-z* is pronounced [ts], also spelled *-tz: toz/totz, maritz, amanz, parlatz, tertz.*

For intervocalic *-z-,* see above under *d.*

Vowels

Occitan vowels remain close to their Latin origins, like those of Italian and Spanish. The tonic vowels are normally pure in articulation, without the "glides" that typify English vowel sounds. There are no nasal vowels, at least not with phonemic value. Non-accented vowels maintain their full sound and clarity of articulation, even in final atonic position.

a The pronunciation of *a* is almost always anterior [a], called "open" by some linguists, or in the Old Occitan theoretical treatises *larc;* there is a posterior variety [ɑ], sometimes referred to as "closed," or *estreit,* which occurs before an unstable *-n,* whether written or not, as in *pa/pan, ca/can, lonhda/lonhdan.* Sometimes [ɑ] may occur when *a* is tonic and final, as in *va (he goes), cantara (she will sing), esta (is),* and sporadically before *-m* and *-n.*

e Accented *e* must be distinguished as closed [e] *(e estreit)* or open [ɛ] *(e larc),* according to its original state in Latin, or sometimes by analogy. There is no convenient way to determine which vowel to use without recourse to etymology or to a helpful dictionary, but a few modern editors have chosen to follow the dictionary practice of distinguishing them with diacritical marks. The distinction is important for the integrity of the rhyme and because the difference may be phonemic: *ser (evening), pel (hair), mes (mouth), pres (taken),* all with [e], are distinct from *ser (servant), pel (skin), mes (harvest), pres (near),* all with [ɛ].

In unaccented position, all cases of *e* should be pronounced with a short but clear median sound, probably closer to [e] than to [ɛ].

i/j/y Some editors follow the manuscript usage in writing *i* for the vowel [i] as well as for the semi-vowel [j] and for the consonant [dʒ]. For the problems caused by this practice, particularly in distinguishing the semi-vowel from the consonant, see above, "Consonants," under *i/j.*

o Accented *o* must be distinguished as closed [o] *(o estreit)* or open [ɔ] *(o larc),* according to its pronunciation in Latin, or sometimes by analogy. As with the two varieties of *e*, the reader must rely on dictionaries or on extraordinarily helpful editors to furnish the necessary notations: e.g., with [o]: *flor, amor, jorn, mot;* with [ɔ]: *cor, mort, joi, joc, cors.* In pretonic position, the closed [o] evolved to [u] during the twelfth century, undoubtedly in connection with the shift of [u] to [y]. The same shift occurred later for [o] in tonic position, but not until at least the thirteenth century, after the period of flowering of the troubadour poetry. The texts show both spellings interchangeably for pretonic [o], but usually have only *o* for the tonic vowel. It is possible to pronounce the sounds as written, but it is preferable to pronounce [o] consistently for the tonic *o* and [u] for the pretonic: *Toloza* [tuloza], *dolor* [dulor], *amorosa* [amuroza], *dolent* [dulɛn].

u The vowel [u] shifted to [y], as in French, though it is not clear how widespread the phenomenon was or at what date it took place. The shift did not affect the Catalan area.

The front rounded pronunciation [y] should be used consistently for the vowel that represents the Latin *u* (but not where *u* represents the closing of a pretonic closed *o*). The corresponding semi-vowel [ɥ] is used only in the diphthongs *uo* and *ue* [ɥɔ], [ɥɛ].

Diphthongs and Triphthongs

Only one diphthong was maintained from Latin: [aw] in *causa, lauzar;* but at least a dozen new ones were formed during the evolution of the language, along with four triphthongs. All of them consisted of a full vowel preceded and/or followed by a semi-vowel, thus never forming more than one syllable in pronunciation.

The semivowel *u* as the second element in a diphthong is pronounced [w], as in *laus, leu, mezeus, viu, nou, roure* [laws], [lɛw], [mezews], [viw], [nɔw], [rrowr̩e]. As the first element in the two rising diphthongs *uo, ue,* it is pronounced [ɥ], as in *fuoc, nueva* [fɥɔk], [nɥɛva].

The semivowel *i* as the second element in a falling diphthong is pronounced [j], as in *verai, peitz, meitat, pois, conoisser, duire* [ver̩aj], [pɛjts], [mejtat], [pɔjs], [kunojser̩], [dyjr̩e]; as the first element in the diphthong *ie* it is also [j], as in *vielh, lieg* [vjɛʎ], [ljɛtʃ].

Four triphthongs may occur in Old Occitan, all consisting of a central vowel preceded and followed by a semivowel, as in *lieu, miei, nuoit, nuou* [ljɛw], [mjɛj], [nɥɔjt], [nɥɔw].

SAMPLE TEXTS

Bernart de Ventadorn, "Quan vei la lauseta mover"

CD #25.

Quan vei la lauseta mover
De joi sas alas contra·l rai,
Que s'oblid' e·s laissa cazer
Per la doussor qu'al cor li vai,
Ailas! quals enveja m'en ve
De cui qu'eu veja jauzion!
Meravilhas ai, quar desse
Lo cors de dezirier no·m fon.

Ailas! tan cujava saber
D'amor, e tan petit en sai!
Quar eu d'amar no·m posc tener
Celeis don ja pro non aurai;
Tout m'a mon cor, e tout m'a se
E mi mezeis e tot lo mon;
E quan si·m tolc, no·m laisset re
Mas dezirier e cor volon.

Anc non agui de mi poder
Ni no fui meus deslor en çai,
Que·m laisset en sos olhs vezer
En un miralh que mout mi plai.
Miralhs, pos me mirei en te,
M'an mort li sospir de preon,
Qu'aissi·m perdei com perdet se
Lo belhs Narcisus en la fon.

De las domnas mi dezesper,
Jamais en lor no·m fiarai,
Qu'aissi com las solh captener,
Enaissi las descaptenrai:
Pos vei que nulha pro no·m te
Ab leis que·m destrui e·m cofon,
Totas las dopt e las mescre,
Car sai que atretals se son.

D'aisso·s fai ben femna parer
Ma domna, per qu'eu l'o retrai,
Que vol ço qu'om no deu voler,
E ço qu'om li deveda fai.

Cazutz sui en mala merce
Et ai ben fait com fols en pon,
E no sai perque m'esdeve,
Mas quar trop pogei contra mon.

Merces es perduda per ver,
Et eu non o saubi ancmai,
Car cil que plus en degr'aver
Non a ges, et on la querrai?
A! quan mal sembla, qui la ve,
Que aquest caitiu deziron,
Que ja ses leis non aura be,
Laisse morir, que no l'aon.

Pos ab midons no·m pot valer
Precs ni merces ni·l dreitz qu'eu ai,
Ni a leis no ven a plazer
Qu'eu l'am, ja mais no lo·i dirai.
Aissi·m part d'amor e·m recre:
Mort m'a, e per mort li respon,
E vau m'en, pos ilh no·m rete,
Caitius en eissilh, no sai on.

Tristans, ges non auretz de me,
Qu'eu m'en vau caitius, no sai on:
De chantar me gic e·m recre,
E de joi e d'amor m'escon.

kan vɛj la lawzeta muveṛ
de dʒɔj saz alas kontṛalṛaj
ke sublid es lajsa kazeṛ
peṛ la dɔwsoṛ kal kɔṛ li vaj
ajlas kalz envedʒa men ve
de kuj kɛw vedʒa dʒawzi·on
meraviλaz aj kaṛ dese
lu kɔṛs de deziṛjɛṛ num fon

ajlas tan kujava sabeṛ
damoṛ e tan petit en saj
kaṛ ɛw damaṛ num pɔsk teneṛ
se lɛjs dun dʒa pṛo nun awṛaj
tɔwt ma mun kɔr e tɔwt ma se
e mi mezɛjs e tot lu mon
e kan sim tɔlk num lajsɛt rre
mas deziṛjɛṛ e kɔṛ vulon

ank nun agi de mi pudeṛ
ni nu fwi mews dez lɔṛ en saj
kem lajsɛt en sos ɔλs vezeṛ
en yn miṛaλ ke mowt mi plaj
miraλs pɔs me miṛɛj en te
man mɔṛt li suspiṛ de pṛe·on
kajsim pɛṛdɛj kum pɛṛdɛt se
lu bɛλs naṛsisys en la fon

de las domnas mi dezespeṛ
dʒamajs en luṛ num fi·aṛaj
kajsi kum las sɔλ kapteneṛ
enajsi las deskaptenṛaj
pɔs vej ke nyλa pṛo numte
ab lɛjs kem destṛyj em kufon
totas laz dopt e laz meskṛe
kaṛ saj ke·atṛetals se son

dajsɔ sfaj ben femna paṛeṛ
ma domna per kɛw lo rretṛaj
ke vɔl sɔ kom nu dew vuleṛ
e sɔ kom li deveda faj
kazyts syj en mala meṛse
ez aj ben fajt kum fɔls en pon
e nu saj peṛke mezdeve
mas kaṛ tṛɔp pudʒɛj kuntṛa mon

meṛses es peṛdyda peṛ veṛ
ez ɛw nun o sawbi ankmaj
kaṛ sil ke plys en degṛ aveṛ
nun a dʒes ez un la kerraj
a kan mal sembla kuj la ve
ke akɛst kajtiw deziṛon
ke dʒa ses lɛjs nun auṛa be
lajse muṛiṛ ke nu la·on

pɔs ab midons num pɔt valeṛ
pṛɛks ni meṛses nil drɛjts kɛw aj
ni a lɛjs nu ven a plazeṛ
kɛw lam dʒamajs nu lu·i diṛaj
ajsim paṛt damoṛ em rrekṛe
mɔṛt ma e peṛ mɔṛt li rrespon
e vaw men pɔs iλ num rrete
kajtiws en ɛjsiλ nu saj on

tṛistans dʒes nun awṛets de me
kew men vaw kajtiws nu saj on

de tʃantar̩ me dʒik em rrekr̩e
e de dʒɔj e damor̩ meskon

Raimbaut de Vaqueyras, "Kalenda maia"

Paris, Bib. Nat. fonds Fr. 22543, Fol. 62r. CD #26.

Kalenda maia
Ni fuelhs de faia,
Ni chans d'auzel ni flors de glaia
Non es que·m plaia,
Pros dona gaia,
Tro qu'un isnel messatgier aia
Del vostre bel cors, qui·m retraia
Plazer novel qu'amors m'atraia
e jaia
E·m traia
Vas vos, domna veraia,
e chaia
De plaia
'L gelos, anz que·m n'estraia.

Ma bel' amia,
Per Dieu non sia
Que ja·l gelos de mon dan ria,
Que car vendria
Sa gelosia,
Si aitals dos amantz partia;
Qu'ieu ja joios mais non seria,
Ni jois ses vos pro no·m tenria;
Tal via
Faria
Qu'oms ja mais no·m veiria;
Cel dia
Morria,
Domna pros, qu'ie·us perdria.

kalenda maja
ni fyɛλz de faja
ni tʃanz dawzɛl ni flor̩s de glaja
nun es kem plaja
pr̩os dona gaja
tr̩o kyn iznɛl mesadʒɛr̩ aja
del vɔstr̩e bɛl kɔr̩s kim retr̩aja
plazer̩ nuvɛl kamor̩s matr̩aja

e dʒaja
em traja
vas vos domna veṛaja
e tʃaja
de plaja
ldʒelos ants kem nestṛaja

ma bɛl ami·a
peṛ djɛw nun si·a
ke dʒal dʒelos de mun dan rri·a
ke kaṛ vendṛi·a
sa dʒelozi·a
si ajtals dos amants paṛti·a
kjɛw dʒa dʒɔjos majs nun seṛi·a
ni dʒɔjs ses vos pṛo num tenṛi·a
tal vi·a
faṛi·a
koms dʒa majs num vɛjṛi·a
sɛl di·a
mɔrri·a
domna pṛos kjɛws pɛṛdṛi·a

Anonymous, "A l'entrada del temps clar, eya"

Paris, Bibl. Nat. fonds Fr. 844, fol. 191b.

A l'entrada del temps clar, eya
Per joia recomençar, eya
E per jelos irritar, eya
Vol la regina mostrar
Qu'el es si amorosa.

A la vi', a la via, jelos,
Laissatz nos, laissatz nos
Balar entre nos, entre nos.

El' a fait pertot mandar, eya
Non sia jusqu'a la mar, eya
Piucela ni bachalar, eya
Que tuit non vengan dançar
En la dança joiosa.

Lo reis i ven d'autra part, eya
Per la dança destorbar, eya
Que el es en cremetar, eya
Que om no li volh' emblar
la regin' aurilhosa.

Mais per nient lo vol far, eya
Qu'ela n'a sonh de vielhart, eya
Mais d'un leugier bachalar, eya
Qui ben sapcha solaçar
La domna saborosa.

Qui donc la vezes dançar, eya
E son gent cors deportar, eya
Ben pogra dir de vertat, eya
Qu'el mont non aja sa par
La regina joiosa.

a lentṛada del temps klaṛ e·i·a
peṛ dʒɔja rrekumensar e·i·a
e peṛ dʒelos iṛitaṛ e·i·a
vɔl la rredʒina mustṛaṛ
kel es si amuṛoza

a la vi a la vi·a dʒelos
lajsats nos lajsats nos
balaṛ entṛe nos entṛe nos

ela fajt peṛtot mandaṛ e·i·a
nun si·a dʒyska la maṛ e·i·a
pjysɛla ni batʃalaṛ e·i·a
ke tɥjt nun vengan dansaṛ
en la dansa dʒɔjoza

lu rrɛjs i ven dawtṛa paṛt e·i·a
peṛ la dansa destuṛbaṛ e·i·a
ke el es en kṛemetaṛ e·i·a
ke om nu li vɔʎ emblaṛ
la rredʒin awṛiʎoza

majs per njɛnt lu vɔl faṛ e·i·a
kela na soɲ de vjɛʎaṛt e·i·a
majs dyn lɛwdʒeṛ batʃalaṛ e·i·a
ki ben saptʃa sulasaṛ
la domna sabuṛoza

ki donk la vezes dansaṛ e·i·a
e sun dʒent kɔṛs depuṛtaṛ e·i·a
ben pɔgṛa diṛ de veṛtat e·i·a
kel mont nun aja sa paṛ
la rredʒina dʒɔjoza

Arnaut Daniel, "Lo ferm voler"

CD #27.

Lo ferm voler qu'el cor m'intra
No·m pot ges becs escoissendre ni ongla
De lauzengier, qui pert per mal dir s'arma;
E car non l'aus batr' ab ram ni ab verga,
Sivals a frau, lai on non aurai oncle,
Jauzirai joi, en vergier o dinz cambra.

Quan mi soven de la cambra
On a mon dan sai que nulhs om non intra
Anz me son tuch plus que fraire ni oncle,
Non ai membre no·m fremisca, neis l'ongla,
Aissi com fai l'enfas denant la verga:
Tal paor ai no·l sia trop de l'arma.

lo feṛm vuleṛ kel kɔṛ mintṛa
num pɔt dʒes bɛks eskɔjsendṛe ni ongla
de lawzendʒɛṛ ki pɛṛt peṛ mal diṛ saṛma
e kaṛ nun lawz batṛab rram ni ab veṛga
sivals a fṛaw laj un nun awṛaj onkle
dʒawziṛaj dʒɔj en veṛdʒɛṛ o dints kambṛa

kan mi suven de la kambṛa
un a mun dan saj ke nyλz om nun intṛa
ants me sun tutʃ plys ke frajṛe ni onkle
nun aj membṛe num fṛemiska nɛjs longla
ajsi kum faj lenfas denant la veṛga
tal pa·oṛ aj nul si·a tṛɔp de laṛma

Iberian Peninsula

8

Catalan

BEATA FITZPATRICK

Catalan, like French, Provençal, Spanish, Portuguese, and Italian, is a Romance language that developed from Vulgar Latin. It is spoken today by some six million people in an area that encompasses the northeastern triangle of the Iberian Peninsula, including the province of Roussillon on the French side of the Pyrenees; extends southward to Valencia; and includes the Balearic Islands of Mallorca, Minorca, and Ibiza. Catalan is spoken in two major dialects, Eastern (or standard) Catalan, which is typified by the speech of the educated people of Barcelona, and Western Catalan, known also as the Lerida variety, which includes the speech of Valencia. Although Mallorcan differs in a few ways from standard Catalan, it falls within the eastern group.

Created as a province out of the Carolingian Spanish March, Catalonia was closely linked ecclesiastically and politically to the south of France throughout much of the Middle Ages. In the early twelfth century, under the Catalan counts of Barcelona, its territories north of the Pyrenees stretched from Nice to the Ariège and included the suzerainties of Carcassonne, Razès, and Provence. Northward expansion was halted by the defeat of Peter II (Pere el Catòlic) at the hands of Simon de Montfort at the battle of Muret in 1213.

Catalonia's expansion southward was aided by its alliance with Aragon in 1137. Under this union, in which the counts of Barcelona also became kings of Aragon, reconquest from the Moors and resettlement spread to the Balearic Islands (1229–1235) and to the Valencian lands (1233–1244). In the thirteenth and fourteenth centuries, the crown of Aragon became an important Mediterranean power, gaining control over Sicily, Sardinia, Corsica, Naples, and the greater part of Greece. As a remnant of those times, Catalan is still spoken in the town of Alghero on the west coast of Sardinia. In the fifteenth century, the political fortunes of Catalonia began to wane as those of Castile grew.

Catalan is sometimes characterized as a *llengua-pont,* a bridge between Gallo-Romance to the north and Ibero-Romance to the south. Its lexicon has more affinity with Occitan (Provençal) than with Spanish and Portuguese. Its phonetic solutions are sometimes common to both Occitan and Spanish and at other times coincide with only one of them. It is, however, a distinct language with a character of its own and an independent status.

Catalonia's early ties to the South of France are reflected in its literary conventions, which prescribed that poetry be written in Occitan and prose in Catalan. The troubadour *corpus,* beginning with the poems of William of Poitiers (1071–1126) and ending with the songs of Giraut Riquier (composed between 1254 and 1292), contains about two hundred songs contributed by some twenty-five Catalan troubadours. These troubadours wrote in the "koiné," the literary language of the poetry of the courts (see Chapter 7, "Occitan"). Their followers continued the tradition of Occitan as the language of poetry, but their works show a growing Catalan influence. From the last quarter of the thirteenth century, this progression can be described as moving from Occitan-with-Catalan influences to Catalan-with-Occitan vestiges. Although Catalan poetry in the fourteenth century, and even into the fifteenth, continued to be influenced by the Consistori de la Gaya Ciència, founded at Toulouse in 1323 to keep troubadour traditions alive (a Barcelona chapter was founded in 1393), an autochthonous poetry was springing up alongside it, creating a fully "de-Occitanized" tradition for Catalan poetry in the fifteenth century.

Alongside the literary, or "cultural," poetic tradition there must have existed a "popular" tradition of poetry transmitted at first orally and later written down. Vestiges of this tradition are seen in the liturgical dramas, the best known being the *Cant de la Sibil·la,* presented at Christmas, and the *Misteri D'Elx,* performed at the Feast of the Assumption. Additional examples include the *epístoles farcides,* epistles amplified with an addition in Catalan, used to enliven liturgical readings, and a few other popular devotional and religious verses. Further, there is some evidence of the existence, in the vernacular, of a strong tradition of songs and dances with refrain.

Prose was written in Catalan from the outset, with the earliest works dating from the end of the twelfth century. The writing of Catalonia's most eminent writer of the Middle Ages, Ramon Llull (1233–1315), displays a fully developed, sophisticated, and rich language. The influence of the royal chancery in the fourteenth century helped standardize the language.

Yet, by the end of the fifteenth century, Catalan faded as a literary language. The subtle social pressures of the court led to the abandonment of Catalan in favor of Castilian. Popular Catalan poetry and plays for religious feasts continued to be passed on orally in great part for the next three centuries.

In the nineteenth century, Catalan language and literature achieved a renaissance ("Renaixença") as a consequence of an awakened consciousness of Catalonia's separate and unique identity. But in 1939 the teaching of Catalan in schools and the publishing of materials in Catalan were banned by General Franco. Since his death in 1976, Catalan has once more emerged as a vibrant and thriving written, as well as spoken, language. It has now co-official status, along with Spanish, in the autonomous Catalan government.

In spite of the fact that, in the Middle Ages, Catalonia was the home of several important centers of music, including the famous monasteries of Ripoll and Montserrat, very few songs in the vernacular have come down to us with musical notation. They are mainly religious songs associated with liturgical performances.* Possibly the earliest is *Cant de la Sibil·la,* performed as a liturgical drama at the monastery of Ripoll from the tenth to the sixteenth century. Versions are known in Latin, Castilian, French, Italian, Aragonese, and Catalan. The Catalan version probably dates no earlier than the thirteenth century. *Cant de la Sibil·la,* based on the Latin text *Judiciis Signum,* was performed after the sixth or ninth reading in the matins of Christmas morning.

Another popular liturgical drama, *Misteri d'Elx,* has come down to us in a manuscript dating from the fifteenth century, which indicates melodies by reference to songs that must have been well known at the time but have been lost. The one exception is the response "Seynora, tot nostre voler," which was to be sung to the tune of Bernart de Ventadorn's "Quant vey la lauzeta mover."

The feasts of St. Stephen (Sant Esteve) and of St. John (Sant Joan) were celebrated with musical performances in the form of *epístoles farcides* in France and Catalonia, until the end of the fifteenth century. For the reading for the feast of St. Stephen, the Catalan text was sung to the hymn *Veni creator spiritus* and the Latin text to another melody. The one exception to the music for the Catalan text is found in a fourteenth-century manuscript from Sant Llorenç d'Hortus in Barcelona. Although it was not as popular as the *epístola farcida* of St. Stephen, the *epístola farcida* of St. John was also practiced in Barcelona. The only extant musical version of the Catalan text comes from the Cathedral at Perpinyà and dates from the fifteenth century.

In addition, three religious songs have survived with musical notation: one, which begins "Quant ay lo mon," in Madrid, B.N., Ms 105; and two songs in the *Llibre Vermell* at Montserrat. This famous manuscript, which was copied at the end of the fourteenth century, contains ten songs to be sung by pilgrims during their vigil in the Church of Our Lady of Montserrat. Seven are in Latin, and two of the three songs written in the vernacular—"Los set gotxs recomptarem" and "Inperayritz de la ciutat joyosa"—have musical notation. One is clearly a Catalan text. The other two are written in Occitan, as was the norm for poetry, but had been copied by a Catalan scribe.

As for profane music, only one manuscript conserved in Catalonia contains Occitan (Provençal) melodies. A fragment found in the parochial archives of Sant Joan de Les Abadesses includes four popular songs from the thirteenth century, one of which is incomplete. The text is very Italianized.

Of the 264 melodies that have survived in the troubadour *corpus,* only nine belong to Catalan troubadours: eight songs by Berenguer de Palou (composed between 1150 and 1185) and one by Ponç d'Ortafa (composed between 1240 and 1247) appear in the Provençal songbook R. This manuscript also has lines drawn to accommodate melodies by Guillem de Cabestany, Rey d'Anfos, Guillem de Berguedà, Cerverí de Girona, and an additional three songs by Berenguer de Palou. Unfortunately they were never completed.

* The following description of sources for Catalan music in the Middle Ages is based on H. Anglès, *La Música a Catalunya fins al segle XIII* (Barcelona, 1988; reproduction of the 1935 edition).

The singer interested in medieval Catalan song should refer to the guidelines in Chapter 7, "Occitan," for the pronunciation of the troubadour songs. For the songs of the *Llibre Vermell,* an excellent edition and study has been prepared by Ramon Aramon i Serra.

Musical works with Catalan text for the sixteenth and seventeenth centuries are also very rare. A brief summary of the very few texts available is given in Miguel Querol i Gavaldà, *Cançoner català dels segles XVI–XVII,* which provides an edition of twenty-seven texts, eight of them from the sixteenth century.

Dialects

As described above, Catalan is divided into two main linguistic zones; East *(català oriental),* comprising the province of Barcelona, part of Tarragona and Roussillon, and the Balearic Islands of Mallorca, Minorca, and Ibiza; and West *(català occidental),* which includes Lerida, the rest of Tarragona, and Valencia.

Major Vocalic Differences

IN STRESSED OR TONIC POSITION

The major difference centers around the pronunciation of *e.* In Catalan, contrary to Romance language tendencies, some time during the eleventh century, open [ɛ] from Latin *ĕ, ae* closed to [e], with some exceptions.* In the eastern regions, this closing caused the [e] from Latin *ē, ĭ, oe* to shift to the center and become the neutral vowel [ə]. Thus, in eastern Catalan, until about the mid-fourteenth century, there existed three *e'*s in tonic position—[e], [ɛ], and [ə]—a distinction maintained to this day in some localities in Mallorca. By roughly the second half of the fourteenth century, [ɛ] and [ə] merged to [ɛ], leaving eastern Catalan with two *e'*s—[e] and [ɛ] in stressed position. The western region did not participate in the change. In western Catalan, although open [ɛ] was closed to [e], with some exceptions, however, closed [e] maintained its timbre, giving western Catalan more words with closed [e] than with open [ɛ]. Thus, western Catalan often pronounces with a closed [e] words that eastern Catalan pronounces with an open [ɛ]. For example, *plēnu* gave [plɛ] in eastern Catalan and [ple] in western Catalan and likewise, *sĭccu* gave [sɛk] in eastern Catalan and [sek] in western Catalan. There are exceptions. One example found frequently in medieval texts is *verge* (Latin *vĭrginem*), which has an open [ɛ] in both eastern and western Catalan.

IN UNSTRESSED OR ATONIC POSITION

In the eastern region, unstressed *a* and *e* merged into [ə] in the fourteenth century. The written language generally maintained the original vowel, as in *segle* and *dona,* although medieval texts vacillated between writing *a* and *e.* For example, one finds *segle* and *segla, dona* and *done.* Both the *a* and the *e* are pronounced [ə].

A further change occurred in the post-medieval period, with atonic *o* closing to *u* in the sixteenth century in eastern Catalan, although the Balearic Islands did not participate

* For a concise discussion of this phenomenon, see Joseph Gulsoy, "Catalan Language," *Dictionary of the Middle Ages,* vol. 3, p. 159.

in the change. As with *a* and *e,* the written language generally maintained the original vowel, so that atonic *o,* as in *mortal,* would be pronounced [u]. The western region has kept atonic *o* and *u* distinct as [o] and [u], although the pronunciation of [o] in atonic position is more closed than in tonic position.

Major Consonantal Differences

Old Catalan distinguished between [b] from Latin *b-, -p-* and [v] from Latin *v, -b-, -f-,* until the fifteenth century, when labio-dental [v] > [β]. This change did not occur in the Valencian territories or in the Balearic Islands, where labio-dental [v] is still heard.

In the fifteenth century, final *r* was muted under certain conditions (see "Mute Consonants," below). Final *r* was maintained and pronounced in Valencia.

In the group finals *-nt, -lt, -rts,* and *-mp* the *t* and *p* are no longer heard except in Valencia and the Balearic Islands. An exact dating of this muting has not been fixed. In his study of the thirteenth-century text *Vides de Sants Rosselloneses,* Joan Coromines notes that the reduction of *-nt* in the singular seems to be starting, while in plural forms, it appears to be well established. He cites examples such as *falimens* (for *faliments*), *gens* (for *gents*), *parens* (for *parents*) which appear with *-ns* rather than with *-nts.**

In order to illustrate some of these dialectal developments, I have chosen texts from both the eastern and the western region. The *Diccionari* by Alcover and Moll gives phonetic transcriptions and indicates pronunciation for each dialect, labeled as follows: or = *català oriental* (eastern); occ = *català occidental* (western); val = *valencià;* bal = *balear.*

Evidence

Although Catalan writers of the thirteenth and fourteenth centuries composed several treatises on Provençal grammar and poetry, including a rhyme dictionary, no equivalent works exist for Catalan. However, the great abundance of medieval Catalan texts have made it possible for philologists to study and date the evolution of Catalan with some accuracy. For example, dating the muting of *r* can be documented through study of rhymes, where words ending in *-r* rhyme with words without *r.* Variant spelling of *a* and *e,* for example, *casa* and *case, segle* and *segla,* are indicative of changes occurring in the pronunciation of atonic *a* and *e.* The consistent separation of etymological *b* and *v* in texts up to the fifteenth century supports the dating of the existence of the two phonemes in eastern Catalan up to the fifteenth century.

Bibliography

Joan Gili. *Introductory Catalan Grammar.* 4th ed. Oxford: Dolphin, 1974.
J. Gulsoy. "Catalan Language." In *Dictionary of the Middle Ages,* vol. 3, pp. 157–64.
C. Wittlin. "Catalan Literature." In *Dictionary of the Middle Ages,* vol. 3, pp. 164–72.
Dictionaries:
A. Alcover and F. Moll. *Diccionari Català-Valencià-Balear.* 10 vols. 1962–1968.
J. Coromines. *Diccionari etimològic i complementari de la llengua catalana.* 9 vols. Barcelona: Curial, 1980–1991.
[These two dictionaries are the only ones that give information about old Catalan. While Alcover and Moll will simply indicate that a word is old and no longer in use, Coromines gives a very rich documentation of old usage.]

* Joan Coromines, *Lleures i converses d'un filòleg* (Barcelona, 1971), p. 305.

Salvador Oliva and Angela Buxton. *Diccionari Català-Anglès.* Barcelona: Enciclopèdia Catalana, 1986.
[This is the only Catalan-English dictionary for the modern language; unfortunately, it does not give phonetic transcriptions.]
For Catalan texts with music see:
Higini Anglès. *La música a Catalunya fins al segle XIII.* Barcelona: Biblioteca de Catalunya, 1988. Reproduction of the 1935 edition.
R. Aramon i Serra. "Els cants en vulgar del *Llibre Vermell* de Montserrat." *Analecta Montserratensia* 10 (1964):9–54.
Miguel Querol i Gavaldà. *Cançoner català dels segles XVI–XVII.* Barcelona: Consejo superior de investigaciones científicas, Instituto español de musicología, 1979.
General music history:
Higinio Anglés. *La música española desde la edad media hasta nuestros dias.* Barcelona: Biblioteca Central, 1941.
Manuel Valls i Gorina. *Història de la música catalana.* Barcelona: Taber, 1969.

Sounds and Spellings

Vowels

IN STRESSED OR TONIC POSITION

As of the mid-fourteenth century, Catalan had, as it does today, seven vowels in stressed syllables: [a], [ɛ], [e], [i], [ɔ], [o], and [u]. Open [ɛ] and closed [e] and open [ɔ] and closed [o] are not distinguished by different orthographic symbols in medieval manuscripts. Most editors follow the modern rules of accentuation. When *e* and *o* are marked with a grave accent, *è* and *ò,* they are pronounced [ɛ] and [ɔ]. When marked by an acute accent, *é* and *ó* are pronounced [e] and [o]. However, in many cases, they are not marked and the correct timbre must be learned by observation.

IN UNSTRESSED OR ATONIC POSITION

In the thirteenth century, Catalan had five vowels in unstressed position: [a], [e], [i], [o], and [u]; but, by the second half of the fourteenth century unstressed [a] and [e] were reduced to the neutral vowel schwa [ə] in eastern Catalan. Therefore, in unstressed position both *a* and *e* should be pronounced [ə]. For example, *jutjamen* becomes [ʒudʒəmen] and *servici* becomes [sərβisi].

In the sixteenth century the unstressed vowels were reduced to three in eastern Catalan by the passage of *o* to *u.* For example, *Josep* would be pronounced [ʒuzɛp].*

Consonants

Catalan had the following consonants in the thirteenth century: [p], [b], [t], [d], [k], [g], [f], [v], [s], [z], [ts], [dz], [ʃ], [ʒ], [tʃ], [dʒ], [l], [ʎ], [m], [n], [ɲ], [r̥], [rr]. In the thirteenth century the sound represented orthographically by *ç* and *c* before *e* and *i* was [ts], which became fricative and merged with [s] in the fourteenth century.

* In providing examples throughout this chapter, unless otherwise indicated, I give the standard (eastern) Catalan transcription. In words that went out of use after the medieval period, I have transcribed atonic *o* as [o].

In standard Catalan, labiodental [v] became fricative [β] in the fifteenth century although it continued to be written as *v*.*

MUTE CONSONANTS

The final *t* in words written with the endings *-nt* and *-lt* may not have been pronounced in standard Catalan by the fourteenth century (see p. 125). Also in the group *-mp*, *p* is not pronounced. Some examples of mute *t* and *p* are: *faliment, molt, camp, recomptarem.*

Final [ṛ], although written, became mute as of the fifteenth century in standard Catalan. It is, however, pronounced in certain monosyllabic words and is heard in infinitives followed by a pronoun object, i.e., *saber* [səβe] but *saber-ho* [səβeru]. This phenomenon probably began in plurals ending in *-rs,* since in fourteenth-century texts, forms such as *carrés* are found alongside *carrers.*

DOUBLED CONSONANTS

Doubled sounds are a feature of Catalan: double *m,* written as *mm, tm, dm;* double *n* written as *nn, tn;* double *l* written as *tl;* and [λλ] written as *tll.* Today there are regions that double the first consonant in the groups *-bl, -cl,* and *-gl.* Although this doubling is not reflected much in old orthography, it must have existed regionally in Old Catalan.

DIGRAPHS

By the thirteenth century, Catalan orthography had developed a series of digraphs (two letters representing a single sound), some of which are in use today. Among the common digraphs found in medieval texts are:

ig for the affricate [tʃ] as in *goig* [gɔtʃ]

ix between vowels and after a vowel in final position, for the prepalatal voiceless fricative [ʃ] as in *peix* [peʃ] and *baixar* [bəʃa]

tg before *e* and *i* and *-tj* before *a, o,* and *u,* for the prepalatal voiced affricate [dʒ] as in *jutjamen* [ʒudʒəmen] and as in *gradatge* [gṛəd̮adʒə], *Olivatge* [olivadʒə], *alegratge* [ələgṛadʒə], and *coratge* [koṛadʒə], which appear as rhyme words in “Los set gotxs”

tz for the alveolar voiced affricate [dz] as in *tretze* [tṛedzə]

Medieval texts contain many variant spellings for the prepalatal fricatives and the affricates, as scribes attempted to find ways to record sounds for which there were no Latin equivalents. One finds many examples of *x* alongside *-ix* for the prepalatal voiceless fricative [ʃ], as in the old forms *vexell* [bəʃeλ], *merexets* [məṛəʃɛts], and *axi* [əʃi]. Instances of *g* as well as *-ig* can be found for the prepalatal voiceless affricate [tʃ], as in the archaic verb form *pug* [putʃ] or *puig* [putʃ]. Plurals of nouns ending in [tʃ] and [ʃ] can appear with an *s* added, as in *gotxs* [gɔtʃ], where one would not pronounce the *s;* or in forms such as *peis,* where one would expect *peixs,* and should be pronounced [peis].** The prepalatal voiced affricate [dʒ] represents the sound of *tg* and *tj,* and often of *g* alone,

* I have followed standard Catalan practice of transcribing *v* as the phoneme /b/ in the words given as examples throughout this chapter, except as noted in old forms of the verbs *voler, venir,* and *veer* (modern *veure*).

** Today many of these words have plurals ending in *-os,* as in *peix, peixos.*

as in *jugament* [ʒudʒəmen]. It may be helpful to remember that *-tg* derives from *t'c* and *d'c,* e.g., *iudicare* > *jutgar.*

ll, yl for the palatal lateral [ʎ], as in *millor* [miʎo], *uyl* [uʎ]. *yll* and *ly* are also found, although *ly* is rare in Old Catalan. Catalan also has a geminate palatal lateral [ʎʎ] represented by *tll* as in *espatlla.*

ny and *yn* for the palatal nasal [ɲ], as in *tany* [taɲ] and *seynoria* [səɲuriə].

VOICED AND VOICELESS CONSONANTS

Because the final vowel of Latin words was dropped in Catalan, the language has many words ending in consonants. The unvoicing of final voiced stops and sibilants was completed around the third quarter of the thirteenth century. Thus in final position Catalan admits only voiceless stops, fricatives, and affricates, that is, the sounds [p], [t], [k], [f], [s], [ʃ], [ts], and [tʃ].* The orthography may retain the etymological spelling, for example, *fred* for [frɛt] and *llarg* for [ʎark].

However, in breath groups, that is, in contact with another word, pronunciation is modified. The final voiceless consonants are usually voiced before a voiced consonant, that is, [p], [t], [k], [f], [s], [ʃ], [ts], and [tʃ] are pronounced [b], [d], [g], [v], [z], [ʒ], [dz], and [dʒ] respectively. The voiceless fricatives [s] and [ʃ] and the affricates [ts] and [tʃ] are also voiced before a vowel. For example: the first line of the song "Los set gotxs recomptarem" in *Llibre Vermell* is pronounced [los sed gɔdʒ rrəkomtəɾ̣ɛm]. The phonemes */b/, /d/,* and */g/* have stop [b], [d], and [g] and fricative counterparts [β], [d̯], and [ɣ], which may be heard between vowels and in contact with certain other consonants.

In general, the slower and more careful the speech, the less consonants are altered by their environment. In the transcriptions at the end of this chapter, I have left some of the final consonants in their voiceless form. Normal pronunciation will result in a voiced or half-voiced consonant, without the singer's being conscious of voicing the consonant. Emphatic pronunciation, especially in a musical context, would have final consonants voiceless.

SPELLING

Some editors may regularize *i, y,* and *j* in accordance with current spelling, while others render the form found in the manuscript. For example, one may find *jutgament* and *iutgament* for [ʒudʒəmen], *jorn* and *iorn* for [ʒorn], *mai* and *may* for [mai], and *oir* and *oyr* for [u·i]. Medieval scribes did not distinguish between *u* and *v.* It is conventional for editors to make that distinction for the reader.

Stress and Accent

Catalan words may be stressed on the final, penultimate, or antepenultimate syllable, although the majority of Catalan words are oxytonic, that is, stressed on the final syllable, giving Catalan the appearance of a Gallo-Romance language. However, unlike French, Catalan is characterized by a continuous falling and rising of the tone, the result of a binary stress pattern: Polysyllabic words have a main stress (´) and a secondary stress,

* [ts] is not heard today in final position in standard Catalan.

or counterstress (`), every second syllable from the main one, as in *corrùmpimént.* In unstressed position the neutral vowel schwa [ə] is present in abundance. This tonality is reinforced by a preponderance of falling diphthongs in *-i* and *-u.* Catalan has very few rising diphthongs. Functional words of one syllable, that is, articles, pronouns, prepositions, possessives, etc., are weakly stressed.

Although accent marks do not appear in medieval texts, editors generally follow the modern system of accentuation to indicate the stressed syllable of polysyllabic words. The stress is on the final syllable if the word ends with a diphthong, a consonant, or two consonants. Plural forms with *-s* of words ending with one or two consonants are also stressed on the final syllable: e.g., *espai, voleu, peccat, peccats, hivern, hiverns.* The stress is on the penultimate syllable if the word ends with a vowel, a vowel + *s, -en,* or *-in:* e.g., *Maria, missa, segle, pares, volen.*

Consonants

b The Catalan phoneme /b/ has both a stop [b] and a fricative [β] allophone. Although it is unclear to what extent medieval practice coincided with modern custom, as a rule, [b] is heard in absolute initial position, after the nasals *m* or *n,* and after another *b.* [β] occurs in intervocalic position or after a consonant other than *m, n,* or *b;* for example, *combat* [kumbat], *treballar* [trəβəλa], *bé* [be], *tot bé* [tod βe].

At the end of a word or at the end of a syllable before a voiceless consonant, *b* is pronounced [p] as in *Jacob* [ʒəkɔp], *corb* [kɔr̥p], *absent* [əpsen], *dubtança* [duptansə].

Note that in the consonant cluster *-bl* after a vowel, *b* is doubled as in *poble* [pɔbblə].

c Pronounced [k] before *a, o,* and *u* as in *cavalcant* [kəβəlkan], *com* [kɔm], *cuc* [kuk]. Medieval texts alternate between *can* and *quan (quando). Quan* is always pronounced [kwan], but it is not certain whether the form *can,* which is not in use today, should be pronounced in the same way. Given the very extended usage of the form *can* in medieval Catalan texts, it is perhaps best to say [kan].

Pronounced [ts] before *e* and *i* until the fourteenth century, by which time it had merged with [s] as in *cel, certament, esforcem, ciutat, servici, resuscitar.*

ç Originally pronounced [ts], but pronounced [s] as of the fourteenth century, as in *encenç* [ənsɛns], *dolça* [dolsə] and *cobegança* [koβəʒansə], the common medieval word for "envy" (today Catalan has *cobdícia*). Pronounced [z] in medial syllable final before a voiced consonant, as in *feliçment* [fəlizmen].

ch Pronounced [k] as in the old verb forms *volch* [vɔlk] and *estich* [əstik] and is voiced as [g] before a voiced consonant.

cl Doubled as [kkl] as in *article.*

d Catalan *d* differs from the English *d* in its point of articulation, as the latter is formed in the gum ridge while the former is articulated with the tip of the tongue touching the inner surface of the incisors. Although today Catalan has two allophonic variations, a stop plosive [d] and a fricative [d̯], like the *d* in Spanish *cada,* articulated by gently placing the tip of the tongue on the edges of the upper incisors, the extent to which medieval Catalan coincided with modern practice for pronunciation of [d] and [d̪] is difficult to determine. Correct pronunciation of the surrounding vowels and/or consonants should be sufficient to produce the right sound. In absolute initial position and after *m, n,* and *l, d* is always pronounced [d] as in *devotament* [dəβɔtəmen], *dolorosa* [dulurozə], *al dissapte* [əldisaptə] and in *endenyosa* [əndəɲozə], an old word for "scornful." When it is word final, *d* should be pronounced [t] as in *verd* [bɛrt].

dm Pronounced *mm* as in *admirar* [əmmira].

f Pronounced similarly to English *f.*

g Before *a, o,* and *u* or before a consonant, *g* was usually pronounced [g], which today has a stop and a fricative allophone. As with fricative [d̪], the extent to which medieval pronunciation corresponded with modern practice for pronunciation of [g] and [ɣ] is difficult to determine. Fricative *g* [ɣ] is articulated with the back of the tongue gently touching the velum without making a complete closure. In absolute initial position or after *n, g* is pronounced [g], similar to English *g* in *go* or *get.* For example, *gaire* [gaiɽə], *gotxs* [gɔtʃ], *gran* [gɽan], and the old verb form *vengren* [veŋgɽən]; *pregar* [pɽəɣa] and *negun* [nəɣun], an old variant of the indefinite adjective *ningun.*

Note, however, that confusion between *g* and *j* before *a, o,* and *u* to indicate the prepalatal voiced fricative [ʒ] from Latin *j, di,* and *g* followed by *e* or *i* is common; for example, *mengar* alongside *menjar* [mənʒa], *bategar* alongside *batejar* [bətəʒa].

Medieval texts may also have *g* in place of *gu* before *a* (see below, under *gu*).

Before *e* and *i, g* is generally pronounced [ʒ], as in *gent* [ʒen], *gitar* [ʒita], *verge* [bɛɽʒə], *regina* [rrəʒinə]. In word final position, *g* should be pronounced [k] as in *llarg* [λaɽk] except after a stressed *i,* in which case *g* is pronounced [tʃ], as in *desig* [dəzitʃ], *mig* [mitʃ].

gl Occurring between vowels, *g* is doubled to [ggl]. The first *g* is implosive, that is, strongly articulated. One must be careful to maintain an almost doubled pronunciation, as in *segle* [seg·glə].

gu Before *e* and *i* pronounced [g] as in *guerra* [gɛrrə], *guia* [giə], and in the old verb form *romangués* [rromaŋges]. Before *a, gu* is pronounced [gw] as in *llengua* [λeŋgwə]. Words in [gw] are sometimes spelled with *g* before *a.* Some words commonly found in medieval texts are *gardar* for *guardar, ganyar* for *guanyar, garnir* for *guarnir, aiga* for *aigua, egal* for *egual,* and *llenga* for *llengua.*

h Not pronounced but may sometimes indicate hiatus, as in *vehés* and *yohel.*

j Pronounced [ʒ], as in *joyosa* [ʒujosə], *jorn* [ʒoɽn].

k Occurs occasionally in place of *c* before *a,* as in *karitat.*

l In texts of the thirteenth and fourteenth centuries, *l* at the beginning of a word, except in articles and pronouns, may be a palatal [λ]. Initial Latin *l* mostly became a palatal [λ] in Catalan in the thirteenth and fourteenth centuries, and this pronunciation was generalized by the fifteenth century although it was normally written as a single *l* until then. In many medieval texts, palatal *l* [λ] is not distinguished from non-palatal *l* [l]. Examples of *l* to indicate [λ] abound: *batala* [bətaλə], *trebalar* [trəbəλa], *ul* [uλ], *vel* [beλ], *aquel* [əkɛλ], *falimens* [fəλimens], *caval* [kəβaλ].*

Otherwise, single *l* is generally pronounced [l], which in Catalan has a velar quality and is not articulated in the same way as in French and Spanish or as in the English word *lip*. Catalan *l* is pronounced with the tip of the tongue in the gum ridge and the body of the tongue raised toward the back of the mouth. This gives it a distinct velar quality, which is most noted after a stressed syllable, especially in final position, and before labial consonants *(m, b, p, f)* and velar consonants *(k, g)* in any position. It is similar to the *l* sound in English *tall, tell, milk* and to Portuguese *l* in final position. It is sometimes described as a "dark" *l*. Some examples in the sample texts that follow are *dolça, molt, cel, perpetual, tal, mortal, humilment, cavalcan, volch.*

Before a stressed *e* or *i*, the *l* is less velar, as in *voleu, soleta, complitz,* but it never approaches the light timbre of English *l* as in *leave, let, lit* or of Spanish or French *l*. In Valencia the velar quality of *l* is not as noticeable, but it is still different from Spanish *l*, which has a palatal element.

ll Represents the palatal [λ] (see "digraphs"). In "Los set gotxs" we find an example of *cell* for *cel (caelum)* when *ll* is not palatal.

m Pronounced like English *m*.

n Catalan *n* frequently assimilates to the point of articulation of the following sound. Before a labial it is pronounced [m], as in *convenir* [kumbəni], *un pa* [um pa]. Before [f] it has a labio-dental pronunciation, and before [k] or [g] it becomes velarized and is similar to the *ng* [ŋ] in English *sing;* for example, *blanca* [blaŋkə]. However, when the group /nk/ represented by *nc* or *ng* is final, *k* is assimilated to *n* as in *blanc* [blaŋ], *sang* [saŋ]. Before a palatal consonant, *n* is palatalized as [ɲ], as in *enlloc* [əɲλɔk].

ny Represents the palatal *n* [ɲ], which is pronounced like *n* of Spanish *baño,* the *gn* of French *agneau,* or the *ni* of English *onion.*

p In initial position it does not have the strong aspiration it has before a stressed vowel in English *part* or *push;* however, in final position before a pause its release is usually strong. In the word *temps* the *p* is purely orthographic; in the group *-mp* the *p* is mute, as in *recomptarem* [rrəkumtərɛm] and *camp* [kam]. In a breath group and in compound words *p* is voiced before a voiced consonant and is pronounced [b] as in *cap de* [kabdə] and *capdal* [kəbdal], written as *cabdal* today.

q/qu Generally pronounced [k] before *e* or *i,* as in *que* [kə] or *quin* [kin]. Before *a* it is generally pronounced [kw] as in *quan* [kwan].

r Trilled as [rr] in initial position and after the consonants *n, l,* and *s*. Otherwise it is pronounced as a simple vibrant [ɾ̣]. This *r* does not have the quasi-vocalic sound of

* See Joan Coromines, *Lleures i converses d'un filòleg,* pp. 289–91, for a detailed explanation of the history of the orthography of palatal *l*.

English *r* in *forest* and *worry.* It is similar to the Castilian *r* in *verdad.* For example, *rei* [rrei], *honra* [onrrə], *volrien* [volrriən]—an old form of the conditional of *voler; trenca* [tɾ̣ɛŋkə], *grans* [gɾ̣ans], *quarta* [kwaɾ̣tə], *paraules* [pəɾ̣auləs], *serà* [səɾ̣a].

In standard Catalan final *r* was generally not pronounced after the fifteenth century (see section "Mute Consonants"). By the fourteenth century final *r* was weak and may have had a fricative timbre.

rr Trilled, as in *mirre* [mirrə], *parrà* [pərra], *corrumpiment* [kurrumpimen].

s Pronounced [s], which like the Spanish *s,* is apical and has a slight shrill. It is produced with the tip of the tongue raised toward the upper part of the gum ridge, forming a slightly concave curve.

Pronounced [z] when *s* is between two vowels and in medial syllable final before a voiced consonant, as in *piadosa* [pi·əd̯ozə], *desmai* [dəzmai].

Final *s* before a vowel or a voiced consonant is voiced as [z], as in the following two examples in "Los set gotxs": *si per nós vos plau* [si pəɾ̣ nos vox plau] and *agués en* [əɣezən].

ss Pronounced [s], as in *destrossar* [dəstɾ̣usa], *missa* [misə].

t The dental voiceless stop [t] is similar to the *t* of Spanish and French and is articulated with the tip of the tongue touching the inner surface of the incisors. Initial *t* in Catalan is not as strongly aspirated as the English initial *t* before a stressed vowel. In a breath group, final *t* before a voiced consonant is voiced as [d]; for example, *tot fallimen* [totfəλimen] but *tot bé* [todβe].

In words ending in *-nt* and *-lt, t* is not pronounced in standard Catalan. There are some exceptions in expressions where the following word begins with a vowel, for example, in saints' names, one says *Sant Joan* [san ʒuan] but *Sant Andreu* [santəndreu]. In the song "Los set gotxs," the phrase *lo quint alegrage* should probably be pronounced [lo kint ələgɾ̣adʒə]. Also, the *t* may have been preserved in *Munt d'Olivatge.*

tg, tj Generally pronounced [dʒ] (see "Digraphs"). However, *setgle* should be pronounced [segglə] (see *gl* above).

tl, tll *tl* generally indicates [ll], while *tll* is pronounced [λλ] (see "Digraphs").

tm Pronounced with double *mm,* as in *setmana* [səmmanə].

ts This spelling is found in second person plural verb forms such as *cantats, volets,* until about 1440, when the normal ending in *-u* (from Latin *-tis*) was generalized to give *cantau, voleu.* It is pronounced [ts] and is voiced to [dz] before a vowel or a voiced consonant. It is also found in past participles such as *aünits, venguts, complits.*

tx Pronounced [tʃ] and is voiced as [dʒ] (see "Digraphs").

tz In texts influenced by Occitan, many words ending in *-ts* also appear written with *-tz,* which was the normal form in Occitan, as in *mostratz, avetz, complitz.* It should be pronounced [ts] and is voiced as [dz]. In Catalan [dz] is found only between vowels in words such as *dotze, tretze.*

v Pronounced in standard Catalan as [v] until the fifteenth century, after which it is pronounced [b] or [β] (see under *b* above). Valencian and Mallorcan retain the pronunciation [v].

x Initially, *x* may be pronounced [ʃ], as in *xisclar* [ʃiskla], however, the *x* in *xantant* is an Occitan influence, and this word should probably be pronounced [kəntan], as would be normal in Catalan. After a consonant *x* may be pronounced [ʃ] as in *clenxa* [klɛɲʃə], *portxe* [pɔrʃə].

When *x* is followed by a voiceless consonant, it represents the combination [ks], as in *mixta* [mikstə]. Intervocalic *x* may also be pronounced [ks] in learned words such as *flexió* [fləksi·o] or voiced to [gz] as in *exaltar* [əgzəlta].

The digraph *ix* between vowels and after a vowel in final position indicates the affricate [ʃ] as in *caixa* [kaʃə], *peix* [peʃ]. [ʃ] is voiced to [ʒ] in a breath group when followed by a vowel or a voiced consonant, as in *peix viu* [peʒ βiu].

y Between vowels *y* can be the palatal glide [j] found in rising diphthongs, which are not frequent in Catalan. It should have more the timbre of a vowel than of a consonant, for example, *joyosa* [ʒojozə] in "Los set gotxs." It can also indicate the semi-vocalic glide [i] in falling diphthongs or the vowel [i] (see *i, j,* and *y* above). Because Catalan did not have a consonant phoneme /y/ or /i/, *y* indicated [ʒ], as in the old infinitive forms *puyar* [puʒa], *cobeyar* [koβəʒa] or the adverb *mayorment* [məʒormen].

yl Pronounced as palatal [λ] as is *yll* (see "Digraphs").

yn Palatal [ɲ] (see "Digraphs").

z May be found between vowels, as in *riquezes, nozent, cozes,* although *s* is more common in Catalan. It is pronounced [z].

Vowels

In general Catalan vowels have a pure and simple sound. Single vowels should not be diphthongized as often happens in English.

a Pronounced [a] when it is stressed, but as of the mid-fourteenth century, pronounced [ə] in standard Catalan when unstressed. Stressed [a] takes on a velar timbre in the diphthong *au* and before an *o* or *l* and in these cases is pronounced similar to the *a* in English *calm* or *father.*

e Pronounced either open [ɛ] or closed [e] in stressed syllable. As of the mid-fourteenth century, generally pronounced [ə] in unstressed position in eastern Catalan and [e] in western Catalan. There are some exceptions in unstressed position, such as in adverbs formed with *-ment,* in which the timbre of the stressed vowel in the root word is maintained; for example, *cert* [sɛrt] and *certament* [sɛrtəmen].

i Pronounced like the English *i* in *marine.*

o In stressed position can be an open [ɔ], similar to the *o* of French *sol,* Italian *cosa,* or a closed [o] similar to the *o* in French *beau.* As of the sixteenth century, in unstressed position it is pronounced [u] in standard Catalan and [o] in western Catalan and in Mallorca. As with [e], there are some exceptions in unstressed position, for example, in adverbs formed with *-ment,* as in *devotament* [dəβɔtəmen] from *devot* [dəβɔt].

u A relatively open vowel found in stressed and unstressed position; similar to the *u* of English *put, push.*

Diphthongs

A diphthong is usually defined as the combination of a full vowel with a glide vowel (semivowel or semiconsonant) before or after it, articulated in one syllable. Diphthongs with the vowel first and the glide second are called falling diphthongs, as the shift is from the prominent, or the stressed, to the less prominent. Rising diphthongs have the glide first and the vowel second. Catalan is characterized by an abundance of falling diphthongs and comparatively few rising ones. Its structure permits a great many vocalic combinations in hiatus. Vocalic combinations that lend themselves to rising diphthongs are usually in hiatus. Triphthongs are not common in Catalan.

Various combinations of falling diphthongs with the semivowel [i] and the semivowel [u] are possible, for example: *mai* [mai], *rey* [rrei], *servei* [sər̩βɛi], *aytal* [əital], *boira* [bɔir̩ə], *plau* [plau], *Déu* [deu], *peu* [pɛu], *aurem* [əur̩ɛm], *moure* [mɔur̩ə], *duu* [duu].

Rising diphthongs are formed with the semiconsonant [j] in combinations with *a, e,* and *o* after a vowel, as in *reyal* [rrəjal], *seiem* [səjem], *joyosa* [ʒojozə]. After a consonant the combinations *ia, ie,* and *io* are in hiatus. Rising diphthongs with the semiconsonant [w] occur in the combinations *gua, guo, güe, güi, qua, quo,* and *qüe* and medially after a vowel, as in *diuen* [diwən]. Some examples with [kw] and [gw] are *quatre* [kwatr̩ə], *quan* [kwan], *guanya* [gwaɲə], *llengües* [ʎeŋgwəs].* After other consonants *ua* and *ue* do not form diphthongs, and the two vowels are in hiatus. Some examples of hiatus are *Maria* [mər̩i·ə], *celestial* [sələsti·al], *Orient* [ur̩i·en] or [or̩i·en] in the Middle Ages, *graciosa* [gr̩əsi·ozə], *perpetual* [pər̩pətu·al], *aünits* [ə·units], *duent* [du·en], and the old verb form *vehés* [və·es].

* Dieresis in modern Catalan is used with *i* and *u* to indicate hiatus or to indicate pronunciation of *qu* [kw] and *gu* [gw].

DIACHRONIC SOUND CHART FOR CATALAN

1100 1200 1300 1400 1500 1600 1700

VOWELS

IN STRESSED POSITION

Eastern dialect

a [a] -------→

e [e] --------→

[ɛ] --------→

[ə] --------------------- [ɛ] ---→ (some localities in Mallorca retain [ə])

i [i] --------→

o [ɔ] --------→

[o] -------→

u [u] -------→

Western dialect

a [a] -------→

e [e] --------→

[ɛ] --------→ (Western dialect has more words with closed [e] and often has [e] where eastern dialect has [ɛ], see p. 124.)

i [i] --------→

o [ɔ] --------→

[o] -------→

u [u] -------→

IN UNSTRESSED POSTITION

Eastern (standard) dialect

a [a] -------------------- [ə] ---→

e [e] --------------------- [ə] ---→

i [i] --------→

o [o] ---------------------------------[u] ------→ (except in Balearic Islands)

u [u] -------→

Western dialect

a [a] -------→

e [e] --------→

i [i] --------→

o [o] -------→ (Has a more closed pronunciation than [o] in stressed position.)

u [u] -------→

DIPHTHONGS

Falling diphthongs are formed with a stressed or an unstressed vowel plus the glide vowel *i* or *u* and follow the evolution of the vowels; e.g., [əi] and [əu] would have been heard as of the mid-fourteenth century in standard Catalan, and unstressed *oi* would have sounded [ui] as of the sixteenth century. Rising diphthongs are far less common in Catalan and occur under limited circumstances in the combination *i* [j] or *u* [w] plus a vowel (see p. 134).

1200 1300 1400 1500 1600 1700

CONSONANTS

An asterisk* indicates that a voiceless consonant has a voiced correlative or that a stop has a fricative allophone. The reader should consult the general section on voiced and voiceless consonants, p. 128, and the detailed description of the consonant for the conditions under which voicing occurs.

b	[b][β]* -------------→(for final b, see p. 129)
-bl	[bbl] ---------------→
c	[k] before *a, o, u* ------→
	[ts] before *e, i* [s] -----→
ç	[ts] ------- [s][z]* ----→
ch	[k][g]* -------------→
-cl	[kkl] ---------------→
d	[d][d̯]* -------------→(for final d, see p. 130)
dm	[mm] --------------→
f	[f][v]* --------------→
g	[g][γ]* before *a, o, u,* or a consonant (for exceptions see p. 130) (for final *g,* see p. 130)
	[ʒ] before *e, i* --------→(for the digraph *-ig* as [tʃ], see p. 127)
-gl	[ggl] ---------------→
gu	[g] before *e, i* --------→
	[gw] before *a* --------→
h	not pronounced
j	[ʒ] ----------------→(see also p. 130)
k	[k] ----------------→
l	[l] ----------------→(Catalan *l* has a velar quality.)
	[λ] (see p. 130)
ll	[λ] ----------------→
n	[n] ----------------→
	(*n* assimilates to the point of articulation of the following sound, see p. 131)
ny	[ɲ] ----------------→
p	[p][b]* -------------→(mute in the group *-mp* except in Valencia and the Balearic Islands)
q/qu	[k] before *e, i* --------→
	[kw] before *a*
r	[rr] ----------------→(in initial position and after *n, l, s*)
	[ṛ] ----------------→
	(final *r* was mute in eastern dialect by the fifteenth century and may have already been weakly pronounced in the fourteenth)
rr	[rr] ---------------→
s	[s][z]* --------------→
ss	[s] ----------------→
t	[t][d]* --------------→
	(mute in words ending in *-nt, -lt, -rts,* as of the fourteenth century, except in Valencia and the Balearic Islands, see p. 125)
tg/tj	[dʒ] ---------------→
-tl	[ll] ----------------→
-tll	[λλ] ---------------→
tm	[mm] --------------→
ts	[ts][dz]* ------------→
tx	[tʃ][dʒ]* ------------→
tz	[dz] ---------------→(see p. 132)
v	[v] ----------------→in Valencia and the Balearic Islands
	[v] ---------------- [β] in eastern Catalan. By late fifteenth century eastern Catalan had one phoneme /b/ with fricative and stop allophones.

	1200	1300	1400	1500	1600	1700
x	[ks][gz]* ------------→ (see p. 133)					
x/-ix	[ʃ][ʒ]* --------------→ (see p. 133)					
y	[j] -----------------→ (see p. 133)					
	[ʒ] -----------------→ (see p. 133)					
yl	[λ] ----------------→					
yn	[ɲ] ----------------→					
z	[z] -----------------→					

SAMPLE TEXTS

Los set gotxs

From *Llibre Vermell* of Montserrat, fol. 23v–r, copied at the end of the fourteenth century and believed to date after the first third of the fourteenth century. I have used the edition by Aramon i Serra,* which regularizes the use of *i* and *j* and places accent marks on words in accordance with modern usage, but is otherwise faithful to the spellings of the manuscript. Although musical notation appears in the manuscript only for the first four lines of Catalan text and for the Latin refrain, Aramon i Serra believes that the music and the rhymes coincide in the pattern ab ab ab ab, although not all the stanzas have consistently maintained these rhymes. CD #28.

I Los set gotxs recomptarem
Et, devotament xantant,
Humilment saludarem
La dolça verge Maria
. . .
. . .
Ave Maria, gracia plena,
Dominus tecum, Virgo serena.

II . . .

III Verge: fos anans del part
Pura, e sens falliment
En lo part, e prés lo part
Sens negun corrumpiment;
Lo Fill de Déus, Verge pia,
De vós nasqué verament.
Ave Maria, gracia plena,
Dominus tecum, Virgo serena.

IV Verge: tres reys d'Orient,
Cavalcan ab gran corage,
Ab l'estella precedent,
Vengren al vostre·bitage,
Offerint-vos de gradatge
Aur et mirre et encenç.
Ave Maria, gracia plena,
Dominus tecum, Virgo serena.

V Verge: [e]stant dolorosa
Per la mort del Fill molt car,
Romangués tota joyosa
Can lo vis resuscitar;

* "Els cants en vulgar del *Llibre Vermell* de Montserrat," pp. 41–44.

A vós, mare piadosa,
Primer se volch demostrar.
Ave Maria, gracia plena,
Dominus tecum, Virgo serena.

VI Verge: lo quint alegrage
Que·n agués del Fill molt car,
Estant al Munt d'Olivatge,
Al cell lo·n vehés puyar,
On aurem tots alegratge,
Si per nós vos plau pregar.
Ave Maria, gracia plena,
Dominus tecum, Virgo serena.

VII Verge: quan foren complitz
Los dies de Pentacosta,
Ab vós eren aünits
Los apòstols, et decosta,
Sobre tots, sens nuylla costa,
Devallà l'Espirit Sant.
Ave Maria, gracia plena,
Dominus tecum, Virgo serena.

VIII Verge: ·l derrer alegratge
Que·n agues en aquest món,
Vostre Fill ab gran coratge
Vos muntà al cel pregon,
On sóts tots temps coronada
Regina perpetual.
Ave Maria, gracia plena,
Dominus tecum, Virgo serena.

IX Tots, donques, nos esforcem,
En aquesta present vida,
Que peccats foragitem
De nostr' anima mesquina,
E vós, dolçe Verge pia,
Vullats-nos-ho empetrar.
Ave Maria, gracia plena,
Dominus tecum, Virgo serena.

Polysyllabic words are marked with a ˈ before the accented syllable, and a ˈˈ before the secondary stressed syllable.

I Los ˈsɛd ˈgɔdʒ rrəˈˈkomtəˈr̩ɛm
e dəˈˈvɔtəˈmen kənˈtan
ˈˈumilˈmɛn səˈludˈˈəˈr̩ɛm

lə ˈdolsə ˈvɛṛʒə məˈṛi·ə
. . .
. . .

II
. . .

III ˈvɛṛʒə ˈfoz əˈnanz dəl ˈpaṛt
ˈpuṛə e ˈsens fəλiˈmen
ən lo ˈpaṛt e ˈpṛez lo ˈpaṛt
ˈsens nəˈγuŋ koˈˈrrumpiˈmen
lo ˈfiλ də ˈdeuz ˈvɛṛʒə ˈpi·ə
də voz nəsˈke vəṛəˈmen

IV ˈvɛṛʒə ˈtṛɛz ˈrreiz doṛi·ˈen
kəvəlˈkan əb ˈgraŋ koˈṛadʒə
əb ləˈsteλə pṛəsəˈden
ˈveŋgṛən əl ˈvɔstṛə biˈtadʒə
ofəˈṛin voz də gṛəˈdadʒə
ˈəuṛ e ˈmirrə e ənˈsɛns

V ˈvɛṛʒə əsˈtan doloˈṛozə
pəṛ lə ˈmɔṛt dɔl ˈfiλ ˈmol ˈkaṛ
rromənˈges ˈtotə ʒoˈjozə
ˈkan lo ˈviz rrəˈˈsussiˈtaṛ
ə voz ˈmaṛə pi·əˈḓozə
pṛiˈmeṛ sə ˈvɔlg dəmosˈtṛaṛ

VI ˈvɛṛʒə lo ˈkint ələˈgṛadʒə
kən əˈγez dəl ˈfiλ ˈmol ˈkaṛ
əsˈtan əl ˈmunt doliˈvadʒə
əl ˈsɛl lon və·ˈes puˈʒaṛ
on əuˈṛɛm ˈtodz ələˈgṛadʒə
si pəṛ noz vos ˈplau pṛəˈγaṛ

VII ˈvɛṛʒə ˈkwan ˈfoṛəŋ komˈplits
loz ˈdi·əz də pəntəˈkɔstə
əb voz ˈeṛən ə·uˈnits
loz əˈpɔstols e dəˈkɔstə
ˈsobṛə ˈtots ˈsens ˈnuλə ˈkɔstə
dəvəˈλa ləspiˈṛit ˈsan

VIII ˈvɛṛʒəl dəˈrreṛ ələˈgṛadʒə
kən əˈγez ən əˈkɛst ˈmon
ˈvɔstṛə ˈfiλ əb ˈgṛaŋ koˈṛadʒə
voz munˈta əl ˈsɛl pṛəˈγǫŋ
on ˈsots ˈtots ˈtems koṛoˈnadə
rrəˈʒinə pəṛpətu·ˈal

IX ˈtodz ˈdoŋkəz noz əsforˈsɛm
ən əˈkɛstə prəˈzen ˈvidə
kə pəˈkats fɔrəʒiˈtɛm
də ˈnɔsˈtr animə məsˈkinə
e voz ˈdolsə ˈvɛrʒə ˈpi·ə
vuˈʎatznozo* əmpəˈtrar

Soleta y verge estich

A sixteenth-century text attributed to Càrceres, who is believed to have been a Valencian composer in the service of the Duke of Calabria. Barcelona, Bibioteca de Catalunya, Ms. 1166, fols. 10v–13. I have used the edition by Miguel Querol,** which is faithful to the spellings of the manuscript with the addition of accents as required by modern usage. The phonetic transcription is in Classical Valencian, as described above, not the sub-dialectal "apixat" speech also heard in Valencia. CD #29.

Soleta y verge estich,
si m voleu veure parir.
Ara que n'és hora,
si voleu venir.

Soleta en esta nit,
só verge y mare
parint Déu infinit,
y, sent ell lo meu pare,
tanbé vostre, e yo mare
que glòria us dó sense fi.
Ara que n'es hora,
si voleu venir.

O, com se alegraven
de tal nova oyr
los pares que esperaven
de les tenebres exir!
La missa volen dir
de la sol, fa, re, mi.
Ara que n'és hora,
si voleu venir.

Cantem tots en est dia
molt devotament,
lloant la verge Maria

* The pronunciation of *o* in the pronouns *nos* and *ho* in *vullats-nos-ho* was probably already very closed and may have approximated [vuʎatznuzu].
** *Cançoner català dels segles XVI–XVII,* p. 13.

y son fill omnipotent,
que.ns dó tal sentiment
que.ns porte a bona fi.
Ara [que n'és hora,
si voleu venir].

soˈleta i ˈvɛṛʒe esˈtik
sim voˈleu ˈveuṛe paˈṛiṛ
ˈaṛa ke ˈnez ˈɔṛa
si voˈleu veˈniṛ

soˈleta en ˈesta ˈnit
ˈso ˈvɛṛʒe i ˈmaṛe
paˈṛint ˈdeu infiˈnit
i ˈsent eλ lo meu ˈpaṛe
tamˈbe ˈvɔstṛe e ˈjo ˈmaṛe
ke ˈglɔṛi·a uz ˈdo ˈsense ˈfi
ˈaṛa ke ˈnez ˈɔṛa
si voˈleu veˈniṛ

ˈo ˈkɔm se aleˈgṛaven
de ˈtal ˈnɔva o·ˈiṛ
los ˈpaṛes ke espeˈṛaven
de les teˈnebṛez eˈʃiṛ
la ˈmisa voˈlen ˈdiṛ
de la ˈsɔl ˈfa ˈrrɛ ˈmi
ˈaṛa ke ˈnez ˈɔṛa
si voˈleu veˈniṛ

kanˈtem ˈtodz en ˈest ˈdi·a
ˈmolt deˈˈvɔtaˈment
λo·ˈant la ˈvɛṛʒe maˈṛi·a
i son ˈfiλ omˈˈnipoˈtent
kens ˈdo ˈtal sentiˈment
kens ˈpoṛte a ˈbɔna ˈfi
ˈaṛa ke ˈnez ˈɔṛa
si voˈleu veˈniṛ

From *Cant de la Sibil·la*

The texts are those provided by Anglès,* presented as they appear in the manuscripts, without accents and without regularizing *i, j,* and *y.* In order to point up some of the major dialectal differences, I have juxtaposed three texts: a fourteenth-century text from Palma de Mallorca (*Cantorale,* s.xiv), a sixteenth-century text from the eastern linguistic

* *La música a Catalunya fins al segle XIII,* p. 301.

zone (*Ordinarium Barcinonense* of 1569, fol. 285v), and a sixteenth-century text from the western linguistic zone (*Ordinarium Urgellinum* of 1548, fol. 180v). CD #30.

Palma	Al jorn del judici parra qui haura fet servici
Barcelona	Al iorn del iudici parra qui haura fet servici
Urgell	Al iorn del iudici parra qui aura fet servici
Palma	Un rey vindra perpetual
Barcelona	Un rey vindra perpetual
Urgell	Un rey vindra perpetual
Palma	Vestit de nostra carn mortal
Barcelona	Vestit de nostra carn mortal
Urgell	Vestit de nostra carn mortal
Palma	Del cel vindra tot certament
Barcelona	Del cel vindra tot certament
Urgell	Del cel vindra tot certament
Palma	Per fer del setgle jutjament
Barcelona	Per fer de tots lo jutjament
Urgell	Per fer del setgle jutjament

əl ˈʒoṛn dəl ʒuˈd̯isi pəˈrra ki əuˈṛa ˈfet səṛˈvisi
əl ˈʒoṛn dəl ʒuˈd̯isi pəˈrra ki əuˈṛa ˈfet səṛˈβisi
al ˈʒorn del ʒuˈd̯isi paˈrra ki auˈṛa ˈfet seṛˈβisi

un ˈrrei vinˈdṛa pərpətu·ˈal
un ˈrrei βinˈdṛa pərpətu·ˈal
un ˈrrei βinˈdṛa perpetu·ˈal

vəsˈtit də ˈnɔstrə ˈkaṛn morˈtal
bəsˈtit də ˈnɔstrə ˈkaṛn murˈtal
besˈtit de ˈnɔstra ˈkaṛn morˈtal

dəl ˈsɛl vinˈdṛa ˈtot ˈˈsɛṛtəˈment
dəl ˈsɛl βinˈdra ˈtot ˈˈsɛṛtəˈmen
del ˈsɛl βinˈdra ˈtot ˈˈsɛṛtaˈmen

pəṛ ˈfeṛ dəl ˈsegglə ʒudʒəˈment
pəṛ ˈfe də ˈtodz lu ʒudʒəˈmen
peṛ ˈfe del ˈseggle ʒudʒaˈmen

9

Spanish (Castilian)

JAMES F. BURKE

With the exception of a small area next to the Pyrenees Mountains in the north, where Basque (which is not an Indo-European language) is spoken, the entire Iberian Peninsula since Roman times has used dialects of Latin. Muslim conquerors crossed the Strait of Gibraltar in A.D. 711 and rapidly overran almost all of what had been Roman Hispania. Small nuclei of Christians managed to maintain their independence in tiny protected pockets in the Pyrenees and in the Cantabrian Mountains. Within a few years after the Muslims' arrival, the Christians were able to initiate wars of Reconquest, which continued until the end of the fifteenth century.

During this exercise of Reconquest there evolved five distinct military and political entities, which slowly extended themselves southward throughout the Middle Ages. This movement resulted in five different dialects of Hispano-Romance, all related to one another to some degree. From east to west they were Catalan, Aragonese, Castilian, Leonese, and Galician-Portuguese.

A sixth language entity, Mozarabic, also existed in Iberia in the Middle Ages and survived in one form or another until the sixteenth century. In very simplified terms, it was a Romance dialect that developed among Christians living under Muslim rule. The earliest literary writings in a Romance dialect from the Peninsula are the *xarchas* (also spelled *jarchas* and *kharjas*). They are the final lines of a long poem, known as the *muwashshahat,* composed in either Arabic or Hebrew. The last lines were written in Mozarabic instead of the language of the body of the poem. The rules for the pronunciation of Spanish from the earliest period also serve for Mozarabic and for these brief poems.

Because of historical and political developments, Castilian has become the national tongue of Spain. It is an important international language, which is now spoken by more than three hundred million people beyond the borders of the mother country. Often referred to as "Spanish," Castilian had its origins around the headwaters of the Ebro River, probably in the ninth century. This region is very close to areas in which Basque is spoken, and the influence of that language may explain some of the exotic characteristics of Castilian. By the time of Alfonso X, called the Wise (1252–1284), Castilian had become the most important dialect in the central portion of the Peninsula. The language of the first significant work in Castilian, the *Poem of the Cid* (ca. 1207), is very similar to that of modern Spanish, doubtless because intellectual developments during Alfonso's reign had a stabilizing effect on linguistic forms and usages.

The Renaissance in Spain arrived at the end of the fifteenth century and merged imperceptibly into the era of the Golden Age, the highest period of cultural achievement Spain has ever known. An important cycle of changes in the language began near the end of the fifteenth century and continued until almost the end of the Golden Age, around 1700.

There are no comprehensive commentaries on pronunciation of medieval or Renaissance Castilian and very few references to the subject in early texts. After the advent of printing, a number of grammars and studies of the language were produced that analyzed its structure from the perspective of the period, but none of them treated pronunciation in a systematic manner. However, philologists, by using a wide variety of tools and sources, have been able to determine very effectively the characteristics of oral usage as it has varied across the centuries.

Bibliography

R.S. Boggs. *Tentative Dictionary of Medieval Spanish.* Chapel Hill, N.C.: n. p., 1946.
Collins Spanish-English English-Spanish Dictionary. Ed. Colin Smith. London and Glasgow: 1971. (Any edition may be used.)
J. Corominas. *Diccionario crítico etimológico de la lengua castellana.* 4 vols. Madrid: Gredos, 1956.
A.D. Deyermond. *A Literary History of Spain: The Middle Ages.* London: Ernest Benn, 1971.
William J. Entwistle. *The Spanish Language together with Portuguese, Catalan and Basque.* London: Faber & Faber, 1936.
Rafael Lapesa. *Historia de la lengua española.* 8th ed. Madrid: Gredos, 1980.
Yakov Malkiel. "Spanish Language." In *Dictionary of the Middle Ages,* vol. 11, pp. 390–405.
Tomás Navarro Tomás. *Manual de pronunciación española.* New York: Hafner Publishing Company, 1957.
Robert K. Spaulding. *How Spanish Grew.* Berkeley and Los Angeles: University of California Press, 1943.
Vox inglés-español español-inglés. 4th ed. Barcelona: Bibliograf, 1980. (Any edition may be used.)
Edwin B. Williams. *Dictionary Spanish & English.* New York: Holt, Rinehart and Winston, 1963.

Spelling

Orthography in medieval and Renaissance Spanish is reasonably regular and remarkably similar to that of the modern language with, of course, some major exceptions.

The principal problems are the interchange of the consonants *b* and *v* and the occasional use of the vowel *u* for either of them: *abia/avia/auia.* The consonant *q* is sometimes used for what would be a *c* in the modern language: *quando/cuando.* A *y* may on occasion be substituted for the vowel *i: veynte/veinte.* Between 1300 and 1500 the consonants *f* and *h* had a very similar sound in certain words and were interchanged:

fasta/hasta. Sometimes the initial consonant *f* or *h* was omitted altogether (e.g., *asta*), indicating that for the scribe the sound had vanished, as was eventually the case in modern Spanish. For further information on this subject see the discussion of individual vowels and consonants below.

Rhyming

Rhyme in medieval and Renaissance Castilian is of two types, assonant and consonant. Consonant rhyme is what we normally have in English. Because of the relatively pure nature of the vowels in Spanish, it is simple to see when such rhyme occurs. Comparable combinations of consonant plus vowel will rhyme in Spanish.

Assonant rhyme in the medieval language normally depended on the occurrence of the same last accented vowel plus the same final unaccented vowel through a number of lines. The pattern can be seen in the opening stanza from the *Poem of the Cid,* where the assonance is in *á–o.* The italicized syllables carry the assonance.

De los sos ojos tan fuertemientre llor*ando,*
tornava la cabeça e estávalos cat*ando:*
vio puertas abiertas e uços sin cañ*ados.*
Alcándaras vazías, sin pielles e sin m*antos*
e sin falcones e sin adtores mud*ados.*

With tears streaming from his eyes, he turned his head and looked at them. He saw open doors and unlocked gates, empty pegs without coverings or cloaks, perches without falcons or molted hawks.

Such epic lines were undoubtedly sung or chanted in performance, but unfortunately we have no music showing how that was done. We do possess a great deal of notation for the *romances,* or ballads, the earliest examples of which are from the fourteenth century. Previously unknown *romances,* often suspected to be hundreds of years old, are still being gathered today. Although there must have been some relation between the epic and the *romance,* there is considerable disagreement as to what it might have been.

Each line of an epic consisted of about sixteen syllables and had a relation of assonance with every other line in its group. In the *romance* one finds lines of eight syllables, resulting in assonance in alternate lines. Some scholars believe that the *romance* resulted from dividing the epic line in half. The following example from the famous *romance* "El Prisionero" demonstrates this point:

Por el mes era de mayo
cuando hace la ca*lor,*
cuando canta la calandria
y responde el ruise*ñor,*
cuando los enamorados
van a servir el a*mor,*
sino yo triste, cuitado,
que vivo en esta pri*sión,*
que ni sé cuándo es de día,
ni cuando las noches *son.* . . .

It was in the month of May/ when it is hot/ when the lark sings/ and the nightingale answers/ when lovers go out in the service of love/ but I, sad, unfortunate,/ who live in this prison,/ do not know when it is day/ nor when it is night. . . .

Here the assonance is in *ó* without a final syllable. In the first three examples—*calor, ruiseñor, amor*—there is also consonant rhyme. This enhances the poetic effect, but the next words, *prisión* and *son,* show that we are really dealing with assonance, where the important point is again the *ó.*

Stress and Accent

Medieval Spanish placed a strong stress on one of the vowels in a word but such an accent did not diminish the clarity and quality of the unaccented vowels. The rules for syllabification in order to determine accentuation in modern Spanish are quite simple and also serve for the medieval and Renaissance language:

1. If a word ends in a vowel, [n], or [s], the accent falls naturally on the penultimate syllable. In *libro* the accent is on *i.*

2. If a word ends with any other consonant, the accent falls on the last syllable. In *amor* the accent is on *o.*

3. Any deviation from such a rule requires the placing of a written acute accent over the accented syllable: thus *eléboro,* showing that the accent falls on the second *e,* not on the penultimate vowel, as would be expected since the word ends in a vowel.

4. The vowels [a], [e], and [o] are considered strong and do not form diphthongs with each other: *a·e·ro·bio.* They each combine with [u] and [i] to form diphthongs, and [u] and [i] combine to create a diphthong: *ai·re, rui·do·so.* The strong vowel normally carries the accent, so if the weak vowel of a diphthong is the one to be accented, it must be marked, as in María.

5. The first syllable in a Spanish word consists of the first vowel and any preceding consonant, for example: *e·lé·bo·ro.* When a vowel is preceded by [b], [c], [d], [f], [g], [p], or [t] plus [r] or [l], such a combination is called a "group." The vowel and this "group" form one syllable: *blan·co.*

The second and subsequent vowels in a word are dealt with in the same manner as the first one. A diphthong counts as one syllable: *rui·do.* The final consonant in a word forms part of the preceding syllable. All combinations of consonants within a word, save those that form a "group," divide, the first going with the preceding syllable and the second with the next syllable; for example: *er·va·je, fi·li·gra·na.*

A well-edited text from the medieval or Renaissance period should have accent marks placed according to the modern system. If they are lacking or if one has suspicions concerning the accents that are present in a text, a good modern Spanish dictionary can be consulted.

Consonants

In many cases the pronunciation of consonants in medieval Spanish approximates that of their English equivalents, but because many individuals have studied modern Spanish, it is essential to indicate where medieval or Renaissance practice differs from the modern. Sibilants present a special problem in medieval and Renaissance Spanish and are dealt with in a special summary section below.

There are a number of allophones in Spanish, phonemes that are altered by the circumstances around them. Such an alteration occurs naturally and does not concern the student. For example, the *n* in *donde* takes on the dental characteristics of the adjacent *d,* thus differing from the normal phoneme [n], which is very similar to the one in English.

b [b] is bilabial and occlusive, that is, the lips are completely closed. Between vowels, *b* became fricative at the end of the Middle Ages, that is, the lips no longer close tightly, and air passes between them to produce [β]. Initial *b* also becomes fricative if it follows a word that ends in a vowel; e.g., *Es una boba* [e:s u:nɑ: βo:βɑ:].

c Pronounced [k] before *a, o,* and *u,* with a hard articulation, as in *cat;* e.g., *conquistan* [kɔ:nki:stɑ:n].

c Pronounced [ts] before *e* and *i.* See "Sibilants" below.

ch Pronounced [tʃ] as in English *cheese;* e.g., *chico* [tʃi:ko:].

d [d]. In the medieval period this consonant was an occlusive in all positions, similar to the *d* in English. At the end of the Middle Ages it became fricative between vowels: [d̪]. At the end of a word it becomes equivalent to *th* in *then;* e.g., *ciudad* [θju:d̪ɑ:ð]. As with *b,* an initial *d* following a vowel in the preceding word becomes fricative; e.g., *Menga la del Bustar* [me:ŋgɑ: lɑ: d̪e:l bu:st:ɑ:r].

f [h]. In the early period, in initial position before a vowel this consonant had an aspirated pronunciation originating in the pharynx. A harsh articulation of the *h* in *have* gives a rough equivalent; e.g., *forro* [ho:rro:]. By the fifteenth century it has become silent and may be found written as *h;* e.g., *horro.* In the interior of words and in ones of learned origin the voiceless, labio-dental articulation we know in English obtained [f]; e.g., *falsa, familia, fe (faith), feo (ugly), infinito (infinite).*

g Pronounced [g] before *a, o,* and *u,* and was given a "hard" enunciation similar to that of the *g* in *gate,* e.g, *gato* [gɑ:to:]. At the end of the Middle Ages this sound also became fricative between vowels: [g̪].
Pronounced [ʒ] before *e* and *i*—a sibilant, see below.

h Originally had practically the same pronunciation as the *f* described above, and the two are sometimes confused orthographically in the earlier periods. Between 1475 and 1525 this consonant became silent in Old Castile, the area north of the mountains immediately above Madrid. The change then slowly spread southward and was eventually accepted in Latin America also. One would not pronounce the *h* in texts from northern Spain from the sixteenth century but might do so for works from Andalucía or Latin America from the same period.

j Before *a, o,* and *u* pronounced [ʒ], equivalent to *ge, gi* in the lists of sibilants below; e.g., *junta* [ʒu:ntɑ:]. In the Middle Ages this phoneme was occasionally written as *i,* as in *consejo* or *conseio; oreja* or *oreia.*

k [k] is almost non-existent in medieval Spanish save for a few words of foreign origin, such as *kyrie.* The number of such words increases in the Renaissance and later. Pronounced like the *c* in English *cat.*

l Pronounced [l] as in English *lip.*

ll In early Spanish, this was probably pronounced [λ], like the modern Spanish voiced palatal lateral—a sound similar to the *lli* in English *colliery.* Occasionally in the earlier periods it was written as a single *l.* A modern dictionary of Spanish would show whether the letter concerned was *l* or *ll;* e.g., *lleno* [λe:no:]. In the late fifteenth century in many areas this consonant began to be pronounced [j]. These two pronunciations are now intermixed across the Spanish-speaking world. For texts later than the late fifteenth century, the second pronunciation is acceptable for works from all areas.

In Argentina and Uruguay, in the region along the River Plate (Río de la Plata), at the end of the eighteenth century, *ll* took on a pronunciation roughly equivalent to the old sound of *ge, gi,* and *j:* [ʒ] as in modern French *je.*

m Pronounced [m] as in English *month.*

n Pronounced [n] as in English *night.*

ñ Pronounced ɲ as in modern Spanish *señor* and English *onion.*

n [ŋ] a velar *n,* an allophone, which occurs naturally whenever an *n* occurs before a velar consonant such as a *k;* e.g., *cinco* [θi:ŋko:].

p Pronounced [p] as in English *pit.*

q Pronounced [k] as in modern Spanish; e.g. *porque* [po:ɾke:]. It is always followed by the vowel *u,* which is silent. The Old Spanish spelling *qu* (as in *quando*) is sometimes adjusted to *cu,* as in the modern language: *cuando.*

r Pronounced [ɾ] as in modern Spanish, a simple vibrant or trill, with one flip of the tip of the tongue; e.g., *quiero* [kje:ɾo:].

rr Pronounced [rr] as in modern Spanish, strongly vibrated or trilled; e.g., *carro* [kɑ:rro:].

s A sibilant, pronounced [z] as in English *zipper* in the medieval period—see the discussion of sibilants below for change. This phoneme disappears before the multiple [rr].

ss Pronounced [s] as in English *silly.* This phoneme disappears before [rr]. There is no double *s* in modern Spanish orthography.

t Pronounced [t] as in English *tip.*

v Pronounced [v] in the earlier language, as in English *vine.* Very early in the north of Spain this labio-dental began to be confused with [b], and the confusion spread to the center and south by the second half of the sixteenth century. It also becomes the fricative [β] between vowels: *cava* [kɑ:βɑ:]. As with *b* and *d,* initial *v* becomes fricative when it follows a word that ends in a vowel; e.g., *Que yo nunca vy serrana* [ke: jo: nu:ŋkɑ: βi: se:rrɑ:nɑ:]. It is sometimes found written as *u.* The sound [u] between vowels is unusual in Spanish except in some Amerindian words. Most well-edited texts resolve such a *u* to [v]; a modern dictionary can help in case of doubt.

x In the early language *x* is pronounced [ʃ] as in English *ship;* e.g., *dexar* [de:ʃɑ:r]. It is found in words of a learned origin, particularly in the Renaissance and later, pronounced [ks] or [gz], as in English *exam* or Spanish *examen.* Note also *ecelente* [e:kse:le:nte:], *asfisia* [ɑ:sfi:gsjɑ:], where the same pronunciation obtains.

y Equivalent to modern English *y* [j] but is sometimes used orthographically for *i* in words such as *soy, estoy, voy.* In the area along the River Plate (Río de la Plata) in South America after about 1750 this phoneme took on the pronunciation described for *ll* above, that of the *j* in modern French *je.*

z The sibilant [dz] as in English re*d z*ipper. (See "sibilants," below.)

A voiceless consonant at the end of a word changes to its voiced equivalent when the next word has an initial voiced consonant; e.g., *Quando mas descanso da* [kwɑ:ndo: mɑ:z de:skɑ:nso: d̪ɑ:].

Vowels

Medieval Spanish had five basic vowels, which were pronounced as in the modern language, in a more clipped and closed manner than their English equivalent. Care should be taken to permit no diphthongization of the vowel at all:

a [ɑ:] as in *father*
e [e:] as in *date*
i [i:] as in *eat*
o [o:] as in *go*
u [u:] as in *moot*

There are variations in vowel quality in Spanish, but they occur naturally because of context. For example, the [i:] in *mira* [mi:ɾɑ:] has the extremely closed enunciation characteristic of the language. The [i:] in *mirra* [mɪrrɑ:] is open—roughly equivalent to the vowel of English *veer*—because the adjacent *rr* causes the buccal cavity to expand.

The semi-consonant *i* [j] and the semi-consonant *u* [w], which occur in diphthong combinations in such words as *bien* and *fuente,* are not problematic because the timbre of the adjacent strong vowel (in these cases *e*) automatically diminishes the force of the following semi-vowel or semi-consonant. The semi-vowel *i* as in *aire* and *u* as in *caudal* are transcribed in the texts as pure vowels since they are close enough to pass for such, particularly in singing.

In adjacent words, a vowel at the end of one word always elides with any vowel at the beginning of the next one unless a definite pause is indicated, for example, by a comma. The result is a kind of diphthong. Note the elisions in the phrase *De‿Antequera sale‿un moro, de‿Antequera‿aquessa villa.*

Development and Changes in the Language

The language of a people will often experience noticeable phonetic and morphological evolution when the group undergoes periods of great political, social, and cultural transformation and upheaval. Toward the end of the fifteenth century in Spain, the kingdoms of Aragón-Catalunya and Castile were united by the marriage of Ferdinand

and Isabella. In 1492 Granada was recaptured from the Muslims, ending the long period of Islamic involvement in the Peninsula. In the same year the two monarchs decided to expel all practicing Jews from the joint kingdom, an action that adversely affected the economics and culture of the country. Columbus reached the New World in 1492, and almost immediately the energies of the Castilian-Andalusian portion of the realm were devoted to exploration and conquest in the Americas.

The late fifteenth century was also a time of significant cultural activity in the Spanish-speaking areas of the Peninsula. In 1499 the great literary masterpiece *Celestina* was published, the first in a series of fine works from the Spanish Renaissance and Golden Age. In architecture the ornate plateresque style produced numerous interesting examples. Painting as an art form attained new brilliance in the representations of El Greco and Velázquez. Spanish music from this period has not received the notice accorded to that of Italy, France, England, and a bit later Germany, but few would question its quality.

Around the middle of the fifteenth century, just before the beginning of this great epoch of cultural, social, and economic ferment, the Spanish language began to undergo a series of changes. They accelerated toward the end of the century, when so many other developments were taking place, and a period of flux in the language continued until the end of the seventeenth century. Early in the eighteenth century, with the establishment of the Royal Academy of the Language by the new Bourbon dynasty, Spanish was fixed and regularized in the form it retains to the present.

The most important and problematic group of phonemes during this period of evolution are the sibilants, which underwent extensive modification before stasis was achieved. One system operated in the Middle Ages, until about 1450. After this two important shifts occurred, one after the other, which produced the sound system of modern Spanish. In the medieval period, one group of six sibilants divided into three pairs, each comprising a voiced and a voiceless form:

-s- was voiced [z], equivalent to *z* in English *zipper;* e.g., *casa* [kɑ:zɑ:].

-ss- was voiceless [s], equivalent to *s* in English *save;* e.g., *priessa* [prje:sɑ:].

-ge, gi, and *j* (before *a, o,* and *u*) were the voiced, prepalatal fricative [ʒ] roughly equivalent to modern English *s* in *leisure* or French *j* in *je;* e.g., [mu:ʒe:ɽ], *inojos* [i:no:ʒo:s].

-x- was the voiceless, prepalatal fricative [ʃ] roughly equivalent to *sh* in English *ship;* e.g., *dixo* [di:ʃo:].

-z- was the voiced, dental, affricative [dz]. This sound is roughly equivalent to that in English produced by the *-d-* and the *-z-* when the words *red zipper* are pronounced rapidly; e.g., *dezir* [de:dzi:ɽ].

-ce, ci, ç was the voiceless, dental, affricative [ts], which corresponds to some degree to the one produced in English by the *-t-* and *-s-* when the words *cat soup* are pronounced rapidly; e.g., *recibio* [rre:tsi:βjo:], *esforçad* [e:sfo:ɽtsɑ:ð].

About the year 1450 the three voiced phonemes [z], [ʒ], and [dz] begin to merge with their voiceless counterparts so that by 1620 only the voiceless forms [s], [ʃ], and [ts] remained. In the early sixteenth century a second series of sound shifts began, resulting in the pronunciation common to standard modern Spanish. Pronunciation of words in texts before the standardization of Spanish is problematic because for about a century and a half the two processes were mixed both geographically and temporally.

In the second series of permutations two changes are of particular importance. The first occurred in Spain only to the north of the Sierra Morena Mountains (a line of hills some twenty-five miles above Seville running from the Portuguese border eastward toward the Mediterranean). The voiceless dental affricative which remained after the absorption of its voiced twin (re*d* *z*ipper is gone, leaving only ca*t* *s*oup) and which was now represented by orthographic *ce, ci, ç,* and *z,* began to move toward an interdental articulation roughly equivalent to that of English *th* [θ]. By the end of the seventeenth century this change was complete.

It is important to note, however, that to the south of the Sierra Morena, the phoneme lost only its affricative qualities and became a sound produced on the alveolar ridge (the line of skin just above the teeth) roughly equivalent to English [s]. This pronunciation also took root in Latin America. Thus in rendering a song from the late Golden Age (after 1625), it is important to know whether it originated north of the Sierra Morena in Castile or La Mancha, or in the south in Andalusia, or in Latin America.

The voiceless prepalatal fricative [ʃ] (pronounced *sh*) had started to absorb its voiced counterpart about 1450. The point of articulation of this phoneme slowly moved toward the rear of the roof of the mouth eventually attaining a velar position; this change was completed by the end of the first third of the seventeenth century. It is the modern Spanish pronunciation in all areas of *ge, gi,* and *j,* and it is roughly equivalent to a very strong ejaculation of an English [h]. England took the name of one of her favorite wines from Spanish before this change was effected, and thus it is that we say *sherry* instead of *harry.* The city after which this ambrosia is called is Jerez, and the initial *j* is now equivalent to an explosively and harshly rendered *h* in English.

Because of the overlapping and intermingling of older and newer uses in different Spanish-speaking areas of Spain and, after 1500, in the New World, the correct pronunciation of sibilants is difficult to ascertain until the end of the seventeenth century. To determine the pronunciation for a particular piece, find out its provenance and probable date, and consult reference works to see what developments had occurred in regard to each of the sibilants in the geographical area and period.

To simplify matters, observe the medieval system until about 1475, the second structure (the merger of the voiced sibilants with their unvoiced counterparts) until about 1650, and the modern system thereafter.

The rules given above serve for all Spanish-speaking areas in regard to a specific time period as long as the problems listed for the sibilants are taken into consideration. Thus pronunciation of the words of a song from Barcelona written in Spanish in 1600 should be roughly equivalent to that of a song from Madrid or Valladolid or Toledo. (Barcelona is of course in a Catalan-speaking area, but Spanish was also used there from the early sixteenth century onward.) For a song from Seville or Mexico City of the same date, one would have to take into account the differences in the pronunciation of certain sibilants as indicated above.

DIACHRONIC SOUND CHART FOR SPANISH

The pronunciation of vowels in Spanish remains roughly the same during this entire period save for some allophonic variation that occurs naturally in the context of certain consonants.

	1100 1200 1300 1400 1500 1600 1700
b	[b] (initial) --
	[β] between vowels --------
c	[k] before *a, o, u* --
	Sibilant before *e, i* [ts] -------------------------- [θ]-north ------
	-------------------------- [s]-south ------
ch	[tʃ] --
d	[d] (initial) --
	[d̪] between vowels --------
	[ð] at end of words -------
f	[h] (initial) ------------------ [disappears] --------------------
f	[f] appears in learned words --------------------------
g	[g] before *a, o, u* (initial) --
	[g̪] between vowels --------
g	sibilant before *e, i* [ʒ] ---------------- [x] --------- [h] ------------
	transition over a period of 100 years
h	[h] ------------------------ [disappears] --------------------
j	before *a, o, u* is equivalent to *ge, gi* ------------------------------
k	[k] --
l	[l] --
ll	[λ] --
	[j] in many areas -----------------
	passes to [ʒ] along River Plate after 1750
m	[m] --
n	[n] --
ñ	[ɲ] --
p	[p] --
q	(followed by *u*) [k] --
r	[r̝] --
rr	[rr] --
s	[z] ----------------------------- [s] ---------------------
ss	[s] --
	begins to be written as single *s* after 1700
t	[t] --
v	[v] ---------------- (north) [b] ------------------------------
	------------------------------------ (south) [b] --------------
	see *b* above when intervocalic
x	[ʃ] -- [h] ----------
	transition over a period of 100 years
y	[j] --
	passes to [ʒ] along River Plate after 1750
z	[dz] ----------------------------- [ts] ---------- [θ]-north ------
	-------- [s]-south ------

SAMPLE TEXTS

Transcriptions of the texts are done according to the rules of pronunciation which obtained during the middle period—1475–1650. Sibilants are transcribed as follows:

s or *ss* as [s], equivalent to *s* in English *save.*
ge, gi, x, and *j* (before *a, o, u*) as [ʃ], equivalent to *sh* in English *ship.*
z, ce, ci, and *ç* as [ts], equivalent to ca*t s*oup.

An orthographic *v* should be pronounced [b] or [β], depending on its position in the word or phrase, in a text from the area north of Madrid later than 1300. It should be pronounced in the same manner in any text dating after 1550 from the area south of Madrid. If one is unsure concerning the date and origin of the text, the modern Spanish pronunciation [b] or [β] may be used.

Menga, la del Bustar

Late fifteenth century. Madrid, Bibl. del Palacio Real, 2–1–5, fol. 210v–211. CD #31.

Menga, la del Bustar
Que yo nunca vy serrana
De tan bonico baylar.

Yo me iva, a la mi madre
A Santa María del Pino;
Vi andar una serrana
Bien acerca del camino;

Saya traya pretada
De un verde florentino,
Bien allá la viera andar
Gurriando su ganado
Y diziendo este cantar.

I hablava i dezia:
-Domingo, ¿por qué no vienes,
Pues que saltas bien y corres,
En la lucha bien te tienes?
Contigo me quiero andar
Gurriando este ganado
I diziendo este cantar.-

Tanto bien me pareçiera,
Que de amores la fui ablar.
¿Mi amor queréis que os diga
Quien a mi haze penar?
Grande amor que a mi fatiga
De Miguel del Colmenar.
Que me oyó este cantar.

me:ŋga: la: d̪e:l bu:sta:ṛ
ke: jo: nu:ŋka: βi: se:rra:na:
d̪e: ta:n bo:ni:ko: βa:i:la:ṛ

jo: me: i:βa: a: la: mi: ma:dṛe:
a: santa: ma:ṛˈi:a: d̪e:l pi:no:
bi: a:nda:ṛ u:na: se:rr:a:na:
bje:n a:tse:ṛka: d̪e:l ka:mi:no:

sa:ja: tṛa:ˈi:a: pṛe:ta:d̪a:
d̪e: u:n be:ṛde: flo:ṛe:nti:no:
bje:n a:λˈα: la: βje:ṛa: a:nda:ṛ
gu:rrja:ndo: su: g̪a:na:d̪o:
i: d̪i:tsje:ndo: e:ste: ka:nta:ṛ

i: a:bla:βa: i: d̪e:tsˈi:a:
do:mi:ŋgo: po:ṛkˈe: no: bje:ne:s
pwe:s ke: sa:lta:z bje:n i: ko:rre:s
e:n la: lu:tʃa: bje:n te: tje:ne:s
ko:nti:g̪o: me: kje:ro: a:nda:ṛ
gu:rrja:ndo: e:ste: g̪a:na:d̪o:
i: d̪i:tsje:ndo: e:ste: ka:nta:ṛ

ta:nto: bje:n me: pa:ṛe:tsje:ṛa:
ke: d̪e: a:mo:ṛe:z la: fwi: a:bla:ṛ
mi: a:mo:ṛ ke:ṛˈe:i:s ke: o:z di:g̪a:
kjˈe:n a: mˈi: a:tse: pe:na:ṛ
gra:nde: a:mo:ṛ ke: a: mi: fa:ti:g̪a:
d̪e: mi:g̪e:l de:l ko:lme:na:ṛ
ke: me: o:jˈo: e:ste: ka:nta:ṛ

Otro bien si a vos no tengo

Early sixteenth century. Madrid, Bibl. del Palacio Real, 2–1–5, fol. 258v. CD #32.

Otro bien si a vos no tengo,
Y la noche se me irá,
¡Ay Dios! ¿quién la dormirá?

La bien andança que tengo
Tal bida la dexará
Que otras muchas llorará.

Gozando del galardón
Que gané con mil enojos,
¿Cómo dormirán los ojos
Pues que vela el coraçón?

Que si muestro yo dolores
Ante vuestra perfeción,
Es porque saben d'amores
Pocos on*bres lo que son;
Es una gloria que pena
Quando más descanso da.
Pues triste ¿quién la dormirá?

I la gloria que poseo
Estando juntos los dos,
Hará más bivo el deseo
Quando me parta de vos.
Estonçe toda vitoria
Con sus bienes dormirá
Y tristeza velará.

I queriendo por serviros
Todo el mal que me desdeña,
Para mis quexas deziros
Es la noche muy pequeña:
Pues gos**aros y adoraros
Lo poco que durará,
¡Ay triste! ¿quién la dormirá?

o:tṛo: βje:n si: ɑ: βo:z no: te:ŋgo:
i: lɑ: no:tʃe: se: me: i:ṛˈɑ:
ɑ:j djo:s kjˈe:n lɑ: d̯o:ṛmi:ṛˈɑ:

lɑ: βje:n ɑ:ndɑ:ntsɑ: ke: te:ŋgo:
tɑ:l bi:d̯ɑ: lɑ: d̯e:ʃɑ:ṛˈɑ:
ke: o:tṛɑ:z mu:tʃɑ:z λo:ṛɑ:ṛˈɑ:

go:tsɑ:ndo: d̯e:l gɑ:lɑ:ṛdˈo:n
ke: g̯ɑ:nˈe: ko:n mi:l e:no:ʃo:s
kˈo:mo: do:ṛmi:ṛˈɑ:n lo:s o:ʃo:s

pwe:s ke: βe:lɑ: e:l ko:ṛɑ:tsˈo:n
ke: si: mwe:stṛo: jo: d̯o:lo:ṛe:s
ɑ:nte: bwe:stṛɑ: pe:ṛfe:tsjˈo:n
e:s po:ṛke: sɑ:βe:n dɑ:mo:ṛe:s
po:ko:s o:mbṛe:z lo: ke: so:n
e:s u:nɑ: glo:ṛjɑ: ke: pe:nɑ:
kwɑ:ndo: mˈɑ:z de:sk:ɑ:nso: d̯ɑ:

* scribal error for *m*
** scribal error for *z*

pwe:s tr̥i:ste: kj̍e:n lɑ: d̯o:r̥mi:r̥ˈɑ:

i: lɑ: glo:r̥jɑ: ke: po:se:o:
e:stɑ:ndo: ʃu:nto:z lo:z do:s
ɑ:r̥ˈɑ: mˈɑ:z bi:β o: e:l de:se:o:
kwɑ:ndo: me: pɑ:r̥tɑ: d̯e: βo:s
e:sto:ntse:*to:d̯ɑ: βi:to:r̥jɑ:
ko:n su:z bje:ne:z do:r̥mi:r̥ˈɑ:
i: tr̥i:ste:tsɑ: βe:lɑ:r̥ˈɑ:

i: ke:r̥je:ndo: po:r̥ se:r̥bi:r̥o:s
to:d̯o: e:l mɑ:l ke: me: d̯e:zde:ɲɑ:
pɑ:r̥ɑ: mi:s ke:ʃɑ:z de:tsi:r̥o:s
e:z lɑ: no:tʃe: mwi: pe:ke:ɲɑ:
pwe:z go:tʃɑ:ro:s i: ɑ:d̯o:r̥ɑ:r̥o:s
lo: po:ko: ke: d̯u:r̥ɑ:r̥ˈɑ:
ɑ:j tr̥i:ste: kj̍e:n lɑ: d̯o:r̥mi:r̥ˈɑ:

Peynándose estava

Early seventeenth century. Madrid, Bibl. Nac., MS 3880, fol. 20. CD #33.

Peinándose estava un olmo
sus nuevas guedejas verdes
y se las rizava el ayre
al espejo de una fuente.

Por verle galán del prado,
las flores se desvanecen,
que vanidades infunden
aun la hermosura silvestre.

Y viéndole alegre,
viéndole alegre,
se iba de risa
cayendo una fuente de cristal,
murmurando,
murmurando,
murmurando
entre dientes.

pe:i:nˈɑ:ndo:se: e:stɑ:βɑ: u:n o:lmo:
su:z nwe:βɑ:z ge:d̯e:ʃɑ:z be:r̥de:s

* Variant form, *ct* reduced to *t*.

i: se: la:*rri:tsa:βa: e:l a:i:ṛe:
a:l e:spe:ʃo: de: u:na: fwe:nte:

po:ṛ be:ṛle: g̯a:lˈa:n de:l pṛa:d̯o:
la:s flo:ṛe:s se: d̯e:zba:ne:tse:n
ke: βa:ni:d̯a:d̯e:s i:nfu:nde:n
a:u:n la: e:ṛmo:su:ṛa: si:lbe:stṛe:

i: βjˈe:n do:le: a:le:gṛe:
βjˈe:n do:le: a:le:gṛe:
se: i:βa: d̯e: rri:sa:
ka:je:ndo: u:na: fwe:nte: d̯e: kṛi:sta:l
mu:rmu:ṛa:ndo:
mu:rmu:ṛa:ndo:
mu:rmu:ṛa:ndo:
e:ntṛe: d̯je:nte:s

Ya desengaño mío

Early seventeenth century. Madrid, Bibl. Nac., MS 3381, fol. 41. CD #34.

Ya, desengaño mío,
havéis llegado al puerto,
donde perdido y roto
days a la vela el remo.

Y viviréis seguro
de los pasados riesgos
de las inquietas
olas del mar de amor y celos.

Ay de mí,
Ay de mí,
Ay de mí,
pues llego a estar tan çiego,
pues llego a estar tan çiego,
que en tantos desengaños,
que en tantos desengaños
no logro un escarmiento.

ja: d̯e:se:ŋga:ɲo: mˈi:o:
a:βˈe:i:z λe:ga:d̯o: a:l pwe:ṛto:
do:nde: pe:ṛdi:d̯o: i: rro:to:
da:i:s a: la: βe:la: e:l rre:mo:

---
* *s* disappears before *rr*

i: βi:βi:ɾ̥ˈe:i:s se:g̑u:ɾ̥o:
de: lo:s pɑ:sɑ:d̑o:* rrje:zgo:s
de: lɑ:s i:nkje:tɑ:s
o:lɑ:z de:l mɑ:ɾ̥ de: ɑ:mo:ɾ̥ i: tse:lo:s

ɑ:j d̑e: mˈi:
ɑ:j d̑e: mˈi:
ɑ:j d̑e: mˈi:
pwe:z ʎe:g̑o: ɑ: e:stɑ:ɾ̥ tɑ:n tsje:g̑o:
pwe:z ʎe:g̑o: ɑ: e:stɑ:ɾ̥ tɑ:n tsje:g̑o:
ke: e:n tɑ:nto:z de:se:ŋgɑ:ɲo:s
ke: e:n tɑ:nto:z de:se:ŋgɑ:ɲo:s
no: lo:gɾ̥o: u:n e:skɑ:ɾ̥mje:nto:

* *s* before *rr* disappears

10

Spanish Latin

HAROLD COPEMAN

In Spain, as in France under Charlemagne in the early ninth century, adherence to the Roman rite meant that the priests had to read and understand Latin as well as the Romance vernacular (derived from Vulgar Latin over the centuries) in which they preached to their flocks and lived their ordinary lives. How exactly this was pronounced depended on the vowel and consonant sounds of the local dialect, which was influenced by the presence of many French clergy who gave instruction in the new liturgy and in Latin. This French influence came originally from the monks of Cluny, who organized the Compostela pilgrimage, and on papal authority introduced the Roman rite into northern Spain in the late eleventh century.

Meanwhile, spoken Romance developed a grammar and a written form and what is now known as Old Spanish (including Old Castilian) emerged about 1200. As the Spanish words and their pronunciation continued to develop, however, there must have been pressure to pronounce liturgical (and other) Latin words as if they were the vernacular words which had developed from them: to say, for instance, *hombre* instead of Latin *homine,* or to make Latin *miraculo* into Old Spanish *miraglo* or Middle Spanish *milagro,* and Latin *formosa* and *plenum* into Spanish *hermosa* and *lleno.* However, a number of words classed as "learned," taken from Latin in the Middle Ages or Renaissance, have kept close to the Latin pronunciation of the time of borrowing. For instance, Latin *iam* ("already") becomes Spanish *ya,* still pronounced [ja], but *iam magis* ("never") becomes Spanish *jamas,* now pronounced with initial [x]. Latin *plenus* is close to Spanish *pleno* (pronounced with [pl]) but *lleno* also exists; Latin *anima* appears in Spanish unchanged, but there is also *alma.* (See "Sounds and Spellings," below, on the way these linguistic developments affect Latin pronunciation during the period 1200–1650.)

Renaissance learning and culture blossomed in Spain in the sixteenth century before the intensification of religious intolerance which followed the birth of Protestantism and the onset of the Spanish Inquisition and the Jesuits' attempt to reinstate Catholicism throughout Europe. Nebrija at Salamanca retrieved the traditions of Classical Latin pronunciation (see below); and the King brought singers from the (Spanish) Netherlands to his court chapels. During the sixteenth and early seventeenth centuries, the "Golden Age" of Spanish music, a tremendous number of attractive polyphonic works were written (on both sides of the Atlantic). Among the composers at Spanish cathedrals and royal chapels were Morales (at Toledo, the literary center of Spain), Guerrero (in the south at Seville), and Victoria (who worked in Rome and later in Madrid).

The pronunciation described below is suggested as being suitable for this period (and reasonably so for the earlier centuries of our period). But it should be noted that during the sixteenth and seventeenth centuries changes were taking place in the pronunciation of Spanish itself. This process started with lower-class speech in northern Castile, and gradually worked south and became accepted by the educated population. Particular attention needs to be given to the sibilants, which changed as modern Spanish emerged.

Regional varieties

Early in our period Castilian, from the north-central districts of Spain, gradually became the prestige dialect of the whole country, though other dialects continued to be used. In most districts Latin pronunciation was probably based on the Castilian of the time, though with local flavors: but Catalonia may have had a strong French flavor (its dialect was similar to the Occitan of southern France and had developed long before Castilian). Galicia, in the northwest, had a dialect close to that of Portugal, whose Latin pronunciation may be more relevant than that of Spain. The exact sounds of the broadly standard Castilian Latin speech depended, as in any country, on the local speech.

Evidence

The phonological history of Castilian Spanish is a major field of modern linguistic study, drawing on contemporary writers, on orthographic and literary evidence (including rhymes and meter), and on the analysis of dialects and related or neighboring languages (e.g., French and Basque). To establish past pronunciations of Castilian Latin, we need to draw on this vernacular phonology, applying the remarks above about the different development of learned and of popular words and checking the conclusions against the existing fragments of contemporary evidence. This is found in English, Welsh, and Continental writing, from the late fifteenth to the seventeenth century. The first of these grammarians was Antonio of Lebrixa (or Nebrissensis), now usually known as Nebrija, who was an early campaigner for humanist studies and for the Classical pronunciation of the ancient languages. During a stay at Bologna University he drew on knowledge accumulated by Italian humanists and recovered the details of Classical Latin pronunciation as propounded by grammarians in the early centuries A.D. He gives instances, though only a few, of the way Latin was actually pronounced in France and Italy in his time. In the sixteenth and seventeenth centuries there are more references by a number of writers.

Bibliography

Antonio of Lebrixa [Nebrissensis] / E. A. Nebrija. *Secunda repetitio.* A lecture on reform of pronunciation of Latin, 1486. In *Aelii Antonii Nebressensis ars nova grammatices. . . ,* 1509 (and presumably in other editions of Nebrija's Latin grammar).

———. *Gramatica.* A grammar in Spanish, 1492. Chap. IV is entitled "Delas letras & pronunciaciones dela lengua latina"; Chap. V covers Castilian in a comparable way. Printed, with a substantial introduction, in I. G. Gonzalez-Llubera, *Nebrija Gramatica* (Oxford, 1926: text on pp. 20–27).

———. *De vi ac potestatae litterarum,* 1503. Another *repetitio.* A very legible copy is in the Bodleian Library: Byw. A4. 1 (1512). (This lecture was given at Salamanca before Nebrija returned as Professor of Grammar. He left the new University of Alcalá, where he was Latin editor for a "Polyglot Bible." He had sought to apply the humanist approach to biblical scholarship, which led to disagreement with the theologians. This may suggest—but does not prove—that the Church did not automatically accept Nebrija's reformed Latin pronunciation.)

Other Renaissance grammarians (including Erasmus and Hart) are detailed and abstracted in Harold Copeman, *Singing in Latin* (Oxford, 1990), indexed under "Spain: Latin." Many extracts are in A. Alonso, *De la Pronunciación Medieval a la Moderna* (Madrid, 1955). A phonetic guide by the Junta de Andalucia, Consejeria de Educación y Ciencia, in *La música en la era del descubrimiento: la escuela sevillana,* pp. 110–11, quotes Giovanni Miranda (1566) and Cristóbal de las Casas (1597).

Recent Romance philology (a sometimes controversial and fast-moving area):

J. N. Green. "Spanish." In M. Harris and N. Vincent, *The Romance Languages.* London, 1990. Pp. 79–92.

P. M. Lloyd. *From Latin to Spanish.* Philadelphia, 1987.

R. Wright. *Late Latin and Early Romance.* Liverpool, 1982. Esp. pp. 208–260; and the review of this book by T. J. Walsh in *Romance Philology.* 1986–87, pp. 199–214.

R. Wright, ed. *Latin and the Romance Languages in the Early Middle Ages.* London, 1991. Pp. 175–247.

Sounds and Spellings

Many "learned" words were borrowed (from the Cluniacs or other foreign speakers of Latin) into Spanish from the twelfth century on, and so they escaped the Romance developments in Spain in the preceding centuries. For instance, in modern Spanish the *t* has not been voiced to [d] in *espirito,* from Latin *spiritus,* or in the (unchanged) *beato* and *mente.*

With some words the general form remains, but Spanish pronunciation has been modified; e.g., *superbos* (to which Spanish *sobra, soberbia* are closely related), but Spanish *superar* exists, with [p]); *secundum* (Spanish *según*); and words ending in *-atum,* etc. *(peccata, advocata:* cf. Spanish *pecado, abogado).*

For other words there is a clear Latin ancestry, but the form has changed more radically; e.g., *quomodo, homo/homine, sanguine* (Spanish *como, hombre, sangre).* There are intermediate cases like *regina, nostro* (Spanish *reina, nuestro*) where singers may wish to make their own adaptations.

In a few important instances the sound depends also on neighboring letters: Vowels indicated by *e* and *o* are, as in many languages, produced differently according to whether the syllable is open or closed (see above, p. 92); and in Spanish and Spanish Latin the sound of *e* depends on which consonant closes a syllable. Though in initial positions and after [m] or [n], *b, d,* and *g* may sound as the "voiced stops" [b], [d], and [g], in other positions they are likely to be the fricatives [β], [d̰], [ɣ], in Late Latin and in Old and

Modern Spanish, and in Spanish Latin from before the start of our period. So in Spanish *boca* is [boka] but *cabo* is [kaβo]. But *la boca* would have *b* = [β] because it falls between vowels within a breath-group (see J. N. Green in *The Romance Languages,* p. 81). So in the sample text *Magnificat* I suggest that in *ex hoc beatam me dicent* the *b* might have the plosive [b] (depending on the musical phrasing) but the *d* is likely to be the soft fricative [d̯].

Consonants

b Erasmus (1528) tells us that the Spaniards say *bibit* for *vivit,* and vice versa. Lipsius (1586) says they soften *b* to a labial [v]. Sanford (1611), however, says that in the middle of a Spanish word derived from Latin the sound is [b] (cf. Latin *superbos* and Spanish *soberbia*). Initial *b* and *v* are alternative spellings over a long period *(boluntatis/voluntatis).* The commonest usage is perhaps [β], but [b] (gently plosive) after a pause (e.g., *Benedictus qui venit)* or a nasal consonant (in *Beati . . . qui ambulabant* the initial and second *b* could be [b], but not the third). See Lloyd, pp. 239–41. Outside Castille, [v] is possible.

c [k] before *a, o, u,* or a consonant.

Before *e, i,* or when written *ç,* pronounced as a sibilant whose exact sound is uncertain. Hart (1569), giving examples of various countries' usages "both in Latin and in their mother tongue," says that Spaniards make *ce, ci* into [se], [si]. ("The *c* they use is *s,* without any note of difference, before *e* and *i.*") But a variety of other witnesses (detailed in Copeman, p. 178) refer to an element of [t]. The sound [ts] is to be recommended, with the [t] faint; the front of the tongue (behind the tip) lies against the front of the hard palate (Lloyd, p. 258). The modern Spanish [θ] is an alternative for the sixteenth century, and from 1600 on this was the main pronunciation.

cc [kts] before *e* and *i (ecce, accipit),* probably simplified to [ts]; elsewhere [k].

ch Generally [tʃ] (though Nebrija wanted [kh]). [k] before a consonant; *Christe* (if so printed) can be read as *Criste,* the Spanish spelling.

d [d] as an initial consonant after a pause, or when following *l, m,* or *n.*

Between vowels and elsewhere (and in *Deus*) there is a strong tendency to soften to [d̯] (cf. the behavior of *b, g*). So *Magnificat anima mea Dominum . . . in Deo salutari* has [d̯] for *Dominum* but [d] for *in Deo; dispersit superbos . . . Deposuit potentes* has [d] twice; *et divites dimisit* is probably better with [d̯].

f In Spanish itself the sound of initial [f] often developed into [h], later becoming mute: thus, Latin *factum* has led to two Spanish words, *hecho* ("done"), and (as a survival of medieval *f*) *fecha* ("date"). Following the example of "learned" borrowings of Latin words into Spanish, and on the principle discussed above, we can assume that when Latin was used, the sound [f] was retained (probably from twelfth-century Cluniac example).

g [g] before *a, o, u,* or a consonant; perhaps [γ] between these vowels.

Before *e* and *i,* [g] palatalized to [dʒ] in Late Latin, a sound which weakened in Early Spanish to [j] before a stressed vowel (and otherwise disappeared). But the ecclesiastical

Latin taught by the Cluniacs would use [dʒ], and this probably developed to [ʒ] by the sixteenth century. (Sanford, 1611, discussing Spanish, refers to *sh,* [ʃ]; this is the voiceless equivalent of [ʒ], which he would have had no easy way of denoting.)

gn Before 1500, probably [ɲ]; thereafter [gn] with a light [g]. Spanish music printers used *ag·nus,* not *a·gnus,* no doubt following Nebrija's teaching.

h The development of Spanish (confirmed by Sanford for words derived from Latin) suggests that *h* was probably silent; this applies also to *mihi, nihil,* which were pronounced [mi·i], [ni·il].

Consonantal *i/j* Probably [j], but biblical names, at least, used [ʒ] *(Iesus, Ierusalem, Ieremias).*

k [k].

l [l]. (English speakers need to produce this sound on the ridge behind the teeth, not as a dark semivowel.)

m Generally [m]; *mn* (in *omnia*) as [n]; word-final *m* (except before *p* and *b*) as [n].

n [n]; *nct* probably pronounced [nt] (e.g., *sanctus*); *nf, nv* pronounced [mf], [mβ] (e.g., *infernum, invenit*); *np, nb* probably [mp], [mb].

p [p], but voiced to [b] between vowels. Probably dropped in consonantal groups like *sumpturi.*

qu [k] before *e, ae, i.* [kw] before *a* and probably *o;* e.g., *quum* [kum].

r Trilled when written double, but otherwise pronounced as a single "flap": [ɾ].

s In medieval Spain, unlike the present day, sibilants could be voiced or unvoiced. In the center and south the change in pronunciation was not completed until the seventeenth century; it had started in the north at a much earlier date. Given conservative pronunciation by church musicians, the earlier sibilant system may have persisted throughout our period.

Subject to this last proviso, *s* between vowels was [z] until perhaps 1500, then [s]; *ss,* too was [s]. But both [z] and [s] were "blunt" compared with English [z] and [s]: the tongue is concave upwards, resonance is reduced, and the sound moves somewhat toward the "shushing" [ʃ]. Nebrija (1503) compared Spanish *s* with the Hebrew letter *sama* (*samech* seems to have been a dull [s]) and distinguished it from the letters *sin* ([ʃ]) and *sadic* (a harsh [s]). Before a voiced consonant (e.g., *et divites dimisit:* see *d* above) *s* in the earlier period would have been pronounced [z].

This difficult question of the Spanish sibilants is discussed at length in Lloyd, pp. 267–68 and 336–42, including analogies with Arabic letters, and by Green in *The Romance Languages,* pp. 82–83.

t A light [t], on the teeth; *ti-* + vowel is [tsi-] (despite Nebrija's wish to return to Classical [ti-]). Between vowels *t* is sometimes voiced and fricated to [d̞], but not when words borrowed into Spanish retain *t* pronounced [t] *(spiritus,* etc.); the [-t] was possibly also retained at the ends of words *(Magnificat anima, et exsultavit).*

The voicing to [d] may extend to *t* before a voiced consonant *(et misericordia; et nunc).*

Consonantal u/v [β, b]: see note on *b*. Outside Castile, possibly [v].

x [ks] if a final letter, or before another consonant; but it may simplify to [s] if a comparable Spanish word does so: Latin *expecto,* Spanish *espeto.* [ʃ] between vowels (including initial vowels of words in the same breath); *excelsis* probably has [-ts-] (and from perhaps the later period of the Golden Age, [-θ-]).

z Probably [dz] before 1450, then (as shown by contemporary comparisons with Tuscan), devoiced to [ts].

Double consonants are pronounced single in most cases, but see above for *cc, rr, ss.*

Vowels

a [a].

e A fairly closed vowel, indicated here by [e], is used in syllables which are open or which are closed by *d, m, n, s,* or *z.* In Castilian Latin the difference for other closed syllables is slight; the more open vowel is indicated by [ɛ]. This is also used before or after *rr.* But *Amen* is now heard as [amin], and this may have a long tradition.

i Close [i] in all positions.

o In open syllables, the close vowel [o]. In closed syllables (and before and after *rr: terrorem*), the vowel is a very open [ɔ], as in British English *not.*

u Probably the general usage was [u]. But Hart reports (1569) that "the French and Scottish sound" ([y] or [iu]) was often used in Spanish Latin and vernacular—conceivably, one may guess, a relic of Cluniac French Latin.

Latin unaccented *u* tended to become [o] in vernacular Spanish (though not in "learned" words), and this may be assumed to have affected Latin pronunciation. So in the text below we suggest [o] in *superbos* [soberbos] (cf. *soberbia*) but [u] in *secula* [sekula] (cf. Spanish *secúlar*).

SAMPLE TEXTS

These texts relate to polyphony in the "Golden Age" (say 1500–1650). For words ending in *-t,* see above.

Magnificat

CD #35.

Magnificat anima mea Dominum, et exsultavit spiritus meus:
in Deo salutari meo. Quia respexit humilitatem ancillae suae:
ecce enim ex hoc beatam me dicent omnes generationes.
Quia fecit mihi magna qui potens est: et sanctum nomen eius.
et misericordia eius a progenie in progenies: timentibus eum.
Fecit potentiam in brachio suo:
dispersit superbos mente cordis sui.
Deposuit potentes de sede et exaltavit humiles.
Esurientes implevit bonis: et divites dimisit inanes.
Suscepit Israel puerum suum: recordatus misericordiae suae.
Sicut locutus est ad patres nostros:
Abraham et semini eius in saecula.
Gloria Patri, et Filio: et Spiritui Sancto.
Sicut erat in principio, et nunc et semper:
et in saecula saeculorum, Amen.

magnifikaḓ anima me·a ḓɔminum eḓ eʃuldaβit spiṛitus me·us
in de·o saluḓaṛi me·o ki·a ṛɛspeʃiḓ omiliḓaḓem ansile su·e
ɛtse enim ɛks ɔk βe·ata‿me ḓitsent ɔnes ʒeneṛatsi·ones
ki·a fetsit mi·i magna ki potens est ɛt santo‿nomen ejus
ɛd mizeṛikɔṛḓi·a ejus a pṛoʒeni·e im pṛoʒeni·es timentiβus e·um
fetsit potentsi·am im bṛatʃi·o su·o
dispɛṛsit sobɛṛbos mente kɔṛdi‿su·i
deposu·it potentes de seḓe eḓ eʃaltaβiḓ omiles
esuṛi·entes impleβiḓ bonis e‿ḓivitɛs dimisiḓ inanes
sutsebiḓ isṛa·ɛl pu·ɛṛum su·um ṛɛkɔṛḓaḓus miseṛikɔṛḓi·e su·e
sikut lokuḓus est ad patṛez nɔstṛɔs
abṛa·an ɛt semini ejus in sekula
gloṛi·a batṛi ɛt fili·o ɛt spiṛitu·i santo
sikuḓ ɛṛaḓ in pṛintsipi·o ɛḓ nuŋk ɛt sempɛṛ
eḓ in sekula sekuloṛum amin

Salve regina

CD #36.

Salve, regina mater misericordie
vita, dulcedo et spes nostra, salve!
ad te clamamus exsules filii Eve,
ad te suspiramus gementes et flentes
in hac lacrimarum valle.
eia ergo, advocata nostra,
illos tuos misericordes oculos ad nos converte
et Iesum, benedictum fructum ventris tui,
nobis post hoc exsilium ostende,
o clemens, o pia,
o dulcis Maria [*or:* o dulcis virgo semper Maria.]

salβe ṛeʒina maḓɛṛ miseṛikɔṛdi·e
biḓa ḓultseḓo et spes nɔstṛa salβe
aḓ te klamamus ɛksules fili·i eβe
aḓ te suspiṛamus ʒementes ɛt flentes
in ak lakṛimaṛum βale
eja ɛṛgo aβokaḓa nɔstṛa
ilɔs tuɔs miseṛikɔrḓes ɔkulɔs aḓ nɔs kɔmβɛṛte
ɛt ʒesum beneḓiktum fṛuktum bentṛis tu·i
nɔβis pɔst ɔk eʃili·um ɔstende
o klemens o pi·a
o ḓultsis maṛia [Or: o ḓultsis βiṛgo sɛmpɛṛ maṛia]

11—

Galician-Portuguese

JOSEPH T. SNOW AND
JAMES F. BURKE

Today, Galician-Portuguese is a vital and vibrant dialect of Iberian Romance, a survival of centuries of shifting political and cultural upheavals. In early modern Iberia, Galicia has run a course with many parallels to Catalonia, both regions enjoying—after many centuries of official neglect and political and cultural demotion—a literary renaissance in the mid-nineteenth century. In the latter half of the twentieth century, they both earned new cultural respect and, now, political autonomy.

The earliest Galician-Portuguese texts to survive date from the 1180s. The cultural center for this Romance vernacular was Santiago de Compostela, one of the three main pilgrimage destinations of the Middle Ages (with Rome and Jerusalem), famed for its reverence for the remains of St. James the Greater. Foreigners would arrive there overland via the *camino francés* (the French road), which passed through a wide swath of northern Spain from Jaca—below the Pyrenees in Aragon—all the way west to Santiago. Thus, to the local store of folklore, legend, and song were added many elements of the major cultural trends of lands both east and north. The indigenous lyric was enriched by that of the troubadour poets and minstrels from France, for example. The lyric voice developed in Galicia with great freedom, since politically it participated less energetically and was more distant geographically from the battleground between Moor and Christian, to the south. It is fair to say that almost all lyric poetry was composed in Galician-Portuguese by poets from the western two-thirds of the Iberian Peninsula to about the end of the thirteenth century (the eastern third was singing in varieties of Provençal and Catalan). Meanwhile, composition of poetry in Latin meters, as well as verse in the non-Romance strains of Arabic, continued without interruption.

With the increased importance of Galician-Portuguese as a literary standard for Peninsular lyric poetry, and the acquisition of those skills by a fair number of non-native versifiers and singers, the literary language does not evidence many of the changes found in the more dynamic language of prose documents. In some sense, the Galician-Portuguese literary style was becoming fossilized more rapidly, much as had that of the literary *koiné* of Provence, and was recognized more for its beauty and poetical efficiency than as a true reflection of the spoken language and the changes it was experiencing. Thus, in the early decades of the fourteenth century, fewer poets used this increasingly stylized language, preferring the newly mature lyric voice of Castile or the more natural and less artificial one developing in Portugal. Indeed, as the fourteenth century wore on, the recollections of Galician-Portuguese became increasingly laced with nostalgia—as for a time gone by—and, in the *Cancionero general* of 1511, it is clearly perceived as an older art practiced only now and again by a few poets and on special occasions.

Politically, Portugal had been going its own way since the early years of the twelfth century. Alfonso VI, king of León and Castile, had recaptured the capital city of Toledo for the Christian forces in 1085–86, and was noted for his on-again, off-again relationship with the national hero of Castile, Rodrigo Díaz de Vivar (known as El Cid). Alfonso had given his daughter Teresa and her French husband, Henry, from the house of Burgundy, the trust of *Terra Portucale*. His other daughter, Urraca, with *her* Burgundian husband, Raymond, had been given the trust of Galicia. Teresa and her husband did much to foster the independence of their lands from the Castilian crown, and Teresa even fought to bring Galicia under her aegis after her husband died. In this enterprise she was opposed by many nobles and even by her own son, Afonso Henriques. They eventually won the day, and in 1139 Afonso Henriques, as Afonso I, became the first king of the independent-minded Portugal. Galicia—that is, the area north of the Minho River—continued to be allied with the Leonese-Castilian monarchy.

It is generally believed that the major sound changes that characterize Galician-Portuguese originated in the more developed Galicia and then spread southward with the Reconquest, a process begun some time in the eighth century. In the medieval period, at least the period for which the musical record speaks, Galician and Portuguese were not far apart. As time passed, the political fortunes of Galicia, more allied with the provinces and kingdoms to the east, and Portugal, whose political center was shifting from Oporto southward to Lisbon, were reflected in progressively differentiated linguistic norms. Today Galician is the mother tongue of much of the autonomous region of Galicia within the Spanish monarchy. Portuguese, meanwhile, is the national tongue not only of Portugal but also of Brazil, Angola, Mozambique, the Azores, and Cape Verde, and is vestigial in Goa and Macao. Modern Portuguese makes the best standard for comparison when dealing with medieval Galician language and is used below when appropriate.

From the standpoint of music and medieval Galician song, the truly central work is the collection of Marian praise and miracle accounts set to music in the reign of Alfonso X of Castile and León (1252–1284), titled *Cantigas de Santa Maria*. The collection comprises some 420 texts with music, a few from the hand of the king, but most from unnamed collaborators at his court who shared in his vision. There are, additionally, about 1,600 secular poetic texts in the medieval canon of Galician-Portuguese. They are found in three song books, or *cancioneiros (Ajuda, Vaticana,* and *Biblioteca Nacional, olim Colocci-Brancuti).* None of these texts is accompanied by music. However, six of these texts, by Martin Codax, were found in a manuscript fragment by F. Vindel earlier in the twentieth century and do have music. In 1990, another six texts, these by King Diniz of Portugal (1279–1325), a grandson of Alfonso X, were discovered with music in Lisbon's Torre de Tombo library archives by Harvey L. Sharrer. In sum, only about 20 percent of the extant texts survive with their music: of these, practically all are religious in nature, preserved through the happy confluence of a rich patron (who was also an author and composer) and the fervor to leave behind a legacy of complete manuscript works of art (text, music, and miniatures). Like many other poets in Castile who wrote lyric songs, Alfonso chose to write in Galician-Portuguese, having had the additional advantage of spending part of his youth in Galicia.

Bibliography

Higinio Anglès. *La música de las "Cantigas" del Rey Alfonso el Sabio: Facsímil, transcripción y estudio crítico,* II. Barcelona: Diputación Provincial de Barcelona-Biblioteca Central, 1943. (Musical version of Cantiga 167.)
Kurt Baldinger. *La formación de los dominios lingüísticos en la Península Ibérica.* Madrid: Gredos, 1972. ["El gallego-portugués y sus relaciones de substrato con la Aquitania."]
Steven N. Dworkin. "Portuguese Language." In *Dictionary of the Middle Ages,* ed. J. Strayer. Vol. 10. New York: Scribner's, 1988. Pp. 56–58.
José Pedro Machado. *Dicionário Etimológico da Lingua Portuguesa.* 3 vols., 2d ed. Lisbon: Ed. Confluência, 1967.
Walter Mettmann, ed. *Afonso X, Cantigas de Santa Maria.* 4 vols. Coimbra: University of Coimbra, 1959–1972. (Vol. 4 is an extensive glossary of medieval Galician-Portuguese to modern Portuguese.)
The New Appleton Dictionary of the English and Portuguese Languages. Antonio Houaiss and Catherine B. Avery, eds. New York: Appleton, Century, Crofts, 1967.
Francisco da Silveira Bueno. *A formação histórica da língua portuguesa.* 3d ed.
Paul Teyssier. *Histoire de la langue portugaise.* Paris: Presses Universitaires de France, 1980.
Edwin B. Williams. *From Latin to Portuguese: Historical Phonology and Morphology of the Portuguese Language.* 2d ed. Philadelphia: University of Pennsylvania Press, 1962.

Spelling and Accents

Spelling conventions vary between the medieval and modern language and will be noted as needed in the discussions. Edited texts in Galician or Galician-Portuguese of the Middle Ages may or may not carry accents in accord with modern notation. If markings are not present, use a good dictionary as a guide. Some rules, such as those below, can be used as a pronunciation guide for most edited texts, particularly marked ones, but they can also help in abstracting pronunciation from a modern dictionary (with markings):

1. In words of more than one syllable terminating in *-a, -as, -e, -es, -o, -os, -am, -em,* and *-ens,* the vocal stress is normally on the penultimate syllable. Such words carry no accent marking.

2. In words of more than one syllable ending in *-i, -is, -u, -us,* or a nasal vowel (*-ã, -ẽ,* etc.), as well as in words ending in consonants (other than *-s* plurals and nasal markers *-m, -n*), the vocal stress is normally on the final syllable. No special markings are needed in such cases.

3. In words that have a diphthong in the penultimate syllable *(-oi-, -au-, -ai-, -ei-, -eu-, -ou-, -iu-,* and *-ui-),* it is normal to stress the first element of these diphthongs, except when they are followed by a nasal (e.g., *reina,* in which case the second element, *-i-*, receives the stress).

4. In words of two syllables ending in *-a, -as, -o, -os, -am,* and *-em* that have in the preceding stressed syllable any of the following: *-ia, -ie-, -io-, -oa-, -oe-, -ua,* or *-ue-*, the second element is also stressed; e.g., the *e* in *doença* and the *a* in *criava* and *loades.*

5. Stress is placed on the first element of the diphthong in word-final position (singular or plurals with *-s*): *-ai, -ei, -au, -eu, -ou, -ui, -ao, -ae,* or *-oe.*

When vocal stress does not follow these patterns, a written accent in marked texts indicates where vocal stress is to be placed. A circumflex marks a closed vowel *(â, ê,* and *ô),* while an acute accent denotes the open vowels *(á, é,* and *ó).* Either an acute or a grave accent may appear over an *unstressed i* or *u* to prevent the formation of a diphthong.

Syllable Division

Galician-Portuguese syllables normally consist of a vowel and its preceding consonant(s): *miragre = mi·ra·gre.* However, keep the following considerations in mind:

1. Double consonants sometimes reflect an original Latin form but may represent a new sound. Double *-ss-* is phonemic, undivided, as in *nosso = no·sso* (unvoiced, and distinct from *-s-* [z]). Double *-nn-* is most often palatal [ɲ], *tenno* = [tɛɲu]. The *-mm-*, as in *commo,* is graphic only, and may be treated as a single consonant, *co·mo.* Double *-rr-*, as in *torre,* is also phonemic, *to·rre* (trilled).

2. A two-consonant cluster (exceptions: consonant groups with *l* and *r* as the second member, such as *bl, cl, fr,* etc.; see the following paragraph for others) will also divide, as *femença = fe·men·ça, desta = des·ta, encender = en·cen·der.* A three-consonant cluster example would be *desastroso = de·sas·tro·so* (dividing two and one).

3. Special consonant clusters form inseparable units: *ch, lh, nh, sc, br, bl, cr, cl, dr, dl, fr, fl, gr, gl, pr, pl, tr, tl,* and *vr, vl* (= *br, bl*). Examples are easy to identify: *achar = a·char; filho = fi·lho; tenho = te·nho; olhos = o·lhos; miragre = mi·ra·gre; quebra = que·bra; ladrão = la·drão*; and *refrão = re·frão.*

Consonants

Pronunciation of consonants in medieval Galician-Portuguese, with the few exceptions noted below, is much as in modern Portuguese. Only the double consonants *ss* and *rr* are phonemic; others appearing in older texts are treated as if single.

b [b]. A bilabial occlusive, like English *bid.*

c [k] when followed by *a, o,* or *u,* as in English *cat.*

c [ts] when followed by *e* or *i,* as in English *hits.* By the mid-sixteenth century, this sound was reduced to a simple sibilant [s].

ç [ts] essentially as in *-ce-* and *-ci-;* e.g., *faça* [fɑ:tsa].

ch [tʃ] as in English po*t sh*ot. About the middle of the sixteenth century, the earlier medieval affricate lost its dental element and became [ʃ].

d [d] in initial position *(doença)* or following a consonant *(ainda)*, as in English *dog.*

f [f] as in English *fish.*

g The voiced velar stop [g] when followed by *a, o, u, ue,* and *ui;* a hard sound, as in English *good.* When followed by *e* or *i,* pronounced [dʒ], the affricate of English *judge.* Rare orthographic forms do turn up: *lingoa* would be [-gwa], and both *gisa* and *guisa* would be [giza]. In verb paradigms, as well, orthographic or scribal varieties can be puzzling. *Fugir* [fudʒir] may, in the first person singular, be spelled *fugo,* but would still be pronounced [fudʒu] and not [fugu]. Later the affricate (with *e* and *i*) simplifies into the simple [ʒ].

h Not pronounced, but present at times, often designating a hiatus between vowels *(sahir* for *sair).* It may be seen following a consonant, used in place of stressed *i* (*sabha* for *sabia*).

j [dʒ] when followed by *a, o,* and *u,* as in English *edge.* It could alternate with *g* when followed by *e* and *i,* also pronounced [dʒ] (see remarks under *g*). Occasionally the graph was replaced by *i (iulgar* for *julgar).*

k [k]. Exists in Galician-Portuguese only in foreign terms like *kyrie eleison.*

l [l] when initial or intervocalic, as in English *light.* When word-final or before a consonant, it sounds more velar, like the *l* in English *cool.*

lh [ʎ], the palatal sound in English *million.* Frequently, the variant *-ll- (moller* for *molher)* is used instead.

m [m] as in English *mist,* in initial and intervocalic position. The combination *mn (damno* or *somno)* makes the sound of the palatal [so:ɲu]. In syllable-final and word-final position, *m* serves to nasalize the preceding vowel (see "Nasalization," below).

n [n] as in English *nag,* in initial and intervocalic positions. Before stop consonants (*d* for example), the *n* is heard but extends its nasal quality to a preceding vowel: *grande* [grãnde]. Before other kinds of consonants, however, *n* disappears even as it nasalizes the preceding vowel: *tenso* [tẽsu].

nh [ŋ] is the normal grapheme (with *nn* and *mn* as variants in certain manuscripts) for the palatal sound heard in English *onion.*

p [p], similar in all ways to English pronunciation, though perhaps less breathy.

q [k] when followed by *u.* In *que* and *qui* the sound is hard, these two groups being the phonetic equivalents of English *Kay* and *key.* In *quando,* however, the initial sound is [kw]. *Quo* [kwo] is rare, in any case.

r The voiced alveolar flap [ṛ] is the most common form, as in Spanish *caro.* It is intervocalic, word-final, and remains unchanged when combined with all consonants except *n, l,* and *s;* e.g., *Maria* [maṛija], *quer* [kɛṛ], *criava* [kṛijava].

The strongly trilled and voiced apico-alveolar sound [rr] is found at the beginning of a word, internally after *n, l,* and *s,* and when written as *-rr-;* e.g., *rosa* [rrɔza], *onra* or *onrra* [onrra], *morrer* [mɔrrɛr].

A third type of *r,* somewhere between the two, is found before *l* and *n;* e.g., *parlar, carnal.*

s [s] is the sound of *s* in both initial and final position, and of *-ss-* in medial position, like the voiceless alveolar fricative of English *silly.* Intervocalic *-s-* is the voiced alveolar fricative [z], as in English *zebra.*

t [t] as in English *tip,* but, as with the *p,* less breathy.

v [v], equivalent to the voiced labio-dental fricative of English *vine.*

x [ʃ], the voiceless, palato-alveolar fricative akin to that of English *ship.* Exceptions are found in the pronunciation of words closely tied to official Latin; e.g., *existir* [ɛgzistir].

z is the voiced affricate [dz] of English *bids;* e.g., *razon* [radzon], *fazer* [fazɛr].

Vowels

The vowel system of modern Portuguese can be used as a guide to medieval pronunciation. Differences can be learned quickly.

a When this vowel is tonic (in stressed position) it is like the *a* in English *father* [ɑ:]. When unstressed (as in the pre- or post-tonic vowel) it is the de-emphasized [a], but it does not fall to become a "schwa." It has this same de-emphasized sound before the nasals *n, m,* and *nh* as well: *ama* [ama].

e When tonic (stressed), it may be pronounced as open [ɛ:], as in English *there,* Galician-Portuguese *quer* [kɛ:r], or closed [e], as in French *été* and Galician-Portuguese *quen* [kẽ:]. As with *a,* in unstressed (pre- or post-tonic) positions *e* may be shortened slightly. In final position, it can be sounded [ɪ], as in English *bid, sit, fish;* e.g., *pede* [pɛdɪ].

Study of rhyme schemes tells us that in Galician-Portuguese, the *e* in the diphthong *eu* was open [ɛ] in possessive forms *(meu, teu, seu,* and in the word for God, *deus),* whereas it was the closed [e] in the *eu* of the preterit verb endings.

i In stressed position similar to the high, front, unrounded [i:] in English *machine, bead.* In unstressed position, *i* is effectively weakened to the sound of the vowel in English *bid* [ɪ]; e.g., *simonia* [sɪmoni:a].

o In stressed position, may be pronounced as open [ɔ:] as in English *broad,* Galician-Portuguese *por* [pɔ:r], or closed [o:] as in English *go,* and even a bit more tense, as in French *beau* [o]. If the text is not marked, a good dictionary will be of help. When *o* is word-final (plural *-s* does not have any effect) or in pre- or post-tonic position, it is pronounced like the vowel in English *boot.*

u In stressed position, almost exactly like the high back rounded sound in French *foule* [u]; e.g., *alguma* [alguma]. In unstressed positions, there is simply less tension.

Digraphs

Galician-Portuguese has many digraphs. They consist of a strong first element *(a, e, o)* and a weak second element *(i, u)* which is heard as a semi-consonant.

GROUPINGS WITH *i* AS THE SECOND ELEMENT

ai In stressed, or tonic, position, this diphthong is like the vowel in English *ride* [ai]. In unstressed positions, duration is curtailed.

ei In stressed position, the first element can be open or closed. When it is closed the sound is that of English *day* [dei]. When unstressed, duration is curtailed.

oi In stressed position, the first element is either open or closed: if open, the sound is like the *aw* in English *sawyer* and when closed, like the *oy* in English *boy.*

ui Both are weak vowels; the combination produces a sound like the *ui* in English *Bedouin.*

GROUPINGS WITH *u* AS THE SECOND ELEMENT

au Sounded like the *ou* in English *house* [au].

eu Varies since the first element is open [ɛu] or closed [eu]. A marked text will have *éu* for the open variety. If not, consult a good dictionary (one that gives pronunciations).

ou In stressed position, sounded like the English word *owe.* It is slightly weaker in unstressed positions.

iu Both are weak vowels; the combination produces a sound like the *iu* in Provençal *viu* [viu].

GROUPINGS WITH *i* OR *u* AS THE FIRST ELEMENT

ia In tonic, or stressed, position, the semi-vowel *i* is combined with open *a;* e.g., *fiar* [fjar]. In unstressed positions, the articulation is similar and the shortening produces a closed *a* (the same is true for *ea*).

ie In stressed position, we have the semi-vowel plus an open *e* [iɛ]. In unstressed positions, the articulation is similar, but the shortening produces a closed *e.*

io In stressed position, *io* (and frequently *eo,* a graphemic variant) produces the semi-vowel plus either open [jɔ] or closed [jo] (when unstressed, and especially in word-final position, this *io* is like *iu,* above; e.g., *Antonio* [ãntonju].

GROUPINGS WITH *o* OR *u* AS THE FIRST ELEMENT

ua, oa In stressed position *(quando),* pronounced like *wa* in English *swan* [swɑn]. In unstressed positions, the shape of the sound is similar, but shortening relaxes the intensity of the *a.*

ue, oe In stressed position, the semi-vowel is combined with an *e* that is either open [wɛ] or closed [we]. In unstressed position, both sounds are shortened somewhat.

ui, oi [iw] See above, under "Groupings with *i* as the Second Element."

Nasalization

Nasalization is one of the most distinctive features of Galician-Portuguese. It occurs when an original *m* or *n* is lost. To produce a nasal sound, keep the expelled air from exiting through the mouth by directing the air column up past the velar area and through the nose.

Nasals are signaled most often with a tilde [~]. It may appear over any of the vowels: *lã* [lã] ("wool"); *bẽes* [bɛ̃:es] ("good things, qualities"); *dões* [dões] ("gifts"); *vĩir* [vĩ:ĩr] ("to come"); *ũ* or *ũu* [ũ] ("one"). If a tilde appears over either element of a diphthong, the entire diphthong is nasalized: *leão* [leãũ] ("lion").

Another common sign of nasalization (this time of the preceding vowel) is word-final *m,* which is simply a graph and has no consonantal value. All that remains is its nasal quality, transferred to the preceding vowel; e.g., *som* [sõ]; *fazem* [fazẽĩ]. There are occasions when a final *m,* in adopting the point of articulation of a following consonant—i.e., the next word in a breath group—has some consonantal value. For example, a following word beginning with *b* or *p* will provide a bilabial to bolster the *m.* Similarly, a following word with initial *d* or *t* will attract the *m* to the dental position [n]. With a following hard *c (ca-, co-, cu-)* or hard *g- (ga-, go-, gu-),* the *m* will be drawn to the more velar articulation [ŋ]. In such cases, there is, as it were, a reconstituted consonant; e.g., *lã branca* [lã(m)brãka]. When such words are made plural, e.g., *parabens,* the *m* will graphically appear as *n* and the sound will be close to [-ɛ̃nts].

Within a word, an *m* or *n* in contact with a following *b, p, d, t,* hard *c,* or hard *g* will *both* nasalize the preceding vowel and retain its consonantal identity; e.g., *importância* [ĩmpɔrtã(n)tsja]; *encender* [ensẽ(n)der]. If the consonant involved is not one of these, the *m* and *n* nasalize the preceding vowel but also lose their identity as consonants; e.g., *onrra, onra,* or *honra* will be pronounced [õrra].

Nasal diphthongs are easily spotted when a tilde is the marker. Other cases to note are the following: When a word ends in unstressed *-em, -en,* or *-ens* (e.g., *dizem*), the nasal consonant becomes a glide and it and the preceding consonant are nasalized: [ẽĩ] ẽĩs]. In the word *muito* (an exception), *-ũĩ-* is nasalized. Final unstressed *-am,* in third-person plural verb forms (present tense of *-ar* verbs; subjunctive of *-er* and *-ir* verbs, etc.) produces a nasal diphthong: *passam* [pasãũ]; *passaram* [pasarãũ].

Nasalization was more common in medieval Galician-Portuguese than in modern Galician or Portuguese. Normally, a well-edited text will mark these instances with a tilde: *lũa* (modern *lua,* "moon"); *bõa* (modern *boa,* "good, kind"); *tẽer* (modern *ter,* "to have"); *põer* (modern *pôr,* "to put"), and *vĩir* (modern *vir,* "to come"). In these cases, the medieval language reflects the loss of an original *n* while the modern language does not.

Nasalization of the high palatal vowel *i* could produce a palatal consonant between it and the following vowel: Latin > Galician-Portuguese *vio* or *vinho* [viɲu] ("wine"). The feminine possessive *minha* ("my, mine") has the same nasal consonant, but unlike cases such as *vinum,* where an original *n* is responsible, there is none in *minha* to account for it. Finally, a few sporadic occurrences affect a discussion of nasals. In the older language, a doubling of the vowel was sometimes used to indicate nasalization; e.g., *maao* for *mão.* Occasionally, perhaps through Spanish influence, an etymological *n* (and sometimes *m*) alternated with the tilde marker; e.g., *põer/poner, bẽeita/beneita.*

DIACHRONIC SOUND CHART FOR GALICIAN-PORTUGUESE

	1100	1200	1300	1400	1500	1600	1700
VOWELS							
a	[a]						→
	[ɑ] (before nasals)						→
e	[e] (closed)						→
	[ɛ] (open)						→
i	[i]						→
o	[o] (closed)						→
	[ɔ] (open)						→
u	[u]						→
DIPHTHONGS							
ai	[ai]						→
ei	[ei] or [ɛi]						→
oi	[oi] or [ɔi]						→
ui	[ui]						→
au	[au]						→
eu	[eu] or [ɛu]						→
ou	[ou]						→
iu	[iu]						→
CONSONANTS							
b	[b]						→
c	[k] before *a, o, u*						→
	[ts] before *i, e*				→ [s]		→
ç	[ts] before *a, o, u*				→ [s]		→
ch	[tʃ]				→ [ʃ]		→
d	[d]						→
f	[f]						→
g	[g] before *a, o, u, ue, ui*						→
	[dʒ] before *e, i*				→ [ʒ]		→
h	not pronounced; preserves hiatus				lost		→
j	[dʒ] or [ʒ] before *a, o, u;* interchangeable with i						→
k	[k] (rare)						→
l	[l]						→
lh, ll	[ʎ]						→
m	[m] (except word-final) See, for word-final, p. 172.						→
n	[n]						→
nn, nh	[ɲ]						→
p	[p]						→
q	[k]						→
r	[ɾ] or [rr]						→
s	[s] or [z], see p. 173						→
t	[t]						→
v	[v]						→
x	[ʃ] or [ks], [gs]						→
z	[dz]						→

SAMPLE TEXTS

Cantiga 167

From *Cantigas de Santa Maria,* by Alfonso X, the Learned, of Castile and León, reigned 1252–84. Spain, Bibl. Escorial, Cantigas de Santa Maria. CD #37.

Refrain

Quen quer que na Virgen fia e a roga de femença,
valler-ll-á pero que seja d'outra lee en creença.

Stanza

Desta razon fez miragre Santa Maria, fremoso,
de Salas, por hũa moura de Borja, e piadoso,
ca un fillo que avia, que criava, mui viçoso,
lle morrera mui coitado dũa muy forte doença.

kẽin kɛ:ṛ kɛ nɑ vi:ṛdʒẽ fi:a ɪ a rrɔga dɛ fɛmentsa
valɛ:ṛ λjɑ: pɛṛu kɛ se:dʒa doutṛa lɛ:e ẽn kṛe·ẽntsa

dɛsta rrɑzõn fez miṛɑ:grɪ sãnta maṛi:a fṛɛmo:zu
dɛ sɑ:las pɔṛ ũma mouṛa dɛ βɔṛdʒa e pjado:zu
ka ũn fi:λu kɛ avi:a kɛ kṛiɑva mwi vitso:zu
λɛ mɔrre:ṛa mwi kɔitɑ:du dũma mwi fɔṛtɪ duẽntsa

Minina dos olhos verdes

Sixteenth century. Paris, Bibl. de l'Ecole Nationale Supérieure des Beaux-Arts, Chansonnier Masson, fol. 96v-97. CD #38.

Minina dos olhos verdes,
Porque me não vedes?
Porque me não vedes?
Porque me não vedes?
Vede-me, senhora,
Olhai que vos vejo.
Serdes crua agora,
Não hé d'olhos verdes
Pois que me não vedes,
Pois que me não vedes,
e que meu desejo
Creçe de ora em ora.

Mɪnina duz ɔ:λus vɛ:ṛdɪs
pɔṛkɛ mɪ nɑ͡ũ ve:dɪs

pɔr̩kɛ mɪ nãũ ve:dɪs
pɔr̩kɛ mɪ nãũ ve:dɪs
vedɪ mi seɲɔ:r̩a
ɔλai kɛ vos veʒu
sɛ:r̩dɪs kru·a agɔ:ra
nãũ ei dɔλus vɛ:r̩dɪs
pɔis kɛ mɪ nãũ vedɪs
pɔis kɛ mɪ nãũ vedɪs
ɛkɛ mɛu dezɛʒu
kr̩etse dɛ ɔ:r̩a ẽn ɔ:r̩a

Pois tudo tam pouco dura

Sixteenth century. Paris, Bibl. de l'Ecole Nationale Supérieure des Beaux-Arts, Chansonnier Masson, fol. 92v-93. CD #39.

Pois tudo tam pouco dura
Como pasado prazer
Isso me da ter ventura
Como deixa-la de ter.
Acaba-se com a vida
juntamente mal e bem
E quem milhor dito tem
Tem mais penada partida.
E pois he cousa sabyda
Que tudo fim a da ver
Isso me da ter ventura
Como deixa-la de ter.

pɔis tudu tãũ(m)pouku dur̩a
komu pasɑ:du pr̩azɛ:r̩
isu mɪ da tɛr ventura
komu deiʃa la di tɛ:r̩
akaba si kõn a vi:da
ʒũntamenti mal ɪ bẽĩn
i kẽĩn mɪλɔ:r di:tu tẽĩn
tẽĩn mais penada par̩ti:da
i pɔis ɛ kouza sabi:da
kɛ tudu fĩn a da vɛ:r̩
isu mɪ da tɛr̩ ventur̩a
komu deiʃa la dɪ tɛ:r̩

Mis ojos tristes lhorando

Mixed Spanish-Portuguese, sixteenth century. Lisbon, BN. C.I.C. no. 60, fol. 41v–42. CD #40.

Mis ojos tristes lhorando
Quando non podem calhar,
descansam, descansam, pera lhorar.
Cuidados [y] mil enojos,
quantos males causa el ver
Tantos tiene mi querer
Com que vive com antojos
Por isso lhoram mis ojos
I por mas pena me dar,
descansam, descansam, pera lhorar.

mis oʒos tṛistɪs λɔṛɑ̃:ndu
kwã:ndu non pɔ:dẽn kaλɑ:ṛ
dɛskãnsa͡ũ dɛskɑ̃nsa͡ũ pɛṛa λorɑ:ṛ
kwidados i mil enoʒos
kwãntos ma:les kausa ɛl vɛ:ṛ
tãntos tiɛne mi keṛɛ:ṛ
kõn kɛ vive kõn ãntoʒos
pɔṛ isu λɔ:ṛa͡ũ mis oʒos
i pɔṛ mas pe:na mɪ da:ṛ
dɛskãnsa͡ũ dɛskãnsa͡ũ pɛṛa λorɑ:ṛ

12

Portuguese Latin

HAROLD COPEMAN

Under Roman occupation in the early Middle Ages, (Vulgar) Latin gradually came to be spoken alongside the earlier languages, adopting their phonetic coloring. This Latin developed, as elsewhere, into Romance dialects, and (Old) Portuguese emerged as a recognizably separate language in the late twelfth century. Modern Portuguese, with intensified stresses, dates from the late sixteenth century. In the fifteenth century Portuguese poets began writing in Spanish; they were criticized on the humanistic grounds that Portuguese was a less corrupt form of Latin than Spanish or other Romance languages.

The two principal regional varieties are the speech of the center and south, which has for some centuries provided the educated standard Portuguese; and the dialect or dialects of the north (the Minho), speech which is shared with neighboring Galicia. We shall concentrate on the former, where the pronunciation is relevant to Portuguese Renaissance music. The northern speech has undergone less change since early medieval times; notably, the system of sibilants is more complicated than in standard Portuguese (they were reduced from eight to four by the sixteenth century). Also the sounds of *b* and *v* are confused in the north (as in Castilian Spanish); and the nasal vowels differ. A map summarizing the differences can be found in Teyssier (see Bibliography), p. 48.

Bibliography

James Howell. *A new English Grammar* (1662). Extracts from the section "Of the Portuguese Language, or sub-dialect" are given in notes to Harold Copeman, *Singing in Latin* (Oxford, 1990), pp. 180, 182.

S. Parkinson, "Portuguese." In M. Harris and N. Vincent, *The Romance Languages* (London, 1988). See pp. 131–44 on phonetics and historical phonology. (Several points of judgment on Portuguese Latin rely on Parkinson's advice as linguist and singer.)

P. Teyssier. *História da língua Portuguesa.* Lisbon, 1984; in French, Paris, 1980. Pp. 40–65.

E. B. Williams. *From Latin to Portuguese.* 2d ed. Philadelphia, 1980. Esp. pp. 12–17.

Sounds and Spellings

As in other Romance countries, we may expect Latin pronunciation to have developed in parallel with the changes associated with individual vowels and consonants in the vernacular, and also (among the less sophisticated) often in accordance with changes in the shape and spelling of the vernacular word. Detailed evidence is lacking, but we may, for instance, expect that *regina* in a liturgical text was often sung as *"reinha/rainha."* However, in standard educated Portuguese such changes may have been somewhat less prevalent than in medieval France and Spain. In the Renaissance Portuguese was viewed as a Romance language that was comparatively close to Latin (Latin *advocatus,* French *avocat,* Spanish *abogado,* Portuguese *advogado*).

There is not sufficient evidence to suggest the sound of medieval Portuguese Latin, but in performing the music of the Renaissance, the Latin texts may be sung with simple transliteration into the phonetic equivalents given below, keeping in mind that the stress is strong and its placement is the same as for Italian Latin.

Consonants

b [b]. (Note that in Portuguese the weakening, and sometimes disappearance, of *b, d,* and *g* between vowels is relatively modern.)

c [s] before *e, i,* silent before *t* or *ce, ci,* so *cc* = [s] in *ecce, accipiat.* Elsewhere *c* = [k].

ch [k]

d [d]. See note under *b.*

f [f]

g [ʒ] before *e* and *i;* otherwise [g]. See note under *b.*

gn [gn]

h Silent, but in *mihi* and *nihil* pronounced [ʃ] or (in Roman style) [k].

i/j [ʒ], including *cujus, eius,* and probably *eia.*

l, ll [l] (despite the tendency to substitute [ɽ] in forming vernacular words).

m, n [m,n], but see "Nasal vowels" below.

nc (except before *e, i*), nq [ŋk].

p [p] but probably silent in *mpt.*

qu [kw] before *a, o,* and *u;* [k] before *e* and *i.*

r [ɽ]. Trilled, strongly at the beginning or end of a word, the end of a syllable, or in *rr* or *sr (Israel).*

s [z] between vowels (within a word or phrase); elsewhere [s] (and not the modern [-ʃ]).

t [t]; but *ti* followed by a vowel is [si].

u/v [v]

x [ks] but [gz] between vowels; *xc* before *e* and *i* is [ks].

z [z]

Double consonants are pronounced as single sounds.

Consonantal Groups

The extent to which consonants were dropped depended on the context of the music. In a village church or small monastery the sound might have resembled that reported by A. F. G. Bell in *Portuguese Literature* (Oxford, 1922), p. 24: *"Stabat mater doloroza/ Jussa crussa larimosa/ Du penebat Filius."* But in sophisticated music the pronunciation of words borrowed from Latin may give an indication of the educated Latin pronunciation. Most clusters are maintained (in European Portuguese the consonants are pronounced in *facto, absurdo, advogado*). But after a nasal vowel (see below) only a sibilant sounds at the end of a syllable: thus the *m* and *p* are silent in *re·demp·tor,* as is the *n* in *plo·rans.*

Vowels

Non-nasal

a When stressed, [a]; unstressed, it resembles the [ə] at the end of *sofa.*

au The diphthong [ou].

e When stressed, usually [ɛ], despite a complicated situation in Portuguese itself. In unstressed final syllables (*-e, -es, -et,* etc.) with short note values, may tend to [e], [i].

i [i]

o When stressed, [ɔ], but tends to [u] in an unstressed final syllable with short note values.

u [u]

Nasal

In a final syllable, a vowel followed by *m* or *n* is nasalized to [ã], [ɛ̃], [ĩ], [ɔ̃], [ũ]; e.g., *Amen* [amɛ̃].

If a vowel in a medial syllable is followed by *m* or *n* and a consonant *(gementes, flentes, Redemptor),* it is nasalized and the *m/n* is sounded weakly. This also applies in *ancillae.*

If there are two nasal consonants *(omnes, perennis, flammis)* the vowel retains slight nasality, and the second consonant is sounded.

SAMPLE TEXTS

These texts relate to music of the Portuguese Renaissance, 1600–1650.

Salve regina

CD #41.

Salve, regina misericordie
vita, dulcedo et spes nostra, salve!
ad te clamamus exsules filii Evae,
ad te suspiramus gementes et flentes
in hac lacrimarum valle.
eia ergo, advocata nostra,
illos tuos misericordes oculos ad nos converte
et Iesum, benedictum fructum ventris tui,
nobis post hoc exsilium ostende,
o clemens, o pia,
o dulcus Maria.

salvi ṛeʒinə mizəṛikɔrdi·i
vitə dulsɛdu ɛt spɛs nɔstṛə salvə
ad tɛ klamamuz ɛgzulis fili·i ɛvi
ad tɛ suspiṛamus ʒemẽtiz ɛt flẽtis
in ak lakṛimaṛũm vali
ɛʒə ɛrgu advukatə nɔstṛə
ilɔs tuɔs mizəṛikɔṛdiz ɔkulɔs ad nɔs kɔ̃vɛṛti
ɛt ʒɛzũm beneditũm fṛutũm vẽtṛis tui
nɔbis pɔst ɔk ɛgzili·ũm ɔstẽdi
ɔ klɛmẽs ɔ pi·a
ɔ dulsis maṛi·a

Crux fidelis

Crux fidelis, inter omnes arbor una nobilis
nulla silva talem profert fronde, flore, germine:
dulce lignum, dulces clavos, dulce pondus sustinet.

kṛuks fidɛlis ĩntɛr ɔ̃niz aṛbɔṛ una nɔbilis
nula silva talẽm pṛofɛṛt frɔ̃di flɔṛi ʒɛṛmini
dulsi lignũm dulsis klavɔs dulsi pɔ̃dus sustinɛt

Italy

13—

Italian

GIANRENZO P. CLIVIO

Latin was originally the language of only a small tribe that settled in the borderland of Latium and Etruria, in a rather inhospitable environment not far from the Tiber estuary, and—according to the legendary date—founded the city of Rome in 753 B.C. This tribe was of Indo-European stock and its language was related not only to Sanskrit, Germanic, and Balto-Slavic but also to several of Italy's ancient languages, such as Celtic (spoken in the north) and Greek (spoken in the south). The might of the Roman armies and fleets, as well as very skillful diplomacy, eventually carried the Latin language to a vast territory, comprising much of Europe, North Africa, and Asia Minor.[1] It continued to be widely used in its Classical form as an international language of culture until less than two hundred years ago. However, in the mouths of the people and in everyday usage, it began to undergo increasingly rapid changes in the course of the Middle Ages, splitting into regional and local dialects which eventually became mutually unintelligible, though all clearly were the recognizable offsprings of a common ancestor. By the year A.D. 1000 at the latest, the Romance languages were beginning to emerge in written form,[2] while Latin continued to be the language of the educated.

Italian is a direct continuation of ancient Latin, indeed a modern form of Latin,[3] just like French, Provençal, Catalan, Spanish, Portuguese, Romanian, and the other Romance languages and dialects.

In its present form, Italian evolved from thirteenth-century Florentine. Apart from numerous lexical additions and minor syntactic restructuring,[4] it has not changed very much since then, chiefly because until fairly recently it was primarily a written language. Therefore, while the sound systems and hence the pronunciation of other European languages, such as English and French, have undergone vast changes from medieval times to the Renaissance and on to the present, this has not happened to the language of Dante. Medieval and Renaissance Italian are pronounced exactly the same as the contemporary language. As the well-known Italian linguist Tristano Bolelli recently put it:

> In contrast to French, English, and German, with Italian we are not obliged to study a different language if we wish to read our ancient authors, starting with the fourteenth century. This distinction can be explained by the particular history of the Italian language, whose structure has remained practically unchanged over the centuries because of the literary character of its origins and because of the general acceptance of a single model (the Tuscan of Dante, Petrarch and Boccaccio) on the part of the great writers, from Ariosto to Leopardi, and thanks to the important contribution of Manzoni.[5]

The Florentine dialect soon began to enjoy immense prestige as a medium of belletristic literature, largely because of the three very great fourteenth-century writers—Dante, Petrarch, and Boccaccio—who employed it in their masterpieces.[6] Therefore it could be used in writing, chiefly as an alternative to Latin, but also to other local dialects. Its eventual triumph over the other dialects of the Peninsula can also be attributed in part to the fact that it remained closer to Latin and was hence easier to understand in other regions.

Extensive efforts to standardize the language by defining its rules were made in the sixteenth century. Controversy was intense, with some scholars insisting on adhering strictly to fourteenth-century Florentine as used by Dante, Petrarch, and Boccaccio, while others favored solutions that would take into account changes that had occurred since then and the linguistic reality of Italy. The conservative position was championed by Giovanni Francesco Fortunio (ca. 1470–1517), who published the first grammar, *Regole grammaticali della volgar lingua,* in 1516. By and large, the same opinion was held by Pietro Bembo (1470–1547), whose very influential *Prose della volgar lingua* appeared in 1525. An opposing school of thought, which may perhaps be called eclectic, rejected all archaisms and maintained that Italian should be based on the living language of the Italian courts. Its most distinguished proponents were Count Baldassarre Castiglione (1478–1529), the famous author of the *Cortegiano,* and Giangiorgio Trissino (1478–1550). Finally, several other writers, and most notably Niccolò Machiavelli (1470–1527), whose *Dialogo della lingua* was published around 1505, favored adopting contemporary Tuscan, and especially Florentine, usage. In the sixteenth century many grammars and treatises on the "vulgar" language were published.

In the end, it was Bembo's archaizing school that turned out to be the most influential until the first half of the nineteenth century. Heated controversy, however, did not cease, and the *questione della lingua,* that of defining in all of its particulars Italy's literary language, occasioned countless books and publications.[7] Outside of Tuscany, however, only the highly educated could master Florentine Italian, and they used it almost exclusively in writing or on very formal, solemn occasions. Latin remained very much alive for several more centuries.[8]

In Italy, standard Italian coexists to this day with a large number of regional and local dialects, also derived from Latin,[9] and some of them—such as Milanese, Neapolitan, Piedmontese, Sicilian, and Venetian—still enjoy a certain amount of social prestige and can boast of a not inconsiderable literary tradition.

In the Italian linguistic context, the term "dialect" may designate what is in fact a separate—though unofficial—language, diverging from Italian to such an extent that mutual intelligibility is impossible and differing from it as radically as Italian differs from

French or Spanish. This is indeed the case with the northern and southern dialects, while the dialects of central Italy are closer to Italian, though by no means devoid of their own peculiarities. For example, the simple Italian sentences *andò a parlargli* ("he went to speak to him"), *il bambino piange* ("the child is crying"), and *non gridare* ("do not shout"), correspond in Piedmontese to *a l'é andàit a parleje, ël cit a piora,* and *braja nen;* and in Neapolitan to *jette pe nce parla', 'o ninno chiagne,* and *n'allucca'.* Because poetic texts with musical settings from the relevant period are not to be found in these and other dialects, we need not concern ourselves here with their pronunciation.

Standard Italian is blessed with a spelling system which represents actual pronunciation in a fairly accurate, though not always straightforward way and leaves little doubt. This is not to say that an English speaker will not encounter some significant difficulties, for Italian is not pronounced in exactly the same way in every region of the country, though mutual intelligibility is generally not a problem.[10]

There are two major models for Italian pronunciation, and they differ considerably. We shall deal first with cultivated Florentine (FIt), not only in homage to tradition, but also because the northern system (NIt) can readily be described in terms of simplification of various aspects of the Florentine-type pronunciation in that it corresponds much more closely to the standard orthography.

However, before undertaking a detailed examination of FIt and NIt phonemes, a summary overview of the spelling system and of the correspondence between letters and sounds is in order.

Spelling

As pointed out by Agard and Di Pietro, "although Italian spelling does not represent Italian phonemes in a perfect one-to-one relationship, it nevertheless is close enough to provide a striking contrast with English."[11] The correspondences between sounds and letters or letter combinations are shown in Table I. While modern Italian spelling is fully standardized, older Italian texts often contain spelling peculiarities due largely to Latin graphic influence and to uncertainty about how to write the vulgar tongue in the absence of fixed norms. For example, *u* and *v* were not graphically distinguished, as in modern usage, as late as the seventeenth century; and spellings such as *bvono, uero, uoi* for *buono, vero, voi* were normal. Etymological *h* was often retained in writing *(honesto, honore, huomo),* again well into the seventeenth century, though it was certainly not pronounced; it was often omitted in verb forms that now require it and sometimes replaced by a stress mark *(ò, à).* The conjunction "and" was written *et* as in Latin, though the *t* was not pronounced; *k* and *ch* were common in place of velar *c* in any position; *ph* was often written instead of *f* in learned words; and *ç* or *ti* (less commonly *cz* or *th*) were frequently used instead of *z* or *zz (dolçemente, treçe, amicitia, avaritia).*[12] These older graphemes, together with a few others, and their phonetic values are summarized and exemplified in Table II. Several of them occur in the texts in phonetic transcription at the end of this chapter.

Modern editors of older texts tend to eliminate to a lesser or greater extent some of the peculiarities of old Italian spelling (according to stated or unstated criteria). As for

Table I

Modern standard spellings		Pronunciation
a		[a]
b		[b]
c	(before *a, o, u*)	[k]
c	(before *i, e*)	[tʃ]
ch	(before *i, e*)	[k]
ci	(before *a, o, u*)	[tʃ]
cq	(used only before *u*)	[kk] (e.g., *acqua* = ['akkwa]
d		[d]
e		[e], [ɛ]
é	(only in word-final position)	[e]
è	(only in word-final position)	[ɛ]
f		[f]
g	(before *a, o, u*)	[g]
g	(before *i, e*)	[dʒ]
gh	(before *i, e*)	[g]
gi	(before *a, o, u*)	[dʒ]
gli		[ʎ]
gn		[ɲ]
i		[i], [j] before or after stressed vowel
l		[l]
m		[m]
n		[n], [ŋ] before velar stops ([k], [g])
o		[o], [ɔ]
ò	(only in word-final position)	stressed ['ɔ]
p		[p]
q	(before *u* in many words)*	[k]
r		[r]
s		[z] before voiced consonant, [s] word-initially before vowel or before voiceless consonant, [s] or [z] elsewhere (always [z] intervocalically in NIt)
sc	(before *i, e*)	[ʃ]
sci	(before *a, o, u*)	[ʃ]
t		[t]
u		[u], [w] before or after stressed vowel
v		[v]
z	(intervocalically zz in some words)	[ts] or [dz]

punctuation (including accent marks and the use of the apostrophe), in medieval texts it was either almost entirely absent or much reduced; modern norms did not become established until approximately the beginning of the seventeenth century. Again, contemporary editors tend to modernize punctuation in order to facilitate reading.

Note that in a few cases *gl* is not pronounced [ʎ] but [gl] as in English *glad;* this applies word-initially *(glauco, gloria, gleba)* except in the word *gli* and its compounds *(glielo, gliene,* etc.) and in *gliommero* ("a type of poetical composition"). In word-internal position *gl* is pronounced [gl] when it is preceded by *n (ganglio),* in *negligente* and *negligenza,* in all forms of the verb *siglare,* and in a few other rare words.

* The use of *c* or *q* before *u* in Italian spelling depends largely on etymology: thus *quando* < Lat. *quando* ("when") but *cuore* < Lat. *cor* ("heart"). Common words spelled with *cu* are *cuocere, cuoco, cuoio, percuotere, scuotere,* and *scuola.*

Table II

Older spellings		Pronunciation
bs		[ss] (e.g., *absentia* for *assenza*)
ç		[dz] or [ts] (e.g., *çappatore* = *zappatore, treççe* = *trezze*), rarely [z]
ch		[k] (used before any vowel, e.g., *bocha, chosa*)
ci	before vowel	[ts] (e.g., *ocio* = *ozio, gracia* = *grazia*)
cz	(used primarily in south Italy)	[ts] or [ttʃ] (e.g., *saczo* = *saccio*)
et		[e] (only in the meaning "and")
h		no phonetic value (e.g., *homo, honore*)
î	(only in word-final position)	[i]
j		[j] (used word-initially or intervocalically, e.g., *jeri, ajo*)
k		[k] (e.g., *kiese* = ['kjeze])
lgl(i)		[λ] (e.g., *filglio* = *figlio, folglia* = *foglia*)
ngn(i)		[ɲ] (e.g., *dengno* = *degno*)
ph		[f] (e.g., *philosophia*)
ps		[ss] (e.g., *epso* = *esso*)
pt		[tt] (e.g., *apto* = *atto, rapto* = *ratto*)
th		[ts] (e.g., *vethosa* = [*vet'tsoza*]) or [t] (e.g., *theatro* = *teatro, thesoro* = *tesoro*)
ti	(before vowel)	[ts] (e.g., *gratia* = *grazia, spatio* = *spazio*)
u		[u] or [v]
v		[u] or [v]
x		[z] (especially in northern Italy), [ss] in etymological spellings of the type *maximo*)
y		[i] (especially in words of Greek origin)

Until about the first half of the twentieth century some writers employed *j* instead of *i* intervocalically and sometimes in word-initial and word-final positions to write the semivowel [j]; and in the masculine plural of nouns such as *criterio, rimedio, studio* some grammarians recommended the use of *î (criterî, rimedî, studî)* while others preferred *j*.

While Tables I and II provide a quick guide to Italian pronunciation, they may leave the user in doubt about the phonetic values of certain ambiguous letters, e.g., *e, o, z,* and *s*. Also, the tables do not reflect certain other peculiarities of Italian pronunciation, such as the important distinction between short and long consonants and the phenomenon of syntactic doubling. These problems will be dealt with in the examination of the consonant and vowel systems below.

Stress

Stress is written obligatorily when it falls on the last vowel of a word, e.g., *saprò* ("I'll know") and in a few other cases to distinguish homographs, the more common of which are shown in Table III. In modern usage, accent marks on the vowel *e* in word-final position indicate its closed *(é)* or open *(è)* quality, but this distinction was not observed in older texts (though it often is by their modern editors).

Stress position must be shown in either phonetic or phonemic transcription because stress in Italian is a suprasegmental or "simultaneous" phoneme that may differentiate otherwise identical words. See Table IV. Stress may fall on the last, next to the last, or

Table III

ché	"why," "because"	che	"who," "which," "that"
dà	"give!"	da	"from"
è	"is"	e	"and"
là	"there"	la	"the" (f. sing.)
lì	"here"	li	"them" (m. pl.)
né	"neither," "nor"	ne	"of it," "of them"
sé	"oneself"	se	"if"
sì	"yes"	si	"oneself"
tè	"tea"	te	"you" (object)

third last syllable of a word. Less commonly, however, it may also fall on the fourth or the fifth syllable from the end of a word, as in [ˈindikano] ("they indicate"), [ˈkapitano] ("they happen"), [ˈpoṛtamelo] ("bring it to me"), [ˈalteṛamene] ("alter some for me"), [ˈindikatʃene] ("indicate some to us"), etc. Some monosyllables bear a stress in pronunciation while others are either proclitic or enclitic, i.e., in speech they become "attached" to the preceding or the following word. Enclisis is generally shown in normal spelling by writing the enclitic word as one with the preceding word, e.g., [ˈpaṛlami] = *parla* + *mi* ("speak to me"), but proclisis is not indicated. Thus, in phonetic or phonemic transcription stress must be marked on monosyllables that bear it in order to distinguish them from unstressed clitics.

Words stressed on the next to the last syllable (known as *parole piane*) are the most common, while those stressed on the third and fourth from the last are primarily infinitive, imperative, or gerund verb forms with one or two enclitic pronouns. Words stressed on the last syllable *(parole tronche)* will cause no difficulty since a stress mark is obligatory, required by the spelling system (see below). The words that are likely to give problems are those in which the stress falls on the third last syllable *(parole sdrucciole),* since the spelling does not indicate this.[13]

Practice will teach the foreign learner which words are *sdrucciole,* but the following rules will help initially:

Words consisting of three of more syllables are *parole piane* if the vowel of the next to the last syllable is followed in normal spelling by two consonants the second one of

Table IV

[anˈkoṛa]	"yet," "still"	[ˈankoṛa]	"anchor"
[desiˈdeṛi]	"desires"	[deˈsideṛi]	"you wish"
[imˈpaṛi]	"you learn"	[ˈimpaṛi]	"uneven"
[ˈkanto]	"I sing"	[kanˈto]	"he sang"
[kapiˈtano]	"captain"	[kapitaˈno]	"he led"
[paˈgano]	"pagan"	[ˈpagano]	"they pay"
[ˈpenso]	"I think"	[penˈso]	"he thought"
[prinˈtʃipi]	"principles"	[ˈprintʃipi]	"princes"
[ˈsali]	"you go up"	[saˈli]	"he went up"
[ˈspaṛi]	"shots"	[spaˈṛi]	"he disappeared"

which is neither *l* nor *r.* Exceptions are verb forms with enclitic pronouns: such forms retain the stress on the same syllable as the simple infinitive, e.g., [ˈskṛiverti] ("to write to you"), [ˈlɛddʒeṛtʃi] ("to read to us") with stress as in [ˈskṛivere] ("to write") and [ˈlɛddʒeṛe] ("to read"). Many place names and surnames also contradict this rule.[14]

Nouns ending in *-agine (compagine), -igine (caligine), -iggine (fuliggine), -edine (torpedine),* and *-udine (solitudine)* are stressed on the third last syllable.

The same applies to adjectives and nouns ending in *-abile (inabile), -evole (lodevole), -ibile (possibile), -aceo (cartaceo), -ico (tecnico), -ognolo (amarognolo),* and *-oide (pazzoide).*

Further rules could be provided for learned and scientific words; however, most of them are uncommon.[15]

Consonants

In striking contrast with English, in Italian the only consonants that can occur in word-final position are [l], [ṛ], and [n], which are found in a few common monosyllables (e.g., *bel, con, il, in, per, quel*). However, according to the rules of syntax, they can never appear in sentence- or phrase-final position. Hence, as N. Vincent observes, they are "best treated as proclitics rather than independent phonological words."[16] A final vowel may be dropped in other words as well if the preceding consonant is [l], [ṛ], [n], or [m] (e.g., *amabil, cuor, lodan, andiam, partiam*). This is quite common in literary texts and especially in songs and operatic librettos, but it is unusual in normal prose or conversation.

Consonants in Italian may be either short or long. The difference, in word-internal position, is phonemic, that is, it may differentiate one word from another; e.g., *fato* ("fate") vs. *fatto* ("done"), *faremo* ("we shall do") vs. *faremmo* ("we would do"). Long consonants occur not only word-internally but, in FIt as well as in all central and southern varieties, also in word-initial position under certain circumstances. In phonetic or phonemic transcription a long consonant may be transcribed by doubling it as in the normal spelling; e.g., [pp] as in [ˈtappo] ("cork"), [ll] as in [ˈpalla] ("ball").

Word-internal long consonants are indicated in the standard spelling system by writing the long consonant twice, e.g., *palla* ("ball") vs. *pala* ("shovel"). Exceptions are voiced *s* ([z]), which occurs only short; and [ʃ], [ɲ], and [ʎ], which are always long[17] and are spelled respectively *sc(i), gn,* and *gl(i),* as in *lasciare* ("to leave"), *pesce* ("fish"), *bagno* ("bath"), *foglia* ("leaf" of a tree), *figli* ("sons").[18] The *i* after *sc* and *gl* is used, obligatorily, when the following vowel is [u], [o], [ɔ], or [a]. The affricates [ts] and [dz], both written as *z,* are also always pronounced long intervocalically (and transcribed here as [tts] and [ddz]), but the spelling system does not always indicate this because of etymological reasons; hence *pazzo* ("mad") but *vizio* ("vice"), both pronounced [tts].

The process whereby a consonant is lengthened—or in layman's terms, doubled—in initial position (after a preceding word ending in a vowel) is referred to as "syntactic doubling" *(rafforzamento sintattico).* Word-initial long consonants are never indicated by the writing system (in FIt one writes *a cavallo* but says [a kkaˈvallo], for instance), except in a few cases when two words, which frequently occur together, have come to be spelled—optionally or obligatorily—as one word (e.g., *oppure* from *o pure, daccapo* from *da capo*). It should be pointed out, however, that consonant doubling in initial position is frequently found in early Italian texts written before the spelling system had become stabilized.

Syntactic doubling occurs consistently in FIt (and in all central and southern varieties of the language) after any word ending in a stressed vowel (e.g., *andò via* = [an'do 'vvia]), as well as after the monosyllables *a, blu, che, chi, e, è, da, fra, ma, né, o, qui, qua, se, tu, tra* when the following word in the same pitch phrase begins with a single consonant or with a consonant plus [r̥] or [l]. Syntactic doubling is also caused by the monosyllabic verb forms *dò, fa, fu, ha, ho, va;* by all monosyllables that bear a graphic stress, such as *ciò, dà, dì, già, giù, più, sé;* and by *come, dove, qualche, sopra.*

Learning to pronounce long consonants correctly is one of the principal difficulties English speakers encounter in studying Italian (but see below for the situation obtaining in NIt pronunciation).

Long consonants are produced by holding the position of articulation approximately one and a half to two times as long as for short consonants before being released. While English has no long consonants as such, sequences of identical consonants may occur at word boundaries, as in *wet turf, mad dog, enough fun, top pay, leg gear, ten knots.* When these sequences are pronounced rapidly, with no pause between the words, they approximate Italian long [t], [d], [f], [p], [g], [n]. Examples of common Italian words containing long consonants are shown in Table V. Examples of common words which are distinguished only by consonant length are given in Table VI.

Italian consonants may be classified as stops or occlusives, affricates, fricatives, sibilants, laterals, trills, and nasals. Stops, affricates, fricatives, and sibilants may be voiced (i.e., produced with vibration of the vocal chords) or voiceless (i.e., produced with no vibration of the vocal chords). This distinction is unlikely to cause any difficulty since it occurs in English as well.

Concerning the point of articulation (i.e., the point in the mouth where a given consonant is produced), the following positions can be distinguished: bilabial, labio-dental, dental, palatal, and velar. In the production of nasal sounds, part of the air flow exits through the nasal cavity, as in English. Table VII shows Italian consonants in phonetic transcription according to their manner and position of articulation.

Table V

[pp]	*zappa* ("hoe")	[tts]	*mazzo* ("bunch")
[bb]	*babbo* ("father")	[ddz]	*mezzo* ("half")
[tt]	*tetto* ("roof")	[ttʃ]	*faccia* ("face")
[dd]	*addio* ("adieu")	[ddʒ]	*maggio* ("May")
[kk]	*pacco* ("package")	[mm]	*somma* ("sum")
[gg]	*leggo* ("I read")	[nn]	*panno* ("cloth")
[ff]	*affare* ("deal")	[ɲɲ]	*bagno* ("bath")
[vv]	*avvenire* ("future")	[ll]	*bello* ("beautiful")
[ss]	*sasso* ("stone")	[λλ]	*tagliare* ("to cut")
[ʃʃ]	*pesce* ("fish")	[rr]	*terra* ("earth," "land")

When the stress falls on the vowel following a long, or double, consonant, it is traditionally marked as follows: [ap'pare], [seb'bene], [mat'tso], [mɛd'dzo], [at'tʃajo], [mad'dʒore]; that is, between the first and second symbols used to transcribe a long consonant.

Table VI

bruto	"brute"	*brutto*	"ugly"
camino	"chimney"	*cammino*	"path, walkway"
cane	"dog"	*canne*	"reeds"
capello	"hair"	*cappello*	"hat"
caro	"dear"	*carro*	"cart"
copia	"copy"	*coppia*	"couple"
dona	"he gives"	*donna*	"woman"
eco	"echo"	*ecco*	"here"
mola	"grindstone"	*molla*	"(metal) spring"
nono	"ninth"	*nonno*	"grandfather"
pala	"shovel"	*palla*	"ball"
poro	"pore"	*porro*	"wart"
rito	"rite"	*ritto*	"upright"
tufo	"tufa"	*tuffo*	"dive"
vile	"coward"	*ville*	"villas"

It should be noted that in FIt certain consonantal oppositions have a very low functional yield, that is, they distinguish only a very few pairs of words or, perhaps, none at all. Thus, minimal pairs for [s] vs. [z], both spelled *s*, are extremely few and are not found in the speech of all individuals.[19] The same can be said of [ts] vs. [dz], both spelled *z*.[20] Nonetheless, [s] and [z], and [ts] and [dz] respectively occur in similar contexts, and the distinction is unmistakable to a Florentine ear. Complete rules to establish when the letters *s* (representing [s] or [z]), and *z* (representing [ts] or [dz]) should be pronounced voiced or voiceless in intervocalic position are practically impossible to provide; however, the following rules (and lists of exceptions) will help, while at the same time showing how complicated it is to adhere to FIt pronunciation in this regard.

The phonemes [s] and [z] have a partially complementary distribution in FIt in that only [s] can occur word-initially before a vowel, after a consonant (e.g., *forse, penso*), and, initially or internally, before a voiceless consonant. In intervocalic position, however, both [s] and [z] may occur.

In general, the letter *s* corresponds to [z] in FIt only in non-compound words (e.g., *casacca, poesia, uso*) or in words no longer felt to be compounds (e.g., *desinenza, esangue, filosofo*), but words ending in *-es-, -os-* are pronounced with [s] (e.g., *acceso, geloso, inglese, mese, posi, spesa, ripreso*). However, *Agnese, bleso, chiesa, cortese, francese, lesi, leso,*

Table VII

		bilabial	labio-dental	dental	palatal	velar
Stops	voiceless	p		t		k
	voiced	b		d		g
Affricates	voiceless			ts	tʃ	
	voiced			dz	dʒ	
Fricatives	voiceless		f			
	voiced		v			
Sibilants	voiceless			s	ʃ	
	voiced			z		
Laterals				l	ʎ	
Trills				r̥		
Nasals		m		n	ɲ	ŋ

marchese, obeso, paese, palese, rosa, sposo, and others have [z]. In the common endings *-osìa, -osità* the letter *s* is also pronounced [s] (e.g., *bramosia, curiosità, gelosia, golosità*). Words containing the sequences *ras-, res-, ris-* have [s] (e.g., *raso, resa, riso*); among the exceptions are *abrasi, abraso, derisi, deriso, irrisi, irriso, rasente, risico,* and *resina.* The words *asello, asino, casa, chiusi, chiuso, cosa, così, desiderio, difesa, fuso* (noun), *naso, peso, Pisa, pisello, posa, rimasi, rimasuglio, susina,* and others have [s] (also in their inflected and derivative forms) and must be memorized. Furthermore, [z] is found in the ending *-esimo* (e.g., *battesimo, cristianesimo, trentesimo*); in the ending vowel + *-sione* (e.g., *fusione, visione*); in learned words ending in *-asi, -esi, -isi, -osi, -usi* (e.g., *analisi, apoteosi, crasi, crisi, esegesi, metamorfosi, mimesi,* etc.); in the prefixes *bis-* and *dis-* (e.g., *bisunto, disonesto*); in the following common words (besides those already listed): *base, bisogno, caso, causa, chiesa, desinare, elemosina, episodio, esame, esempio, esilio, esercizio, esule, fantasia, fusione, fuso* (past participle of *fondere*), *Giuseppe, isola, misura, museo, musica, osare, poesia, pausa, presentare, prosa, quasi, rosa, uso, usura, visita, viso* (including inflected forms and derivatives), and a few others.

As for the pronunciation of the letter *z,* which between vowels may be written *zz* without any difference in pronunciation, the following general guidelines apply: in word-initial position it is normally pronounced voiceless as [ts], but *zaffiro, zaino, zanzara, Zefiro, zelo, zero, zeta, zigzag, zolla, zotico,* and a few other words have initial [dz], as in general do words whose second syllable begins with a voiced consonant (e.g., *zanzara, zenzero, Zodiaco*), but *zanna, zana,* and *zazzera* have [ts]. It is pronounced [ts] in the endings *-anza, -enza, -zione, -izia, -ezza, -ozzo, -uzzo, -onzolo,* and *-zi* + vowel (e.g., *amicizia, anziano*), *diffidenza, nazione, poetonzolo, predicozzo, speranza,* and *stanchezza;* but *azienda, pranzo, pranzare, ronzio, romanziere,* and derivatives have [dz]. It is also pronounced [ts] after [l] and generally after [r̥] and [n] (e.g., *alzare, calza, danza, terzo*), but *Belzebù, donzella* and a few other words are pronounced with [dz]. The following words have [ts]: *forza, innanzi, menzogna, nozze, pazzo, pezzo, pozzo, prezzo, ragazzo, senza, stanza, tazza, terzo.*

The letter *z* is also voiced in the verbal endings *-ezzare* and *-izzare* and in their inflected or derived forms (e.g., *armonizzare, analizzare, organizzare, organizzazione, battezzare*). However, if *-ezzare, -izzare* are not endings, but part of the stem of a verb, then *z* is voiceless (e.g., *frizzare, guizzare, raccapezzare, schizzare*). It is generally voiced when written as a single consonant between vowels (e.g., *bizantino*), but the surname *Guinizelli* is an exception.[21] Finally the letter *z* is voiced in the following common words: *arzillo, azzurro, bronzo, dozzina, mezzo, orizzonte.*

A non-Florentine wishing to adhere to FIt pronunciation would have to invest a considerable amount of time in memorization and practice. The situation in NIt is much simpler in that intervocalic *s* is always pronounced [z] and word-initial *z* is always [dz] (see below).

Most of the consonant phonemes shown in Table VII occur in English as well and present no problem, but several differences exist:

In English [t], [d], and [n] are apico-alveolar rather than apico-dental. This means that English [t], [d], and [n] are generally produced with the apex, or tip, of the tongue touching the alveolar ridge behind the upper teeth, whereas in Italian the tip of the tongue touches the teeth themselves.

In English the voiceless stops [p], [t], and [k] and the affricate [tʃ] are followed by a puff of air when they occur as the first sound in stressed syllables (compare the [p] of *pot,* which is aspirated, with the [p] of *spot,* which is not).[22] No such aspiration occurs in Italian.

The lateral [l] has two positional variants in English, often referred to as "bright" *l* and "dark" *l.* Dark *l* occurs in syllable-final position, as in *full, Bill;* bright *l* occurs in all other positions (compare the initial sound of *late* with the *l* of *table*). No dark *l* exists in Italian, and care should be taken to avoid it in words such as *altro, del,* and *il.*

The English sequences [ts] and [dz], as in *bets, beds, pats, pads,* are similar to Italian [ts] and [dz]. However, [ts] and [dz] occur in English only in word-internal or word-final position, whereas Italian [ts] and [dz] occur word-initially as well; e.g., *zio* ("uncle") and *zero* ("zero"), so that English speakers may experience some difficulty in this regard.

English [r] is pronounced somewhat differently in different varieties of the language, and it has partly vowel-like variants. It is defined as a voiced alveolar frictionless continuant, exemplified by the initial consonant of *rib.* On the other hand, Italian [r̪] is a voiced dental flap, involving the apex of the tongue moving rapidly near the upper teeth. On the whole, it is a difficult sound for English speakers to imitate and only practice will help. In particular, English [tr] and [dr] sound quite different from Italian [tr̪] and [dr̪], for in English these clusters are articulated noticeably further back in the mouth (compare English *tree* and *drama* with Italian *tre* and *dramma*).

The palatals [ʎ] and [ɲ] do not exist in English. They are similar but not identical to the sequences [lj] and [nj] in *million* and *onion,* also because Italian [ʎ] and [ɲ] are phonetically long. Pronunciations such as [ˈfiljo] and [ˈbanjo], though not desirable, are acceptable. Word-initial [ʎ] is almost nonexistent in lexical words, but is very common in utterance-initial position because of the form *gli* [ʎi], which is both the masculine plural article before nouns or adjectives beginning with a vowel and the third person masculine indirect object pronoun. Palatal [ɲ] is also very rare in word-initial position.

In English, the velar nasal [ŋ] has phonemic status in that it may differentiate words (compare *sin* vs. *sing*). In Italian, it is a positional variant of [n] which occurs only before [k] and [g] as in *anche* and *sangue.*

Both English and Italian have a voiced *s*, transcribed [z], and the sound is almost identical in the two languages. However, its distribution differs; in English there are no words beginning with [z] plus a consonant (words such as *slip, smile, snow* have an initial [s]). In Italian [s] cannot occur before a voiced consonant; that is why Italian speakers tend to pronounce *slip, smile, snow* as [ˈzlip], [ˈzmajl], [ˈznow]. English speakers must learn to pronounce [zb], [zd], [zdʒ], [zv], [zg], [zm], [zn], [zl], and [zr], which in English may occur word-internally[23] but not initially. Examples of Italian words beginning with these clusters are given in Table VIII.

Two-member word-initial clusters are in general limited in Italian to the following types: occlusive or [f] + [r̪]; [p], [b], [k], [g], [f] + [l]; [s] + [p], [t], [k], [f]; and [z] + [b], [d], [g], [v], [l], [r̪], [m], [n], [ɲ]. Only the fourth type is likely to cause English speakers any serious difficulty. The cluster [stʃ] is absent in FIt but is often heard in NIt in words

Table VIII

[zb]	*sbagliare*	"to err"
[zd]	*sdraiarsi*	"to lay down"
[zdʒ]	*sgelare*	"to thaw"
[zv]	*svegliare*	"to wake up"
[zg]	*sgridare*	"to scold"
[zm]	*smettere*	"to cease"
[zn]	*snodare*	"to untie a knot"
[zl]	*slacciare*	"to untie"
[zr]	*srotolare*	"to unwind"

such as *scentrare, scervellare;* it is pronounced with initial [ʃ] in FIt, but generally with [stʃ] in NIt. In loan words and technical terms some additional hetero-organic clusters occur.[24]

Triconsonantal initial clusters may only consist of *s* plus any of the clusters of the first two types listed above, except that [skl], [zgl], and [sfl] do not occur in common words. The following are examples of triconsonantal clusters: *sprecare, sbranare, stremare, sdraiare, scranna, sgridare, sfracassare;* and *splendere, sbloccare, (e)sclamare.*

Vowels

In FIt the vowel system consists of seven vowel phonemes in stressed position (indicated by the symbol ˈ preceding the stressed syllable) and five in unstressed position: [i], [e], [a], [o], and [u]. The seven stressed vowels are [i], [e], [ɛ], [a], [o], [ɔ], and [u] (see Table IX). They may occur initially, medially, or finally (except for [u], which does not occur unstressed in final position). Vowels occurring before a short consonant are phonetically longer than vowels before a long (or "double") consonant: the [a] in *fato,* for example, is longer than the [a] in *fatto.*

The standard spelling system represents both [e] and [ɛ] with the single grapheme *e,*[25] and both [o] and [ɔ] with the single grapheme *o,* yet the distinctions are unmistakable to a Tuscan ear.

All Italian vowels are pronounced without a following glide, which is heard in the pronunciation of several English vowels, and therefore only approximate comparisons can be made.

The phoneme [i] is a front (or anterior) high unrounded vowel; it is produced in the anterior part of the mouth with the tongue elevated and close to the upper teeth and the lips unrounded (if the lips are rounded while the tongue is maintained in the same position the resulting vowel is [y] as in French *pur* or German *Bücher*). Examples of its

Table IX

	Front	Central	Back
High	i		u
High mid	e		o
Low mid	ɛ		ɔ
Low		a	

occurrence in Italian are *isola* [ˈisola] ("island"), *filo* [ˈfilo] ("thread"), and *partì* [parˈti] ("[he] left"). It can be compared to the onset of the vowel nucleus of English *beat* [ˈbijt], and is distinctly higher than the vowel in *bit.* While Italian speakers have difficulty distinguishing between such words as *beat* and *bit,* English speakers learn Italian [i] without significant problems. The phoneme [i], when followed or preceded by a stressed vowel, becomes the semivowel [j] as in *ieri* ("yesterday"), *fiore* ("flower"), *piede* ("foot"), *mai* ("never"), *guaio* ("trouble").

The phoneme [e], often called "closed e" or *e chiusa,*[26] is a front high-mid unrounded vowel; it is produced in the anterior part of the mouth with the tongue elevated toward the upper teeth, but less so than in the case of [i], and with lips unrounded. Examples of its occurrence in Italian are *esse* [ˈesse] ("they" [feminine plural]), *sera* [ˈsera] ("evening"), *perché* [perˈke] ("why" or "because"). It can be roughly compared to the vowel of English *bet,* but is higher and closer to the *é* of French *été.*

The phoneme [ɛ], often called "open e" or *e aperta,* is a front low-mid unrounded vowel; it is produced in the anterior part of the mouth with the tongue elevated toward the upper teeth, but less so than in the case of [e], and with lips unrounded. Examples of its occurrence in Italian are *esse* [ˈɛsse] ("s" [the letter]), *bene* [ˈbɛne] ("well"), *caffè* [kafˈfɛ] ("coffee"). It can be roughly compared to the vowel of English *bed.*

The phoneme [a] is a central low unrounded vowel; it is produced with the tongue in a more or less flat position and with the lips quite open and unrounded. Examples of its occurrence in Italian words are *anima* [ˈanima] ("soul"), *andare* [anˈdare] ("to go"), *città* [tʃitˈta] ("city"). It is comparable to the *a* of German *Mann* or French *patte.*

The phoneme [u] is a back high rounded vowel; it is produced in the posterior part of the mouth with the tongue elevated toward the hard palate and with lips rounded. Examples of its occurrence in Italian are *uno* [ˈuno] ("one"), *pugno* [ˈpuɲɲo] ("fist"), *tribù* [triˈbu] ("tribe"). It can be compared to the onset of the vowel nucleus of English *boot* [ˈbuwt], and is distinctly higher than the vowel heard in *bush.* While Italian speakers have difficulty distinguishing between the vowels of such words as *boot* and *bush,* English speakers easily learn Italian [u]. The phoneme [u], when followed or preceded by a stressed vowel, becomes the semivowel [w] as in *quale* ("which"), *qui* ("here"), *Pasqua* ("Easter"), *causa* ("cause"), *cauto* ("cautious"). The sound [w] is very similar to the *w* of English *water.*

The phoneme [o], often called "closed o" or *o chiusa,* is a back high-mid rounded vowel; it is produced in the posterior part of the mouth with the tongue elevated toward the hard palate, but less so than in the case of [u], and with lips rounded. Examples of its occurrence in Italian are *olmo* [ˈolmo] ("elm") and *ponte* [ˈponte] ("bridge"). It does not occur under stress in final position. It corresponds to the vowel sound of French *beau* and can be compared roughly to the onset of the vowel nucleus of English *boat* [ˈbowt].

The phoneme [ɔ], often called "open o" or *o aperta,* is a back low-mid rounded vowel; it is produced in the posterior part of the mouth with the tongue elevated toward the hard palate, but less so than in the case of [o], and with lips rounded. Examples of its occurrence in Italian are *occhio* [ˈɔkkjo] ("eye"), *porta* [ˈpɔrta] ("door"), *andrò* [anˈdrɔ] ("I'll go"). It can be compared to the first vowel of English *coffee.*

Table X

With Open Vowel		With Closed Vowel	
accetta	"he accepts"	*accetta*	"hatchet"
affetto	"affection"	*affetto*	"I slice"
collega	"colleague"	*collega*	"he joins"
legge	"he reads"	*legge*	"law"
pesca	"peach"	*pesca*	"fishing"
venti	"winds"	*venti*	"twenty"
botte	"beating"	*botte*	"barrel"
colto	"picked"	*colto*	"educated"
volto	"I turn"	*volto*	"face"

The vowel phonemes [e] and [ɛ], and [o] and [ɔ], have an extremely low functional yield even in FIt; that is, these oppositions differentiate only a very few pairs of words, the large majority of which are unlikely to occur in the same syntactic context and thus create ambiguity. This explains why standard spelling does not indicate the distinction between [e] and [ɛ] and between [o] and [ɔ].[27]

Some of the often cited "minimal pairs" (i.e., words which differ only by one phoneme) are shown in Table X. Not many more minimal pairs appear to exist, and some are clearly artificial, consisting of one archaic and one modern word, such as *mele* (modern *miele*) ("honey") vs. *mele* ("apples"), *torre* (modern *togliere*) ("to remove") vs. *torre* ("tower").

In NIt pronunciation little importance is attached to distinguishing between open and closed mid vowels. The distinction does exist, but it is often blurred and occurs under conditions dictated chiefly by sound patterns of the various dialect substrata and thus bear little or no resemblance to the state of affairs obtaining in FIt. For instance, [o] occurs in Milan but not in Turin;[28] and the distribution of mid vowels in Bergamo differs radically from that of FIt.[29] In any event, the matter is not felt to be of any importance, since it is not reflected by the spelling. A non-Italian would be well advised to take the same position and pronounce any *e* as either [e] or [ɛ], and any *o* as either [o] or [ɔ], whichever is easier. In transcribing NIt pronunciation phonetically only [e] and [o] need be used for the mid vowels: whether one pronounces *sole* as [ˈsole] or [ˈsɔle] is irrelevant.

In addition to the simple vowels, FIt has twenty-one diphthongs (see Table XI), i.e., two-vowel sequences occurring in the same syllable, one of which becomes phonetically a semivowel. In Italian, only [i] and [u] may function as the semivowel member of a diphthong. Only a few of the FIt diphthongs may present difficulties for English speakers.[30]

All other bivocalic sequences occurring in Italian are to be regarded as belonging to different syllables (e.g., *aeree, caotico, eroe, epopea, lineetta, zii*) but in poetry or in opera librettos any two-vowel sequence may, by syneresis, contract into a single syllable, just as a diphthong may, by dieresis, count as two syllables. As observed by Agard and Di Pietro, "this is possible, of course, because there exist no phonemic contrasts between vowel sequences and diphthongs; the differences are entirely phonetic."[31]

Italian also possesses five triphthongs, i.e., sequences of three vowels, one of which is a full vowel and the others semivowels: [jɛj]: *miei;* [wej]: *quei;* [waj]: *guai;* [wɔj]: *vuoi, buoi;* [woj]: *cuoiame.*

North Italian Pronunciation

The Romance languages are often classified into western and eastern: the border between these two main groups is an imaginary line that goes from just south of the city of La Spezia on the Thyrrenean Sea to just south of the city of Rimini on the Adriatic. The La Spezia–Rimini line, running along the northern border of Tuscany, corresponds to an impressive bundle of isoglosses marking certain historical linguistic developments, such as the voicing of intervocalic stops, the lack of long consonants, the tendency to drop unstressed vowels, the assibilation of palatals before front vowels.[32] This linguistic border in fact divides Italy into two main linguistic areas. The central and southern dialects have many features in common with FIt and, together with it, belong to eastern Romance (of which the other major member is Romanian). The northern Italian dialects belong to western Romance and, in many ways, have more in common with French than with Italian. Thus, Italian was learned in the North as a foreign language and it is now pronounced "as it is written," though of course with noticeable influences of the various dialect substrata.

Practically all characteristics of NIt pronunciation constitute simplifications of FIt pronunciation; whatever the spelling system does not explicitly indicate is not pronounced, and certain ambiguities of the system itself have either been resolved or are not felt to be important. As a result, NIt pronunciation is much simpler and easier to learn for a non-Italian than FIt:

Syntactic doubling does not exist. A consonant is pronounced long only if it is written double.

The consonants [ʃ], [ʎ], and [ɲ] are pronounced short. The sounds [ʎ] and [ɲ] are practically undistinguishable from the sequences [lj] and [nj], so that *li* in *Italia* and *gl* in *taglia* sound the same.[33]

The distinction between closed and open mid vowels is blurred (since, as mentioned above, the spelling system does not indicate this distinction), and they generally occur in accordance with their distribution patterns in the various dialect substrata. Thus, little or no importance is attached to distinguishing between closed and open *e* and *o*, and either the closed or the open vowels may be used indifferently in any context. This leads

Table XI

[je]	*pietà*	[wi]	*qui*
[jɛ]	*pietra*	[we]	*quello*
[ja]	*chiaro*	[wɛ]	*quercia*
[jo]	*piombo*	[wa]	*guasto*
[jɔ]	*pioggia*	[wo]	*nuotare*
[ju]	*piuma*	[wɔ]	*uovo*
[ej]	*pei (per + i)*	[oj]	*noi*
[ɛj]	*sei*	[ɔj]	*eroico*
[aj]	*sai*	[uj]	*lui*
[ɛw]	*europeo*	[ɛw]	*pneuma*
[aw]	*pausa*		

to the recognition of only two mid vowel phonemes, each with two nondistinctive variants. The distribution of such variants generally follows the patterns of the underlying local dialect but is of no relevance from a distinctive point of view. As a consequence, the twenty-one diphthongs of FIt may be regarded as being reduced in NIt to only fourteen and the five triphthongs to three.

The phonemes [s] and [z] of FIt are reduced to allophones, i.e., positional variants, of the same consonant: voiced *s* occurs before voiced consonants and intervocalically; in all other positions voiceless *s* occurs.

Voiceless [ts] in initial position does not occur; in that position, the letter *z* is always pronounced [dz] (hence ['dzio] vs. FIt ['tsio]). In other positions the pronunciation of the letter *z* is unpredictable, as in FIt; e.g., *pezzo* ("piece") is ['pettso] but *mezzo* ("half") is ['meddzo]. But by and large the general rules given for FIt also apply in NIt.

SAMPLE TEXTS

The first two texts are transcribed twice: alternate lines are in FIt and NIt pronunciation, and differences are highlighted by underlining (note that in the FIt transcription stressed [e] and [o] are closed mid-vowels, while [ɛ] and [ɔ] are open). The transcriptions of the other texts reflect educated NIt pronunciation; for instance, no distinction is made between open and closed mid vowels (only the symbols [e] and [o] are used) nor is syntactic doubling represented. For the sake of clarity normal punctuation and word-division conventions are retained in the phonetic transcription.

Nel chiaro fiume dilettoso e bello

Madrigal, end of the fourteenth century. Florence, Bibl. Nat. Panciatichiana 26. CD #42.

Nel chiaro fiume dilettoso e bello
Andando per pescar tutto soletto,
Trova' bagnar tre donn' a gran diletto
Ragionavan d'amor dolci parole,
Ma le candide man percotien l'onde
Per imollarsi le lor treçe bionde.
Celandom' i' allora 'n fra le foglie,
Una si volse al sonar d'una rama
E con istrida le compagne chiama,
—Omè—dicend'a me—de' vatten via,
Chè 'l partir più che 'l star è cortesia.

nel ˈkjaṛo ˈfjume diletˈtoso e ˈbbɛllo
nel ˈkjaṛo ˈfjume diletˈtozo e ˈbello

anˈdando peṛ peˈskaṛ ˈtutto soˈletto,
anˈdando peṛ peˈskaṛ ˈtutto soˈletto,

troˈva bbaɲˈɲaṛ ˈtṛe ˈddɔnn a ˈggṛan diˈlɛtto.
troˈva baˈɲaṛ ˈtṛe ˈdonn a ˈgṛan diˈletto.

ṛadʒoˈnavan d aˈmoṛ ˈdoltʃi paˈṛɔle,
ṛadʒoˈnavan d aˈmoṛ ˈdoltʃi paˈṛole,

ma lle ˈkandide ˈman peṛkoˈtien l ˈonde
ma le ˈkandide ˈman peṛkoˈtien l ˈonde

peṛ imolˈlaṛsi le loṛ ˈtṛets:e ˈbjonde.
peṛ imolˈlaṛsi le loṛ ˈtṛets:e ˈbjonde.

tʃeˈlandom i alˈloṛa nfṛa l:e ˈfɔλλe,
tʃeˈlandom i alˈloṛa nfṛa le ˈfoλe,

ˈuna si ˈvɔlse al soˈnaṛ d una ˈṛama
ˈuna si ˈvolse al soˈnaṛ d una ˈṛama

e kon iˈstṛida le komˈpaɲɲe ˈkjama,
e kon iˈstṛida le komˈpaɲe ˈkjama,

—oˈmɛ—diˈtʃɛnd a ˈmmɛ—ˈdɛ ˈvvatten ˈvia,
—oˈme—diˈtʃend a ˈme—ˈde ˈvatten ˈvia,

ˈkɛ l paṛˈtiṛ ˈpju kke l ˈstaṛ ˈɛ kkoṛteˈzia.
ˈke l paṛˈtiṛ ˈpju ke l ˈstaṛ ˈe koṛteˈzia.

Povero çappator

Madrigal, end of the fourteenth century. London, Brit. Lib., Add. 29987. CD #42.

Povero çappator, in chiusa valle
Son aportato con diserto legno
Rotto dal mar, al qual dat'ò le spalle.
Et quel pianeto, ch'a fortunal segno
Govername, non veggio ch'a so corso
Pong'ancor fine per darmi soccorso.
Nell'aspettar ognor mi manca LENA,
Pascendo doglia e rinovando pena.

ˈpɔveṛo ts:appaˈtoṛ, in ˈkjsa ˈvalle
ˈpoveṛo dzappaˈtoṛ, in ˈkjuza ˈvalle

ˈson apoṛˈtato kon diˈzɛṛto ˈleɲɲo
ˈson apoṛˈtato kon diˈzeṛto ˈleɲo

ˈṛotto dal ˈmaṛ, al ˈkwal ˈdat ɔ lle ˈspal:e.
ˈṛot:o dal ˈmaṛ, al ˈkwal ˈdat ˈo le ˈspalle.

e ˈkkwel pjaˈneto, k ˈa ffoṛtuˈnal ˈseɲɲo
e ˈkwel pjaˈneto, k ˈa foṛtuˈnal ˈseɲo

goˈvɛṛname, non ˈveddʒo k a ˈsso ˈkkoṛso
goˈveṛname, non ˈveddʒo k a ˈso ˈkoṛso

ˈpong anˈkoṛ ˈfine peṛ ˈdaṛmi sokˈkoṛso.
ˈpong anˈkoṛ ˈfine peṛ ˈdaṛmi sokˈkoṛso.

nell aspetˈtaṛ oɲˈɲoṛ mi ˈmanka ˈlena,
nell aspetˈtaṛ oˈɲoṛ mi ˈmanka ˈlena,

paʃˈʃendo ˈdoʎʎa e rrinoˈvando ˈpena.
paˈʃendo ˈdoʎa e rinoˈvando ˈpena.

De soto ’l verde vidi i ochi vaghi

Madrigal, mid-fourteenth century. Vatican Library, MS Rossi 215. CD #43.

De soto ’l verde vidi i ochi vaghi
Che mi, so servo, cum dexio mirava,
Si che de lor più me inamorava.

de ˈsoto l ˈveṛde ˈvidi j ˈoki ˈvagi
ke ˈmi, so ˈseṛvo kum deˈzio miˈṛava,
si ˈke de ˈloṛ ˈpju me inamoˈṛava.

Seguendo un me’ sparver che me menava

Madrigal, mid-fourteenth century. Vatican Library, MS Rossi 215.

Seguendo un me’ sparver che me menava
De bosco in bosco, a la staxion più bella
Restiti ad una voce che cantava
E presso a me vidi una pasturella.
Per guardar de soe pecore, filava
La lana lor per farse una gonella.
Questa, cantando, pur me vagheçava;*
Ed io lassiai e stientemi cum ella,
Che più che lo sparver me deletava,
Perche con l’una man e con la boca
Disse:—Vien qua—çitando via la roca.

seˈgwendo un me sparˈver ke me meˈnava
de ˈbosko in ˈbosko, a la statˈtsjon ˈpju ˈbella
reˈstiti ad una ˈvotʃe ke kanˈtava
e ˈpresso a me ˈvidi una pastuˈrella
per gwarˈdar de soe ˈpekore, fiˈlava
la ˈlana ˈlor per ˈfarse una goˈnella.
ˈkwesta, kanˈtando, pur ˈme vagetˈtsava,
ed io lassiˈaj e ˈstjentemi kum ˈella
ke ˈpju ke lo sparˈver me deleˈtava,
perˈke kon l ˈuna ˈman e kon la ˈboka
ˈdisse:—ˈvjen ˈkwa—ziˈtando** ˈvia la ˈroka.

* The word *vagheçava* is an archaic and rare variant of *vagheggiava.* It is debatable whether *ç* is to be pronounced [dʒ] or, more probably, [ts] as in *vaghezza.*

** In view of the various northern elements present in this text, it is likely that *ç* of *çitando* (Tuscan *gettando*) represents a voiced *s* rather than an affricate.

Involta d'un bel velo

Madrigal, mid-fourteenth century. Vatican Library, MS Rossi 215. CD #45.

Involta d'un bel velo
Vidi seder colei
La qual spesso me fa cridar:—Oimei!—
Allor(a), tutto tremando
Cum' al mio signor piace,
Disse: —Madona, cum vui sia pace.—
Questa, piena d'argoglio,
Qual freda pietra e dura,
fece risposta piu che morte oscura:
—Mo' là, vilan! mo' là per la via vostra!—

in'volta d un ˈbel ˈvelo
ˈvidi seˈdeṛ koˈlej
la ˈkwal ˈspesso me ˈfa kṛiˈdaṛ: —ojˈmej!—
alˈloṛ(a), tutˈto tṛeˈmando
kum al ˈmjo siˈɲoṛ ˈpjatʃe
ˈdisse: —maˈdona, kum ˈvuj ˈsia ˈpatʃe.—
ˈkwesta, ˈpjena d aṛˈgoʎo
ˈkwal ˈfṛeda ˈpjetṛa e ˈduṛa
ˈfetʃe ṛiˈsposta ˈpju ke ˈmoṛte oˈskuṛa:
—mo ˈla, viˈlan! mo ˈla peṛ la ˈvia ˈvostṛa!—

Rosetta che non cambi may colore

Madrigal, late fourteenth century. Paris, Bibl. Nat. nouv. acq. Fr. 4917. CD #46.

Rosetta che non cambi may colore,
Amar te voglio sopra ogne altro fiore.
Se altruy me fa languire e sospirare,
Tu me resguardi con gran desiderio;
E se turbar o pianger o tristare,
Pensando via per darmi refrigerio.
Non posso piu legere lo salterio
chi'o a costei che non muta colore.

ṛoˈzetta ke non ˈkambi ˈmaj koˈloṛe
aˈmaṛ te ˈvoʎo ˈsopṛa ˈoɲe ˈaltṛo ˈfjoṛe.
se alˈtṛuj me ˈfa lanˈgwiṛe e sospiˈṛaṛe
ˈtu me ṛeˈzgwaṛdi kon ˈgṛan deziˈdeṛio
e se tuṛˈbaṛ o ˈpjandʒeṛ o tṛiˈstaṛe

penˈsando ˈvaj peṛ ˈdaṛmi ṛefṛiˈdʒeṛio.
non ˈposso ˈpju ˈledʒeṛe lo salˈteṛio
ˈki ˈo a koˈstej ke non ˈmuta koˈloṛe.

Plorans ploravi,[*] perché la fortuna

Madrigal, early fifteenth century. Lucca codex.

Plorans ploravi,[*] perché la fortuna
Pur sopra ad me diriça sua potença.
Ploraboque,[*] che a lei força e prudença
Resister(e) non li val(e), tanto è importuna.
Maldetta quella che 'l mondo raduna,
Quella nutrice e l'ora che me'l tolse;
Nature debitum (in) unda[*] persolse,
Suspiri a lo mio cor sempre s'aduna.
In ulnis patris expiro cum pianto[*]
Per rinovar le pen(e) fi questo canto.

ˈploṛans ploˈṛavi, peṛˈke la foṛˈtuna
ˈpuṛ ˈsopṛa a ˈme diˈṛittsa swa poˈtentsa.
ploṛaˈboque, ke a ˈlej ˈfoṛtsa e pṛuˈdentsa
ṛeˈsisteṛ(e) non li ˈval(e), ˈtanto ˈe impoṛˈtuna.
malˈdetta ˈkwella ke l ˈmondo ṛaˈduna,
ˈkwella nuˈtṛitʃe e l ˈoṛa ke ˈme l ˈtolse;
naˈtuṛe ˈdebitum (in) ˈunda peṛˈsolse,
suˈspiṛi a lo ˈmjo ˈcoṛ ˈsempṛe s aˈduna.
in ˈulnis ˈpatṛis ekˈspiṛo kum ˈpjanto
peṛ ṛinoˈvaṛ le ˈpen(e) ˈˈfi ˈkwesto ˈkanto.

(E) vantende, segnor mio

Early fifteenth century. Paris, Bibl. Nat. nouv. acq. Fr. 6771 (Reina MS). CD #47.

(E) vantende, segnor mio, (e) vatene, amore;
Con ti via se ne vene l'alma (mia) e'l core.
(E) gli ochi dolenti piangon sença fine
Cha veder el paradisso[**] e soa belleza.
A cuy ti lasso, amore, ché no me meni?
L'alma me levi e 'l cor e l'alegreça.
La bocha cridava che sentiva dolceça;
Amara lamentarse, oymé, topina!

---

* These words are in Latin.
** The spelling *-ss-* in this word is unusual: it may be interpreted as an attempt to indicate a voiceless *s*.

Altro signor zamay non voglio avere
Perch'io non troverey del suo vallore.

(e) van'tende, se'ɲoṛ 'mio, (e) 'vatene, a'moṛe;
kon 'ti 'via se ne 'vene l 'alma ('mia) e l 'koṛe.
(e) i 'oki do'lenti 'pjangon 'sentsa 'fine
ka ve'deṛ el paṛa'diso e 'soa bel'lettsa.
a 'kuj 'ti 'lasso, a'moṛe, 'ke non me 'meni?
l 'alma me 'levi e l 'koṛ e l ale'gṛettsa.
la 'boka kṛi'dava ke sen'tiva dol'tʃettsa;
a'maṛa lamen'taṛse, oj'me, to'pina!
'altṛo si'ɲoṛ dʒa'maj non 'voʎo a'veṛe
peṛk 'io non tṛove'ṛej del 'suo val'loṛe.

Marchetto Cara (ca. 1500), "A la absentia che me acora"

Petrucci, Frottole Book V, fol. 42v–43. CD #48.

A la absentia che me acora,
Io non trovo altro conforto;
Sol la fe che mia signora
M'ha promesso o vivo o morto.
Lei promisse, et io iurai;
Altri più mai non amare,
Si che donna al mondo mai
Potra lei farme lasciare
Che fa el spirto vivo ogn'hora,
Hor cussì luntan a torto.

Forza fu e non mi pento
L'absentar dal viso santo,
Benchè focho non è spento;
Ançi abruscio in hogni canto
Chi mantien che in cor non mora,
Se fue spinto fuor dal porto?

a la as'sentsa ke me a'koṛa
'io non 'tṛovo 'altṛo kon'foṛto
'sol la 'fe ke 'mia si'ɲoṛa
m 'a pṛo'messo o 'vivo o 'moṛto.
'lej pṛo'misse, e 'io ju'ṛaj;
'altṛi 'pju 'maj non a'maṛe,
'si ke 'donna al 'mondo 'maj
po'tṛa 'lej 'faṛme la'ʃaṛe,

ke ˈfa el ˈspiṛto ˈvivo oˈɲoṛa,
ˈoṛ kusˈsi lunˈtan a ˈtoṛto.

ˈfoṛtsa ˈfu e non ˈmi ˈpento
l assenˈtaṛ dal ˈviso ˈsanto,
benˈke ˈfoko non ˈe ˈspento;
ˈantsi aˈbṛuʃo in ˈoɲi ˈkanto
ˈki manˈtjen ke in ˈkoṛ non ˈmoṛa,
ˈse ˈfuj ˈspinto ˈfwoṛ dal ˈpoṛto?

Donne leggiadr' e voi vaghe donzelle

Mid-sixteenth century. Modena, Bibl. Estense, MS C 311 (Bottegari Lute Book). CD #49.

Donne leggiadr' e voi vaghe donzelle
Che git' ad empier d'acqua le lancelle,
Che non andat' a riv' o font' o fiumi,
M'a questi tristi duoj correnti lumi.
Voi di bellezza pareggiate il sole,
E dir poss'io che sete al mondo sole:
Voi mai non troverete un rio più chiaro
Che quel che stilla dal mio pianto amaro.
E voi che stat' in calm' e mal contenti,
Navigand' aspettand' or fiati or venti,
Venit' a me, che col mio sospirare
Io vi prometto farvi navigare.
E voi donne ch'andate a trovar foco
Mattin' e sera d'un in altro loco,
Deh, per pietà venit' a questo core,
Che troverete foco, fiamm' e ardore.

ˈdonne ledˈdʒadṛ e ˈvoj ˈvage donˈdzelle
ˈke ˈdʒit ad ˈempjeṛ d ˈakkwa le lanˈtʃelle,
ˈke non anˈdat a ˈṛiv o ˈfont o ˈfjumi,
ˈm a ˈkwesti ˈtṛisti ˈdwoj koṛˈṛenti ˈlumi.
ˈvoj di belˈlettsa paṛedˈdʒate il ˈsole,
e ˈdiṛ ˈposs ˈio ke ˈsete al ˈmondo ˈsole:
ˈvoj ˈmaj non tṛoveˈṛete un ˈṛio ˈpju ˈkjaṛo
ke ˈkwel ke ˈstilla dal ˈmjo ˈpjanto aˈmaṛo.
e ˈvoj ke ˈstat in ˈkalm e ˈmal konˈtenti,
naviˈgand aspetˈtand or ˈfjati or ˈventi,
veˈnit a ˈme, ke ˈkol ˈmjo sospiˈṛaṛe
ˈio vi pṛoˈmetto ˈfaṛvi naviˈgaṛe.

e ˈvoj ˈdonne k anˈdate a tṛoˈvaṛ ˈfoko
matˈtin e ˈseṛa d ˈun in ˈaltṛo ˈloko,
ˈde, peṛ pjeˈta veˈnit a ˈkwesto ˈkoṛe,
ˈke tṛoveˈṛete ˈfoko, ˈfjamm e aṛˈdoṛe.

NOTES

1. See G.C. Starr, Jr., *The Emergence of Rome as Ruler of the Western World* (Ithaca, 1953).

2. See H. Lüdtke, "Die Entstehung romanischer Schriftsprachen," *Vox romanica* 23 (1964):3–21.

3. Excellent historical grammars of Italian tracing its development from Latin are G. Rohlfs, *Grammatica storica della lingua italiana e dei suoi dialetti,* 3 vols. (Turin: Einaudi, 1966–69); and P. Tekavčić, *Grammatica storica dell'italiano,* 3 vols. (Bologna: Il Mulino, 1972).

4. On the historical development of literary Italian see P.O. Kristeller, "The Origin and Development of the Language of Italian Prose," *Word* 2 (1946):50–65; B. Migliorini and T.G. Griffith, *The Italian Language* (London: Faber and Faber, 1966); G.L. Beccaria, C. Del Popolo, and C. Marazzini, *L'italiano letterario, profilo storico* (Turin: Einaudi, 1989).

5. T. Bolelli, "Anche Cavour faceva il 'tifo'," *La Stampa* (Turin), August 8, 1991, p. 3 (translation mine).

6. It should be noted that Dante, Petrarch, and Boccaccio also wrote extensively in Latin. While cultivating the *volgare,* the spoken language of the people, they certainly did not envision—or regard as desirable—the disappearance of Latin as an international language of culture.

7. See Th. Labande-Jeanroy, *La question de la langue en Italie* (Strasbourg and Paris, 1925); R.A. Hall Jr., *The Italian "Questione della lingua": An Interpretative Essay* (Chapel Hill, 1942); M. Vitale, *La questione della lingua* (Palermo: Palumbo, 1967).

8. See H.W. Klein, *Latein und Volgare in Italien, Münchner romanistiche Arbeiten* 12 [Munich], 1957.

9. See G.P. Clivio, "The Development of the Italian Language and of Its Dialects," in S.B. Chandler and J. Molinaro, *The Culture of Italy* (Toronto: Griffin House, 1979), pp. 25–41. A concise survey of Italian dialects is provided by G. Devoto and G. Giacomelli, *I dialetti delle regioni d'Italia* (Florence: Sansoni, 1972).

10. For studies on Italian as spoken in specific regions of the country see L. Canepari, *Italiano standard e pronunce regionali* (Padua: CLUEB, 1980); G. Holtus and E. Radtke, eds., *Varietäten Linguistik des Italienischen* (Tübingen: Niemeyer, 1983), and *Gesprochenes Italienisch in Geschichte und Gegenwart* (Tübingen: Niemeyer, 1985).

11. F.B. Agard and R.J. Di Pietro, *The Sounds of English and Italian* (University of Chicago Press, 1965), p. 34.

12. See G. Hartmann, "Zur Geschichte der italienischen Orthographie," *Romanische Forschungen* 20 (1907):199–283; and B. Migliorini, "Note sulla grafia italiana nel Rinascimento," in *Saggi linguistici* (Florence: Le Monnier, 1957), pp. 197–225.

13. In fact, a common way of ridiculing a foreign accent consists of pronouncing *parole sdrucciole* as though they were *piane.*

14. An excellent guide to the pronunciation of place names is T. Cappello and C. Tagliavini, *Dizionario degli etnici e dei toponimi italiani* (Bologna: Patron, 1981).

15. For further details see L. Serianni, *Grammatica italiana* (Turin: UTET, 1988), p. 47; G. Malagoli, "L'accento dei grecismi nella lingua italiana," *Lingua Nostra* 5 (1943):25–29; and E.M. Malcovati, "Accentazione italiana di grecismi e latinismi," *Lingua Nostra* 10 (1949):62–63.

16. M. Harris and N. Vincent, *The Romance Languages* (New York: Oxford University Press, 1988) p. 283.

17. In NIt pronunciation, however, this is not so (see below).

18. In Old Italian, spellings such as *ngn* and *lgl,* as in *vingna, palglia,* were common though not consistently employed. They represented an attempt, soon to be abandoned, to indicate the length of [ɲ] and [ʎ]; see above, Table II.

19. All Florentines appear to distinguish between *chiese* ("he asked") with [s] and *chiese* ("churches") with [z], but I found several speakers who did not differentiate between *fuso* ("spindle"; which should have [s]) and *fuso* ("smelted"; which should have [z]). Only two or three additional minimal pairs can be found.

20. When *razza* is pronounced [ˈrattsa] it means "race," while [ˈraddza] is a "ray" (a type of fish).

21. Guido Guinizelli (ca. 1235–1276) was an early Italian poet greatly admired by Dante.

22. Speakers of English are generally not aware of this detail, which can be observed by holding a thin sheet of paper close to one's mouth while saying words such as *pin, tick, kin* and comparing the effect on the paper when saying *spin, stick, skin.*

23. As in *Lisbon, dismal, Israel.*

24. Most of these are not possible in English and are likely to cause English speakers some initial difficulties. The more common ones are [ps] as in *psallere, psaltero,* and [pn] as in *pneuma.*

25. In word-final position, however, stressed [e] and [ɛ] are nowadays generally distinguished in printed

material by the use of *é* for [e] (as in *perché*) and *è* for [ɛ] (as in *caffè*). Not all editors of older texts, however, adhere to this norm, which, in any case, is not observed when writing in longhand.

26. The terms "closed" and "open" refer in phonetics to the relative degree to which the mouth is open when producing a given vowel. The higher a vowel the more closed it is.

27. Tonic *e* and *o* are always pronounced open in FIt when they occur in learned words, such as Latinisms; see T. Franceschi, *Sulla pronuncia di* e, o, s, z, *nella parole di non diretta tradizione* (Turin: Giappichelli, 1965).

28. See G.P. Clivio, "The Pronunciation of Italian in Piedmont," in *Actes du Xe Congrès international des linguistes,* vol. 4 (Bucharest: Académie de la République Socialiste de Roumanie, 1970), pp. 275–80.

29. See G. Berruto, "L'italiano regionale bergamasco," in G. Sanga, *Lingua e dialetti di Bergamo e delle Valli* (Bergamo: Lubrina, 1987), p. 501.

30. See Agard and Di Pietro, pp. 37–40.

31. Ibid., p. 39. Not all specialists agree completely with this statement.

32. On this see especially W. von Wartburg, *La frammentazione linguistica della Romania,* ed. A. Varvaro (Rome: Salerno, 1980; first published in German in 1950).

33. See G.P. Clivio, "A Note on Two Oppositions of Standard Italian with a Low Functional Yield," in *Studies Presented to Professor Roman Jakobson by His Students* (Cambridge, Mass., 1968), pp. 70–75.

14

Italian Latin

HAROLD COPEMAN

The Latin language developed as one of the dialects of the Italian Peninsula, in the area around Rome, in pre-Classical times. The other "Italic" dialects died out, but some influence on pronunciation remained, for instance, in the northwest region, Gallia Cisalpina, where the substratum was Celtic, as in transalpine Gaul.

Regional dialects of Italian have long persisted in educated speech, and there was and is local differentiation in the speech in the important musical cities. Apart from the alternatives of Florentine and local models, Latin in the important musical cities may have been influenced by the presence, from the thirteenth to the mid-sixteenth centuries, of French and Flemish singers and directors, who had great prestige.

Scholastic Latin, deriving from Charlemagne's initiative throughout western Europe in the early ninth century, may have survived in pockets in Lombardy, and there is a belief that there has been continuity in Italy since that time; possibly the earlier tradition found its way to the early universities (Bologna was founded in 1088).

There had, however, been changes in Latin pronunciation since the Classical period, as in the vernacular dialects and languages. In the early centuries a major change began in the sound of *c* and *g* before the front vowels *e* and *i*. The classical [k] and [g] (used in our "Restored Classical" school Latin), which are stops produced on the soft palate, moved forward to the hard palate and beyond, and came to be sounded in the ranges of [kj], [tj], [tʃ], [ts], [s], and [gj], [dj], [dʒ], and [ʒ] respectively. The exact quality of the sound relevant to Latin (and to the vernacular) depended on the time and place. There were considerable differences in the sounds of these stops between countries and (sometimes) centuries.

Bibliography

M. Bonioli. *La pronuncia del latino nelle scuole.* Turin, 1962.
H. Copeman. *Singing in Latin.* Oxford, 1990; revised as paperback 1992. Pp. 171–75, 272–75.

M. Cortelazzo. *I dialetti e la dialettologia in Italia.* Tübingen, 1980.
Enciclopedia Italiana Treccani, 1933. "Italia," on linguistic history and dialects, pp. 922–25.
A. L. and G. Lepschy. *The Italian Language Today.* London, 1977. Opening chapters.
B. Migliorini and T. G. Griffith. *The Italian Language.* London, 1966.
G. Rohlfs. *Grammatica storica della lingua Italiana e dei suoi dialetti.* Turin, 1966. Also in German as *Historische Grammatik der Italienische Sprache.* Berne, 1949.
V. U. G. Scherr. *Aufführungspraxis Vokalmusik: Handbuch der lateinischen Aussprache.* Bärenreiter, 1991. Pp. 55–92.

Sounds and Spellings

The sounds detailed below are based on the phonetic equivalents of those described in *Liber usualis,* xxxvi–xxxix, with a few variants for those who wish to be more adventurous.* In departing from the standard version decisions are needed on the nature of the palatalization of *ce, ci, ge, gi;* and on the production of the vowels *e* and *o.*

Liber usualis and Italian literary Latin always open *e* and *o.* Standard Italian and some of the dialects, like classical Latin and most Romance languages, make these two vowels closed or open according to their place in the word.

Given the phonetic equivalents of the letters, standard Italian Latin is generally pronounced as spelled; in particular, double consonants are separately articulated as in Italian. Liaison of a consonant with a following initial vowel depends on the continuity of the phrase, but it is less marked than in the French style. (But there is not the deliberate separation with a glottal stop as in German Latin.)

Stress and Accent

The texts with which we are concerned are in medieval Latin, which was (except in France) a stressed language. The placing of the stress broadly followed the Classical rules. To assign stress one has to know whether a syllable is "long" or "short." A syllable was "long" if it ended with a long vowel, or with two consonants (or with *x*), or with a single consonant when the following syllable began with a consonant. The stress accent in a word of two syllables fell on the first *('De·us 'pa·ter);* in longer words it fell on the penultimate syllable if it was long/heavy *lau·'da·mus, cœ·'les·tis, vo·'bis·cum, om·ni·po·'ten·tem):* otherwise on the antepenultimate *('Do·mi·nus, vi·si·'bi·li·um).* In words of four or more syllables there tends to be a secondary stress (here marked") which arises from the natural tendency to alternate stressed and unstressed syllables: *om·"ni·po·'ten·tem, "vi·si·'bi·li·um.* Some longer words follow a different pattern, which is usually clear from the musical setting: *om·'ni·pō·tens* has the primary stress on its second syllable despite its long vowel. The phonetic texts below show the primary stresses (following the mark ').

Consonants

This list contains only consonants that are pronounced differently from English; but some, like *d, l,* and *t,* are produced with less explosion and further forward than in English. Alternatives to the standard "Roman Style" are suggested in parentheses.

* The *Liber usualis* is a twentieth-century hybrid and cannot be considered a good guide to regional influences in pronunciation. See above, p. 5.

c [k] before *a, o, u,* or a consonant. [tʃ] before *e, æ, œ, i,* and *y.* (In north Italy [ts] or [s] may often be more appropriate; in Venice and Mantua, possibly [tj]. The present Milanese dialect uses [tʃ].)

ch [k]

g [g] before *a, o, u,* or a consonant. [dʒ] before *e* and *i.* (In north Italy and sometimes in Roman use [ʒ]; in Venice, Mantua, possibly [dj]; Milan [dʒ].)

gn [ɲ], prolonged in Tuscany and central and southern Italy.

h Always silent in present use, but between vowels *(mihi, nihil)* it was often sounded (*Liber usualis* gives [k], but [ç] may have been used in some cities).

i, j consonantal [j], but in early centuries of our period probably [dʒ].

qu, ngu [kw], [ngw] (probably following the style of *u* in the northwest: see "Vowels," below).

r Slightly rolled [r̩], notably when before another consonant *(carnis, parce, parte).*

s [s], but between two vowels it is "slightly softened" (often not at the end of a word). The general vernacular habit tends toward a voiced sound, [z], in the north but retains [s] in the center and south. Compounds have [-s-]: *desuper, praesepio;* also (in modern use) *eleison.*

sc [sk] before *a, o, u,* or a consonant. [ʃ] or a doubled [ʃ] before *e, æ, œ, i,* and *y.* (For Venice or Mantua, possibly [stj].)

th [t]

ti + vowel [tsi-], including *Pontio.*

u/v consonantal [v]

x [ks] but tending toward [gz] between vowels *(exercitus).*

xc [ksk] before *a, o,* or a consonant. [kʃ] before *e* or *i (excelsis):* or [kstʃ] or [ktʃ].

z [dz]

Consonantal Groups

Double consonants are sounded twice, but not rigorously so; *ecce* is given in *Liber usualis* as *"et-che";* i.e., with [t-tʃ]. However, awkward groups have probably often been simplified, especially in vernacular Latin, for instance *sanctus* may have had [nt] or [ɲt].

Vowels

a [a], an open and warm but not a backward sound, but varies regionally (often more fronted in the north). (In Milan the unaccented vowel is more closed, tending toward [o].)

e, æ, œ [ɛ], but somewhat less open than in "bed." (Regionally, [e] is likely to have been used in some words: the Italian dictionary's pronunciation of a similar word may be the best guide. No English diphthongs should be introduced into Italian Latin.)

i [i], not [ɪ].

o [ɔ] (but regionally [o] in some words: see *e* above). Again no diphthongs.

u [u], not [ʊ] or [ʌ]. (In the northwest the sound given to *u* in an open syllable resembles *ü* or the French [y:]. The present dividing line includes Mantua but excludes Parma [see *Enciclopedia Treccani,* p. 925], but in the Middle Ages the *ü* extended as far east as Emilia.)

y [i], rather than the Classical [y].

SAMPLE TEXTS

Salve regina

Roman Style (e.g., Palestrina). CD #50.

Salve regina mater misericordiae
vita, dulcedo et spes nostra, salve!
ad te clamamus exsules filii Evae,
ad te suspiramus gementes et flentes
in hac lacrimarum valle.
eia ergo, advocata nostra,
illos tuos misericordes oculos ad nos converte
et Iesum, benedictum fructum ventris tui,
nobis post hoc exsilium ostende,
o clemens, o pia,
o dulcis Virgo Maria.

ˈsalvɛ ṛɛˈdʒina matɛṛ mizɛṛiˈkɔṛdi·ɛ
ˈvita dulˈtʃɛdɔ ɛt spɛs ˈnɔstṛa ˈsalvɛ
ad tɛ klaˈmamus ˈɛgzulɛs ˈfili·i ˈɛvɛ
ad tɛ suspiˈṛamus dʒɛˈmɛntɛs ɛt ˈflɛntɛs
in ak lakṛiˈmaṛum ˈvallɛ
ˈɛja ˈɛṛgɔ advɔˈkata ˈnɔstṛa
ˈillɔs ˈtuɔs misɛṛiˈkɔṛdɛz ˈɔkulɔs ad nɔs kɔnˈvɛṛtɛ
ɛt ˈjɛsum bɛnɛˈdiktum ˈfṛuktum ˈvɛntṛis ˈtui
ˈnɔbis pɔst ɔk ɛgˈzili·um ɔsˈtɛndɛ
ɔ ˈklɛmɛnz ɔ ˈpi·a
ɔ ˈdultʃis viṛgɔ maˈ·ṛia

Rorate caeli

Roman Style (e.g., Palestrina).

Rorate caeli desuper, et nubes pluant justum
Aperiatur terra, et germinet Salvatorem.
Ostende nobis, Domine, misericordiam tuam
et salutare tuum da nobis.
Veni Domine, et non tardare. Alleluia.

ṛɔˈṛatɛ ˈtʃɛli ˈdɛsupɛṛ ɛt ˈnubɛs ˈplu·ant ˈjustum
apɛṛi·ˈatuṛ ˈtɛrra ɛt ˈdʒɛṛminɛt salvaˈtɔṛɛm
ɔsˈtɛndɛ ˈnɔbis ˈdɔminɛ mizɛṛiˈkɔṛdi·am ˈtu·am
ɛt saluˈtaṛɛ ˈtu·um da ˈnɔbis
ˈvɛni ˈdɔminɛ ɛt nɔn taṛˈdaṛɛ allɛˈluja

Germany and the Low Countries

15—

Middle High German

PETER FRENZEL

The study of German literature in the Middle Ages is primarily concerned with the brief period 1170–1250, which saw an extraordinary conjunction, especially in the south and central German-speaking areas, of gifted singers and tale-tellers (often called, somewhat erroneously, "poets") who provided courtly entertainments for circles dominated by Hohenstaufen party politics. Singers such as Walther von der Vogelweide, Reinmar, Heinrich von Morungen, and Neidhart, romancers such as Heinrich von Veldeke, Gottfried von Strassburg, and Wolfram von Eschenbach provided a display of verbal virtuosity unmatched again in German culture until the eighteenth century. A substantial amount of the "literature" of the period was in fact sung performance of one sort or another, grounded in melodic monody, as the courtly love song became high fashion and as political and didactic singing *(Sangspruch)* began to dominate the entertainments of the Hohenstaufen courts. The performers of this brief epoch established the southwestern "literary language" which was to provide a linguistic focal point for the writers in the vernacular during the following one hundred years.

Despite the high cultural value of song and singing during this period, only a handful of German tunes for love songs survive from this time, a surprising fact in the light of the nearly 300 troubadour and over 1,800 trouvère melodies extant. The reasons for the paucity of German tunes are complicated and poorly understood; in addition to the normal waves of war and plundering, pillaging and burning, which accompanied the civil and religious unrest of the late Middle Ages, from the mid-thirteenth century on, the Germans set a much higher premium on religious and didactic singing in the vernacular than on the soon passé and probably frequently parodied courtly love song. Manuscripts containing such songs were no doubt regularly discarded or reused as palimpsests for more pious scribal activity.

German dialects were written down sporadically between the sixth and the ninth centuries, and by the Carolingian period the monastic scriptoria were producing vernacular manuscripts in considerable number, though only a few scattered documents remain today. It is only in the twelfth century that texts, largely poetic, were copied down in any magnitude. The Latin-trained scribes used the Latin alphabet as best they could to represent the sounds of their own dialects, and it is not surprising that we find widely divergent phonetic renderings. And yet, in the course of the thirteenth century, as the Hohenstaufen political power coalesced in the southwest regions of the German-speaking area, the scribes tended toward a more consistent orthography reflecting a kind of Alemannic literary dialect. This dialect forms the basis for the normalized Middle High German (abbreviated MHG) of most edited texts. Though perhaps never an "everyday" language, this dialect was spoken (or sung) at the most important administrative centers for the purposes of courtly entertainment. Today it is possible to work out a phonology which allows us to establish clear phonemic distinctions, and with the help of modern dialects we can posit an approximate pronunciation. Because the waning Middle Ages (ca. 1350–1600) present a quite different set of problems in establishing a "correct" phonology, we will turn to this period later.

Regional Dialects

For the purposes of pronunciation it will be helpful to know the linguistic designations for the larger categories of German spoken in the Middle Ages. The principal distinction is between *High German,* consisting of Upper and Middle German dialects, and *Low German,* the dialects of the low-lying northern parts of the German-speaking area.

Upper German means South German, the dialects of the Alps and the southern uplands: Austrian, Bavarian, Tyrolean, Suabian, Alemannic, and certain southern Frankish dialects. Upper German was spoken generally south of a line from a point near Strassburg east to a point somewhat north of Bamberg. It is in this dialect group that most of the song and story seems to have been sung and told during the heyday of courtly entertainment, between 1175 and 1250.

Middle German is represented by a narrower west-east band extending from the old episcopal cities of Mainz, Trier, and Cologne through Thuringia and Silesia, including Fulda, Eisenach, Meissen, and the present-day cities of Leipzig and Dresden. In this dialect group many of the thirteenth- and fourteenth-century *Sangspruch* singers are transmitted, primarily because of the survival of the Jena and Colmar Songbooks.

Low German is spoken above a line running from Aachen through Düsseldorf east to a point level with present-day Berlin and bounded on the north by the Danish-speaking areas and the North and Baltic seas. It includes what we know today as the Flemish and Netherlandic regions. Low German is dramatically removed from both Middle and Upper German because of what philologists call the Old High German sound shift. For example, the Upper and Middle German utterance *Das ist Wasser* would be heard in Low German as *Dat is Water.* Because of the singularity of Low German, the other two and more similar dialect groups (Middle and Upper) are usually referred to by the single term High German *(Hochdeutsch).* The term is used by philologists and linguists not to designate the social class of the speakers or the quality of the language but to indicate the dialects spoken primarily in the uplands and mountains, i.e., at a higher elevation.

Low German singers of the High Middle Ages are not well represented in the manuscripts, though two of them, Heinrich von Veldeke (twelfth century) and Wizlav (fourteenth century), are sometimes found in anthologies. However, their songs were copied into the manuscripts in a High German translation with only occasional reflexes in rhyme or vocabulary of what was originally a Low German text. Some editors today, however, "re-create" a dialect which they think resembles these singers' original Low German.

Specific Dialects

Determining the pronunciation of German during the High and Later Middle Ages is complicated by the range of dialect variation within the geographical areas outlined above. As was the case with most western European languages, German was deeply divided by dialect differences. The disparate qualities of the German dialects were reinforced by lingering tribal loyalties, so that well after the time of Charlemagne, German speakers tended to think of themselves not as Germans but as Saxons, Bavarians, Thuringians, Franks, or members of dozens of other tribes less familiar to us. Accordingly, when we study a song from around 1200 and after, we must be aware of its dialectal background. The various kinds of German changed sporadically but sometimes drastically between 1250 and 1500. There are also complexities and confusions inherent in scribal copying and editing. For example, a Middle German scribe in the year 1320 might decide to copy the song of a contemporary Low German singer. Because of his readership, he would have to translate the song into a Middle German dialect, though he would retain some scattered Low German words for the sake of rhyme and meter. Some years later an Upper German copyist might insert this song into a collection using his own dialect forms. And, if this last recension is the only one to survive, the present-day singer would face a conundrum. Should she sing the song in a reconstructed Low or Middle German version or should she be faithful to the way it appears in the manuscript, that is, a way in which the song was most assuredly not sung? The issue is further muddied by modern editors. In all probability the only access today's singer has to our hypothetical song is through an edition in which the text is normalized into the "classical" MHG of around 1200, more than a century before the song was actually performed. There is unfortunately no satisfactory solution. The singer is faced with difficult, sometimes arbitrary decisions and must often make do with the best compromise.

Obviously we will never be able to reconstruct the sounds of old languages exactly, except by purest chance. Philologists can fairly well determine the basic phonemic differences, but the actual sounds will have to remain approximate. Fortunately, there is enough scattered evidence which, when taken together, permits us to reconstruct at least a skeleton of a phonology for MHG, at least with regard to consonants, vowels, and diphthongs. Unfortunately, certain aspects of stress and intonation, which the scribes could not take into account, but which give a true idiomatic flavor to a language or a dialect, are permanently lost to us.

Evidence

The phonological guide which follows is based on the following evidence: the use of the Latin alphabet and the assumption that there was at least a rough equivalence between certain Latin and German sounds; MHG words transliterated into foreign texts; hypercorrections in manuscripts, showing avoidance of neologisms or undesirable dialectal variants; rhyme or in some cases alliteration; diacritical or orthographic indications of vowel length, primarily in the Old High German (OHG) and early Modern German periods; present-day dialects, which are always conservative and tend to preserve sounds that appear to have existed during the MHG time.

The last kind of evidence is crucial to reconstructing a phonology of "dead" languages that have living descendants. Though it is clear that dialects, too, change, it is nonetheless possible to trace parallels in phonemic relationships which would appear to reflect certain phonetic similarities. For example, present-day speakers of Alemannic in certain parts of Switzerland would express the utterance *du bist mein* of standard German as [du pɪst mi:n], which is just as it is written in a manuscript dating from the early thirteenth century *(du pist mîn)*. We can compare these phonemic alignments and, together with the orthographical evidence, make some informed judgments about pronunciation.

The most perplexing aspect of MHG pronunciation (of an unnormalized text) for a singer or speaker unacquainted with the language is vowel length. The MHG vowel system included a long and a short version of each of the five Latin vowels *(a, e, i, o,* and *u)* as well as three mutated vowels *(ä, ö, ü)* and various diphthongs. Long and short vowels were not marked in the manuscripts during the MHG period. We know, however, that they were present in the phonology from rhyme words and from the fact that writers both before and after the MHG time indicated them in various ways. In the OHG period a few writers marked vowel length. Notker (eleventh century), for example, used a circumflex to indicated long vowels: *wâra* [wɑ:ra]; other eleventh-century scribes used vowel doublings: *leeran* [le:ran]. We can compare these vowel lengths with writers from the fifteenth century and later who began to use various ways to indicate long vowels. For example, vowel doublings *(Meer, Saat); h* after the vowel *(Dehnung, Ruhm);* the use of a following *e* to indicate a long *i (Liebe, Ziel);* the use of a single consonant or *ß* after a vowel *(sagen, Muße)*. Since direct relationships exist between the long vowels of OHG and those of late MHG, and certain predictable sound changes occur in the transition from MHG to Modern German, it is possible to determine with considerable confidence which vowels were long and which were short in MHG.

One of the best clues to both the phonemic system of MHG and its pronunciation lies in rhyme. The works of the "classic" figures of MHG literary and musical activity were set down on parchment or velum between 50 and 200 years after they flourished. The manuscripts, accordingly, reflect not only the native dialect of the singer or storyteller, but also his or the scribe's attempt to conform to the southwestern literary dialect emerging toward the end of the twelfth century. An earlier singer (and his later scribe), such as Dietmar von Eist (fl. ca. 1175), might "rhyme" long with short vowels, such as *gân* and *man* [gɑ:n/man], which conforms to the kind of assonance frequently found in the lyric of the time. This rarely occurs in the next generation, in singers such as Heinrich von Morungen and Reinmar, or in romancers such as Wolfram von Eschenbach and Gottfried von Strassburg. The scribes who set down the works of such figures and, we presume, the composers themselves, were meticulous in their concern for pure rhyme.

Bibliography

Adolf Bach. *Geschichte der deutschen Sprache,* 8th ed. Heidelberg: Quelle & Meyer, 1970. Esp. B.2: "Vom Ausgang des 11. zur Mitte des 14. Jh.s."

Kenneth Brooke. *An Introduction to Early New High German.* Oxford: Blackwell, 1955.

Jean Fourquet. "The Two e's of MHG, a Diachronic Phonemic Approach." *Word* 8 (1952):122–35.

Jacob Grimm. *Geschichte der deutschen Sprache.* 2 vols. 4th ed. Hirzel: Leipzig, 1880.

Paul Kipansky. "Über den deutschen Akzent." *Studia Grammatica* 7 (1966):69–98.

Mathias Lexer. *Mittelhochdeutsches Handwörterbuch.* 3 vols. Leipzig: S. Hirzel Verlag, 1872–78.

William Burley Lockwood. *An Informal History of the German Language with Chapters on Dutch, Afrikaans, Frisian, & Yiddish.* London: Deutsch, 1976.

W.-D. Michael. "Die graphische Entwicklung der s-Laute im Deutschen." *Beiträge zur Geschichte der deutschen Sprache und Literatur* [Halle] 81 (1959):456–80.

Victor Michels. *Mittelhochdeutsches Elementarbuch.* 4th ed. Heidelberg: Winter, 1921. Esp. "Erster Hauptteil: Lautlehre," pp. 41–55.

C.A.M. Noble. *Modern German Dialects.* New York: Lang, 1983. Esp. pp. 33–40: "The Historical Perspective."

Herbert Penzl. "Die mhd. Sibilanten und ihre Weiterentwicklung." *Word* 24 (1968):204–13.

———. *Geschichtliche deutsche Lautlehre.* Munich: Huber, 1969.

———. *Vom Urgermanischen zum Neuhochdeutschen: eine historische Phonologie.* Berlin: E. Schmidt, 1975.

Gerhard Philipp. *Einführung ins Frühneuhochdeutsche.* Heidelberg: Quelle & Meyer, 1980. Esp. Ch. 3: "Lautung (Phonologie)."

Charles V.J. Russ. *Historical German Phonology and Morphology.* Oxford: Clarendon, 1978.

John T. Waterman. *A History of the German Language.* Seattle: University of Washington Press, 1966.

C.J. Wells. *German: A Linguistic History to 1945.* Oxford: Clarendon, 1985. Esp. Ch. 3: "The Medieval Period."

K. Zwierzina. "Mhd. Studien 8: Die e-Laute in den Reimen der mhd. Dichter," *Zeitschrift für deutsches Altertum* 44 (1900):249–316; 45 (1901):19–100.

Stress and Intonation

MHG, unlike the Romance vernaculars, is a strongly stressed language. Its poetry depends less on rhyme and syllable count and more on a rhythmic alternation of stressed and unstressed syllables. Stress falls on the first beat or syllable of each metrical foot of poetry and is followed by one, two, or possibly three unstressed syllables. The standard metrical line, from which all other metrical forms are derived, is much the same as Modern English stress-timed verse or Modern German *Knittelvers:*

/ - - / - - / - /
Listen my children and you shall hear
- - / - / - / - /
Of the midnight ride of Paul Revere;

or, in a similar MHG couplet attributed to Neidhart von Reuental:

/ - / - - / - /
Ûf dem berge und in dem tal

/ - / - - / - - /
hebt sich aber der vogele schal.

By the year 1200 poets and singers were saying and singing relatively regular lines, that is, lines with a regular alternation of stressed and unstressed syllables. In the 1190s Heinrich von Morungen sang:

/ - / - / - / - / - /
Von den elben wirt ensên vil manic man

or experimented with nearly all-dactylic lines:

/ - - / - - / - - / -
Stên ich vor ir unde schouwe daz wunder. . .

MHG words, like the Anglo-Saxon vocabulary of English, are stressed on the root syllable, which, in most cases, is the first syllable of the word. There are some exceptions, and the following guidelines for word-stress should be borne in mind:

1. The stress rules of Modern German generally apply.
2. Almost all words are accented on the first syllable; hence *ˈarebeit, ˈtugent, ˈgeben, ˈmuget, ˈwunder.*
3. Words of more than two syllables are usually compounds; the primary stress falls on the first syllable, the secondary stress on the first syllable of the second part of the compound: *ˈellenˈˈbogen, ˈrosenˈˈvarwe.* If there is a suffix such as *-lîch* or *-keit,* it will bear a secondary stress: *ˈwunderˈˈlîch, ˈwerdeˈˈkeit.*
4. A small number of important prefixes ("inseparable prefixes") are unstressed, just as in the English words *betrothed* or *entwine.* They are *be-, ent-* (sometimes simplified to *en-*), *er-, ge-, ver-,* and *zer-*. Included among these is the negative particle *en-;* e.g., *beˈhagen, erˈkennen, geˈnâde, verˈlân, enˈkan.* Note also that the stressed root syllables of some words begin with the same combinations of letters as some of these prefixes. Beware of such words as *ˈgeben, ˈbeten, ˈzerren, ˈerde.*
5. Loan-words from Romance vernaculars (chiefly Old French) or Latin with German infinitive endings in *-ieren* are stressed on the *-ier-: wandeˈlieren, organˈieren.*
6. Other loan-words are generally accented as in their home languages.

As in most Romance languages, elision frequently occurs in MHG when a terminal vowel precedes the initial vowel of the following word. Thus the phrase *rôse âne dorn* would consist of four syllables: [ˈro:s ɑ:nə dɔr̥n]. The vowel that is pronounced is always the one at the beginning of the second word. Sometimes, however, it is clear from scanning a poetic line that elision does not apply.

Ten Rules of Thumb

These rules will help eliminate the most commonly sung mistakes by both English speakers and native Germans when performing songs in MHG.

1. Roll your *R*s using a tongue-tip trill, [r̥].

2. Do not pronounce *sp-* as [ʃp] or *st-* as [ʃt], as in the case in Modern German. They are pronounced just as they are spelled, [sp] and [st].

3. While the initial and postconsonantal *z* was probably pronounced more or less as it is today [ts], the intervocalic and postvocalic *z* may well have been still a voiceless lisp [θ] well into the thirteenth century in some areas, perhaps somewhat like the initial sound of English *thing.* In the course of the Middle Ages it changed its sound to a fortis, unvoiced sibilant [s]. If you sing it this way, you are likely to be right for any period. But it contrasts phonemically with the historically unvoiced *s* (spelled *s, ss,* or sometimes *ß*), so that the word *was* ("was," with a lenis *s*) was always clearly differentiated from *waz* ("what," with a fortis *s* or, perhaps, a voiceless lisp).

4. Medial and final *h* equals *ch,* that is, the German *ach*-sound of today [x], a velar fricative well toward the back of the mouth. Accordingly, *sehen* would have been pronounced [sɛxən].

5. The digraph *ng* is pronounced [ŋg], as in English *finger.*

6. The character *w* was probably pronounced something like the modern English *w,* that is, a semi-vowel as in *wine,* not as the *w* [v] of Modern German. Thus, *wîp* was [wi:p]. At various times and in various places, this [w] became a bilabial consonant, possibly pronounced as the Spanish *v* in *Cordova* or *Havana* [β]. Oswald von Wolkenstein (fifteenth century) appears in some manuscripts, for example, as *Osbalt von Bolkenstein.* The present-day German sound [v] represented by the letter *w* seems to have developed during the fifteenth century.

7. In a normalized MHG text (favored by most editors), the long vowels will be marked by a circumflex or a long mark; all other vowels are short.

8. Watch out for vowels in open syllables which were short in MHG but were lengthened in the fifteenth century and remain long in German today: *sagen, legen,* and *loben* should be given the medieval pronunciation of [sagən], [legən], and [lɔbən], not the modern articulations [zɑ:gən], [le:gən], and [lo:bən].

9. Diphthongs are written as diphthongs, that is, in almost all cases, the orthography reflects the pronunciation. *Ouch* is [ɔʊχ], z̦ɨ̧ȩɽȩ ɨʂ [ʈʂɪɛrə], and *guot* is [gʊɔt], though sometimes in the southeast (e.g., Vienna), it would have been written *guet* and spoken [guɛt]. Within these diphthongs the first component is the more important sound. Note that *æ, œ,* and *iu* are not diphthongs but the long versions of the short mutated vowels *ä, ö, and ü.* These long mutated vowels should be pronounced [æ:], [ø], and [y:].

10. Beware of *ei,* which should be pronounced as it is written [ɛɪ], not as in Modern German [ai]. Though the present-day articulation began to make some headway in parts of Bavaria and Austria as early as the thirteenth century, the older sound was widespread during the Classical period and, in certain dialects, over the centuries into the modern era. You may find, too, that the older pronunciation, [ɛɪ], is more pleasant to sing.

Consonants

Written double consonants are not infrequent in MHG, but by the end of the thirteenth century they were probably pronounced as single consonants even though they continued in the orthography, often as signals for preceding short vowels. It is difficult to determine exactly at what time and in what place double consonants became single. Accordingly, in the sample texts (all from the thirteenth century and later) they are regarded as single.

b [b]. In Bavarian and Alemannic the *b* sound was probably pronounced as it is in the present-day dialect, as a lenis *p,* a soft but voiceless bilabial stop. Its less plosive sound, however, is phonemically distinct from [p]. There is no need to emulate this pronunciation, since in many, perhaps most High German dialects it was pronounced [b]: *bein* [bɛɪn], *bette* [bɛtə], *bluome* [bluɔmə]. The use of lenis and fortis *p* to represent the phonemically distinct *b* and *p* of standard German persists today in Swabia, Bavaria, Austria, and Switzerland.

c Pronounced [k] as in *tac* [tak], *mac* [mak]. In certain thirteenth- and fourteenth-century manuscripts the digraph *dc* served as an abbreviation of *daz,* to which it is always normalized in edited texts.

ch The voiceless, velar fricative [x] as in modern German *ach* or Scottish *loch.* It was never palatalized, as in modern German *ich* [ɪç]. The MHG word *ich,* spelled exactly the same as the modern form, would have been pronounced [ɪx], as it still is in some dialects: *mich* [mɪx], *doch* [dɔx].

ck [k]. Usually only in interior positions: *stecken* [stɛkən], *dicke* [dɪkə].

d [d]. As with the grapheme *b,* Upper German speakers frequently unvoiced this sound, making it into a lenis *t,* but this is probably too fine a distinction to emulate in singing.

f The labial dental [f]: *liefe* [lɪɛfə], *fuoge* [fuɔgə]. This sound was also represented by *v: finger* or *vinger* [fɪŋgər̩].

g Pronounced [g] initially and after vowels. As with *b* and *d,* the *g* was probably unvoiced in Upper German to a lenis *k,* but for the majority of High German dialects the voiced *g* no doubt prevailed: *gewalt* [gəwalt], *grôz* [gr̩o:s], *ouge* [ɔʊgə].

Pronounced [k] terminally, though in both the manuscripts and the editions it was usually written *k* or *c.*

h Pronounced [x] between and after vowels: *sehen* [sɛxən], *naht* [naxt]. The digraph *ch* represents the same sound.

Pronounced [h] initially: *hân* [hɑ:n], *hiute* [hy:tə].

j [j]. The *j* was used initially and medially between vowels: *jehen* [jɛxən], *jâr* [jɑ:r̩], *wæjen* [wæjən]. The sound may have ranged from something like the present-day German palatal fricative [ç] and the English semi-vowel represented by the spelling *y,* as in *yellow.* In some manuscripts the spelling *j* was interchangeable with *i.*

l Probably the voiced, alveolar lateral [l] as in modern German, and certainly a difficult sound for the native English speaker to pronounce. Place the tongue so that it just touches the hard palate and grin as broadly and as tautly as possible, emitting the sound laterally and equally on both sides. Remember to keep grinning and keep the tongue as tight and as parallel as possible with the roof of the mouth. Do not let it drop as with the American English *l*. There will be allophonic variations of this sound, more than almost any other: *lant* [lant], *ellen* [ɛlən], *vil* [fɪl].

m [m]: *minne* [mɪnə], *arm* [ar̥m], *bestem* [bɛstəm].

n [n]: *nu* [nu:], *begunde* [bəgʊndə], *zweien* [tswɛɪən].

ng [ŋg]. As in English *finger*: *singen* [sɪŋgən], *lange* [laŋgə], *angest* [aŋgəst].

p The bilabial, unvoiced stop [p]: *pîn* [pi:n], *loup* [lɔʊp].

pf The labial affricate [pf] as in modern German: *pfaffe* [pfafə], *apfel* [apfəl].

ph Pronounced [pf]. Sometimes interchanged with *pf*: *phlihte* [pflɪxtə], *phennic* [pfɛnɪk].

Pronounced [f] in loan-words from Greek: *Philippe* [fɪlɪpə].

r [r̥]. Trilled on the tongue and not the uvular *r* [R] of standard German today (the "guttural" *r* sounded in back of the soft palate and trilled by flapping the uvula). The tongue trill imparts the staccato quality to the utterances of Upper German speakers, especially the Swiss: *rôt* [r̥o:t], *braten* [br̥atən], *aber* [abər̥].

s Always the voiceless sibilant [s]. It is not voiced as it is in standard Modern German: *sippe* [sɪpə], *rôse* [r̥o:sə], *geist* [gɛɪst].

sp Pronounced [sp]. The letter *s* always remains [s] before *p;* it is never pronounced [ʃ] as in Modern German.

st [st]. As with the *sp* digraph, the *s* is always pronounced [s].

sch Pronounced [ʃ] as in Modern German. Occasionally, as a reflex of an earlier spelling and pronunciation, this sound is represented by *sc,* though it was probably always [ʃ] from the beginning of the twelfth century: *schîn* [ʃi:n], *wünschen* [wynʃən].

v [f]. The spelling *v* was generally interchangeable with *f*: *vinger* or *finger* [fiŋgər̥], *vröude* or *fröide* [fr̥œʏdə].

Pronounced [v] between vowels and usually voiced: *hoves* [hɔvəs], *vrevel* [fr̥ɛvəl].

w [w]. A bilabial semi-vowel, probably like the modern English *w* in *wine,* but not yet the labial-dental [v] represented by the Modern German *w.* Sometime in the Later Middle Ages an intermediate stage was reflected in the use of a *b,* probably indicating a bilabial *v* [β].

z Pronounced [ts] in initial position and after consonants: *zart* [tsar̥t], *zwîfel* [tswi:fəl], *herze* [hɛr̥tsə].

By the year 1200 most High German speakers must have been pronouncing it as the unvoiced sibilant [s], though no doubt with a fortis quality (with a loud hissing sound?), since it contrasted phonemically with the other *s*-sound represented by the letter *s.* Accordingly, *waz* ("what") and *was* ("was") were not homonyms until well into the fourteenth century, though their pronunciations must have been quite close.

zz [s]. Essentially the same sound as represented by *z* in the intervocalic or post-vocalic position: *wazzer* [wasər̥].

Vowels

Vowels in Accented Syllables

a [a]. Similar to the American English pronunciation of the *o* in *pod* or, better, like the a in Modern German *Mann: kraft* [kṛaft], *adel* [adəl], *vater* [fatəṛ].

â [ɑ:]. Like the *a* in British English *father: jâr* [jɑ:ṛ], *âne* [ɑ:nə], *dâhte* [dɑ:xtə]. Sometimes, especially in Bavaria and Austria, this tends to become a "dark *a*," probably pronounced more like a long *o* [o:]; e.g., in rhymes such as *trâge: synagôge* and *gefrâget: vôget.* This darkening is also reflected in the modern German words (via Bavarian) *ohne* < *âne* and *Mond* < *mâne.* Scribes, however, striving to rise above the regionalism of their dialects, tended to avoid this in the orthography.

e [ɛ]. Like English *bed: leben* [lɛbən], *herze* [hɛṛtsə], *este* [ɛstə].

ê [e:]. A pure long *e* as in Modern German *Tee: êre* [e:ṛə], *sêle* [se:lə], *owê* [ɔwe:].

i [ɪ]. As in English *bit: wizzen* [wɪsən], *silber* [sɪlbəṛ], *visch* [fɪʃ].

î [i:]. Approximately as in English *see: wîp* [wi:p], *vrî* [fṛi:], *schîn* [ʃi:n].

o [ɔ]. As in Modern German *Gott* or (approximately) as the *ou* in American English *fought; got* [gɔt], *vogel* [fɔgəl], *loben* [lɔbən].

ô [o:]. A long, pure *o,* as in Modern German *tot: rôse* [ṛo:sə], *ôsterrîche* [o:stəṛi:xə], *nôt* [no:t].

u [ʊ]. Like the *u* in Modern German *unter: under* [ʊndəṛ], *wurm* [wʊṛm], *tugent* [tʊgənt].

û [u:]. A long, pure *u*-sound, somewhat like that of English *fool,* but without the diphthong glide at the end; probably much like the Modern German vowel in *gut: hûs* [hu:s], *ûf* [u:f], *lûte* [lu:tə].

Mutated Vowels in Accented Syllables

ä [æ]. Somewhat like the English *a* in *man,* but with a more open quality. This sound was rare, since it generally merged with and was replaced in the orthography by *e: mähte* [mæxtə], *mähelen* [mæxələn], *geslähte* [gɛslæxtə].

æ [æ:]. The long version of *ä;* open, like English *air,* but without the diphthong: *mære* [mæ:ṛə], *stæte* [stæ:tə], *jæmerlîche* [jæ:məṛli:xə].

ö [œ]. Open, with rounded lips, as in Modern German *Töchter; möhte* [mœxtə], *töhter* [tœxtəṛ], *löcher* [lœxəṛ].

œ [ø]. The long version of *ö,* probably articulated as the vowel in Modern German *schön: schœne* [ʃønə], *bœse* [bøsə], *hœren* [høṛən].

ü [ʏ]. Open with rounded lips, like German *Brücke: brücke* [bṛʏkə], *würme* [wʏṛmə], *tür* [tʏṛ].

iu [y:]. The closed, long version of *ü,* with rounded lips, like Modern German *über: liute* [ly:tə], *hiuser* [hy:sər], *diu* [dy:].

Diphthongs in Accented Syllables

ei [ɛɪ]. Like the diphthong in English *stain: ein* [ɛɪn], *kleit* [klɛɪt], *stein* [stɛɪn]. The [aɪ] of Modern German, spelled *ei* as in MHG, appears in some dialects in the thirteenth century, though the older sound [ɛɪ] generally persisted until at least the time of Luther and is still found in various dialects throughout German-speaking areas.

ie [ɪɛ]. Approximately like the Modern English *Korean* or *European,* though tenser and a bit more open: *bieten* [bɪɛtən], *liep* [lɪɛp], *fliegen* [flɪɛgən].

ou [ɔʊ]. Similar to the American English pronunciation of *oh,* though the *u* should be heard distinctly: *ouge* [ɔʊgə], *boum* [bɔʊm], *erlouben* [ɛr̥lɔubən]. The Modern German pronunciation [au] as in *Auge* and *Baum* began sporadically toward the end of the thirteenth century.

öu, eu, or öi [œʏ] or possibly [œɪ]. The umlauted version of *ou.* The lips should be puckered for both components of this diphthong: *vröide* (sometimes spelled *freude* or *fröide* or *fröude*) [fr̥œʏdə], *höu* [hœʏ], *söugen* [sœʏgən]. Though the sound was not a common one in MHG words, the word *vröide* ("joy") represents one of the highest positive values in *Minnesang* and, accordingly, occurs very frequently in the songs of the High Middle Ages.

uo [ʊɔ]. Be sure to sound both components: *guot* [gʊɔt], *muoter* [mʊɔtər̥], *bluome* [blʊɔmə]. In some manuscripts this diphthong shows up as *ue* [ʊɛ], reflecting dialects farther to the east.

üe [ʏɛ]. The umlauted form of *uo: müeder* [mʏɛdər̥], *güete* [gʏɛtə], *küele* [kʏɛlə].

Vowels in Unstressed Syllables

Most of the vowels in unaccented syllables of the Old High German period (OHG) underwent weakening in MHG to an *e*-sound which probably varied between a schwa, [ə], and a short, open *e,* [ɛ]. Thus, OHG *zunga* [tsʊŋga] became *zunge* in MHG [tsʊŋgə] or possibly [tsʊŋgɛ]. This sound is almost always represented by the grapheme *e,* which is rendered in this guide by the schwa rather than the open, short *e.* If, however, [ɛ] seems to the singer a more desirable sound, it would not be an inappropriate articulation, as long as the pronunciation is consistent throughout. Accordingly, *loben* could be pronounced [lɔbən] or [lɔbɛn].

In certain suffixes, often in syllables bearing a secondary stress, the old non-*e* vowel forms persist. These vowels can be either short or long and in normalized texts will be so marked. Despite their frequent occurrence in syllables with a secondary stress, for the sake of convenience they are considered here with other vowels in unstressed syllables. In all cases, pronunciation is identical with that of the vowel in stressed syllables.

The following are examples of vowels in suffixes bearing a secondary stress: *-ære: videlære* [ˈfɪdəlˈˈæ:r̥ə]; *-inne: küneginne* [ˈkʏnəgˈˈɪnə]; *-inc: jungelinc* [ˈjʊŋgəˈˈlɪnk]; *-în* and *-lîn:*

magedîn [ˈmagəˈˈdi:n], *wengelîn* [ˈwɛŋgəˈˈli:n]; *-isse: vinsternisse* [ˈfɪnstɛr̩ˈˈnɪsə]; *-unge: wandelunge* [ˈwandəlˈˈʊŋgə]. A few other non-schwa vowels occur regularly in unaccented syllables: *-isch: hövisch* [hœvɪʃ]; *-ic: künic* [kʏnɪk]; *-sal: trüebsal* [tr̩ʏɛbsal]; *-lîch: ritterlîch* [rɪtər̩li:x]; *-rîch: Dietrîch* [dɪɛtr̩i:x].

Another category of unstressed syllables the singer should bear in mind is the group of "inseparable prefixes" (see "Stress and Intonation" above). The unstressed prefixes with a post-consonantal vowel *(be-* and *ge-)* were probably pronounced with a schwa, while those with pre- or inter-consonantal vowel *(ent-, en-, er-, ver-,* and *zer-)* were pronounced with the open, short *e.* Accordingly, the following articulations are probably valid for these prefixes: *be-* [bə], *ge-* [gə], *ent-* [ɛnt], *en-* [ɛn], *er-* [ɛr̩], *ver-* [fɛr̩], *zer-* [tsɛr̩].

The Definite Article

Though the various forms of the definite article look like those used in Modern German, their pronunciation is generally different. These articles can occur as both accented and unaccented syllables but should be pronounced according to the rules for vowels in accented syllables. Accordingly, all vowels in the various inflected forms of the definite article are short except for the word *diu* (which serves as the feminine nominative singular and, generally, the neuter nominative and accusative plural), which has a mutated vowel, and the word *die* (accusative feminine singular and nominative and accusative plural), which has a diphthong. Noting these differences is especially important for singers who know Modern German, since many of the originally short vowels of these definite articles are lengthened in the present-day language, e.g., *den* [de:n]. The following chart of the definite articles may prove useful:

	Masculine	Neuter	Feminine
Singular			
Nominative	*der* [dɛr̩]	*daz* [das]	*diu* [dy:]
Accusative	*den* [dɛn]	*daz* [das]	*die* [diə]
Genitive	*des* [dɛs]	*des* [dɛs]	*der* [dɛr̩]
Dative	*dem* [dɛm]	*dem* [dɛm]	*der* [dɛr̩]
Plural			
Nominative	*die* [diə]	*diu* [dy:]	*die* [diə]
Accusative	*die* [diə]	*diu* [dy:]	*die* [diə]
Genitive	*der* [dɛr̩]	*der* [dɛr̩]	*der* [dɛr̩]
Dative	*den* [dɛn]	*den* [dɛn]	*den* [dɛn]

SAMPLE TEXTS

Each of the following texts has come down to us associated with a melody or clearly related to a separately transmitted tune. A relatively late song by Wizlav, whose language is something of an anomaly, is included because his appealing melodies, much in the tradition of the older *Minnesang,* frequently appear in today's repertoire of early German songs.

Walther von der Vogelweide, "Palästinalied"

It is difficult to date Walther's song, which might have been composed for the Fourth Crusade (1204) or for the Fifth (1227), or for some less militant occasion in between. The version used here (Manesse Manuscript) dates from about 1300. Since the song exists in five other manuscripts, and editors generally base their texts on several, the normalized MHG version that follows will differ somewhat from the many other printed versions available. Of the seven stanzas in Manuscript C, the first, second, and last are given here. CD # 51.

Text from Manuscript C: Universitätsbibliothek Heidelberg, Cod. pal. germ. 848 (Manesse Manuscript).

1 Alrest lebe ich mir w^{er}de
sit min sv̍ndig ŏge siht.
dc reine lant vn̄ ŏch die erde.
der man so vil eren giht.
es ist geschehē des ich ie bat.
ich bin komē an die stat.
da got menschlichē trat.

2 Schŏͤnv̍ lant rich un̄ here
swc ich d^{er}noch han gesehen
so bist dvs ir all^{er}ere.
wc ist wvnders hie geschehen.
das ein magt ein kint gebar.
here vber aller engel schar.
wc das niht ein wvnd^{er} gar.

7 Kristen ivden vn̄ die heidē.
jehent dc dis ir erbe si.
got mvͤsse es ze rehte scheiden.
dur die sine name dri.
al dv̍ welt dv̍ stritet her.
wir sin an d^{er}rehten ger.
reht ist dc er vns gewer.

Normalized MHG

1 Alrêst lebe ich mir werde
sî mîn sündig ouge siht
daz reine lant unde ouch die erde,
der man sô vil êren giht.
Ez ist geschehen des ich ie bat:
ich bin komen an die stat,
dâ got menschlîchen trat.

2 Schœniu lant rîch unt hêre
swaz ich der noch hân gesehen;
sô bist duz ir aller êre:
waz ist wunders hie geschehen!
daz ein magt ein kint gebar,
hêre über aller engel schar;
was daz niht ein wunder gar!

7 Kristen, jûden unt die heiden
jehent daz diz ir erbe sî.
Got müsse ez ze rehte scheiden
dur die sîne namen drî.
Al diu welt diu strîtet her;
wir sîn an der rehten ger:
reht ist daz er uns gewer.

1 ˈalṛˈe:st lɛb ˈɪx mɪṛ ˈwɛṛdə
ˈsi:t mi:n ˈsʏndɪk ˈɔʊgə ˈsɪxt
das ˈṛɛɪnə ˈlant ʊnd ˈɔʊx dɪ ˈɛṛdə
ˈdɛṛ man ˈso: fɪl ˈe:ṛən ˈgɪxt
es ˈɪst gəˈʃɛxən dɛs ˈɪx ɪɛ ˈbat
ˈɪx bɪn ˈkɔmən ˈan dɪə ˈstat
ˈdɑ: gɔt ˈmɛnʃˈli:xən ˈtṛat

2 ˈʃøny: ˈlant ˈṛi:x unt ˈhe:ṛə
ˈswas ɪx ˈdɛṛ nɔx ˈhɑ:n gəˈsɛxən
ˈso: bɪst ˈdʊs ɪṛ ˈaləṛ e:ṛə
ˈwas ɪst ˈwʊndəṛs ˈhiə gəˈʃɛxən
ˈdas ɛɪn ˈmagt ɛɪn ˈkɪnd gəˈbaṛ
ˈhe:ṛ ʏbəṛ ˈaləṛ ˈɛŋgəl ˈʃaṛ
ˈwas das ˈnɪxt ɛɪn ˈwʊndəṛ ˈgaṛ

7 kˈṛɪstən ˈju:dən ˈʊnt dɪə ˈhɛɪdən
ˈjɛxənt das ˈdɪs ɪṛ ˈɛṛbə ˈsi:
ˈgɔt mʏs ˈɛs tsə ˈṛɛxtə ˈʃɛɪdən
ˈdʊṛ dɪə ˈsi:nə ˈnamən ˈdṛi:

ˈal dy: ˈwɛlt dy: ˈstṛi:tət ˈhɛṛ
ˈwɪṛ si:n ˈan dɛṛ ˈṛɛxtən ˈgɛṛ
ˈṛɛxt ɪst ˈdas ɛṛ ˈʊns gəˈwɛṛ

MODERN SOURCES

Horst Brunner, Ulrich Müller, Franz Viktor Spechtler, eds. *Walther von der Vogelweide: Die Gesamte Überlieferung der Texte und Melodien, Abbildungen, Materialien, Melodietranskriptionen.* Göppingen: Kümmerle, 1977 (Litterae, No. 7). Contains manuscript facsimiles of texts and melodies as well as diplomatic editions of both.

Friedrich Mauer, ed. *Die Lieder Walthers von der Vogelweide.* Tübingen: Niemeyer, 1974 (Altdeutsche Textbibliothek, No. 43). The standard edition containing both texts and melody.

Neidhart von Reuental, "Si jehent, daz der winder"

Neidhart sang during the first half of the thirteenth century, first in Bavaria and later at the Austrian courts. He is the earliest singer for whom a substantial body of song is transmitted, though many of the songs attributed to him were composed and sung after his death. The version given here is from the Manesse Manuscript, which differs slightly from most edited versions, which usually include variant readings from other manuscripts. In its various forms the song has between seven and eleven stanzas. Included here are the first and last Manesse stanzas. CD #52.

Text from Manuscript C: Universitätsbibliothek Heidelberg, Cod. pal. germ. 848 (Manesse Manuscript).

1 Si iehent das der winter
keme nie bi siner zit
so scharpfer noh so swinter
noh clag ich min vrowe diu ist herteklich gemuot.
si ist wider mich ze strenge.
got ir ungnade nie mer
gar an mir verhenge
miner frowen über mich si ist wirser danne guot.
ich han miniu iar
ir gedienet ane masse
nieman sol mir wissen ob ich miner frowen lasse
da ist liebes lones niht so tiure als umb ein har.

10 Swer einen vogel hete
der mit sange dur das iar
sinen willen tete
dem solt man under wilent zuo dem vogelhuse sehen
und gebe im guote spise
so koende ouch der selbe vogel
singen suesse wise
so mueste man dem vogel guoter meisterschefte iehen.
sunge er sinen sang

iemer schone gegen dem meigen
so solt man in den summer und den winter lute heigen
guoter handelunge wissen ouch die vogel dank.

Normalized MHG

1 Si jehent, daz der winder
koeme nie bî sîner zît
sô scherpfer noch sô swinder;
noch klag ich, mîn vrouwe diu ist hertichlîch gemuot.
Si ist wider mich ze strenge;
got ir ungenâde niemer
gar an mir verhenge
mîner vrouwen über mich: sist wirser danne guot.
ich hân mîniu jâr
ir gedienet âne mâze;
niemen sol mir wîzen, ob ich mîner vrouwen lâze.
Dâ ist liebes lônes niht sô tiure als umb ein hâr.

10 Swer einen vogel haete
der mit sange dur daz jâr
sînen willen taete:
dem solt man underwîlent zuo dem vogelhûse sehen
und gebe im guote spîse
so künde ouch der selbe vogel
singen süeze wîse;
so müeste man dem vogel guoter meisterschefte jehen.
Sunge er sînen sanc
iemer schône gên dem meien
sô solt man in den summer und den winder lûte heien.
guoter handelunge wîsen ouch die vogel dank.

1 sɪ ˈjɛxənt ˈdas dɛṛ ˈwɪndəṛ
ˈkømə ˈnɪə bi: ˈsi:nəṛ ˈtsi:t
so: ˈʃɛṛpfəṛ ˈnox so: ˈswɪndəṛ
ˈnox klak ˈɪx mi:n ˈfṛɔʊwə ˈdy:st ˈhɛṛtɛ̎li:x gəˈmʊɔt
si:st ˈwɪdəṛ ˈmɪx tsə ˈstṛɛŋgə
ˈgɔt ɪṛ ˈungə̎nɑ:də ˈnɪəməṛ
ˈgaṛ an ˈmɪṛ vɛṛˈhɛŋgə
ˈmi:nəṛ ˈfṛɔʊwən ˈʏbəṛ ˈmɪx si:st ˈwɪṛsəṛ ˈdanə ˈgʊɔt
ˈɪx hɑ:n ˈmi:ny: ˈjɑ:ṛ
ˈɪṛ gəˈdɪɛnət ˈɑ:nə ˈmɑ:sə
ˈnɪɛmən ˈsɔl mɪṛ ˈwi:sən ˈɔp ɪx ˈmi:nəṛ ˈfṛɔʊwə ˈlɑ:sə
ˈdɑ: ɪst ˈlɪɛbəs ˈlo:nəs ˈnɪxt so: ty:ṛ als ˈʊmb ɛɪn ˈhɑ:ṛ

10 swɛṛ ˈɛɪnən ˈfɔgəl ˈhæ:tə
ˈdɛṛ mɪt ˈsaŋgə ˈdʊṛ das ˈjɑ:ṛ
ˈsi:nən ˈwɪlən ˈtæ:tə
dem ˈsɔlt man ˈʊndəṛʺwi:lənt ˈtsʊɔ dɛm ˈfɔgəl ˈhu:sə ˈsɛxən
ʊnt ˈgɛb ɪm ˈgʊɔtə ˈspi:sə
ˈso: kʏnd ˈɔʊx ˈsɛlbə ˈfɔgəl
ˈsɪŋgən ˈsʏɛsə ˈwi:sə
so: ˈmʏəstə ˈman dɛm ˈfɔgəl ˈgʊɔtəṛ ˈmɛɪstəṛʺʃɛftə ˈjɛxən
ˈsʊŋg ɛṛ ˈsi:nən ˈsank
ˈɪɛməṛ ˈʃo:nə ˈge:n dɛm ˈmɛɪən
so: ˈsɔlt man ˈɪn dɛn ˈsʊməṛ ˈʊnd dɛn ˈwɪndəṛ ˈlu:tə ˈhɛɪən
ˈgʊɔtəṛ ˈhandəlʺʊŋgə ˈwi:sən ˈɔʊx diə ˈfɔgəl ˈdank.

MODERN SOURCES

G. Fritz, ed. *Abbildungen zur Neidhart Überlieferung I: Die Berliner Neidhart-Handschrift R und die Pergamentfragmente C^{b}, K, O, und M.* Göppingen: Kümmerle, 1973 (Litterae, No. 11). Photocopy of the text as it appears in the R manuscript.
Die Manessische Liederhandschrift. Insel: Leipzig, 1924–29. Facsimile of the oldest manuscript containing a version of the song (C); text only.
Paul Sappler and Helmut Lomnitzer. *Die Lieder Neidharts.* Tübingen: Niemeyer, 1984 (Altdeutsche Textbibliothek, No. 44). The standard edition of Neidhart's songs, containing texts and melodies.
E. Wenzel, ed. *Abbildungen zur Neidhart-Uberlieferung II: Die Berliner Neidhart-Handschrift c (mfg 779).* Göppingen: Kümmerle, 1976 (Litterae, No. 15). Photocopy of the only manuscript (c) containing a melody.

Der Marner, "Long Melody" (Langer Ton)

Marner was singing between about 1235 and 1270. This is the first of five stanzas in the Colmar Songbook, compiled about 1470. CD #53.

Text from MS. t: Staatsbibliothek München, Cod. germ. 4997 (Colmar Song Manuscript).

Maria muter reine meit
ros one sunden dorn
die heilig schrift uns von dir seit
wir waren alle gar verlorn
da halff din kusch und gottes gut
uns usser ymmerwernder not.
Wir sint in arger zit beteit
milt uns den gottez zorn
din son dir nymmer nit verseit
der helle wir hat es gesworn
er woll uns werffen ewiclich
al in den ymmerwernden tot.
Nu bit got und gebut
dem eingebornen sone din
daz er vns hie nit lass

also verwyset sin
dorch solcher freudenkunft
sît er zu trost gesendet hat
sins todes vrstend in vernunft
und er den grymmen tot
mit sinem tot vor vns herflug
und ab vns zwug
der sunden vngefug
die sich die mentscheit uff ir trug
daz waz der cristenheit zu trost
von irem schopfer me dan gnug
daz er sich zu der martel sin
hie fur vns an daz crucze bot.

Normalized MHG

Marîa, muoter, reiniu meit,
rôse âne sünden dorn:
die heilic schrift uns von dir seit,
wir wâren alle gar verlorn.
dâ half dîn kiusche unt gotes güet
uns ûzer iemerwernder nôt.
Wir sint in arger zît beteit,
milte uns den gotes zorn;
dîn sun dir niemer niht verseit,
der helle wirt hât ez gesworn,
er wolle uns werfen êwiclîch
al in den iemerwernden tôt.
Nû bit got unt gebiut
dem eingebornen sune dîn,
daz er uns hie niht las
alsô verwîset sîn
durch solcher vröiden kunft,
sît er ze trôst gesendet hât
sîns tôdes urstende in vernunft,
unde er den grimmen tôt
mit sînem tôt vor uns hersluoc
unde ab uns zwuoc
der sünden ungevuoc,
die sich die menschheit ûfertruoc,
daz was der kristenheit ze trôst
von irem schöpfer mê dan gnuoc,
daz er sich zuo der martel sîn
vür uns daz kriuze bôt.

maˈṛi:ə ˈmʊɔtəṛ ˈṛɛɪny: ˈmɛɪt
ˈṛo:s ˈɑ:nə ˈsy:ndən ˈdɔṛn
dɪə ˈhɛɪli:k ˈʃṛɪft ʊns ˈfɔn dɪṛ ˈsɛɪt
wɪṛ ˈwɑ:ṛən ˈalə ˈgaṛ fɛṛˈlɔrn
dɑ: ˈhalf di:n ˈky:ʃ ʊnt ˈgɔtəs ˈgʏɛt
ʊns ˈu:səṛ ˈɪɛməṛ ˈwɛṛndəṛ ˈno:t
wɪṛ ˈsɪnt ɪn ˈaṛgəṛ ˈtsi:t bəˈtɛɪt
mɪlt ˈʊns dɛn ˈgɔtəs ˈtsɔṛn
di:n ˈsʊn dɪṛ ˈnɪɛməṛ nɪxt fɛṛsɛɪt
dɛṛ ˈhɛlə ˈwɪṛt hɑ:t ˈɛs gəˈswɔṛn
ɛr ˈwɔl ʊns ˈwɛṛfən ˈe:wɪkˈˈli:x
al ˈɪn dɛn ɪɛməṛˈwɛṛndən ˈto:t
nu: ˈbɪt gɔt ˈʊnt gəˈby:t
dɛm ˈɛɪngəˈbɔṛnəṛ ˈsʊnə ˈdi:n
das ˈɛṛ ʊns ˈhɪə nɪxt ˈlas
aˈlso: fɛṛˈwi:sət ˈsi:n
dʊṛx ˈsɔlxəṛ ˈfṛœʏdən ˈkʊnft
si:t ˈɛṛ tsə ˈtṛo:st gəˈsɛndət ˈhɑ:t
si:ns ˈto:dəs ˈʊṛstɛnd ˈɪn fɛṛˈnʊnft
ʊnd ˈɛṛ dɛn ˈgṛɪmən to:t
mɪt ˈsi:nəm ˈto:t fɔṛ ˈʊns hɛṛˈslʊɔk
ʊnd ˈab ʊns ˈtswʊɔk
dɛṛ ˈsʏndən ˈʊngəˈˈfʊɔk
dɪə ˈsɪx dɪə ˈmɛnʃhɛɪt ˈu:fɛṛˈˈtṛʊɔk
das ˈwas dɛṛ ˈkṛɪstənˈˈhɛɪt tsə ˈtṛo:st
fɔn ˈɪṛəm ˈʃœpfəṛ ˈme: dan ˈgnʊɔk
das ˈɛṛ sɪx ˈtsʊɔ dɛṛ ˈmaṛtəl ˈsi:n
fʏṛ ˈʊns das ˈkṛy:tsə bo:t

MODERN SOURCES

Hugo Moser and Joseph Müller-Blattau. *Deutsche Lieder des Mittelalters von Walther von der Vogelweide bis zum Lochamer Liederbuch: Texte und Melodien.* Stuttgart: Klett, 1968. Edited version of text and melody.

Ulrich Müller, Franz Viktor Spechtler, and Horst Brunner. *Die Kolmarer Liederhandschrift der Bayrischen Staatsbibliothek München (cgm 4997).* Göppingen: Kümmerle, 1976 (Litterae, No. 35). Photocopy of manuscript.

Paul Runge. *Die Sangweisen der Colmarer Handschrift und die Liederhandschrift Donaueschingen.* Hildesheim: Georg Olms, 1965 (reprint of 1896 Leipzig edition). A near-diplomatic version of text and melody.

Alexander, “Hie bevorn dô wir kinder wâren”

Alexander seems to have been singing between 1240 and 1260. His songs are included in the Jena Songbook, which was compiled about a hundred years later. The first four of seven stanzas are given here. CD #54.

Text from MS. J: Universitätsbibliothek Jena, Perg. 133 B11 (Jena Song Manuscript).

1 Hie bevorn do wir kynder waren.
Vnd die tzit was in den iaren.
Daz wir liefen of die wesen.
Von ienen her wider tzv desen.
Da wir vnder stvnden.
viol vunden.
Da sicht man nv rynder besen.

2 Ich gedenke wol daz wir sazen.
In den blumen vnde mazen.
Vvellich die schoneste mvchte syn.
Da scheyn vnser kintlich schyn.
Mit den nuwen krantze.
Tzv dem tantze.
Alsus get die tzit von hyn.

3 Seht do liefe wir ertberen suchen.
Von der tannen tzv der buchen.
Vber stoc und vber steyn
Der wile daz die svnne scheyn.
Do rief ien waltwiser.
durch die riser.
wol dan kinder vnde get heyn.

4 Vvir vntfiengen alle masen.
Gestern do wir ertberen lasen.
Daz was vns ein kintlich spil.
Do erhorte wir so vil.
Vnsen hirten rufen.
unde wufen.
kynder hie get slangen vil.

Normalized MHG

1 Hie bevorn dô wir kinder wâren
unt die zît was in den jâren,
daz wir liefen ûf die wisen,
von jenen her wider zuo disen.
Dâ wir under stunden
vîol vunden,
dâ siht man nû rinder bizen

2 Ich gedenk wol daz wir sâzen
in den bluomen unde mâzen,
welh diu schœneste möhte sîn.
Dâ schein unser kintlich schîn

mit dem niuwen kranze
zuo dem tanze:
alsus gêt diu zît von hin.

3 Seht, dô liefen wir ertberen suochen
von der tannen zuo der buochen
über stock unde über stein
der wîle daz diu sunne schein;
Dô rief ein waltwîser
durch diu rîser:
“wol dan, kinder, unde gêt hein!”

4 Wir enphiengen alle mâsen
gestern dô wir ertberen lâsen:
daz was uns ein kintlich spil.
Dô erhôrten wir sô vil
unsren hirten ruofen
unde wuofen:
“kinder, hie gêt slangen vil!”

1 ˈhɪɛ bəˈfɔṛn do: wɪṛ ˈkɪndəṛ ˈwɑ:ṛən
ˈʊnt dɪə ˈtsi:t was ˈɪn dɛn ˈjɑ:ṛən
ˈdas wɪr ˈlɪɛfən ˈu:f dɪə ˈwɪsən
ˈfɔn jɛnən ˈhɛṛ ˈwɪdəṛ tsʊɔ ˈdɪsən
dɑ: wɪṛ ˈʊndəṛ ˈstʊndən
ˈfi:ɔl ˈfʊndən
dɑ: sɪxt ˈman nu: ˈṛɪndəṛ ˈbɪsən

2 ˈɪx gəˈdɛnkə wɔl ˈdas wɪṛ ˈsɑ:sən
ˈɪn dɛn ˈblʊɔmən ˈʊndə ˈmɑ:sən
ˈwɛlx dy: ˈʃønɛstə ˈmœxtə ˈsi:n
ˈdɑ: ʃɛɪn ˈʊnsəṛ ˈkɪntlɪx ˈʃi:n
ˈmɪt dɛm ˈny:wən ˈkṛantsə
ˈtsʊɔ dɛm ˈtantsə
ˈalsʊs ˈge:t dy: ˈtsi:t fɔn ˈhɪn

3 ˈsɛxt do: ˈlɪɛfən wɪṛ ˈɛṛtbɛṛən ˈsʊɔxən
ˈfɔn dɛṛ ˈtanən ˈtsʊɔ dɛṛ ˈbuɔxən
ˈʏbəṛ ˈstɔk und ˈʏbəṛ ˈstɛɪn
dɛṛ ˈwi:lə ˈdas dy: ˈsʊnə ˈʃɛɪn
ˈdo: ṛɪɛf ˈɛɪn waltˈwi:səṛ
ˈdʊṛx dy: ˈṛi:səṛ
ˈwɔl dan ˈkɪndəṛ ˈʊndə ge:t ˈhɛɪn

4 ˈwɪṛ ɛnˈfɪɛŋgən ˈalə ˈmɑ:sən
ˈgɛstɛṛn ˈdo: wɪṛ ˈɛṛtbɛṛən ˈlɑ:sən

ˈdas was ˈʊns ɛɪn ˈkɪntlɪx ˈspɪl
do: ɛṛˈho:ṛtən ˈwɪṛ so: ˈfɪl
ˈʊnsṛən ˈhɪṛtən ˈṛʊɔfən
ˈʊndə ˈwʊɔfən
kɪndəṛ hɪɛ ge:t ˈslaŋgən ˈfɪl

MODERN SOURCES

Georg Holz, Eduard Bernoulli, and Franz Saran, eds. *Die Jenaer Liederhandschrift.* 2 vols. Leipzig: Hirschfeld, 1901. An excellent diplomatic version of text and melody.

Hugo Moser and Joseph Müller-Blattau. *Deutsche Lieder des Mittelalters von Walther von der Vogelweide bis zum Lochamer Liederbuch: Texte und Melodien.* Stuttgart: Klett, 1968. Edited versions of melody and text.

Helmut Tervooren and Ulrich Müller. *Die Jenaer Liederhandschrift.* Göppingen: Kümmerle, 1972 (Litterae, No. 10). Photocopy of manuscript.

Wizlav, "Nach der senenden klage"

Circumstantial evidence associates the Wizlav of the Jena Songbook with a similarly named prince of Rügen, a Baltic island close to the German coast with dependencies on the mainland. The prince was born in the 1260s, and his death is documented in the year 1325. It would seem that Wizlav's native tongue was Low German, probably more akin to Danish than to the middle and upper German dialects which tended to be the standard language of entertainment at the German courts of his day. The Wizlav of the manuscript, whether princely or not, is represented by songs copied into the Jena Songbook in a Middle German idiom. Here and there they betray what must have been an original Low German dialect. Some editors have tried to recreate the native lowland speech, but it seems more appropriate to sing the songs as they occur in the manuscript, that is, in a Middle German redaction with a Low German flavor added, not through pronunciation but through vocabulary. The following song was copied in relatively "good" MHG, so the singer should encounter few difficulties: however, it lacks the long vowel marks normally supplied by an editor. The letter *h* following *g* probably had no effect on the pronunciation and should be considered a "silent *h*." Wizlav's scribe writes *e* for MHG *ie (we* for *wie, lep* for *liep).* This has been construed in the phonetic transcription as [ɛ:].

Text from MS. J: Universitätsbibliothek Jena, Perg. 133 B11 (Jena Song Manuscript).

1 Nach der senenden claghe muoz ich singhen
kunde ich mir selben bringhen.
vroyde nach dem willen min.
Das ich muochte leben ane swere
so were ich vroyden bere.
hohes muotes wolde ich sin.
So vuorwunne ich alle senende wise.
daz ich wol tzuo prise
ymmer an daz alter vrolich grise
sunder allen pin.

2 In hoher werde eyn leplich abentuore.
tuot mir de minne huore.
wen ich denke ir werdicheyt.
We nach wunsche wol ghetan eyn bilde.
vor minen oughen spilde.
de mich an daz hertze sneyt.
Mit ghewelde clar also de sunne.
Waz ist bezzer wunne.
wen se mit yr scone twinghen kunne.
de de lebe treyt.

3 Se schoz mich durch de oughen in das hertze.
unttzundet sam eyn kertze.
weldilichen tzuo ghevloghen.
Sus berovuet se mich mine sinne.
die minningliche minne.
seth we se hat mich betroghen.
Wen de lebeliche waghe stellet.
und in minne sellet.
so der hertzelebe wol ghevellet.
lep durch lep ghetzogen.

1 ˈnɑːx dɛṛ ˈsɛnəndən ˈklagə ˈmʊɔs ɪx ˈsɪŋgən
ˈkʊnd ɪx mɪṛ ˈsɛlbən bṛɪŋgən
ˈfṛɔɪdə ˈnɑːx dɛm ˈwɪlən ˈmiːn
ˈdas ɪx ˈmʊɔxtə ˈlɛbən anə ˈswæːṛə
soː ˈwæːṛ ɪx ˈfṛɔɪdən ˈbæːṛə
ˈhoːxəs ˈmʊɔtəs ˈwɔld ɪx ˈsiːn
ˈsoː fʊɔṛˈwʊn ɪx ˈalə ˈsɛnəndə ˈwiːsə
ˈdas ɪx ˈwɔl tsʊɔ ˈpṛiːsə
ˈɪməṛ ˈan das ˈaltəṛ ˈfṛɔliːx ˈgṛiːsə
ˈsʊndəṛ ˈalən ˈpiːn

2 ɪn ˈhoːxəṛ ˈwɛṛd ɛɪn ˈlɛːpliːx ˈɑːbɛnˈˈtʊɔṛə
ˈtʊɔt mɪṛ dɛː ˈmɪnə ˈhʊɔṛə
ˈwɛn ɪx ˈdɛnk ɪṛ ˈwɛṛdiːˈxɛɪt
ˈwɛː nɑːx ˈwʊnʃə ˈwɔlgəˈˈtɑːn ɛɪn ˈbɪldə
fɔṛ ˈmiːnən ˈɔʊgən ˈspɪldə
ˈdɛː mɪx ˈan das ˈhɛṛtsə ˈsnɛɪt
ˈmɪt gəˈwɛldə ˈklaṛ alˈsoː dɛː ˈsʊnə
ˈwas ɪst ˈbɛsəṛ ˈwʊnə
ˈwɛn sɛː ˈmɪt ɪṛ ˈʃoːnə ˈtwɪŋgən ˈkʊnə
ˈdɛː dɛː ˈlɛːbə ˈtṛɛɪt

3 sɛ: ˈʃɔs mɪx ˈdʊṛx dɛ: ˈɔʊgən ɪn das ˈhɛṛtsə
untˈtsʊndət ˈsam ɛɪn ˈkɛṛtsə
ˈwɛldiˈˈli:xən ˈtsʊɔ gəˈflɔgən
ˈsʊs bəˈṛɔʊvət ˈsɛ: mɪx ˈmi:nə ˈsɪnə
dɛ: ˈmɪnɪŋgˈˈli:xə ˈmɪnə
ˈse:t wɛ: ˈsɛ: hɑ:t ˈmɪx bəˈtṛɔgən
ˈwɛn dɛ: ˈlɛ:bəli:xə ˈwɑ:gə ˈstɛlət
ˈʊnd ɪn ˈmɪnə ˈsɛlət
ˈso: dɛṛ ˈhɛṛtsə ˈlɛ:bə ˈwɔl gəˈfɛlət
ˈlɛ:p dʊṛx ˈlɛ:p gəˈtsɔgən

MODERN SOURCES

Georg Holz, Eduard Bernoulli, and Franz Saran, eds. *Die Jenaer Liederhandschrift.* 2 vols. Leipzig: Hirschfeld, 1901. An excellent diplomatic version of text and melody.

Hugo Moser and Joseph Müller-Blattau. *Deutsche Lieder des Mittelalters von Walther von der Vogelweide bis zum Lochamer Liederbuch: Texte und Melodien.* Stuttgart: Klett, 1968. An edited version of the melody with a Low German translation of the text.

Helmut Tervooren and Ulrich Müller. *Die Jenaer Liederhandschrift.* Göppingen: Kümmerle, 1972 (Litterae, No. 10). Photocopy of manuscript.

Wesley Thomas and Barbara Garvey Seagrave. *The Songs of the Minnesinger, Prince Wizlaw of Rügen.* Chapel Hill: University of North Carolina Press, 1967. Photocopies of all of Wizlav's songs together with a minimally edited version of the melodies and the texts, that is, they remain close to the Middle German forms in the manuscript.

16

Late Medieval German and Early New High German

PETER FRENZEL

In dealing with an unedited late medieval German text, the singer or speaker must make a number of decisions. Even more than was the case with MHG, the late medieval German dialects, labeled "Late MHG" or Early New High German ("ENHG"), were affected by a lack of a political, cultural, or even geographical center of gravity. There was neither a Germany nor a dominant cultural capital city (like Paris or London) to provide a linguistic standard. The problem was compounded by significant sound changes developing at various rates of speed and in various dialects. With the advent of modern scholarship, in the field of literature MHG came to be regarded as a "classic" language. Thus most of the texts from the period 1150–1350 have been normalized by editors into a standard, though of necessity somewhat artificial, form characterized by a fixed orthography based on the dialects of southwestern German-speaking areas. Late MHG and ENHG texts in nineteenth- and twentieth-century editions appear either roughly as they were in manuscript or in a form in which the editor thinks they should have existed. Because the problem is so complex, and because there is such a perplexing array of dialectal and orthographical uncertainties, the following guidelines for the period 1350–1600 are more general than for MHG and offer possibilities and ranges from which the singer can choose. For the sake of simplicity, both the fading MHG and the developing NHG are subsumed under the rubric of ENHG.

In general the scribes writing ENHG used an orthographical system similar to that of MHG. There were some inconsistencies, but on the whole the letters and groups of letters can be pronounced according to the rules for MHG.

ENHG had various orthographical quirks, which appear in some manuscripts but have been edited out of many of the printed versions available today. The resultant spelling resembles either MHG or the modern language. The following irregularities may occur in the manuscripts or in diplomatic editions: The *i*-sound, long or short, can be represented by *i, j,* or *y;* hence the word *in* can be spelled *in, jn,* or *yn.* The letter *v* is frequently used for *u* at the beginning of a word (vns=uns, vnter=unter), though if it is followed by a vowel it is pronounced [f] (vor, vater). The letter *u* in the middle of a word represents the *u*-sound (mut, darumb), though before vowels it can represent an *f*-sound *(hieuor=hievor; zweiuel=zweifel); w* also can stand for *u: erfrewt=erfreut* [ɛṛfṛɔɪt]. The letter *w* sometimes stands for [b], though it was probably pronounced bi-labially rather than as the more modern labio-dental sound: *wehagen* [βəhagən]. The sibilant took on many interesting orthographic forms: *ſ, s, ss, z, zz, ß,* and *z;* voicing of prevocalic or intervocalic *s* was probably becoming common. The *z* after a consonant or in the initial position was pronounced [ts]; variant orthographic forms for this sound were *cz, tz, czz,* and *ctz.*

The spellings *eu* and *ew* probably represented a sound intermediate between that of the MHG spelling *öi* [œʏ] and the modern pronunciation of *eu* [ɔɪ]. It would be simplest—and not incorrect in most instances—to give it the present-day articulation [ɔɪ].

Superscripts representing umlauted sounds were used in ENHG as in MHG. In the normalized MHG texts they are represented by two letters in their long form *(æ, œ,* and *iu)* and by the modern umlaut for their short versions *(ä, ö, ü).* The ENHG scribe usually represented these sounds, both long and short, as *aͤ, oͤ,* and *uͤ: waͤre=wäre, goͤttelich=göttelîch,* and *gemuͤte=gemüte.* Editors of modern editions frequently indicate the superscript *e* as an umlaut *(ä, ö,* and *ü).*

In manuscripts superscripts *v, o,* and sometimes *e* represent the second component of a diphthong. Therefore *guͦt=guot* and *oͮch=ouch,* and in some cases *guͤt=guet.* The use of the superscript *e* as a diphthong indicator can be confusing, since its more common usage is to indicate umlaut. Fortunately its use is infrequent.

The most severe problem in the pronunciation of ENHG is vowel length. MHG short vowels in open syllables became long in the ENHG period (though exactly when and where is usually difficult to say). Sometimes scribes indicated vowel length by doubling *(gaabe, saat),* by following the vowel with an *h (fahren, befehlen),* or by following an *i* with an *e* (the old MHG diphthong *ie* [ɪɛ] now reduced to a simple long vowel i [i:]: *liegen, krieg* [li:gən], [kṛi:k]). But the most common way of indicating a long vowel, and one which has persisted to the present day, was to follow it with a single rather than a double consonant: *sagen* [sɑ:gən], *haben* [hɑ:bən]. MHG short vowels in open syllables became long in ENHG and NHG. Compare MHG *neben* [nɛbən] and *wider* [wɪdəṛ] with ENHG and NHG *neben* [ne:bən] and *wider* [wi:dəṛ].

In many dialects by the fifteenth century, medial *h* had probably become silent or lightly aspirated. Accordingly, *sehen* would have been pronounced [se:·ən] or [se:·hən]. The digraph *ch,* pronounced generally [x] in MHG, at some point in the early modern period split into the allophones [ç] (after *e* and *i*) and [x] (after *a, o,* and *u*), except in Bavarian and other Upper German dialects, in which [x] has prevailed in all situations up to the present.

As in MHG *v* alternates with *f* or *ff* to represent the voiceless, labio-dental *f*-sound; *vatter* [fatər̥], *volbracht* [fɔlbr̥axt].

The sound of apical *r,* as in MHG, continued, probably in all dialects. It is not until the seventeenth and eighteenth centuries that the uvular *r* became fashionable, largely through the influence of the "Parisian *r.*"

By the late fifteenth century, the letter *h* began to appear sporadically after *t*. There is no linguistic evidence that this altered the pronunciation of the *t* in any way. Accordingly, *thun, garthen,* and *rath* all have the usual *t*-sound: [tu:n], [gar̥tən], and [r̥ɑ:t]. The use of the silent and apparently useless *h* may have been influenced by the increasing knowledge of Greek as well as Greek loan-words among humanists; cf. *theater* and *thesis,* which in German would have been pronounced with an initial *t*-sound. With less frequency, *h* was used following *r, j,* and *v* when these letters occurred initially. As in the case of *t,* it does not alter the pronunciation of the preceding consonant: *rhümen* [r̥y:mən], jhar [jɑ:r̥], *vhest* [fɛst].

The articulation of *ei (ey, ej)* can be problematic. Generally the MHG sound [ɛɪ] was replaced in the thirteenth century in Bavarian and other southern dialects by [aɪ], usually spelled *ai.* Many Middle German dialects retained the [ɛɪ] articulation well into the late Middle Ages, with a corresponding *ei (ey, ej)* spelling. Others changed to the modern [ai] pronunciation while retaining the conventional *ei* spelling, a quirk which continues in the orthography of modern German. Always pronounce *ai* as [aɪ], that is, just as it is spelled. Pronounce *ei* as [ɛɪ] if the text is dated before about 1500; for a later date, give *ei* the modern pronunciation of [aɪ]. While these rules do not guarantee total accuracy, they will ensure consistent and historically appropriate articulations.

DIACHRONIC SOUND CHART FOR GERMAN

The sound changes from Middle High German to New High German took place at different times in different regions between about 1200 and 1500. As a matter of convenience the year 1400 is used here to mark the beginning of the NHG period, though each sound change would have appeared earlier or later in specific regions.

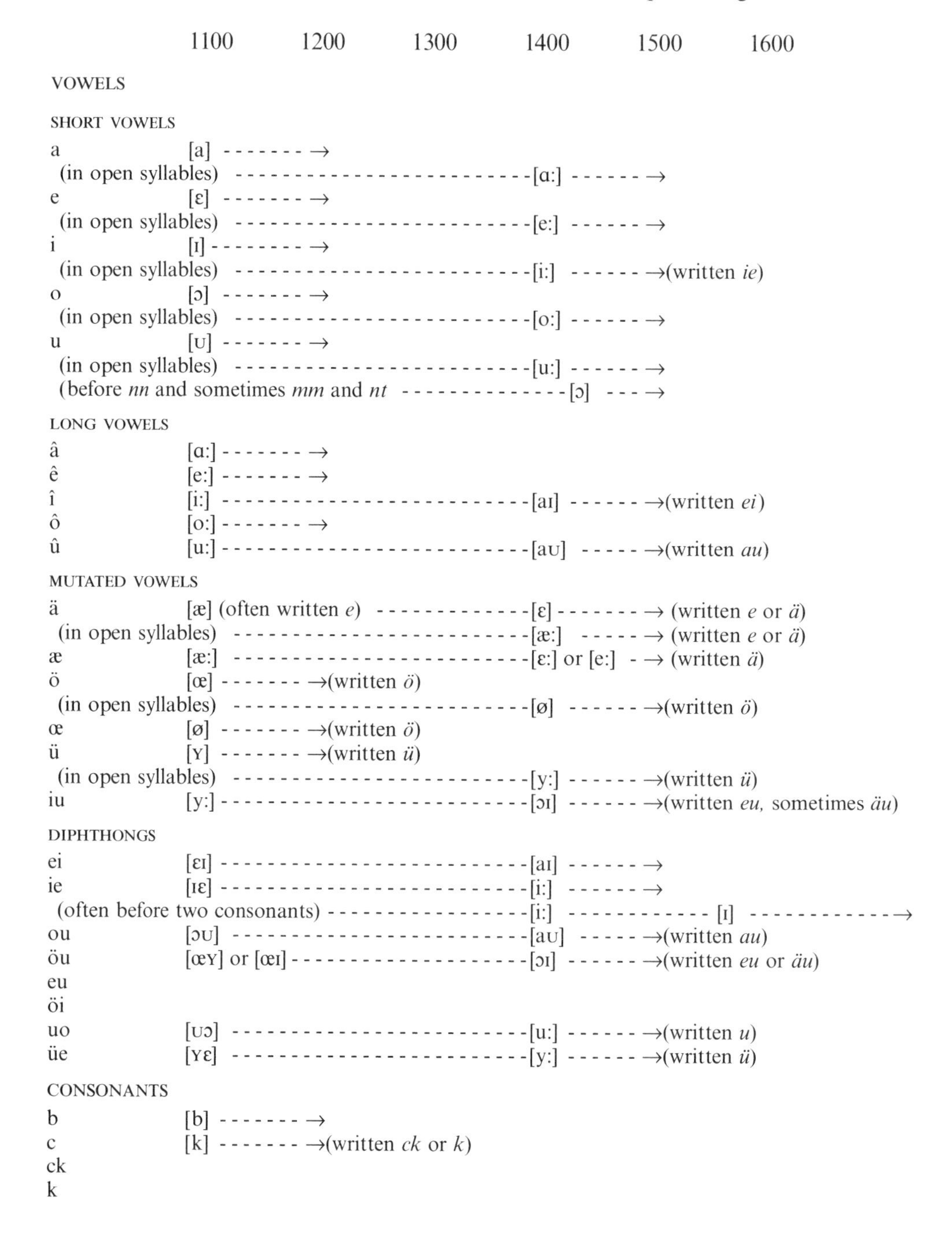

	1100	1400	1500	1600
VOWELS				
SHORT VOWELS				
a	[a] -------→			
(in open syllables)	------------------------	[ɑ:] ------→		
e	[ɛ] -------→			
(in open syllables)	------------------------	[e:] ------→		
i	[ɪ] --------→			
(in open syllables)	------------------------	[i:] ------→	(written *ie*)	
o	[ɔ] -------→			
(in open syllables)	------------------------	[o:] ------→		
u	[ʊ] -------→			
(in open syllables)	------------------------	[u:] ------→		
(before *nn* and sometimes *mm* and *nt*	-------------	[ɔ] ---→		
LONG VOWELS				
â	[ɑ:] -------→			
ê	[e:] -------→			
î	[i:] ------------------------	[aɪ] ------→	(written *ei*)	
ô	[o:] -------→			
û	[u:] ------------------------	[aʊ] -----→	(written *au*)	
MUTATED VOWELS				
ä	[æ] (often written *e*) ------------	[ɛ] -------→	(written *e* or *ä*)	
(in open syllables)	------------------------	[æ:] -----→	(written *e* or *ä*)	
æ	[æ:] ------------------------	[ɛ:] or [e:] --→	(written *ä*)	
ö	[œ] -------→(written *ö*)			
(in open syllables)	------------------------	[ø] ------→	(written *ö*)	
œ	[ø] -------→(written *ö*)			
ü	[ʏ] -------→(written *ü*)			
(in open syllables)	------------------------	[y:] ------→	(written *ü*)	
iu	[y:] ------------------------	[ɔɪ] ------→	(written *eu*, sometimes *äu*)	
DIPHTHONGS				
ei	[ɛɪ] ------------------------	[aɪ] ------→		
ie	[ɪɛ] ------------------------	[i:] ------→		
(often before two consonants)	-----------------	[i:] ------------	[ɪ] ------------→	
ou	[ɔʊ] ------------------------	[aʊ] -----→	(written *au*)	
öu eu öi	[œʏ] or [œɪ] -------------------	[ɔɪ] ------→	(written *eu* or *äu*)	
uo	[ʊɔ] ------------------------	[u:] ------→	(written *u*)	
üe	[ʏɛ] ------------------------	[y:] ------→	(written *ü*)	
CONSONANTS				
b	[b] -------→			
c ck k	[k] -------→(written *ck* or *k*)			

1100 1200 1300 1400 1500 1600

ch (after back vowels) [x] - - - - - - - - - - - →
(after front vowels) [x] -[ç] - - - - →
d [d] - - - - - - - →
f [f] - - - - - - - - →
g (initially and after vowels) [g] - - - - - - →
h (initially) [h] - - - - - - - - - →
(between vowels and
after *l* or *n*) [x] - | (disappears, but "silent *h*" remains)
(before t or s) - [x] - - - - - - - →(written *ch*)
j [j] - - - - - - - - →
l [l] - - - - - - - - →
m [m] - - - - - - - →
n [n] - - - - - - - →
ng [ŋg] - [ŋ] - - - - - - - →
p [p] - - - - - - - →
pf [pf] - - - - - - - →
ph [pf] - |
(in Greek words) [f] - - - - - - - - - - - - - - →
r [r̥] - [R] - - - - - - →
s [s] - - - - - - - - →
(initially before vowels and medially
between voiced sounds) - [z] - - - - - - - →
(initially before *p* and *t*) - [ʃ] - - - →
(initially before *l, m, n,* and *w*) - [ʃ] - - - → (written *sch*)
sch [ʃ] - - - - - - - →
t [t] - - - - - - - - →
v [f] (sometimes written *f*) - - - - - - - - →
(medially) [v] - - - - - - - - - - - - - - - - [f] - - - - - - → (written *f*)
w [w] - - - - - - - - - - - - - - - - [β] - - - - - - - - - - - - - - - - [v] - - - - - - →
z (initially or after consonants) [ts] - - - - - - - - - - - - - → (written *z*)
(after or between
vowels) [s] or [θ] - [s] - - - - - - - → (written *s* or *ss*)
zz [s] or [θ] - - - - - - - - - - - - - [s] - → (written *ss*)

SAMPLE TEXTS

The following texts reflect a range in both dialect and time period. The first two, from the southern German-speaking area and the mid-fifteenth century, contrast with the last two, both of more central German provenance and from the early and late sixteenth century.

Von meiden pin ich dick berawbt

The *Lochamer Liederbuch* (sometimes written *Locheimer Liederbuch*) was set down in Bavaria between 1452 and 1460. The four stanzas given here represent the song as it appears in the manuscript. The phonetic transcription assumes that *b, d,* and *g* were only minimally voiced, and then only in a favorable environment; accordingly, if the orthography indicates a voiceless sound, it is retained in the transcription; that the velar fricative [x] was retained in all positions in Bavarian; and that all other sound changes of ENHG (summarized above) had already occurred.

In the *Lochamer Liederbuch* in general and in this song in particular there is a frequent alternation of *ai* and *ei (ey),* which may at first be confusing. The use of both forms stems from the quality of the vowel in the earlier stage of the language (MHG). The old diphthong [ɛɪ], written *ei* in MHG, changed to [ai], almost always spelled *ai,* just as it sounds. The old long vowel sound of MHG, [i:], written *î,* underwent diphthongization in the late Middle Ages and became [eɪ], written *ei* or *ey.* Therefore sing these diphthongs as they are written. CD #55.

Text from MS: Berlin, Mus. ms. 40613 (Lochamer Songbook).

Von meyden pin ich dick werawbt.
des mueβ mein frewd engellden.
der mir zu sehen ist erlaubt.
den sich ich laider sellden.
Das waiβ got wol das mein wegir
jn rechter lieb sich senckt zu jm,*
und macht mir ein senlich leiden.

Als lang piβ mich ernert dy frist
senenn tut mir verdriessen
als meyden nit gehaissen ist
jch hoff mir süll gelingen.

---

* The lack of rhyme here is probably due to a scribal rewriting for a female voice, or at least a female persona yearning for a male. The earlier version probably contained feminine personal pronouns and, accordingly, lines 3–7 would have been written:

die mire zu sehen ist erlaubt,
die sich ich laider sellden,
das waiβ got wol das mein wegir
jn rechter lieb sich senckt zu jr,
vnd macht mir ein senlich leiden.

so lebt mein hercz nit liebere zeit.
denn das ich dur sehen würd erfrewt.
so wollt ich frölich singen.

O wunigliche zuuersicht.
nu lasß mir meyden nit schaden.
wann ich dich meid so hertiglich.
vnd ich pin ÿberladen
so schwir ich pey meiner lieb so groß
wenn ich dich meid so frewet mich doch
dÿ gunst von deinen gnaden.

Nw mag es ye nit anders gesein.
denn laid durch lieb ze haben.
durch meyden muß ich leiden pein.
dar vmb laß ich nit abe.
wann ich vor offt vernummen han.
das lieb on laid nit mag ergan
jn trewen will ichs tragen.

fɔn ˈmɛɪdən ˈpɪn ɪx ˈdɪx bəˈṛaʊpt
dɛs ˈmʊs mɛɪn ˈfṛɔɪd ɛnˈgɛldən
dɛṛ ˈmɪṛ tsu: ˈse:an ˈɪst ɛṛˈlaʊpt
de:n ˈsɪx ɪx ˈlaɪdəṛ ˈsɛldən
das ˈwaɪs gɔt ˈwo:l das ˈmɛɪn bəˈgi:ṛ
ɪn ˈṛɛxtər ˈli:b sɪx ˈsɛnkt tsu: ˈi:m
ʊnt ˈmaxt mɪṛ ɛɪn ˈse:nli:x ˈlɛɪdən

als ˈlaŋ pɪs ˈmɪx ɛṛˈnɛṛt di: ˈfṛɪst
ˈse:nən ˈtu:t mɪṛ fɛṛˈdṛi:sən
als ˈmɛɪdən ˈnɪt gəˈhaɪsən ˈɪst
ɪx hɔf mɪṛ sʏl gəlɪŋən
so: ˈlɛ:pt mɛɪn ˈhɛṛts nɪt ˈli:bəṛə ˈtsɛɪt
dɛn ˈdas ɪx ˈdʊṛ ˈse:ən ˈwʏṛd ɛrˈfṛɔɪt
so: ˈwɔlt ɪx ˈfṛøli:x ˈsɪŋən

o: ˈwʊnɪkli:xə ˈtsu:fɛṛˈsɪxt
nu: ˈlas mɪṛ ˈmɛɪdən nɪt ˈʃa:dən
wan ˈɪx dɪx ˈmɛɪt so: ˈhɛṛtɪkli:x
ʊnt ˈɪx pɪn ˈy:bəṛˈlɑ:dən
so: ˈʃwɪṛ ɪx pɛɪ ˈmɛɪnəṛ ˈli:p so: gṛo:s
wɛn ˈɪx dɪx ˈmɛɪt so: ˈfṛɔɪwət mɪx ˈdɔx
di: ˈgʊnst fɔn ˈdɛɪnən ˈgnɑ:dən

nu: ˈmak ɛs ˈɪɛ nɪt ˈandəṛs gəˈsɛɪn
dɛn ˈlaɪd dʊṛx ˈli:p tsə ˈhɑ:bən

durx ˈmɛɪdən ˈmʊs ɪx ˈlɛɪdən ˈpɛɪn
daˈrʊmb las ˈɪx nɪt ˈɑ:bə
wan ˈɪx fɔr ˈɔft fɛrˈnʊmən ˈhɑ:n
das ˈli:b ɑ:n ˈlaɪd nɪt ˈmak ɛrˈgɑ:n
ɪn ˈtrɔɪ wən ˈwɪl ɪxs ˈtrɑ:gən

MODERN SOURCES

Friedrich Wilhelm Arnold. *Das Locheimer Liederbuch nebst der Ars Organisandi von Conrad Paumann.* Leipzig: Breitkopf & Härtel, 1926; reprint Wiesbaden: Sändig, 1969. A nearly diplomatic edition of text and melody.

Oswald von Wolkenstein, "Ain mensch von achzehen jaren klüg"

Oswald von Wolkenstein, a South Tyrolean nobleman singing around 1400, is a special case. Since he was the most transmitted German singer of the Middle Ages (over 130 songs, most of them with melody) as well as a gifted maker of appealing tunes, his songs are frequently performed by singers of early music. Nonetheless, his South Tyrolean dialect lies at the periphery of the German-speaking areas and presents difficulties not normally encountered in more mainstream ENHG manuscripts. The reader should keep in mind the guidelines for ENHG, above, as well as the following observations about Oswald's pronunciation.

The two primary scribes who copied Oswald's songs tried to be as accurate as possible in their use of the Latin alphabet to represent his Tyrolean sounds. On the whole, the letters and groups of letters can be pronounced following the rules outlined for ENHG.

As in the *Lochamer Liederbuch* the frequent *ei/ai* alternation may at first cause some confusion, but these two digraphs stem from quite different sounds in an earlier stage of the language and, though changed, continued to be sounded differently. They should be pronounced as written: *ei* as [ɛɪ] and *ai* as [aɪ]. This difficulty is compounded by a relatively frequent conservative spelling (and perhaps pronunciation) in Oswald's songs, reflected in the alternation of [i:] with [ɛɪ] in such suffixes as *-lîch* and *-leich* and *-lîn* and *-lein.* Since these are frequently found as rhyme words, they must be pronounced as they are spelled: [-li:x] and [-lɛɪx], [-li:n] and [-lɛɪn], even if that produces inconsistencies.

The frequent initial *p* in place of *b,* which would occur in other upper and middle German dialects *(prechen* instead of *brechen),* is a reflex of lenis *p,* that is, a softer *p*-sound without aspiration, phonemically different from the fortis *p.* The normal *p*-articulation, however, should serve adequately.

The grapheme *w,* which we regard in MHG as a semi-vowel akin to the modern English sound represented by *w,* appears in Oswald to be about halfway toward the present-day German sound [v], probably (as it also might have been in MHG) a bilabial. In the manuscripts the scribes were not consistent, sometimes representing the sound with *w* and sometimes with *b.* It may have sounded like the Spanish articulation represented by [β], or, as indicated here, like the older MHG [w].

Oswald's rhymes show indications of the "dark *a,*" that is, both short and long *a*-sounds tending toward an *o*-sound (although it is difficult to say how "dark" these vowels were). Accordingly, the grapheme *a* should probably be pronounced [ɔ] in its short version and [ɔ:] in its long version. This will lend what the nineteenth-century philologists called "Trübung" (darkening) to the speech and approximate the tone of certain present-day Bavarian and Tyrolean dialects.

Words which in MHG would have ended with the graphemes *p, t,* and *k* frequently terminate, when written by Oswald's scribe, with *b, d,* and *g.* This spelling results from either an oblique case-ending or a plural formation in which the consonant becomes voiced. The *b-, d-,* and *g-* endings, however, as in modern German, should be unvoiced to *p, t,* and *k: lieb* [lɪɛp], *und* [ʊnt], *gesang* [gəsɔnk], and *aug* [ɔuk]. CD #56.

Text from MS. B: Universitätsbibliothek Innsbruck, Wolkenstein-Handschrift B (without call number).

Ain mensch von achzehen jaren klüg
daß hat mir all mein freud geswaig
dem kund ich nie entwynnen gnüg
seyd mir ein aug sein wandel zaigt
An underlass hab ich kain rü
mich zwingt ir mündlin spat und frü
das sich als lieplich auff und zu
mit worten süss kan lencken

Wie ferr ich bin mir nahet schir
ir rains gesicht durch alle land
ir zärtlich blick umbfahent mir
mein herz inrechter lieb bekannt
Ach got und wesst sy mein gedankh
wenn ich vor ir senlichen krank
hert stän und tar in kainem wanck
desgeleichen rencken

Weiplicher weib menizsch nye gesach
so liederlich an tadels punt
ir schön gepärd tüt mir ungemach
von höch der schaittel über ab den grund
wenn ich bedenck so gar die mass
kürz leng smal brait zwar tün und lass
wer möcht der lieben sein gehass
o wolt sy mich bedencken

Normalized Text

Ain mensch von achzehen jaren klug
das hat mir all mein freud geswaigt
dem kund ich nie entwinnen gnüg
seid mir ain oug sein wandel zaigt.

An underlass hab ich kain rü
mich zwingt ir mündlin spat und fru
das sich als lieplich auff und zu
mit worten süss kan lencken.

Wie ferr ich bin, mir nahet schir
ir rains gesicht durch alle land,
ir zärtlich blick umbfahent mir
mein herz in rechter lieb bekannt.
Ach got, und wesst si mein gedanc
wenn ich vor ir senlichen kranck
hert stän und tar in kainem wanck
desgeleichen rencken.

Weiplicher weib mensch nie gesach
so liederlich an tadels punt.
ir schön gepärd tüt mir ungemach,
von höch der schaittel über ab den grunt
wenn ich bedenck so gar die mass,
kürz, leng, smal, brait, zwar tün und lass
wer möcht der lieben sein gehass?
O, wolt si mich bedencken!

aɪn ˈmɛnʃ fɔn ˈɔxtsɛhən ˈjɔ:ṛən klu:x
dɔs ˈhɔ:t mɪṛ ˈɔl mɛɪn ˈfṛœt gəˈswaɪxt
dɛm ˈkʊnt ɪx ˈnɪɛ ɛntˈwɪnən ˈgnu:x
sɛɪt ˈmɪṛ aɪn ˈɔʊx sɛɪn ˈwandəl ˈtsaɪxt
ɔn ˈʊntəˈlɔs hɔ:p ˈɪx kaɪn ˈṛu:
mɪx ˈtswɪŋgt ɪṛ ˈmʏndli:n ˈspɔ:t ʊnt fṛu:
dɔs ˈsɪx ɔls ˈlɪɛpli:x ˈɔʊf ʊnt ˈtsu:
mɪt ˈwɔṛtən ˈsy:s kɔn ˈlɛnkən

wɪɛ ˈfɛṛ ɪx ˈbɪn mɪṛ ˈnɔ:xət ˈʃɪṛ
ɪṛ ˈṛaɪns gəˈsɪxt dʊṛx ˈɔlə ˈlɔnt
ɪṛ ˈtsæṛtli:x ˈblɪk ʊmbˈfɔ:xənt ˈmɪṛ
mɛɪn ˈhɛṛts ɪn ˈṛɛxtəṛ ˈlɪɛp bəˈkɔnt
ɔx ˈgɔ:t ʊnt ˈwest si: ˈmɛɪn gəˈdɔnk
wɛn ˈɪx fɔṛ ˈɪṛ sɛnˈli:xən ˈkrɔnk
hɛṛt ˈstæ:n ʊnt ˈtɔṛ ɪn ˈkaɪnən ˈwɔnk
ˈdɛs gəˈlɛɪxən ˈṛɛnkən

ˈwɛɪpli:xəṛ ˈwɛɪp mɛnʃ ˈnɪɛ gəˈsɔx
so: ˈlɪɛdəṛˈˈli:x ɔ:n tɔdəls punt
ɪṛ ˈʃœ:n gəˈpæṛt ty:t mɪṛ ˈʊngəˈˈmɔx
vɔn ˈhœ:x dɛṛ ˈʃaɪtəl y:bəṛ ˈɔp dɛn ˈgṛʊnt

wɛn ˈɪx bəˈdɛnk so: ˈgɔṛ dɪə ˈmɔs
kʏṛts ˈlank smɔl ˈbṛaɪt tswɔṛ ˈty:n ʊnt ˈlɔs
wɛṛ ˈmœxt dɛṛ ˈlɪɛbən ˈsɛɪn gəˈhɔs
o: ˈwɔlt si: ˈmɪx bəˈdɛnkən

MODERN SOURCES

Karl Kurt Klein, ed. *Die Lieder Oswalds von Wolkenstein.* 3d ed. Tübingen: Niemeyer, 1987 (Altdeutsche Textbibliothek No. 55). The standard critical edition of text and melody.

Friedrich Maurer. *Beiträge zur Sprache Oswalds von Wolkenstein.* Giessen: Münchow, 1922. A phonetic analysis of Oswald's dialect.

Hans Moser and Ulrich Müller, eds. *Abbildungen zur Überlieferung der Lieder Oswalds von Wolkenstein I: Die Innsbrucker Wolkenstein-Hs. B.* Göppingen: Kümmerle, 1972 (Litterae 12). Photocopies of text and melody.

Hans Sachs, "Golden Melody" (Goldener Ton)

Hans Sachs lived and practiced his craft of shoemaking and his art of music and verse in Nuremberg during the first half of the sixteenth century. His dialect reflects both his lower Bavarian origins and the more Middle German (here: East Franconian) form of the language preferred by the printers who published his works. Several orthographic idiosyncrasies should be noted: The grapheme *ü* seems to represent both the long and the short *u*-umlaut: [y:], the long *u*-sound: [u:], as well as the consonant [v]; initial *d* frequently stood for [t]; *ÿ* represented [ɪ]; and the length of the vowel is generally not indicated by the spelling.

For the phonetic transcription certain assumptions have been made: initial *s* remains unvoiced, as in all southern speech up to the present; the diphthong written *ei* probably represented the sound [aɪ], a characteristic of Bavarian at this time; when the grapheme *w* represented a vowel, it may have assumed its later pronunciation of [v], but it also can stand for [u:], as in the word *zw* [tsu:]. In the choice between long and short vowels, the transcription represents the sound in the modern language. Accordingly, all single vowel sounds in open, accented syllables are shown as long, in contrast to MHG.

The orthography of this song contains exceptional inconsistencies. The song was found in a manuscript probably set down by Sachs himself in the years before his songs and other writings appeared in printed form (MS. 414, about 1515). Consequently, the orthography is more erratic than in the later printed versions of his works. Only the first of the original five stanzas is treated here. CD #57.

Text from MS: Berlin, 414

Da zweÿ vnd fünfczig hündert iar
zwar gar
vergangen was
in gottes has
manch proffet sas
diff in varhelle qüal

Der edel weis künig Daüit
mit pitt
erlicher stim
rüffet in grim
her vns vernim
sendt vns dein sün zw dal
Er hor uns küng sabaotht
sent vns das himelische prot
so wirt geent al vnser not
drot hot got
den sun becleit
mit der menscheit
beÿ einer meit
in irem keuschen sal

da ˈtsvaɪ ʊnt ˈfʏnftsɪx ˈhʊndɛṛt ˈjɑ:ṛ
ˈtsvɑ:ṛ ˈgɑ:ṛ
fɛṛˈgangən ˈvas
ɪn ˈgɔtəs ˈhas
manx pṛɔˈfe:t ˈsas
ˈti:f ɪn ˈfaṛhɛlə ˈkvɑ:l
dɛṛ ˈe:dəl vaɪs ˈky:nɪx ˈdɑ:vɪt
ˈmɪt ˈpɪt
ˈe:ṛli:xəṛ ˈstɪm
ˈṛu:fət ɪn ˈgṛɪm
ˈhɛṛ ʊns fɛṛˈnɪm
ˈsɛnt ʊns daɪn ˈsʊn tsu: ˈtɑ:l
ɛṛ ˈho:ṛ ʊns kʏng ˈsɑ:bɑˈˈo:t
ˈsɛnt ʊns das ˈhɪməlɪʃə ˈpṛo:t
so: ˈvɪṛt gəˈɛnt al ˈʊnsəṛ ˈno:t
ˈdṛo:t ˈho:t ˈgɔt
de:n ˈsʊn bəˈklaɪt
ˈmɪt dɛṛ ˈmɛnʃaɪt
paɪ ˈaɪnəṛ ˈmaɪt
ɪn ˈɪṛəm ˈkɔɪʃən ˈsɑ:l

MODERN SOURCES

Francis H. Ellis. *The Early Meisterlieder of Hans Sachs.* Bloomington: Indiana University Press, 1974. A diplomatic version of the text.
Philipp Wackernagel. *Das deutsche Kirchenlied.* Vol. II. Leipzig: Teubner, 1867.

Buchsbaum und Felbinger

The *Ambraser Songbuch,* printed in Frankfurt am Main in 1582, is a collection of diverse texts without melody. This song occurs in a somewhat different form, with melody, in

Heinrich Fink's Songbook *(Schoene, außgelesene Lieder des hochberuempten Heinrici Finkens . . .)*, published about fifty years earlier in Nuremberg. Other versions appear throughout the seventeenth century in both High and Low German. The language used here is very close to the modern form, and if the orthography is any indication, the pronunciation is probably close to the German spoken today. Note that the voiceless velar fricative [x] has become palatalized [ç] after front vowels. CD #58.

Printed Text: *Lieder-Büchlein. Darin begriffen sind zweihundert und sechtzig allerhand schöner weltlicher Lieder, allen jungen Gesellen und züchtigen Jungfrowen zum newen Jahr, in Druck verfertiget. Auffs newe gemehret mit viel schönen Leidern.* Nic. Basse, Frankfurt, 1582 (Ambraser Songbook).

Nun wölt ir hören newe mär
vom Buchsbaum und vom Felbinger.
Sie zogen mit einander über feld
und kriegten mit einander.

Der Buchsbaum sprach: ich bin so kün,
ich bin sommer und winter grün;
Das tust du, leidiger Felbinger, nicht,
du verleurst dein besten zweige.
Felbinger, wie gefellt dir das?

Der Felbinger sprach: ich bin so fein,
aus mir macht man die langen zeun
Wol umb das korn und umb den wein,
davon wir uns erneren.
Buchsbaum, wie gefeltt dir das?

Der buchsbaum sprach: ich bin so fein,
aus mir macht man die krenzelein,
Mich tregt auf manche schöne jungfraw
mit freuden zu dem tanze.
Felbinger, wie gefellt dir das?

nu:n ˈwœlt i:ṛ ˈhøṛən ˈnɔɪə ˈmɛ:ṛ
fɔm ˈbʊxsbaʊm ˈʊnt fɔm ˈfɛlbɪŋˈˈgəṛ*
si: ˈtso:gən ˈmɪt aɪn ˈandəṛ ˈy:bəṛ ˈfɛlt
unt ˈkṛi:gtən ˈmɪt aɪnˈandəṛ

dɛṛ ˈbʊxsbaʊm ˈspṛɑ:x ɪç ˈbɪn so: ˈky:n
ˈɪç bɪn ˈsɔməṛ ʊnt ˈvɪntəṛ ˈgṛy:n
das ˈtu:st du: ˈlaɪdɪgəṛ ˈfɛlbɪŋgəṛ ˈnɪçt

* This would have been the normal pronunciation of *felbinger*. However, for the sake of the rhyme and the humor of the song it was probably pronounced [ˈfɛlbɪŋˈˈgɛ:ṛ] in this context.

du: fɛr̩ˈlɔɪr̩st daɪn ˈbɛstən ˈtsvaɪgə
ˈfɛlbɪŋgər̩ ˈvi: gəˈfɛlt di:r̩ das

dɛr̩ ˈfɛlbɪŋgər̩ ˈspr̩ɑ:x ɪç ˈbɪn so: ˈfaɪn
aʊs ˈmi:r̩ mɑ:xt ˈman di: ˈlaŋgən ˈtsɔɪn
ˈvo:l ʊmb das ˈkɔr̩n ʊnt ˈʊmb dɛ:n ˈvaɪn
daˈfɔn vi:r̩ ˈʊns ɛr̩ˈne:r̩ən
ˈbʊxsbaʊm ˈvi: gəˈfɛlt di:r̩ ˈdas

dɛr̩ ˈbʊxsbaʊm ˈspr̩ɑ:x ɪç ˈbɪn so: ˈfaɪn
aʊs ˈmi:r̩ ma:xt ˈman di: ˈkr̩ɛntsələɪn
mɪx ˈtr̩e:gt aʊf ˈmançə ˈʃønə jʊŋgˈfr̩aʊ
mɪt ˈfr̩ɔɪdən ˈzu: de:m ˈtantsə
ˈfɛlbɪŋgər̩ ˈvi: gəˈfɛlt di:r̩ ˈdas

MODERN SOURCES

Joseph Bergmann, ed. *Das Ambraser Liederbuch vom Jahre 1582.* Stuttgart: Das literarische Verein, Stuttgart, 1845 (Bibliothek des Literarischen Vereins in Stuttgart, Vol. 12). Nearly diplomatic edition of the text of the Ambraser Liederbuch.

Franz M. Böhme, ed. *Altdeutsches Liederbuch: Volkslieder der Deutschen nach Wort und Weise aus dem 12. bis zum 17 Jahrhundert.* Leipzig: Breitkopf & Härtel, 1877; reprint, Hildesheim: Olms, 1966. Nearly diplomatic edition of the melody of the Heinrich Fink Songbook.

Ludwig Senfl, "Alleyn dein huld"

Though he was born in Switzerland, Ludwig Senfl (1486–ca. 1543) spent most of his active life at courts in Bavaria and Vienna. It is probable that his songs were first sung in the dialect of southern Bavaria (Munich and Augsburg). The language of this song, included in a printed songbook published in Strassburg in 1536 by Petter Schöffer and Mathias Apiarius, seems to reflect more of an Alsatian (southwestern) German than Senfl's adopted Bavarian dialect. In the phonetic rendition of the text the orthography is taken as much as possible at face value. Accordingly, *ei* and *ey* are rendered [ɛɪ], as they are still pronounced today in upper Rhineland dialects. As in later German, *ch* and terminal *g* after *e* and *i* are palatalized to [ç]. Vowels in open syllables are assumed to be long. Hence *geben* would be pronounced more or less as it sounds today: [ge:bən]. CD #59.

Printed Text: Peter Schöffer and Mathias Apiarius, *Fünff und sechzig teutscher Lieder.* Strassburg, 1536.

Allyn dein huld
gebirt die schuld
mich gentzlich dir zergeben
Was moͤglich mir
vnd gfellig dir
demselben will ich leben

Nach deinem gmůͤt
iedoch verhůͤt
kleyn gnies vnd groß argwonen
Laß mich dein sein
lieblich du mein
thů rechter trew verschonen.

Sei gscheid vnd klug
nit saum vnd lůg
die zeit nit leicht verlieren
Biß frölich frei
beger dabei
laß dich keyhns wegs verfieren

aˈlɛɪn dɛɪn ˈhʊlt
gəˈbɪr̩t di: ˈʃʊlt
mɪç ˈgɛntsli:ç ˈdɪr̩ tsɛr̩ˈge:bən
was ˈmœgli:ç ˈmɪr̩
ʊnt ˈgfɛlɪç ˈdɪr̩
dɛmˈsɛlbən ˈvɪl ɪç ˈle:bən

nɑ:x ˈdɛɪnəm ˈgmy:t
je:ˈdɔx fɛr̩ˈhy:t
klɛɪn ˈgni:s ʊnt ˈgr̩o:s ar̩gˈvo:nən
las ˈmɪç dɛɪn ˈsɛɪn
ˈli:pli:ç du: ˈmɛɪn
tʊɔ r̩ɛçtər̩ tr̩ɔɪ fɛr̩ʃo:nən

sɛɪ ˈgʃɛɪt ʊnt ˈklʊɔx
nɪt ˈsaʊm ʊnt ˈlʊɔx
di: ˈtsɛɪt nɪt ˈlɛɪçt fɛr̩ˈli:rən
bɪs ˈfr̩øli:ç ˈfr̩ɛɪ
bəˈge:r̩ daˈbɛɪ
las ˈdɪç kɛɪns ˈwe:gs fɛr̩ˈfi:r̩ən

SOURCES

Peter Schöffer and Mathias Apiarius. *Fünff und sechzig teutscher Lieder.* Strassburg, 1536 (No. 51). The original publication. The song appears in differing forms in two manuscripts: Wolfenbüttel, Herzog-August Bibliothek, Ms. 292 (fol. 27v.); and Zürich, Zentralbibliothek, Ms. Z.XI.301 (No. 57).

Ludwig Senfl. *Deutsche Lieder: erster Teil: Lieder aus handscriftlichen Quellen bis etwa 1535.* ed. Arnold Geering and Wilhelm Altweg. Wolfenbüttel and Berlin: G. Kallmeyer Verlag, 1938 (Reichsdenkmale Deutscher Musik. Abteilung mehrstimmiges Lied, Vol. I).

17—

German Latin

HAROLD COPEMAN AND
VERA U. G. SCHERR

The Roman Empire reached only into the extreme west and south of Germany, that is, the Germanic area which developed through a myriad of political changes into Germany and Austria. Germans who were within the Empire might have learned Latin, the language used for military and civil administration, but most of Germany met Latin only in the seventh and eighth centuries, after the barbarian invasions, when missionaries from the British Isles and northern France penetrated much of the country (see *The Times Concise Atlas of World History,* maps 30/3 and 38/3).

In the late eighth century, Charlemagne, king of the Franks (and from 800 Holy Roman Emperor) sent for Alcuin of York to teach Latin and to build up an educated priesthood in his intended Christian state. Latin was in particular need of reform in the western regions, and Alcuin set up a number of schools. The use of Latin throughout the Holy Roman Empire was expanded in the interests of administration and learning; it was also used in the reformed liturgy, which was as far as possible based on that of Rome.

In this early medieval period, Latin in German areas followed more closely than in other countries the pronunciation of Rome in the early centuries A.D. This was a result of the teaching of the missionaries, whose Irish, British, and Anglo-Saxon Latin exhibited fewer changes than the Latin in France, Spain, Italy, and other countries where a Romance vernacular was gradually emerging from the local Vulgar Latin. In later centuries speech habits in German areas remained relatively stable, though Latin pronunciation no doubt varied with regional and local accents.

Vowels changed less than in England and France, and the palatalization of *c* and *g* ([k] and [g]) before front vowels did not go as far as elsewhere: standard German Latin still uses [g], not [dʒ], before *e* and *i,* and [k] before these vowels only moved as far as [ts], not to [s] or [tʃ]. Over the centuries there do not appear to have been periods of major reform in German Latin pronunciation as there were in England and France. However, following Luther's lead there was in the sixteenth to eighteenth centuries a gradual standardization of educated German over much of the area, to that of the Saxon Chancery; and in 1898 there was a move to the present standard speech as defined in T. Siebs's volume, now entitled *Deutsche Hochsprache* (or *Deutsche Aussprache*). Educated Latin pronunciation followed changes in the standard German speech.

With Luther's Reformation the German states and cities began to divide, for reasons of state, into Protestant and Catholic. This had no direct effect on the pronunciation of Latin (which long continued to be used, together with German, in the Lutheran Church), but there were probably local variations in the sixteenth and seventeenth centuries, as Netherlandish and then Italian singers were engaged for court chapels; indeed, a fashion for the Italian musical style developed in Vienna, Dresden, and other centers and may have affected singing pronunciation at the end of our period.

The Low German of the north, shading off into Dutch, had (as at present) characteristic consonants: *s* was voiced to [z] when it started a syllable. In the northwest *sp-, st-* started with [s] instead of the generally used [ʃ]. The sounds of the stops *b/p, d/t* were close to those in English (but final *-d* was devoiced to [-t] in the whole country); in the south and Saxony these stops were lighter, and the voicing of *b* and *d* was (and is) slight or absent, making the voiced and unvoiced pairs difficult to distinguish. (In the south they are distinguished by aspiration/non-aspiration.) In Saxony the initial and intervocalic *g* were sounded as fricatives, one of which survives in modern German as final *g*. ("Saxony" here refers to the late medieval and modern area.)

Evidence is fairly scarce; the most significant material comes from writers and musicians of the sixteenth and seventeenth centuries. The humanist writers Erasmus (1528) and Lipsius (1586) give a variety of indications; they supplemented descriptions of the way Latin ought to sound (for Classical purposes and for international communication) by remarks on the shortcomings of speakers from the different nations. For instance, Erasmus tells us that the Germans, and excessively the Westphalians, sounded *u* with a roundish lowing *(mugitu);* and the French printer Tory (1529) comments on unexpected fricative sounds in German Latin: *g* before *a, o,* or *u* is given "the sound of I consonant"; *Ego gaudeo Gabrielem* was sounded *Eio iaudeo Iabrielem* ("words far removed from true Latinity").

The young musician Ornithoparcus, from central Germany, whose vernacular name was probably Vogelsang, traveled through Europe listening critically to church musicians before writing his *Micrologus,* 1517 (which seems to have drawn on remarks by Conrad von Zabern, 1474). Nearly a century later John Dowland thought highly enough of this book to publish an English translation. It contains interesting general assessments of the singing in several countries, e.g.:

> The Germanes (which I am ashamed to vtter) doe howle like Wolves. . . . Germany nourisheth many Cantors but few Musitians. For very few, excepting those which are or haue been in the Chappels of Princes, doe truly know the Art of Singing. For those

> Magistrates to whom this charge is giuen, doe appoint . . . Cantors, whom they choose by the shrilnesse of their Voyce . . . thinking that God is pleased with bellowing and braying.

At the end of our period Christoph Bernhard, who trained choirboys for Schütz at Dresden, wrote that Germans must strive to make a clear distinction between *b* and *p*, *d* and *t*, *f* and *v*, and to render *st* as in *besten*, not, in their usual manner, as in *steten*. He also indicated the respect with which Italian Latin was held (at that time and in those circles).

Bibliography

C. Bernhard. *Von der Singe-Kunst oder Manier*, c. 1649; tr. W. Hilse, as *The Music Forum*, III. New York and London, 1973.

J. Bithell. *German Pronunciation and Phonology*. London, 1952.

W. Braune. *Ueber die Einigung der deutschen Aussprache*. Halle, 1905.

Conrad von Zabern. *De modo bene cantandi choralem cantum*. Dresden, 1474; tr. Würzburg, 1509. *Die Musiktraktate Conrads von Zabern*, ed. K.W. Gümpel. Freiburg im Breisgau, 1956.

H. Copeman. *Singing in Latin*. Oxford, 1990. See pp. 56–59, 67–68, 70–73, 81–85, 90, 106–107, 166–70, 214–16, 221; abstracts passages of interest from early writers.

D. Erasmus. *De recta Latini Græcique pronuntatione dialogus*, 1528; tr. M. Pope, as *Collected Works of Erasmus*, 26, Toronto, 1985. Pp. 347–475, 580–625.

A. Ornithoparcus. *Micrologus*, 1517; tr. J. Dowland 1609: facsimile in G. Reese and S. Ledbetter, *Compendium of Musical Practice*. New York, 1973.

C.V.J. Russ. *Historical German Phonology and Morphology*. Oxford, 1978.

———. *Studies in Historical German Phonology*. Berne and Frankfurt, 1982.

V.U.G. Scherr. *Aufführungspraxis Vokalmusik: Handbuch der Lateinischen Aussprache*. Kassel: Bärenreiter, 1991.

Sounds and Spellings

German Latin is fairly simple; if one has some knowledge of German pronunciation the Latin can generally be read accordingly. Syllabification is important: where there is a choice, German syllables start with a consonant or a pronounceable group such as *br, cl, dr, gl, tr;* e.g., *sem·per, be·ne·dic·tus, re·ple·ta, re·qui·em, se·cre·to.* But *s* is separated from a following *c, cr, pl, t, tr,* e.g., *Chris·te* (Erasmus gives this as the Dutch Latin usage, in contrast to the French *Chri·ste*). (For a fuller treatment of word division, see *Singing in Latin*, p. 215.) German regional Latin may have differed, e.g., *Chri·ste, tri·stis* = [kr̥ɪʃte, tr̥ɪʃtɪs]; note also the phonetic rather than etymological placing of stress: [kɔntr̥ɪˈʃta:tɛm], [pɛrtr̥anˈsi:fɪt].

Word division is particularly important in German Latin when a syllable is stressed. In present usage, an *open stressed syllable* is spoken or sung with a long closed, or "tense," vowel: that is, the tongue is closer to the roof of the mouth than for an "open" vowel (in English, the vowel in *bead* rather than that in *bid*). The relevant closed, tense vowels in German are the [e:], [i:], [o:], and [u:] of the Phonetic Chart ([a], [a:] being more or less identical open sounds).

At the time of the Renaissance, these vowels would have been used in stressed open syllables in Latin in several parts of Germany. Earlier, up to the fourteenth century at least, in the center and south, such syllables had short open vowels as in *sibi, spiritum.* (This may still be found today; present dialects can serve as a guide to the probable vernacular Latin pronunciation in much earlier times.)

The corresponding open vowels, [ɛ], [ɪ], [ɔ], [ʊ], are those in *let, bid, Gott* (slightly less open than British English *pot*), and *wood.* A *stressed closed syllable (benedictus)* has a short, open vowel, as in English usage but unlike the tendency of Romance languages to use a closed vowel.

Unstressed vowels are generally open and short, for instance, in endings such as *Domi·nus, pa·cem, ca·nunt.* An unaccented vowel in an open syllable may be closed, e.g., in endings *-e, -i, -o, -u;* this also applies before a stressed syllable *(se·quuntur),* and especially in compound words like *re·cordare* (but *des·cendit* is phonetically so divided). A vowel ending a Latin word would be closed and often lengthened. But *-e* is [e] or, after the sixteenth- and seventeenth-century reforms, [ɛ]. (See below for *-el.*)

Before *r* an unaccented vowel is open *(i·te·rum),* except in *-ur,* which is [u:r̩].

Because the first syllable of *'be·nedic* is stressed, the vowel is closed and long. This influences other forms of the word: the first syllable of *be·ne'dictus* has a fairly closed vowel, [be-]; similarly for other unstressed vowels in these circumstances, e.g., [o] in *po'tentiam* because of [o:] in *'potens,* and the [i] in *vi'dere, vi'demus* because of [i:] in *'video.*

Stress and Accent

In German music, the stress falls on the syllable one would expect from singing Italianate Latin; in measured music this is usually confirmed by the lengths of the notes. The normal stress will fall on a penultimate syllable if, classically, it counted as "long" (or, in less confusing terminology, "heavy"): that is, if it had a long vowel *(salu'tari)* or was closed by a consonant *(po'tentes).* But otherwise (in words of more than two syllables) the main stress falls on the antepenultimate *('Dominus, 'secula).*

In a long word there is likely to be secondary stress; in German Latin this is particularly likely on the initial syllable *''miseri'cordia*). But the composer's word-setting is often the best guide.

Consonants

In the center and south of Germany the plosives [b], [d], [g] were light (lenis) sounds, not voiced. In the south [p], [t], [k] were aspirated, whereas in Saxony there was practically no difference between the lenis consonants *b, d, g* and *p, t, k,* which were unvoiced and unaspirated.

b [b], but [p] when final.

c [k] before *a, o, u,* or *r, l, t, c;* [ts] before *e, ae, oe, i, y.* These sounds are in line with the vernacular pronunciation in words where German uses *c (Cassel, Celle).*

cc [kts] before *e, i.*

ch Usually pronounced as German *ch* ([x] after *a, o, u;* e.g., *brachio, Rachel, eucharistia*). Pronounced [ç] after *e, i,* or consonants; e.g., *Melchisidech, Michael, sepulchrum* ([l] and [r̩] are made by the tip of the tongue, so there is no velar [x]), *pulcher.* As initial, mostly [k], e.g., *Christus.* Sixteenth-century humanism taught [kh], but it was not adopted; Erasmus jokingly distinguished *Christe* and *criste* (cock's comb).

d [d], but [t] when final.

f [f]

g [g] in all positions in standard modern German Latin. Earlier, Erasmus complained of "caudeo" for *gaudeo* (probably an unvoiced south German *g*). In Saxony and parts of the north it was often sounded as one or another of the fricatives akin to German *j/ch*.

gn (between vowels) [ŋn].

h [h], but perhaps [ç] in *mi(c)hi, ni(c)hil,* when spelled with *ch.*

i/j Normally [j], but could be [g] in the north (mainly before *e, i*), and a *ch* fricative in Saxony (e.g., *Jesus* as *Cheses*); this could be [ç], or like the strong initial [h] in *Hugh.* In *eia* it is treated not consonantally but as [ɛi·a].

l [l], produced forward.

m, n [m], [n].

ng, nc/nq [ŋg], [ŋk]; and see *qu.*

p [p]

qu *u* after *q, (n)g, s* ("*v* consonant") was pronounced [f] or, more generally, as "German *w*," which would differ from region to region in the range of [v], [w], [β]. In the transcriptions it seemed appropriate to use [kw] for Bavaria, [kv] for Saxony, and [kf] for the medieval Rhineland; so in this last style *quia* [kfia], *lingua* [lɪŋgfa], and *suavis* [ʃfa:fɪs]. This would make disyllables, with [kv], [sv], out of *pascuae, suavis.*

r Generally rolled [r̩].

s As a final, pronounced [s]. As initial in a syllable, pronounced [s] in the center and south but [z] in the north. The digraph *sc* is pronounced [sts] internally before *e, i;* e.g., *suscipe;* initially it is perhaps shortened to [ts]; e.g., *scimus.* Initial *sc, sp,* and *st,* before *a, o, u,* are pronounced [ʃk], [ʃp], and [ʃt] respectively (except in the northwest). Within a word they are pronounced similarly in the south and perhaps in the west (except in the Rhineland); e.g., *hostes, hospes.* In Saxony either [s] or [ʃ] might be used; Bernhard, c. 1649, under Italian influence, deplored these pronunciations, so [sk], [sp], [st] may have been used by Schütz's choirs.

sch [ʃ] *(paschale).*

t [t]; *ti* + vowel generally pronounced [tsi-].

u/v consonant [f]: and see *qu.*

x [ks]; *xc* is pronounced [ksts] before *e, i.*

z Generally [ts], but [s] in the southwest; [sd], [ds] were also known. (The humanist's choice as a Classical sound was [ds].)

Double consonants are pronounced single in modern German Latin, in contrast to Italian Latin; but they have a function, as an indicator that the preceding vowel is pronounced "short" (i.e., open). The sound may have been double up to say 1500.

With glottal stops, the present practice is that the final consonant or vowel must not liaise (as it may have to in a Romance language) with an initial vowel in the next word (or part of a compound word). So in the sample text below, the words *Et illa apparuerunt omnia* are separated by a glottal stop. In our period, judging by regional dialects, this style would not have been followed in Saxony and south Germany.

Vowels

On the length and quality of vowels for works from around the fifteenth century see notes on stressed and unstressed syllables above.

a [a] in a closed syllable or an open unstressed syllable; pronounced [a:] in an open stressed syllable and as an end vowel. The sound varied greatly by region. In the center and south the vowel tended to be produced at the back of the mouth but to be rounded (an open [ɔ], as in British English "coffeepot"). In the north the sound was forward, [æ]. In Westphalia (northwest Germany) Erasmus says that the mouth is rounded and very open, at the other extreme from the Scots: this was probably for the long vowel, since Ornithoparcus gives the short Westphalian *a* as *ae (aebste* for *abste).*

ae See *e.* Pronounced [ɛ], [ɛ:] in music under humanist influence.

au The diphthong [au], but with different regional developments. Educated Saxon usage may have been nearer [ou], and further south the rising diphthongs [əo], [əʊ] were used. However, especially in words of Greek origin, *au/av* and *eu/ev* were quite generally pronounced [af], [ɛf]; e.g., *autor, evangelium.* This was abandoned fairly soon except in words borrowed from Greek where the *u/v* falls between vowels; e.g., *evangelium.*

e [ɛ] in syllables closed by a strong consonant or group. But in some unstressed endings *(Emanuel, Israel)* [e:l] was used in the south. Pronounced [e:] in stressed open syllables, tending in the north to [i:], but [ɛ:] in Saxony and Austria/Bavaria. Over a wide area in the center and south long *e* became a variety of diphthongs such as *ei* (probably [ɛj]), quoted by Ornithoparcus for Lower Saxony and Swabia, and some of these affected Latin; he gives the example of *Deius* for *Deus.* Pronounced [e] when unstressed in open syllable, but lax and tending to a more open sound. Possibly also [ə] as an ending.

ei diphthong [ɛi] or as the modern standard German diphthong [ai]; e.g., *eleison, eia, dein, deinde;* [əi] is a regional variant.

eu diphthong German diphthong as in *boy* [ɔe]/[ɔi].

i In stressed syllables, [ɪ] if syllable is closed and [i:] if it is open. But long *i* was widely diphthongized in the center and south; Ornithoparcus gives *Mareia* for *Maria* in part of the Rhineland ([ei] or [ej]). Unstressed, it is usually [ɪ] but [i:] in an open ending.

o Sometimes confused, even in educated writing, with *a,* and *oremus* was sung as *aremus* in country churches (a very open unstressed *o* being close to [a]). In a closed syllable short *o* was [ɔ]. But Erasmus reported that among the Franks of western Germany *noster* became *nuster* (the stressed [ɔ] having closed to [ᴜ]). In an open stressed syllable (and in the monosyllable *cor*) the vowel was [o:], particularly in the north. In an open unstressed syllable it was usually [o]; in an open ending [o:].

œ See *e*. When *œ* is printed, German singers today mostly sing a German *ö*, [ø], [œ]. An important instance is *cœli*, but the medieval spelling, until the humanist printing of the sixteenth century, was *celi*, pronounced with [e:] or [ɛ:]. For sixteenth- and seventeenth-century music, at least in Saxony and the south, [ɛ:] is preferable; similarly for *pœnas;* [ø:] is unlikely in most parts in our period; it may only date from the late eighteenth century.

u In closed syllable, [ᴜ]; in open stressed syllable, [u:], but this seems to have resembled the French [y] in the north (reported by Erasmus in Holland). Ornithoparcus/Dowland wrote "The changing of vowels is a signe of an vnlearned singer. . . . They of lower *Germany* doe all expresse *u* & *e*, in steade of the Vowel *u*. [This could mean [y] or [uə].] Which errours, though the *Germane* speech doe often require, yet doth the Latine tongue, which hath the affinitie with ours, exceedingly abhorre them." In open unstressed syllable, usually [ᴜ], but [u:] in open endings *(mugitu)* and [u:r] in *-ur*.

y See *i*. In the north and west, sixteenth- and seventeenth-century reforms probably suggested [y:], [ʏ] (which were not generally used until the nineteenth century).

SAMPLE TEXTS

Hildegarde of Bingen, "O viridissima virga"

Twelfth-century monastic. This part of the Rhineland was not part of the Low German area. Some Hesse dialect is present. This song was recorded by Gothic Voices in 1981 (Hyperion A 66039) using the following edition of the text (by Christopher Page), which is reproduced by kind permission of Hyperion Records Ltd. CD #60.

O viridissima virga ave,
que in ventoso flabro scisciationis
sanctorum prodisti.
Cum venit tempus
quod tu floruisti in ramis tuis;
ave, ave sit tibi
quia calor solis in te sudavit
sicut odor balsami.
Nam in te floruit pulcher flos
qui odorem dedit omnibus aromatibus
que arida erant.
Et illa apparuerunt omnia
in viriditate plena.
Unde celi dederunt rorem super gramen
et omnis terra leta facta sunt
quoniam viscera ipsius
frumentum protulerunt,
et quoniam volucres celi
nidos in ipsa habuerunt.
Deinde facta est esca hominibus,
et gaudium magnum epulantium;
unde, o suavis virgo,
in te non deficit ullum gaudium.
Hec omnia Eva contempsit.
Nunc autem laus sit altissimo.

o: fɪṛˈdɪsɪma fɪṛga: a:fe
kfe: ɪn fɛnˈto:so: ˈfla:bṛo: stsɪstsi·atsi·ˈo:nɪs
saŋkˈto:ṛʊm pṛoˈdɪsti:
kʊm ˈfe:nɪt ˈtɛmpʊs
kfɔt tu: flɔṛu·ˈɪsti: ɪn ˈṛa:mɪs ˈtu:·ɪs (or [floṛu·ˈɪsti:])
ˈa:fe ˈa:fe sɪt ˈti:bi:
ˈkfi·a: ˈka:lɔṛ ˈso:lɪs ɪn te: sʊˈda:fɪt
ˈsi:kʊt ˈo:dɔṛ ˈbalsami:
nam ɪn te: ˈflo:ṛu:·ɪt ˈpʊlçɛṛ flo:s (or [flɔs])

kfi: oˈdo:ṛɛm ˈde:dɪt ˈɔmnɪbʊs aṛoˈma:tɪbʊs
kfe: ˈa:ṛɪda: ˈe:ṛant
ɛt ˈɪla: apaṛu·ˈe:ṛʊnt ˈɔmni·a:
ɪn fɪṛɪdiˈta:te ˈple:na:
ˈʊnde ˈtse:li: deˈde:ṛʊnt ˈṛo:ṛɛm ˈsu:pɛṛ ˈgṛa:mɛn
ɛt ˈɔmnɪs ˈtɛṛa: ˈle:ta: ˈfakta: sʊnt (or [ˈlɛ:ta:])
ˈkfo:ni·am ˈfɪstsɛṛa: ɪpˈsi:·ʊs
fṛʊˈmɛntʊm pṛotʊˈle:ṛʊnt
ɛt ˈkfo:ni·am ˈfo:lʊkṛɛs ˈtse:li:
ˈni:dɔs ɪn ˈɪpsa: habu·ˈe:ṛʊnt
ˈdainde ˈfakta: e:st ˈɛska: hɔˈmi:nɪbʊs
ɛt ˈgaudi·ʊm ˈmaŋnʊm epʊˈlantsi·ʊm (or [ˈgəʊdi·ʊm], or with [ou])
ˈʊnde o: ˈʃfa:fɪs ˈfɪṛgo: (or [ˈsua:fɪs])
In te: no:n ˈde:fɪtsɪt ˈʊlʊm ˈgaudi·ʊm (see *gaudium* above)
hɛ:k ˈɔmni·a: ˈe:fa: kɔnˈtɛmpsɪt
nʊŋk ˈaftɛm laus sɪt alˈtɪsɪmo: (or [ləʊs], [lous])

Orlando Lassus, "Stabat mater"

Bavarian court, late sixteenth century. The difficulties of establishing historic pronunciation are compounded when composer-directors moved around Europe. Lassus came from a French-Picard area, was in Italy as a young man, and moved to a German court which was being "Netherlandized" but later engaged Italian singers also. The version suggested below aims at High German Latin, without regional diphthongs (but we tentatively suggest Bavarian [ɛ:] rather than [e:]). The *s* does not become [z]. In some cases vowel length differs from the general German rule; Bavarian dialect often uses short vowels in place of long closed ones. Final vowels tend to be closed, not much lengthened (except for *-i,* and sometimes *-o*). The edition is from Munich, 1585. CD #61.

Stabat mater dolorosa
Juxta crucem lacrymosa
Dum pendebat Filius.

Cujus animam gementem
Contristatem et dolentem
Pertransivit gladius.

O quam tristis et afflicta
Fuit illa benedicta
Mater unigeniti.

Quae morebat et dolebat
et tremebat cum videbat
Nati poenas inclyti.

Quis est homo qui non fleret
Christi matrem si videret
In tanto supplicio?

Quis posset non contristari
Piam Matrem contemplari
Dolentem cum Filio?

Pro peccatis suae gentis
Vidit Jesum in tormentis
Et flagellis subditum.

Vidit suum dulcem natum
Morientem desolatum,
Dum emisit spiritum.

Eia Mater fons amoris,
Me sentire vim doloris
Fac ut tecum lugeam.

Fac ut ardeat cor meum,
In amando Christum Deum
Ut sibi complaceam.

Sancta Mater istud agas
Crucifixi fige plagas
Corde meo valide.

Tui nati vulnerati
Jam dignati pro me pati
Poenas mecum divide.

Fac me vere tecum flere
Crucifixo condolere
Donec ego vixero

Juxta crucem tecum stare
Te libenter sociare
In planctu desidero.

Virgo, virginum praeclara
Mihi jam, non sis amara
Fac me tecum plangere.

Fac ut portem Christi mortem
Passionis ejus sortem
Et plagas recolere.

Fac me plagis vulnerari
Cruce hac inebriari
Ob amorem Filii

Inflammatus et accensus
Per te Virgo sim defensus
In die judicii.

Fac me Cruce custodiri
Morte Christi praemuniri
Confoveri gratia.

Quando corpus morietur
Fac ut animae donetur
Paradisi gloria. Amen.

ˈʃta:bat[*] ˈma:tɛṛ doloˈṛo:sa:
ˈjʊkʃta:[**] ˈkṛu:tsɛm lakṛˈimo:sa:
dʊm pɛnˈdɛ:bat ˈfi:li·ʊs

ˈkʊɪjʊs ˈa:nɪmam geˈmɛntɛm
kɔntṛɪˈʃta:tɛm et doˈlɛntɛm (or [ɛt], here and below)
pɛrtṛanˈsi:fɪt ˈgla:di·ʊs

o: kwam ˈtṛɪʃtɪs et aˈflɪkta:
ˈfu·ɪt ˈɪla: bɛnɛˈdɪkta:
ˈma:tɛṛ ʊnɪˈgɛ:nɪti:

kwɛ: mɔˈṛɛ:bat et doˈlɛ:bat
et tṛeˈmɛ:bat kʊm fiˈdɛ:bat
ˈna:ti: ˈpɛ:nas ˈɪŋklɪti:

kwɪs ɛ:ʃt ˈho:mo: kwi: nɔn ˈflɛ:ṛɛt
ˈkṛɪʃti: ˈma:tṛɛm si: fiˈdɛ:ṛɛt
ɪn ˈtanto: sʊˈpli:tsi·o:

kwɪs ˈpɔsɛt nɔn kɔntṛɪˈʃta:ṛi:
ˈpi:·am ˈma:tṛɛm kɔntɛmˈpla:ṛi:
doˈlɛntɛm kʊm ˈfi:li·o:

pṛo: pɛˈka:tɪs ˈsu·ɛ: ˈgɛntɪs
ˈfi:dɪt ˈjɛ:sʊm ɪn tɔṛ·mɛntɪs
et fla·ˈgɛlɪs ˈsʊbdɪtʊm

ˈfi:dɪt ˈsu:·ʊm ˈdʊltsɛm ˈna:tʊm
mɔṛi·ˈɛntɛm desoˈla:tʊm
dʊm eˈmi:sɪt ˈʃpɪṛɪtʊm

ˈɛi·a: ˈma:tɛṛ fɔns aˈmo:ṛɪs
mɛ: sɛnˈti:ṛe fɪm doˈlo:ṛɪs
fak ʊt ˈtɛ:kʊm ˈlu:ge·am

fak ʊt ˈaṛde·at ko:ṛ ˈmɛ:·ʊm
ɪn aˈmando: ˈkṛɪʃtʊm ˈdɛ:·ʊm
ʊt ˈsɪbi:[***] kɔmˈpla:tse·am

* Word-initial [ʃt-] was general practice.
** Medial [ʃt-] was a regional usage, but general for southern Germany.
*** Regional usage even today.

ˈsaŋkta: ˈma:tɛṛ ˈɪʃtʊt ˈa:gas
kṛʊtsɪˈfɪksi: ˈfi:ge ˈpla:gas
ˈkɔṛde ˈmɛ:·o: ˈfa:lɪde

ˈtu:·i: ˈna:ti: fʊlnɛˈṛa:ti:
jam dɪŋˈna:ti: pṛo: mɛ: ˈpa:ti:
ˈpɛ:nas ˈmɛ:kʊm ˈdi:fɪde

fak mɛ: ˈfɛ:ṛe ˈtɛ:kʊm ˈflɛ:ṛe
krʊtsɪˈfɪkso: kɔndoˈlɛ:ṛe
ˈdo:nɛk ˈɛ:go: ˈfɪksɛṛo:

ˈjʊkʃta: ˈkṛu:tsɛm ˈtɛ:kʊm ˈʃta:ṛe
tɛ: lɪˈbɛntɛṛ sɔtsi·ˈa:ṛe
ɪn ˈplaŋktu: deˈsi:dɛṛo:

ˈfɪṛgo: ˈfɪṛgɪnʊm pṛɛˈkla:ṛa:
ˈmi:hi: jam nɔn sɪs aˈma:ṛa:
fak mɛ: ˈtɛ:kʊm ˈplaŋgɛṛe

fak ʊt ˈpɔṛtɛm ˈkṛɪʃti: ˈmɔṛtɛm
pasi·ˈo:nɪs ˈɛ:jʊs ˈsɔṛtɛm
et* ˈpla:gas ṛeˈko:lɛṛe

fak mɛ: ˈpla:gɪs fʊlnɛˈṛa:ṛi:
ˈkṛu:tse ha:k ɪnɛbṛi·ˈa:ṛi:
ɔb aˈmo:ṛɛm ˈfi:li·i:

ɪnflaˈma:tʊs et akˈtsɛnsʊs
pɛṛ tɛ: ˈfɪṛgo sɪm deˈfɛnsʊs
ɪn ˈdi:·e jʊˈdi:tsi·i:

fak mɛ: ˈkṛu:tse kʊʃtoˈdi:ṛi:
ˈmɔṛte ˈkṛɪʃti: pṛemʊˈni:ṛi:
kɔnfoˈfɛ:ṛi: ˈgṛa:tsi·a:

ˈkwando: ˈkɔṛpʊs mɔṛi·ˈɛ:tʊṛ
fak ʊt ˈanɪmɛ doˈnɛ:tʊṛ
paṛaˈdi:si: ˈglo:ṛi·a: a:mɛn

Heinrich Schütz, "Jubilate Deo"

Saxon, seventeenth century. The educated Saxon dialect was the literary standard through much of Germany at this time and for long afterwards. How Latin was actually pronounced is less than clear. The main question is how *g* and *j* were pronounced in various positions. (The German consonant *j,* I.P.A. [j], is articulated with more friction than English *y.*)

* Regional southern German (standard German Latin has [ɛt]).

In Saxon phonetics *t/p/k* are non-aspirated and the sounds are more or less the same as for initial *d/b/g.* In this example non-aspirated [t], [p], [k] and unvoiced [d], [b], [g] are shown as [d°], [b°], [g°]; [t] in [ts] is in any case unaspirated. So we have, for example, *laetitia* as [lɛd°i:tsi·a:]. CD #62.

Jubilate Deo omnis terra, servite Domino in lætitia.
Introite in conspectu ejus in exultatione,
scitote, quoniam Dominus ipse est Deus,
ipse fecit nos, et non ipsi nos,
populus ejus et oves pascuæ ejus.
Introite portas ejus in confessione,
atria ejus, in hymnis confitemini illi.
Laudate nomen ejus.
Quoniam suavis est Dominus,
in æternum misericordia ejus,
et usque in generationem et generationem veritas ejus.

jubˈilad°e ˈde:·o ˈɔmnɪs ˈd°ɛṛa: sɛṛˈfi:d°e ˈdo:mɪno: ɪn lɛˈd°i:tsi·a:
ɪnd°ṛo·ˈi:d°e ɪn g°ɔnˈʃb°ɛg°d°u: ˈe:jʊs ɪn ɛksʊld°attsi·ˈo:ne
stɪˈd°o:d°e ˈg°vo:niam ˈdo:mɪnʊs ˈɪb°se e:sd° ˈd°e:ʊs (or [e:ʃd°])
ˈɪb°se ˈfe:tsɪd° no:s ɛd° nɔn ˈɪb°si: no:s
ˈb°o:b°ʊlʊs ˈe:jus ɛd° ˈo:fɛs ˈb°asg°u·ɛ:* ˈe:jʊs (or ˈɛ:jʊs])
ɪnd°ṛo·i:d°e ˈb°ɔṛd°as ˈe:jʊs ɪn g°ɔnfɛsi·ˈo:ne
ˈa:d°ṛia: ˈe:jʊs ɪn ˈhɪmnɪs g°ɔnfɪˈd°e:mɪni: ˈɪli:
lauˈd°a:d°e ˈno:mɛn ˈe:jʊs (or [louˈda:d°e])
ˈg°vo:ni:·am su·a:fɪs* e:sd° ˈd°o:mɪnʊs
ɪn ɛˈd°ɛṛnʊm mɪsɛṛiˈg°ɔrd°i·a: ˈe:jʊs
ɛd° ˈʊsg°ve ɪn çenɛratsi·ˈo:nɛm ɛd° çenɛratsi·ˈo:nɛm ˈfe:ṛɪd°as ˈe:jʊs

* Schütz sets these words as three syllables; see entry for *qu,* p. 262.

18

Flemish (Dutch)

WILLIAM Z. SHETTER

There is probably no region of the world that throughout its history has been so vexed by terminological confusion as the Low Countries. The word "Flemish" today, strictly speaking, refers to the two Belgian provinces of East Flanders and West Flanders, with their respective capitals Ghent and Bruges. It is more commonly used in the broader meaning of all of Dutch-speaking Belgium as far east as the German language area. In the period we are dealing with, however, the political unit known as Flanders comprised a rather differently shaped area, stopping short of Brussels to the east but extending well south into what is now northern France. In other words, in the Middle Ages Flanders did not include the duchy of Brabant immediately to the east but straddled the two language areas.

"Low Countries" refers generally to the cultural unit west of the German area and north of the French, and "Netherlands" in the fifteenth and sixteenth centuries covered more or less the same area—including the French-speaking—but did not yet connote any nationality, as it does today. "Holland" and "Flanders" were simply the names of two of the Low Countries mini-states under counts or dukes. "Burgundy" is appropriate only while some of these states were under the political control of the French dukes of Burgundy, which effectively ended by the close of the fifteenth century, although the name is frequently used to refer to the Burgundian domains on into the sixteenth century, after they had been incorporated into the Habsburg Empire.

As for the adjectives derived from these names, "Flemish" refers to anything associated with the political unit Flanders and "Burgundian" with Burgundy in certain periods. "Netherlandish" is used mainly by historians of art and music to refer to the Netherlands or Low Countries in the widest sense. In practice, the three words are used with considerable overlapping and for the most part synonymously.

Much of this does not apply to the language. Contrary to an almost universal assumption in the English-speaking world, there is no such entity as the Flemish language. The language is Dutch, the same language that developed in Flanders, Brabant to the east, and Holland and other states to the north—in other words all of present-day Belgium north of the French-speaking area plus the whole of the Netherlands. There were three principal dialects in the area, Flemish, Brabant, and Holland, but it will not be necessary here to enter into the specific features distinguishing them. Since in the medieval period the first was the most influential, in modern times among historians (though not among linguists) it has lent its name to the rest.[1]

In terms of dialect geography, the forms of language in the Low Countries form a continuum with dialects across northern Germany all the way east to a meeting with the Slavic languages. But the Dutch-speaking people began to acquire a distinct cultural identity in the Middle Ages, and their writings in the late twelfth and early thirteenth centuries—poems, romances, didactic pieces, chronicles, saints' lives—showed signs of a common written language with features quite distinct from the Low German area to the east. Before long they had developed a culture famous all over Europe in music, art, and literature.

About 1150 the cultural center of gravity of the Dutch-speaking area was Flanders, especially the cities Bruges, Ghent, Ypres, Courtrai, Lille, and Cambrai (only the last two French-speaking), which were becoming prosperous and semi-autonomous trade and manufacturing centers. The whole of the Low Countries was a patchwork of duchies, counties, seigniories, and bishoprics. As elsewhere, social divisions tended to be horizontal between classes rather than vertical between countries, and since these highly permeable borders allowed a considerable flow of tradesmen, students, scholars, clerics, and knights, linguistic and cultural influences naturally went with them.

These urbanized regions reached the height of their prominence in the Burgundian period, in the 1300s and 1400s. In fact, the economic prosperity and cultural luster of the northern half of the Burgundian duchy tended to eclipse the southern half, the original Burgundy in France, until the late 1500s. In the late sixteenth century cities in the north—centered on Amsterdam—began to overtake the southern ones, and by 1600 the south had receded into Spanish control while the independent republic in the north (the United Provinces) went on to a new cultural prominence.

There is therefore no real cultural or linguistic break between the earlier "Flemish" texts and the later "Dutch" or "Netherlandish" ones. Though there were many linguistic changes in some four centuries, only an indispensable few of them will be outlined here. Tendencies toward a standard usage can be found back in the Middle Ages, though it is only toward 1600 that something like a true standard language began to develop—and this happened in the northern Dutch republic but bypassed the South.

Bibliography

Johannes Franck, *Mittelniederländische Grammatik mit Lesestücken und Glossar.* Arnhem: Gijsbers & Van Loon, 1971 (reprint of the 1910 edition). The standard, thorough Dutch-language grammar.

There are several other reliable Dutch-language grammars of Middle Dutch, including those of A. van Loey and T. Le Roux and the following two easy-to-use school texts:

Maaike Hogenhout-Mulder. *Cursus Middelnederlands.* Groningen: Wolters-Noordhoff, 1985.
Cornelis van de Ketterij. *Grammaticale interpretatie van Middelnederlandse teksten.* 3 vols. Vol. 3: *Instructiegrammatica.* Groningen: Wolters-Noordhoff, 1985.
W. Martin and G. Tops. *Van Dale Groot Woordenboek Nederlands-Engels.* Utrecht and Antwerp: Van Dale Lexicografie, 1986. The most complete and up-to-date Dutch-English dictionary available.
Colette Van Kerckvoorde. *An Introduction to Middle Dutch.* Berlin and New York: Mouton–De Gruyter, 1992. The only Middle Dutch grammar in English.
J. Verdam. *Middelnederlandsch Handwoordenboek.* 's-Gravenhage: Martinus Nijhoff, 1979. The standard Middle Dutch dictionary (there is no Middle Dutch–English dictionary). The reader needing more detail should refer to the same author's *Middelnederlandsch Woordenboek,* 9 vols.

Linguistic Changes

1. By the time the earliest vernacular texts appeared, vowels in open syllables had been lengthened (unlike Middle High German, for instance, where this had not taken place yet). *Draghet* is therefore [dr̩a:ɣət], *voghel* is [vo:ɣəl], and *wesen* is [we:zən]. It is possible that lengthened *a* was widely distinguished from original long *â* (possibly as [æ:] versus [ɔ:]), since many modern dialects still distinguish them, but the spellings do not reliably indicate this so it is better ignored. The qualitative difference between short and long *a* implied by their transcription here as [ɑ] and [a:] is based on their respective phonetic qualities in modern Dutch. It is reasonable to assume that this may have been true in the Middle Ages as well, even though the spellings give no reliable evidence of it.

2. Widespread in this area—though probably not everywhere—was the raising of the inherited Germanic *ê* [e:] and *ô* [o:] to [i:] and [u:]. The most common spellings are *ie* and *oe,* suggesting that they had first become, and perhaps still were, diphthongs. The words *lieden* and *verdriet* are probably best pronounced [li:dən] and [vɛrdri:t], and *goed* and *roept* [ɣu:t] and [r̩u:pt]. In the modern Dutch pronunciation these are pronounced somewhat shorter but still tense: *lied* is [lit] and *roept* is [r̩upt], but in the early period this shortening had almost certainly not yet taken place.

3. The vowels *u* [ʊ] and *û* [u:] had been fronted at a very early date (probably through contact with French), and accordingly *stuck* was [stʏk] and *vuur* was [vy:r].

4. The Germanic vowels *î* and *û* had therefore (in light of paragraph 3) become [i:] and [y:], and they retained this quality until they were diphthongized probably sometime after 1600. While there is considerable evidence of diphthongs in the sixteenth century, there is equally abundant evidence of pure long vowels in the seventeenth, so in spite of the similarity in spelling, using the modern pronunciations *zij* [zɛɪ] and *spijzen* [spɛɪzən], *duizend* [dœyzent] and *uit* [œyt] should be considered an anachronism.

This leaves the vexing question how this [i:] was distinguished from the [i:] that had evolved from *ê.* There is no doubt that there was a distinction, since texts normally do not confuse them, and the former later developed a diphthongal pronunciation while the latter never did; in addition some modern dialects distinguish them. Though there was probably some qualitative distinction, an equally good guess is that the distinction was one of quantity, the original *î* having become slightly shorter. So *ziis* and *spise* were [zis] and [spizə] (compare *lieden* [li:dən]), and *duysent* and *wt* were [dyzənt] and [yt]. The Dutch today normally ignore this distinction when reading Middle Dutch texts, saying *spise* [spizə] but also *lieden* [lidən], and the reader might well be inclined to do likewise.

5. Dutch had, and has, terminal devoicing, i.e., the consonants *b, d,* and occasionally *g* when at the end of a syllable, whether or not followed by a voiceless consonant, were pronounced [p], [t], [k]. The fricatives [v], [z], [ɣ] participate in this alternation as well, though since the letters *v* and *w* are never written in final position in any case, there is little temptation to mispronounce them: *lieve* [li:və] but *lief* [li:f]. But it should be remembered that although *s* is more commonly written between vowels than is *z,* when not in syllable-final position or followed by a consonant it must usually be given the voiced pronunciation [z]: *prisen* is [pṛizən]. Often the spelling indicates these alternations (*quade* [kwa:də] but *quaet* [kwa:t]), though not reliably: *god* [ɣɔt]; *menighe* [me:nɪɣə] but *menich* [me:nɪx], though one also finds the spelling *menighe,* likewise [me:nɪx].

6. Another serious problem is how *g* was pronounced. It can reliably be assumed to have been [ɣ] in voiced environment and [x] in word- and syllable-final position (according to paragraph 5), although there must have been considerable regional variation. So we find *gheen* [ɣe:n], *gheslaghen* [ɣəsla:ɣən] but *slach* [slɑx], *menich* [me:nɪx] though *menighe* [me:nɪɣə]. The voiced stop [g] is usually assumed in gemination and following [ŋ]: *seggen* [zɛg:ən] and *zinghen* [zɪŋgən] (this is no longer true today; the pronunciations are *zeggen* [zɛɣən] or [zɛxən] and *zingen* [zɪŋən]).

7. The earlier cluster *sk* had developed into [sx] by the time of these texts, which in syllable-initial position is still its pronunciation today. From spellings such as hypercorrect forms it is deduced that this was probably also pronounced in syllable-final position, where it would not be today. *Schepper* is [sxɛp:əṛ], *gheschent* is [ɣəsxɛnt], *waschen* [wɑsxən] (modern *wassen* [vɑsən]), *visch* [vɪsx] (modern *vis* [vɪs]).

8. The consonants *b, d, g, p, t, k, f, s, x, m, n, l,* and *r* can all occur as geminates following a short vowel. This is not merely a spelling convention, for they were still pronounced long up to 1600. Thus we find *hadden* [hɑd:ən], *schepper* [sxɛp:əṛ], *stucken* [stʏk:ən], *mannen* [mɑn:ən], *verre* [vɛṛ:ə]. In Modern Dutch all geminated consonants have been simplified; e.g., *hadden* [hɑdən].

9. Flemish spellings such as *angen, ebben, ondert,* instead of *hangen, hebben, hondert* indicate that there was widespread loss of *h* in these dialects. As a predictable result of this, *h* is often written hypercorrectly: *hedel, honder, huut* for *edel, onder, uut.*

While all the above refer to sound changes, there were of course many morphological and syntactic changes as well. But since these grammatical changes between the medieval and the modern language (such as noun inflection, which has largely become obsolete) seldom interfere with the understanding of the meaning of texts, none will be singled out here. Readers needing to translate a text are referred to a Middle Dutch grammar and Middle Dutch dictionaries in the Bibliography.

Spelling Conventions

For the most part, the considerable variation and occasional whimsicality in spellings is only what is to be expected everywhere in this period. While most can be seen through fairly readily, assuming some knowledge of the meaning of the text, it will be helpful to point out two matters:

The spellings *o, oo,* and *oe* commonly indicate any of the three sounds [o:], [ø:], and [u:]. To look at it the other way around, [ko:mən] will be found spelled *comen, coomen, coemen* (among other ways); [dø:ɣət] can be expected to be *doghet, dooghet, doeghet,* as well as the more recognizable *dueghet* and *deughet;* and [ru:pən] is found spelled *ropen, roopen, roepen* as well as *ruepen.* Without a knowledge of etymology, the most practical means of distinguishing them is to pronounce them as they would be in modern Dutch, where they are unambiguously distinguished: the sound [o:] will always be *o* or *oo* depending on the rule stated in the next paragraph ([ko:mən] is *komen* and [ho:x] is *hoog*), the sound [ø:] is always *eu* ([dø:xt] is *deugd*), and the sound [u] or [u:] is always *oe* ([rupt] is *roept* and [vu:r] is *voer*[2]).

The Dutch language has evolved the orthographical rule that the long vowels spelled with a doubled letter *(aa, ee, oo, uu)* become single in open syllables (thus modern *jaar* but *jaren, heet* but *hete, groot* but *grote, vuur* but *vuren*). This habit appears to have been fairly well established in the older period, though as one would expect, with considerable inconsistency. We find *draecht* but *draghen, heet* but *hete, hooch* or *hoech* but *hoghe, huus, hues* or *huys* but *huse.*

Conversely short vowels followed by a single consonant must double this consonant when another syllable beginning with a vowel is added: *al* but *allen, ver* but *verre, verlos* but *verlossen, cust* but *cussen.* Accordingly a single vowel followed by a single consonant and then an ending beginning with a vowel, can normally be expected to be long, whereas a single vowel followed by any two consonants will normally be short. Here as well as in the vowels *o, oo,* and *oe,* modern Dutch can serve as a reliable guide.

Consonants

p, b [p] *party, schepper, heb*

t, d [t] *toe, moet, letten, god*

k, ck, c, kw [k] *klein, ick, comen, stucken, quamen*
(The three voiceless stops are unaspirated in Dutch, unlike *p, t, k* in English and German.)

b [b] *by, hebben*

d [d] *die, hadden*

g, gh [g] *zinghen, seggen* (See above, "Linguistic changes," 6.)

f [f] *fel, brief, heffen*

s [s] *stucken, schepper, voghels, mossel*

ch [x] *menich, schepper*

v, u [v] *van, veruolchde*

s, z [z] *sere, spise, vreesde, zanghe*

g, gh [ɣ] *god, tegen, ghi, eyghen*

m [m] *moet*

n [n] *niet*

n(g), n(gh) [ŋ] *lange, zanghes*

j [j] *jeghens*

w [w] *wylen*
(The contactless *w* of modern English and most Flemish dialects, not the fricative *w* of modern Dutch.)

l [l] *let, fel, ellende*

r [r̥] *ryc, waert, verre*

h [h] *hart, hedel* (See above, "Linguistic changes," 9.)

Vowels

i [ɪ] *zinghen, ic*

u [ʏ] *stucken*

e [ɛ] *verre, heb, ellende*

o [ɔ] *noch, com, hondert*

a [ɑ] *ach, langhe, van*

i, ii, y [i] *vri, ziis, ryc*

u (v), uu (w), ue, uy [y] *v, wt, duysent*

ie [i:] *lieden, niet, verdriet*

oe, o/oo, ou, ue [u:] *goede, ropen, versouc, ruepen*

e/ee [e:] *edel, eenich, heet*

o/oo, oe [o:] *voghel, groote, soe*

o/oo, oe, ue, eu [ø:] *doghet, doeghet, vruechde, vreuchde*

a/ae [a:] *draghet, ghehaet*

(a/ae [ɔ:] *quamen, waer*)

ei, ey [ɛɪ] *paleis, eyghen*

ou [ɔʊ] *stout*

oi, oy [o:ɪ] *strois, noyt*

eu, ew, eeu(w) [e:ʊ] *ewelic, eeu*

aei, ey [a:ɪ] *maeit, dreyen*

aeu(w) [a:ʊ] *graeu*

Most Frequent Ambiguities

Spelling	Pronunciation	Conditions	Modern Dutch spelling
a	[ɑ]	closed syllable	a
	[a:]	open syllable	a
b	[b]	initial and medial	b
	[p]	syllable-final	b
d	[d]	initial and medial	d
	[t]	syllable-final	d
e	[ɛ]	closed syllable	e
	[e:]	open syllable	e
ei	[ɛɪ]		ei
	[a:ɪ]		aai
eu	[ø:]		eu
	[e:ʊ]		eeuw
g(h)	[g]	geminated and following [ŋ]	g
	[ɣ]	initially (including clusters), medially	g
	[x]	finally	g
i	[ɪ]	closed syllable	i
	[i]	open syllable	ij
	[i:]	open syllable before *r*	ie
ii	[i]		ij
	[i:]	before *r*	ij
	[i:]		ie
ij	[i]		ij
	[i:]	before *r*	ie
o	[ɔ]	closed syllable	o
	[o:]	open syllable	o
	[u:]		oe
oe	[o:]		oo
	[ø:]		eu
	[u:]		oe
oo	[o:]		oo
	[ø:]		eu
	[u:]		oe
ou	[u:]		oe
	[ɔʊ]		ou

s	[s]	initially before consonant, syllable-final, gemination	s(s)
	[z]	initially before vowel, medially between vowels	z
u	[ʏ]	closed syllable	u
	[y]	open syllable	ui
	[y:]	open syllable before *r*	ui
	[u:]		oe
	[v]	preceding a vowel	v
ue	[u:]		oe
	[y]		ui
	[y:]	before *r*	uu
v	[v]	preceding a vowel	v
	[y]	alone or followed by consonant	ui
w	[w]	preceding a vowel	w
	[y]	preceding a consonant	ui
y	[i]		ij

SAMPLE TEXTS

In the phonetic transcriptions a few adjustments for the "stream of speech" have been made: some unstressed function words have been transcribed as shorter, and a few voicing assimilations have been made; these are meant to be suggestive only.

Ach Vlaendere vrie

Heiligenkreuz, Archiv des Zisterzienserstiftes, fragment, folio 1'f. Printed in Reinhard Strohm, *Music in Late Medieval Bruges* (Oxford: Clarendon Press, 1985), pp. 208 ff. CD #63.

I Ach Vlaendere vrie hedel aert
wylen werstu verre bekent.
Zo ziis tu noch, maer te di waert
draghet niit menich fel serpent

Du wes omtrent langhe gheschent
werstu van herte . . . sy.

Ach, Vlaendre, Vlaendre, wat let dy.

II Ach, Vlaendern, wat mach 't bedreden*
dattu zo sere ziis ghehaet,
en du ne daets noyt goede lieden,
die te di quamen, eenich quaet,

maer hoghen staet hebsi hoe 't gaet
comsi van verren of van by.

Ach, Vlaendre, Vlaendre, wat let dy.

I ax vla:ndərə vriə (h)e:dəl a:rt
wilən werstu ver:ə bəkent
zo zistu nɔx ma:r tə di wa:rt
dra:ɣət ni:t me:nɪx fɛl sɛrpɛnt
du wɛs ɔmtrɛnt laŋgə ɣəsxɛnt
wɛrstu van hɛrtə si
ax vla:ndrə vla:ndrə wat lɛt di

II ax vla:ndərə** wat maxt bədi:dən
dat:u zo ze:rə zis ɣəha:t
ɛn du nə da:ts no:ɪt ɣu:də li:dən
di tə di kwa:mən e:nɪx kwa:t

* Probably a misspelling or a miscopy of *bedieden* or *bedueden* (to indicate).

** The *-n* of the common inflectional ending *-en* is normally dropped today in casual speech throughout the western part of the Dutch-speaking area, and there is reliable evidence that this was true of colloquial speech as early as the Middle Ages. This would account for the variant spellings *Vlaend[e]re* and *Vlaender[e]n* for what was almost certainly [vla:ndərə].

maːr hoːɣən staːt hɛpsi hut ɣaːt
kɔmzi vɑn vɛrːən ɔf vɑn bi
ɑx vlaːndrə vlaːndrə wɑt lɛt di

Tzinghen van der nachtegale

Leiden fragment, BPL 2720 fol. 7'. Published by Hélène Wagenaar-Nolthenius in "De Leidse fragmenten: Nederlandse polifonie uit het einde der 14e eeuw," in Jozef Robijns, ed., *Renaissance-Muziek 1400–1600* (Leuven: Katholieke Universiteit, 1969), pp. 303–22.

Tzinghen van der nachtegale
Can ic niet gheprisen wale
noch gheen voghels zanghes ryc

Jeghens haer die mi te dale
Heeft ghetoghen tesen male
in ellende misselyc

Haer so moet ic ewelic
eyghen wesen ho soe 't gheet
Nochtans roept si wonderlic:
"Hale mosselkyn al heet!
Die beste spise die ic weet
dat syn mosselkin al heet!"

ət sɪŋgən vɑn dɛr nɑxtəɣaːlə
kɑn ɪk niːt ɣəprizən waːlə
nɔx xeːn voːɣəls zɑŋgəs rik

jeːɣəns haːr di mi tə daːlə
heːft ɣətoːɣən teːzən maːlə
ɪn ɛlːɛndə mɪsːəlik

haːr zo muːt ɪk eːwəlik
ɛɪɣən weːzən hu zot ɣeːt
nɔxtans ruːpt si wɔndərlik
haːlə mɔsːəlkin al heːt
di bɛstə spizə di ɪk weːt
dɑt sin mɔsːəlkin ɑl heːt

Souterliedekens, Psalm 3

J. Clemens non Papa, *Souterliedekens I. Het vierde musyck boexken mit dry parthien* (Antwerp: T. Susato, 1556). Published in *Corpus of Early Music* (Brussels: Editions Culture et Civilisation 1160, 1972), vol. 16, Psalm 3. CD #64.

I Heer hoe zynse so menichfout
Myn vyanden seer fel en stout

staen tegens my
Veel seggen tot mynder silen
Dat ick van god verlaten sy.

V Al waer ick van hondert duysent man
besinghelt, die mi quamen an,
ick en vreesde niet.
myn heer, myn god, myn schepper
staet op: verlost mi wt verdriet.

VI Want ghi gheslaghen hebt myn party
die sonder saeck veruolchden my.
haer tanden fel
hebt ghi in stucken ghebroken
o groote god van Israel.

I he:r hu zin zə zo me:nɪxfɔʊt
min viandən ze:r fɛl ən stɔʊt
sta:n te:ɣəns mi
ve:l zɛg:ən tɔt mindər zilən
dɑt ɪk vɑn ɣɔt vɛrla:tən zi

V ɑl wa:r ɪk vɑn hɔndərt dyzənt mɑn
bəsɪŋgəlt di mi kwa:mən ɑn
ɪk ɛn vre:zdə ni:t
min he:r min ɣɔt min sxɛp:ər
sta:t ɔp vɛrlɔst mi yt vɛrdri:t

VI wɑnt ɣi ɣəsla:ɣən hɛpt min pɑrti
di zɔndər za:k vɛrvɔlʏdən mi
ha:r tɑndən fɛl
hɛpt ɣi ɪn stʏk:ən ɣəbro:kən
o ɣro:tə ɣɔt vɑn israɛl

NOTES

1. The Dutch terminology is hardly less chaotic. Vlaanderen, Brabant, and Holland are the names of the three main political units and of their dialects; today each of the three has been divided into two provinces, and Brabant is divided as well by a national frontier. The first and third have lent their names—officially in the case of the first and informally by the third—to an entire country. "De Nederlanden" is generally used to refer to all the Dutch-speaking lands, while "Nederland" is the common name of the kingdom to the north of Belgium—except that in its official name it goes back to the plural in "Koninkrijk der Nederlanden." "De Lage Landen" is slightly broader, usually including French-speaking areas in the same geographical-cultural area.

Parallel to this are the adjectives "Vlaams," "Brabants," and "Hollands." When the word "Nederlands" is applied to the language—and only then—it refers not just to Nederland but to the entire Dutch-speaking area, in other words Vlaanderen as well. The word "Diets" was often used in the Middle Ages to distinguish southern Dutch speech from "Duuts," northern speech and German undifferentiated, but just as often it referred to all Dutch speech, leading many to claim it today as early evidence of a consciousness of linguistic distinctiveness from German. The term is occasionally used today in this latter meaning.

2. Note the examples here and in paragraph 2 under "Linguistic Changes," above, of the fact that in modern Dutch the vowels [i:], [y:], [u:] are long only before *r* (*vier* [vi:r], *vuur* [vy:r], and *voer* [vu:r]) but somewhat shorter though just as tense everywhere else (*verdriet* [vɛrdṛit], *minuut* [minyt] and *roepen* [rupən]).

19—

Netherlands Latin

HAROLD COPEMAN

Regional Varieties

The great Franco-Flemish, or "Netherlandish," musicians of the fourteenth to sixteenth centuries came from the region south of what is now the central Netherlands, reaching through Belgium to the northernmost part of France. These singers, composers, and directors served all over Europe, particularly in the courts and cathedrals of northern Italy at the crest of the Renaissance. They influenced the European choral style, especially in Italy and Germany, and in turn trained many of the Italian singers who moved to other countries from the mid-sixteenth century.

The vernacular language of the southern part of this region is French; but the dialect, which differs markedly from standard French, is called Picard in France, and Walloon in Belgium. In the north the dialects and language are Germanic; they are known as Flemish in Belgium, and Dutch in Holland. The historic linguistic border between these two groups lies across what is now Belgium, just south of Brussels.

For much of our period the Low Countries were ruled by the Burgundian dukes, who lived mainly at local courts, notably in Brussels and Mechelen ("Malines" in French). Their own culture was French, and courtly speech in Burgundy was probably close to the standard Francien, but the ducal families entered into local life and came to speak local dialects. Art and music flourished under their patronage. We may therefore be fairly sure that one of the styles of Latin was French. Furthermore the vernacular language used in church affairs in much of the extensive and ancient Archdiocese of Rheims was French.

It seems likely that in the important provincial cathedrals and abbeys south of the linguistic dividing line, Latin pronunciation was based on the regional dialects rather than on Francien French. Those dialects were varieties of Old Picard, then of Middle Picard; these were literary languages as well as forms of everyday speech. One important difference between the dialects and French Latin was that the sound of *c* before *e* or *i* had remained closer to the [k] of Roman times than in French and French Latin, which had developed to [s].

North of the linguistic line, the independently minded northern towns—Bruges, Ghent, Antwerp—were strongly Flemish/Dutch in culture (though French was spoken and written fluently by educated people), and Latin was likely to have been pronounced according to the local (Germanic) dialects. (Between Dutch and Low German the linguistic frontier was quite gradual.)

The Low Countries suffered severely from wars, religious oppression, and revolt, and political changes may have added to the linguistic complications. The Burgundian territories (with Spain and Germany) were inherited in 1520 by Charles V, who became Holy Roman Emperor (a largely nominal primacy over the German princes and prince-bishops). Like the Burgundians, Charles engaged in continual struggles with the French. He also was determined to put down the rising Protestant religion; his son Philip II of Spain (Mary Tudor's husband) continued this attack, and introduced the Spanish Inquisition into the Netherlands. There was war between the Dutch Protestants and the Spanish Catholic troops for eighty years starting in 1568, and large numbers of Protestants moved north to central Holland.

There are a very few contemporary references to Latin pronunciation in the Low Countries. Geofroy Tory, a French humanist scholar and printer, remarked in 1529 that in Latin the Picards pronounced *c* better than the French, for they made it thick, and as if aspirated, saying "Amiche," "Sochie," "Chichero." Erasmus (1528) and Mekerchus (1565) discussed, inter alia, the Dutch pronunciation of *u,* and there are also (confusing) references by Lipsius (1586). These passages are assembled in Copeman, *Singing in Latin,* pp. 57, 66–68, and 96–101.

Apart from this, the only guides are the sounds of currently surviving dialects and the historical phonology of these vernaculars, which in the absence of deliberate reform would also apply to the local pronunciation of Latin.

Bibliography

French: See Bibliography in Chapter 6, "French Latin," especially M. K. Pope, pp. 487–92.

Picard:

J. Darras, ed. *La forêt invisible . . . le picard.* Amiens, 1985. A discursive background book with literary examples of Picard; see pp. 55–60 on the status of the language, and an incomplete account of phonetics, pp. 77–79.

L.-F. Flutre. *Le moyen picard.* Amiens, 1970. See also other studies by this author.

Dutch/Flemish:

B. C. Donaldson. *Dutch: A Linguistic History of Holland and Belgium.* Leiden, 1983.

Sounds, Spellings, and Accents

Latin spelling was of course broadly the same in all countries. Where the local language was unconnected with Latin, the latter, when used, had to be learned; its pronunciation would be affected by local vowels and consonants. But pronunciation developed differently where the vernacular itself emerged from Latin (that is, in French and Picard/Walloon), since these vernaculars were changing the Latin words themselves. Syllables (especially Latin endings) were abbreviated or dropped entirely—in French Latin to such an extent that there might eventually be nothing left after the stressed or lengthened syllable. This end-accentuation remained in the French word, and when Latin came to be learned (from Charlemagne's time, for purposes of church and state) the habit of lengthening a syllable late in the word was applied, inappropriately, to the Latin word. Erasmus said that the French spoke their endings so obscurely that you could hardly hear them, inordinately stretching out the vowel; in *dominus* the *u* "has the space of three vowels" (i.e., for him, the duration of a Classical long vowel joined to a short vowel).

In the Picard/Walloon area the stress was stronger than in central France, though its placement seems likely to have followed the French pattern of end-lengthening. On the other hand, Dutch/Flemish Latin would generally have maintained the same stress pattern as in earlier Latin (similar to English, German, and Italian Latin).

Elision: Middle Picard (1500–1700) seems to have elided consonants freely: French *il ressemble* = Middle Picard *i rsãn;* similarly *il tremble* = *i trãn, plus* = *pu.* This habit suggests that some elision took place in Picard Latin also. The phonetic transcriptions of the sample texts below (except for one case) follow the practice suggested for French Latin. It attempts to simplify sequences of consonants which involve sharp and repeated changes in articulation, which French-speaking people avoided; e.g., *est de* becomes [ezde] (‿ indicating elision at the end of a word). The exception is that Picard maintained later than French the sound [s] before [p] or [t], so that (at the end of a phrase or before a vowel) I suggest Picard Latin [est] where French Latin would have [ɛt]. (On [e] and [ɛ] see below.)

For the pronunciation of French Latin, see Chapter 6. In the following sections the pronunciation of Picard/Walloon Latin is labeled *P,* that of Dutch/Flemish Latin *D.**

Consonants

c before *e, i* P. Probably around [kj]; D. Around [tj].

c otherwise [k].

g before *e, i* P. Probably [dʒ] to about 1250, then [ʒ]. D. A light sound between [ʒ] and [ʃ].

g otherwise P. [g]. D. Broadly [ɣ], [ç], or [ʃ] in Holland; [h], [x], or [ɣ] in Flanders.

h P. Silent. D. [h] in Holland, tending to drop in Flanders.

i/j consonantal P. Probably [dʒ] to about 1250, then [ʒ]; D. [j], or as for *ge, gi.*

qu P. [k]; D. [kɥ]

r P. and D. Short trill, [r̥], but a uvular sound is heard in Brabant and some other regions.

s initial P. [s]. D. [s] but with a flavor of [z], especially in Holland.

---

* I am indebted to Rebecca Stewart of The Hague for suggestions arising from experiments with her professional choir in the Netherlands.

s otherwise P. Between vowels [z]; final, [s]. Before *p, t,* [s] persisted in Picard later than in French. D. Between vowels within a word, [z] (because initial in new syllable); end of syllable, [s].

sc before *e, i* P. [k] (French *je descends* = Middle Picard *je déquen*). D. [sj] or [tj].

t P. final [t] was retained after a tonic vowel, thus *et* [et]; D. [t].

ti + vowel P. probably [tʃi]; D. [ts], [tj].

v P. [v]; D. [β].

x, xc P. probably [z]; *xt* pronounced [st]. D. probably [ks], or [kz] before a vowel.

z P. [z]; D. similar to (initial) *s* above.

Double consonants are pronounced single in both P. and D.

Vowels

a P. [a]. D. [ɑ] in closed syllables; [a:] in open syllables; unaccented, [ə].

e P. [e] (cf. French [ɛ] in closed syllables); stressed *er* probably [ar]. D. [ɛ] in closed syllables (but *est* perhaps [e:st]); [e:] in open syllables; unaccented, [ə].

i P. [i]; D. [ɪ] in closed syllables, [i] in open syllables (when accented, perhaps [ɛi]).

o P. [ɔ] in closed syllables (but *-or* as [-ur]); [o] in open syllables, moving to [u] by the sixteenth century. D. [ɔ] in closed syllables, [o] (half long) in open syllables.

u P. The Roman [u] was palatalized later here than in central France, and may not have reached [y]; I suggest [ʏ]. D. In a syllable closed by *n* or *m,* varying sounds between [ə] and [y] (*-unt* perhaps [ont]); in other positions, [y] *(Domin·us, u·nigenite).*

Picard Nasalization

(Based largely on Middle Picard, 1500–1700)

am = [ãm]; *an* = [ã] but [ãn] before a vowel.

In the sample texts below, the following features occur: 1. The vowel [a] is nasalized (as in Middle French), even in some positions when *m*/*n* is followed by a vowel. This occurred before a final *ne, me* (French *da·me,* Middle Picard *dãm*), and so probably also before Latin endings like *lauda·mus.* 2. But before a vowel which has been nasalized in the same word, the initial vowel is denasalized; the Old Picard *grantement* became Middle Picard *gramẽ:* so we can expect, for instance, *Amen* to have a non-nasal [a]. These two patterns may apply to other vowels as well, though there is no evidence to hand. But we have made the assumption that, for instance in *omnipotentem,* nasalization of *-em* means that the preceding *-ent* does not have a nasal vowel. 3. The sounds *am, an* are denasalized before [k], [g], [p], in accordance with the French pattern.

em, en were [ɛ̃m], [ɛ̃n] (not with French [ã]). Assuming nasalization follows pattern 1. above, the first vowel in *ple·na, e·misit* is [ɛ̃].

im, in were nasalized, starting in the fifteenth and sixteenth centuries, to [ĩ] or [ẽ] or became [eim], [ein].

For *i, o, u,* nasalization was late and evidently weaker, and possibly absent in vowels in open syllables *(fi·nis, ho·mo, u·num)*. This would apply within a phrase: in *Credo in unum Deum,* the [n] becomes an initial consonantal sound, and the [i] is non-nasal.

om, on gradually nasalized in closed syllables to [ũm], [ũn] (but see previous paragraph). Before *f* or *v, n* might become *m: confiteor, converte.*

um, un. From 1400 [ỹm], [ỹn]; in the seventeenth century the sound moved through [œ̃m], [œ̃n] to [ɛ̃m], [ɛ̃n].

SAMPLE TEXTS

For French Latin, see *Credo* in Chapter 6.

Picard/Walloon Latin

Style P., around 1500. For medieval Picard, see "Picard Sounds" in Chapter 5. Compare the following *Credo* with that in Chapter 6; see also Copeman, *Singing in Latin,* pp. 285–87, and detailed notes above. CD #65.

Credo

Credo in unum Deum, Patrem omnipotentem,
Factorem celi et terre,
Visibilium omnium et invisibilium.
Et in unum Dominum Jesum Christum, Filium Dei unigenitum.
Et ex Patre natum ante omnia secula.
Deum de Deo, Lumen de lumine, Deum verum de Deo vero.
Genitum, non factum, Consubstantialem Patri:
Per quem omnia facta sunt.
Qui propter nos homines et propter nostram salutem
descendit de cælis; et incarnatus est de Spiritu Sancto
ex Maria Virgine, et Homo factus est.
Crucifixus etiam pro nobis sub Pontio Pilato
passus et sepultus est.
Et resurrexit tertia die secundam Scripturas et ascendit in caelum.
Sedet ad dexteram Patris, et iterum venturus est
cum gloria judicare vivos et mortuos
cujus regni non erit finis.
Et in spiritum sanctum Dominum et vivificantem,
qui ex Patre Filioque procedit.
Qui cum Patre et Filio simul adoratur, et conglorificatur,
qui locutus est per prophetas.
Et unam sanctam catholicam et apostolicam ecclesiam.
Confiteor unum baptisma in remissionem peccatorum.
Et exspecto resurrectionem mortuorum.
Et vitam venturi seculi. Amen.

ˈkṛedu in ˈʏnʏ̃‿ˈdeʏ̃m ˈpatṛɛ̃m unipoˈtentɛ̃m
faˈtuṛɛ̃m ˈkjeli e‿ˈtaṛe
viziˈbili·ʏm ˈuni·ʏm et inviziˈbili·ʏ̃m
et in ˈʏnʏ̃‿ˈduminʏ̃m ˈʒesʏ̃‿ˈkṛistʏ̃m ˈfili·ʏ̃‿ˈde·i ʏniˈʒenitʏ̃m
et ez ˈpatṛe ˈnatʏ̃m ˈãte ˈũni·a ˈsekʏla
ˈde·ʏ̃‿de ˈde·u ˈlʏmɛ̃n de ˈlʏmine ˈde·ʏ̃‿ˈvɛṛʏ̃‿de ˈde·u ˈvɛṛu
ˈʒenitʏ̃‿nũ‿ˈfatʏ̃m kusʏstantʃi·ˈalɛ̃m ˈpatṛi

pa‿kɛ̃m ˈũni·a ˈfata sʏ̃nt
ki ˈpṛute‿nus ˈumĩnez e ˈpṛute‿ˈnustṛãm saˈlʏtɛ̃m
deˈkɛ̃ndi‿de ˈkjelis et ĩkaˈṛnatʏz ez‿de spiˈṛitʏ ˈzãtu
ez‿maˈṛi·a ˈviṛʒine et ˈũmu ˈfatʏz est
kṛʏkjiˈfizʏz ˈetʃi·am pṛu ˈnubi‿sʏ‿ˈpũtʃi·u piˈlatu
ˈpasʏz e‿seˈpʏltʏz est
e‿rezʏˈṛezi‿ˈtaṛtʃi·a ˈdi·e seˈkʏndãm skṛiˈtʏras et aˈkɛ̃ndit ĩ‿ˈkjelʏ̃m
ˈsedet a‿ˈdesteṛam ˈpatṛis et ˈiteṛʏ̃‿vɛ̃nˈtʏṛʏz est
kʏ̃‿ˈgluṛi·a ʒʏdiˈkaṛe ˈvivuz‿e‿ˈmuṛtʏ·us
ˈkʏʒʏz ˈṛegni nun eṛi‿ˈfinis
et ĩ‿spiˈṛitʏ̃‿ˈsantʏ̃‿ˈduminʏm e‿vivifiˈkantɛ̃m
ki ez‿ˈpatṛe fili·ˈuke pṛuˈkjedit
ki kʏ̃‿ˈpatṛe e‿ˈfili·u ˈsimʏl aduˈṛatʏṛ e‿kɔ̃gluṛifiˈkatʏṛ
ki luˈkʏtʏz ez‿pa‿pṛuˈfetas
et ˈʏnãm ˈsantam kaˈtulikãm et apɔsˈtulikãm eˈklezi·ãm
kũmˈfite·ɔṛ ˈʏnʏ̃‿baˈtima ĩ‿remizi·ˈunɛ̃m pekaˈtuṛʏ̃m
et ezˈpetu ṛezʏṛezi·ˈunɛ̃‿muṛtʏ·ˈuṛʏ̃m
e‿ˈvitãm vɛ̃nˈtʏṛi ˈsekʏli aˈmɛ̃n

Dutch/Flemish Latin

Style D., sixteenth-seventeenth centuries.

Jan Sweelinck, "Hodie"

CD #66.

Hodie Christus natus est (noe),
Salvator apparuit . . . in terra canunt angeli, laetentur archangeli
exultent justi, dicentes Gloria in excelsis Deo. Alleluia.

ˈhɔdi·e ˈkṛɪstys ˈna:tys e:st no·ˈe
zɑlˈβa:tɔṛ əˈpa:ṛyɪt ɪn ˈtɛṛə ˈka:nont ˈɑŋɣəli leˈtɛntyṛ ɑṛˈxɑŋɣəli
ɛkˈzyltɛnt ˈjysti diˈsɛntɛs ˈɣloṛi·a ɪn ɛkˈzɛlzɪs ˈde·o ɑleˈly:ja

GLOSSARY

Fuller discussions of many of these terms may be found in the individual chapters and, especially, in the section on phonetics in the Introduction. Many of the terms occur in several forms: noun, adjective, verb. In general, the principal entry is under the noun form, and (where they are not immediately obvious) the adjective and verb forms are given at the end of the entry.

ACCENT. Stress. Words of more than two syllables may have more than one stress; in such cases there is usually a distinction between primary and secondary stress. Note that verbal stress may or may not have anything to do with musical accent.

AFFRICATE. A sound consisting of a stop followed by a fricative, such as [tʃ] as in "church." A stop which develops into an affricate is said to be affricated.

ALLOPHONE. A variant of a single phoneme.

ALVEOLAR. The bony alveolar ridge lies just behind the teeth. Sounds articulated between the tongue and this point are called alveolar.

ANTEPENULTIMATE SYLLABLE. The third syllable back from the end of a word. *See* PENULTIMATE SYLLABLE.

ANTERIOR. Toward the front of the mouth, usually used to describe vowel position. *See* BACK; FRONT; POSTERIOR.

APEX. The tip of the tongue. Adjectival and prefix forms: apical, apico-.

APPROXIMANT. A sound articulated with an air passage narrower than that of a vowel and wider than that of a fricative; [l], [r], [j], and [w] are approximants.

ARTICULATION. The parts of the mouth used to form a consonant define its point of articulation.

ASPIRATE. A more or less sharp outward breath, either as a separate sound *(ha!)* or accompanying a voiceless stop (Eng. *too* as opposed to Fr. *tout*). *See* LENIS; FORTIS.

ASSIMILATION. The process by which one sound becomes more like, or assimilates to, another.

ASSONANCE. In rhyme, an agreement between vowels but not between consonants. *See* CONSONANCE.

ATONIC. Unstressed.

BACK. Toward the back of the mouth, usually used to describe vowel position. *See* ANTERIOR; FRONT; POSTERIOR.

BILABIAL. Articulated by the upper and lower lips.

BIVOCALIC. Consisting of two vowels.

CLOSE, CLOSED. Some vowel letter-forms may indicate two slightly different sounds. The one with the higher tongue position is called "close" or "closed." *See also* OPEN.

CLOSED SYLLABLE. A syllable ending in a consonant. *See also* OPEN SYLLABLE.

CONSONANCE. In rhyme, an agreement between both vowels and consonants. *See* ASSONANCE.

CONTINUANT. Consonants in which the air passage is not stopped; includes both fricatives and approximants. *See* STOP.

DENTAL. Articulated by placing the tip of the tongue on the teeth.

DEVOICING. The process by which a voiced consonant becomes unvoiced. *See also* VOICED; UNVOICED.

DIALECT. The form of a language prevailing in a particular district and marked by peculiarities of vocabulary and pronunciation; adj. dialectal.

DIGRAPH. A pair of letter-forms, usually representing a single sound, such as *ch*.

DIPHTHONG. A compound vowel consisting of two vowel sounds joined by a glide. The process by which a pure vowel becomes a diphthong is called diphthongization. A diphthong in which the first element is stressed is called a falling diphthong; one in which the second element is stressed is called a rising diphthong.

DISJUNCTIVE. Tending to separate syllables.

DISYLLABLIC. Consisting of two syllables.

ELISION. The omission of a final vowel before a word with an initial vowel, as in Fr. *l'amour (le + amour)*.

ENCLITIC. An unaccented word attached in meaning to the preceding word, such as Lat. *-que (and)* and It. parla<u>mi</u>.

ETYMOLOGY. The derivation of a word; an explanation of its origin and the linguistic changes it has undergone.

FALLING. *See* DIPHTHONG.

FEMININE RHYME. In scansion, a rhyme ending in an unstressed syllable. *See* MASCULINE.

FINAL. A sound occurring at the end of a word is in final position; also called terminal. *See also* INITIAL; MEDIAL.

FLAP. Usually referring to [r̥], an articulation in which the tip of the tongue makes a single flap against the alveolar ridge or the teeth. *See* TRILL.

FORTIS. Strong; usually used to describe aspiration or articulation. *See* LENIS.

FRICATIVE. A consonant articulation in which the sound is produced by forcing the air through a narrow passage; e.g., [s], [z], [f], and [v]. Also called spirants.

FRONT. Toward the front of the mouth, usually used to describe vowel position. A vowel is said to be fronted when it moves forward in the mouth. *See* ANTERIOR; BACK; POSTERIOR.

GEMINATE. A doubled consonant, as in It. *canne* (as opposed to *cane*).

GLIDE. A continuous movement from one vowel to another; a normal component of a diphthong.

GLOTTIS. The gap between the vocal cords. A stop caused by the full closure of the glottis is called a glottal stop.

GRAPHEME. A letter-form.

GUTTURAL. Produced in the back of the throat.

HIATUS. The boundary between syllables; especially a syllabic boundary between two vowels.

HIGH. Describes a vowel produced with the tongue high in the mouth. *See* LOW.

HOMOGRAPH. Two words with the same spelling but different meanings; e.g., *lead* (verb) and *lead* (noun). The pronunciation may or may not be different.

HOMOPHONE. Two words with the same sound but different spellings and meanings; e.g., *meat* and *meet*.

IMPLOSIVE. A consonant at the end of a syllable, preceding a syllable which begins with a consonant, as in Fr. su<u>b</u>til.

INFLECTION. An ending added to a word to indicate its syntactic or grammatical function. A word to which such an ending has been added is said to be inflected.

INITIAL. A sound occurring at the beginning of a word is in initial position. *See also* FINAL; MEDIAL.

INTERVOCALIC. Occurring between two vowels.

LABIAL. Produced by using the lips. *See* BILABIAL; LABIODENTAL.

LABIODENTAL. A consonant in which the point of articulation is between the upper teeth and the lower lip; e.g., Eng. [f] and [v].

LARYNX. The voice box; the organ in the throat which produces vocal sounds by means of the vibration of the vocal cords.

LATERAL. A consonant in which the tongue is placed against the alveolar ridge and the air exits from one or both sides of the mouth; e.g., [l].

LENGTHENING. The process by which a short vowel becomes longer. *See* LONG.

LENIS. Weak; usually used to describe aspiration or articulation. *See* FORTIS.

LEXICON. Vocabulary.

LIAISON. The pronunciation of an otherwise silent final consonant before a word with an initial vowel (or nonaspirated h), esp. in Fr. (compare *les femmes* and *les hommes*).

LONG. All languages make a distinction between long and short vowels, though the nature of the distinction varies considerably. In some languages the difference may originally have been merely temporal—long vowels sounding longer than short vowels—but that is rarely the case now. In many languages (English is a good example) a long vowel represents a sound quite distinct from a short vowel. Compare the vowels of *mane* (long) and *man* (short), or *meet* (long) and *met* (short).

LOW. Describes a vowel produced with the tongue low in the mouth. *See* HIGH.
LOWERING. The process by which the production of a vowel moves lower in the mouth.
MASCULINE RHYME. In scansion, a rhyme which ends in a stressed syllable. *See* FEMININE.
MEDIAL. A sound occurring in the middle of a word is in medial position. *See also* FINAL; INITIAL.
METATHESIS. The transposition of adjacent sounds.
MONOPHTHONG. A single, or pure, vowel sound.
MONOSYLLABIC. Consisting of one syllable.
MUTE. Not pronounced. The process by which a sound becomes mute is called "muting."
NASAL. A sound produced by the air being redirected partially or completely into the nose; e.g., [n] and [m].
NASALIZED. A vowel may be nasalized by opening up the nasal passage and allowing air to pass through it without closing the mouth.
NEOLOGISM. A newly created form.
OCCLUSIVE. *See* STOP.
OPEN. Some vowel letter-forms may indicate two slightly different sounds. The one with the lower tongue placement is called "open." *See also* CLOSE; CLOSED.
OPEN SYLLABLE. A syllable ending in a vowel. *See also* CLOSED SYLLABLE.
ORTHOEPIST. A scholar of pronunciation; usually refers to scholars of the sixteenth to eighteenth centuries.
ORTHOGRAPHY. Spelling.
PALATE. The hard palate; the bony part of the roof of the mouth. A sound produced by raising the tongue toward the palate is said to be palatal (as in the [j] of *yes*). A sound that is moved in that direction is said to be palatalized (compare Eng. *cheese* and Ger. *Käse*).
PENULTIMATE SYLLABLE. The second syllable back from the end of a word. *See* ANTEPENULTIMATE SYLLABLE.
PHONEME. The smallest functional unit of speech. A phoneme may be a single sound, such as [o], or a sound cluster, such as [dʒ] in *edge,* but it is functionally indivisible. *See also* ALLOPHONE.
PLOSIVE. A consonant produced by full closure of the air passage, followed by rapid exhalation; e.g., [p] and [b]. *See* STOP.
POLYSYLLABIC. Consisting of two or more syllables.
POSTERIOR. Toward the back of the mouth, usually used to describe vowel position. *See* ANTERIOR; BACK; FRONT.
POST-TONIC. Immediately following a stressed syllable.
POSTVOCALIC. Immediately following a vowel.
PRECONSONANTAL. Immediately preceding a consonant.
PREPALATAL. Produced toward the front of the palate.
PRETONIC. Immediately preceding a stressed syllable.
PREVOCALIC. Immediately preceding a vowel.
PROCLITIC. An unaccented word attached in meaning to the following word, such as "*to* go."
PURE. Describes a vowel consisting of only one sound; the mouth does not change during its production.
QUANTITATIVE. A type of Latin verse (and its vernacular derivatives) in which a precise number and pattern of long and short syllables is maintained in each line. Quantitative verse frequently does not rhyme.
RAISING. The process by which a vowel is moved higher in the mouth. *See* LOWERING.
RISING. *See* DIPHTHONG.
ROLL. *See* TRILL.
ROUNDED VOWEL. A vowel whose production involves the tensed rounding of the lips; e.g., [u] as in *pool. See also* UNROUNDED.
SCHWA. The relatively neutral vowel [ə] produced by the mouth in a state of relaxation; the first and third vowel of *banana.*
SEMICONSONANT. *See* SEMIVOWEL.

SEMIVOWEL. A letter which in different circumstances can act either as a vowel or a consonant; refers particularly to *y* [j] and *w* [w]. Also called semiconsonant.

SHORT. *See* LONG for a brief explanation of the distinction between long and short vowels.

SIBILANTS. The sounds [s] and [z]. The process by which a sound moves in a "hissing" direction is called sibilization.

SPIRANT. *See* FRICATIVE.

STOP. A consonant articulation in which the air passage is completely closed, e.g., [p], [t], [k], [b], [d], and [g]. Also called occlusive. Stops may be voiced or unvoiced.

SYNAERESIS. The contraction of two vowels into a diphthong or a single vowel.

TERMINAL. A sound occurring at the end of a word is in terminal position. Also called final. *See also* INITIAL; MEDIAL.

TONIC. Stressed. Note that this has no connection with the musical meaning of the word.

TRILL. Usually refers to [rr], an articulation in which the tip of the tongue makes a series of brief contacts with the alveolar ridge or, in some languages, with the uvula. Also called roll. *See* FLAP.

TRIPHTHONG. A compound vowel consisting of three elements. *See* DIPHTHONG.

UMLAUT. The process by which a back vowel becomes a front vowel. In Mod. Ger., commonly indicated by a dieresis (¨), which has also come to be called an umlaut.

UNROUNDED VOWEL. A vowel in which the lips are in a relaxed and unrounded position; e.g., the first *e* of *these. See also* ROUNDED VOWEL.

UNVOICED. A sound produced without the vibration of the larynx; e.g., [s] in *save* or [f] in *feel.* Also called voiceless. *See also* DEVOICING; VOICED.

UVULA. The small flap of flesh which hangs down at the back of the soft palate; a sound produced there is said to be uvular.

VELUM. The soft palate; the back part of the roof of the mouth in which the flesh is not supported by bone. A sound produced by raising the tongue toward the velum is said to be velar; e.g., [g] as in *gone.*

VERNACULAR. Native languages, as opposed to scholarly languages like Latin.

VOICED. A sound produced with the vibration of the larynx; e.g., [z] as in *maze* and [v] as in *veal. See* UNVOICED.

VOICELESS. *See* UNVOICED.

CONTENTS OF THE COMPACT DISK

Read by David Klausner
Recorded and edited by Bryden Baird

1. Phonetic chart at the back of the book

English

2. A St. Godric hymn
3. Miri it is
4. Edi beo thu
5. Owt of your slepe (Pre-vowel shift version)
6. Owt of your slepe (Post-vowel shift version)
7. Henry VIII, Pastime with good company
8. John Bennet, All creatures now are merry-minded

Scots

9. Balulalow

Anglo-Latin

10. Hymn to St. Oswald
11. O potores exquisiti
12. Risum fecit Sare
13. Robert Fayrfax, O Maria Deo grata
14. William Byrd, Suscepimus

Old French

15. Gace Brulé, De bone amour
16. Roman de Fauvel, Se mes desirs
17. Guillaume de Machaut, Phyton, le mervilleus serpent
18. Baude Cordier, Belle, bonne, sage
19. Josquin des Prés, Entre je suis
20. Johannes Ockeghem, J'en ay dueil
21. Orlando di Lasso, Que dis-tu?
22. Perrin d'Angicourt, Il couvient k'en la candeille

French Latin

23. Salve regina
24. Credo in unum Deum

Occitan

25. Bernart de Ventadorn, Quan vei la lauseta mover

26. Raimbaut de Vaqueyras, Kalenda maia
27. Arnault Daniel, Lo ferm voler

Catalan

28. Los set gotxs
29. Càrceres, Soleta y verge estich
30. Cant de la Sibilla (Palma version)
    Cant de la Sibilla (Barcelona version)
    Cant de la Sibilla (Urgell version)

Spanish

31. Menga, la del Bustar
32. Otro bien si a vos no tengo
33. Peynádose estava
34. Ya desengaño mío

Spanish Latin

35. Magnificat
36. Salve regina

Portuguese

37. Alfonso X, Cantiga 167
38. Minina dos olhos verdes
39. Pois tudo tam pouco dura
40. Mis ojos tristes lhorando

Portuguese Latin

41. Salve regina

Italian

42. Nel chiaro fiume dilettoso e bello (Florentine version)
42. Povero çappator (Northern version)
43. De soto 'l verde vidi i ochi vaghi
45. Involta d'un bel velo
46. Rosetta che non cambi may colore
47. (E) vantende, segnor mio
48. Marchetto Cara, A la absentia che me acora
49. Donne leggiadr' e voi vaghe donzelle

Italian Latin

50. Salve regina

Middle High German

51. Walther von der Vogelweide, Palästinalied
52. Neidhart von Reuental, Si jehent, daz der winder
53. Der Marner, Langer Ton
54. Alexander, Hie bevorn dô wir kinder wâren

Late Medieval German and Early New High German

55. Von meiden pin ich dick berawbt.
56. Oswald von Wolkenstein, Ain mensch von achzehen jaren klüg
57. Hans Sachs, Goldener Ton
58. Buchsbaum und Felbinger
59. Ludwig Senfl, Alleyn dein huld

German Latin

60. Hildegarde of Bingen, O viridissima virga
61. Orlando Lassus, Stabat mater
62. Heinrich Schütz, Jubilate Deo

Flemish

63. Ach Vlaendere vrie
64. Clemens non Papa, Souterliedekens, Psalm 3

Netherlands Latin

65. Credo (Picard/Walloon version)
66. Jan Sweelinck, Hodie

CONTRIBUTORS

JAMES F. BURKE is professor of Spanish at the University of Toronto. His specialty is early medieval Spanish literature and language. His most recent book is *Structures from the Trivium in the Cantar de Mio Cid* (1991).

GIANRENZO P. CLIVIO is a professor in the Department of Italian Studies at the University of Toronto. His major fields of expertise are the history of the Italian language, Italian phonology, and Italian dialectology. He has published numerous books, including critical editions, as well as scholarly articles in such journals as *Zeitschrift für romanische Philologie, Romanische Forschungen, L'Italia dialettale,* and *Studi Piemontesi.*

HAROLD COPEMAN is retired from Her Majesty's Treasury, London. He is the author of *Singing in Latin* (1990).

BEATA FITZPATRICK is a former student of Joseph Gulsoy. She is co-author with Joan Coromines of *Cerveri de Girona: Lirica* (1988).

PETER FRENZEL is the Marcus L. Taft Professor of German and Medieval Studies at Wesleyan University, specializing in the literature of the Middle Ages and its musical context.

DAVID N. KLAUSNER is professor in the Department of English and the Centre for Medieval Studies, University of Toronto. He has written widely on Old and Middle English, Middle Welsh, and, especially, on medieval and Tudor drama.

TIMOTHY J. MCGEE is professor of musicology at the Faculty of Music, University of Toronto, specializing in performance practices before 1700. He is the author of *Medieval and Renaissance Music; A Performer's Guide* (1985) and *Medieval Instrumental Dances* (1989).

A.G. RIGG is professor of Medieval Latin and the History of the English Language at the Centre for Medieval Studies, University of Toronto. Among his recent publications is *A History of Anglo-Latin Literature 1066–1422* (1992), which contains an Appendix on Metre.

VERA U.G. SCHERR is professor of singing at Staatliche Hochschule für Musik Heidelberg-Mannheim and the author of *Aufführungspraxis Vokalmusik: Handbuch der Lateinischen Aussprache* (1991).

WILLIAM Z. SHETTER is professor emeritus of Germanic Studies at Indiana University. His field of specialization is the language and culture of the Low Countries. He is the author of a grammar of modern Dutch and of *The Netherlands in Perspective* (1987).

JOSEPH T. SNOW is professor of Romance Languages at Michigan State University, where he teaches courses in medieval Spanish language and literature. His research is almost evenly divided between the *Cantigas de Santa Maria* of Alfonso X and the late Spanish medieval masterpiece *Celestina.*

ROBERT TAYLOR is professor of French at Victoria College, University of Toronto. He specializes in Romance philology, in particular medieval French and Occitan language and literature, textual criticism, and bibliography. Among his recent publications is "The Old French 'Cistercian' Translations," in Jeanette Beer, ed., *Medieval Translators and Their Craft* (1989).

PHONETIC CHART

David N. Klausner

This chart is based on the International Phonetic Alphabet, though in some cases choices have been made between British and North American IPA usage on practical and typographic grounds. The numbering of symbols is arbitrary and is intended merely to facilitate connecting this chart with the phonetic demonstration on the accompanying CD. CD #1.

Consonants

	Symbol	*Description*	*Example*
1	[b]	voiced bilabial stop	bid
2	[β]	voiced bilabial fricative	Sp. haba
3	[p]	voiceless bilabial stop	pit
4	[d]	voiced alveolar stop	deed
5	[t]	voiceless alveolar stop	tip
6	[d̪]	voiced dental fricative (weak)	Sp. cada
7	[ð]	voiced interdental fricative	then
8	[θ]	voiceless interdental fricative	thin
9	[dz]	voiced alveolar affricate	heads
10	[ts]	voiceless alveolar affricate	cats
11	[dʒ]	voiced palato-alveolar affricate	jeer, magic
12	[tʃ]	voiceless palato-alveolar affricate	church
13	[g]	voiced velar stop	good
14	[k]	voiceless velar stop	kiss, calm
15	[γ]	voiced velar fricative	Flem. god
16	[g̑]	voiced velar fricative (weak)	Sp. vago
17	[x]	voiceless velar fricative	Scots loch, Ger. noch
18	[ç]	voiceless palatal fricative	Ger. ich
19	[v]	voiced labiodental fricative	vine
20	[f]	voiceless labiodental fricative	fine
21	[z]	voiced alveolar fricative	zebra, as
22	[s]	voiceless alveolar fricative	silly, ass
23	[ʒ]	voiced palato-alveolar fricative	leisure
24	[ʃ]	voiceless palato-alveolar fricative	ship, ash
25	[h]	voiceless glottal fricative	have, cohabit
26	[m]	voiced bilabial nasal	month
27	[n]	voiced alveolar nasal	night
28	[ŋ]	voiced velar nasal	sing
29	[ɲ]	voiced palatal nasal	vignette, barnyard
30	[l]	voiced alveolar lateral approximant	lip
31	[λ]	voiced palatal lateral approximant	colliery
32	[r]	voiced alveolar continuant	rib
33	[R]	voiced uvular continuant or trill	Fr. rouge, Ger. rein
34	[ɾ]	voiced apico-alveolar flap	Sp. or It. caro
35	[rr]	voiced apico-alveolar trill	Sp. carro

36	[j]	voiced unrounded palatal central approximant (sometimes called "semivowel")	yet
37	[w]	voiced rounded labiovelar approximant (sometimes called "semivowel")	worry, between
38	[ɥ]	voiced rounded palatal approximant (sometimes called "semivowel")	Fr. lui

Vowels

Vowels are generally given in pairs, short and long, to make their relationship clearer, with a colon indicating the long form. The exceptions, of course, are those short (or long) vowels for which there were no long (or short) equivalents in common use.

A-forms

1	[ɑ]	low back unrounded	Fr. pas
2	[ɑ:]		father
3	[a]	low front unrounded	Ger. Mann, Fr. patte
4	[æ]	semi-low front unrounded	at
5	[æ:]		bad

E-forms

6	[e]	upper-mid front unrounded	Fr. été
7	[e:]		Ger. See
8	[ɛ]	lower-mid front unrounded	bed
9	[ɛ:]		there, Fr. bête
10	[ə]	mid-central unrounded, "schwa"	about
11	[ə:]		fur, mirth

I-forms

12	[ɪ]	semi-high front unrounded	bid, sit
13	[i]	high front unrounded	Fr. si
14	[i:]		bead, feel, machine

O-forms

15	[o]	upper-mid back rounded	Fr. beau
16	[o:]		go, Ger. Sohn
17	[ɔ]	lower-mid back rounded	coffee, Ger. Gott
18	[ɔ:]		broad, all, saw
19	[ø]	upper-mid front rounded	Fr. peu
20	[ø:]		Ger. schön
21	[œ]	lower-mid front rounded	Fr. oeuf, Ger. Mönch

U-forms

22	[u]	high back rounded	Fr. foule, ou
23	[u:]		boot, Ger. gut
24	[ʊ]	semi-high back rounded	good, put
25	[ʌ]	lower-mid back unrounded	but, love
26	[y]	high front rounded	Fr. tu
27	[y:]		Fr. littérature, Ger. grün
28	[ʏ]	semi-front high rounded	Ger. Küche

Diphthongs and Triphthongs

Diphthongs consist of two vowel elements. Pronunciation involves a glide from the first to the second element; the first element is usually longer than the second. Note that after the fifteenth century, diphthongs are not necessarily indicated in spelling. Triphthongs, consisting of three vowel elements, involve a glide through the second to the third element. In phonetic transcriptions, diphthongs are indicated by a pair of vowels; adjacent vowels which are not diphthongs (where hiatus occurs) are separated by a raised dot. Thus [ˈai] is a diphthong, as in *ride;* while [a·ˈi] is not a diphthong, as in *Aida.* The following list of diphthongs and triphthongs is not exhaustive, but lists the more common ones found in the various chapters. Some contributors make a distinction between "rising" and "falling" diphthongs; in these cases the description above is valid for falling diphthongs, in which the first vowel element is the more important. Rising diphthongs usually begin with a semivowel *(y* or *w),* and phoneticians differ in considering them true diphthongs or a semivowel followed by a vowel.

Diphthongs

1	[ai]	ride
2	[ʌi]	EModEng ride
3	[au]	house
4	[ɛu]	ME reu
5	[ʌu]	EModEng house
6	[ɔi]	boy
7	[ei]	day
8	[eu]	OFr fleur
9	[ue]	OFr nuef
10	[ɥi]	Fr lui
11	[iu]	Prov viu
12	[ou]	Prov nou
13	[ɥɔ]	Prov fuoc
14	[ɥɛ]	Prov nueva

Triphthongs

1	[eau]	OFr beau
2	[ieu]	OFr dieu

Nasalization

Nasalization of a vowel or diphthong is indicated by a tilde (~) over the vowel or the second element of the diphthong. Thus French *on* is represented by [ɔ̃], *an* by [ɑ̃].

Elision

Elision is shown by the symbol ‿; e.g., French Latin *spes nostra* [spɛ̃‿nɔtra], see p. 100.

Other Symbols

·	separates syllables
ˈ	precedes stressed syllable
ˈˈ	precedes secondary stressed syllable
<	derives from
>	changes to